A WILD LIFE

Mare Carter

Also by Mare Carter:
The Complete Guide to Central Australia
Central Australia – the New Complete Guide

A WILD LIFE
BRINGING UP A BUSH MENAGERIE

Mare Carter

BANTAM BOOKS
SYDNEY • AUCKLAND • TORONTO • NEW YORK • LONDON

A WILD LIFE
A BANTAM BOOK

First published in Australia and New Zealand in 2001
by Bantam

National Library of Australia
Cataloguing-in-Publication Entry

Carter, Mare.
    A wild life: bringing up a bush menagerie.

    ISBN 1 86325 293 2.

    1. Carter family. 2. Menageries – New South Wales. 3. Glenrock Farm Wildlife
    Refuge, New South Wales. 4. Wildlife refuges – New South Wales. I. Title.

636.083209944

Transworld Publishers,
a division of Random House Australia Pty Ltd
20 Alfred Street, Milsons Point, NSW 2061
http://www.randomhouse.com.au

Random House New Zealand Limited
18 Poland Road, Glenfield, Auckland

Transworld Publishers,
a division of The Random House Group Ltd
61-63 Uxbridge Road, London W5 5SA

Random House Inc
1540 Broadway, New York, New York 10036

Edited by Jo Jarrah
Cover design by Noel Pennington/Cusp Creative Pty Ltd
Cover photographs by Jeff Carter
Maps of Foxground and Wild Country Park by Lauren Jaye Carter and Aaron Westenberg
Typeset by Midland Typesetters, Maryborough, Victoria
Printed and bound by Griffin Press, Netley, South Australia

10 9 8 7 6 5 4 3 2 1

This is the story of Glenrock Wildlife Refuge, which included Wild Country Park, at Foxground on the New South Wales south coast.

It is also the story of the Carter family, my version of their lives and times, and I dedicate this book to them.

CONVERSION CHART

Weights

Imperial	Metric
1 pound	454 grams

Measures

Imperial	Metric
1 inch	25.4 millimetres
1 foot	30.5 centimetres
1 yard	0.914 metres
1 mile	1.61 kilometres
1 acre	0.405 hectares

CONTENTS

Glenrock Farm Wildlife Refuge, Wild Country Park and surrounds at the top of the Foxground valley, NSW.

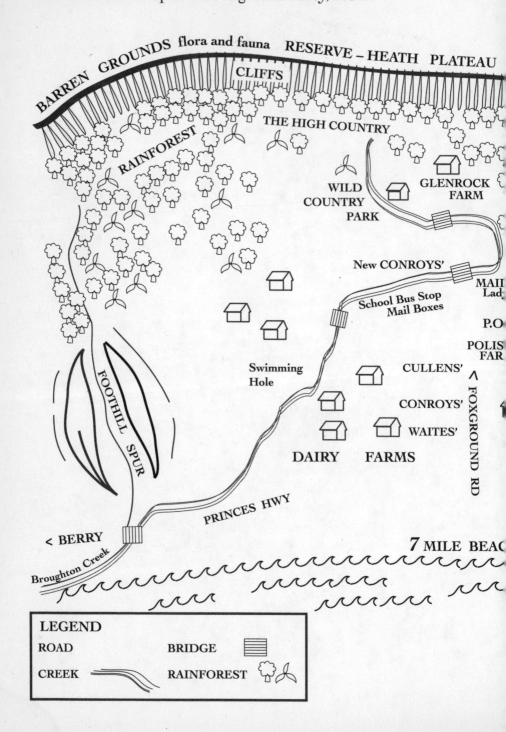

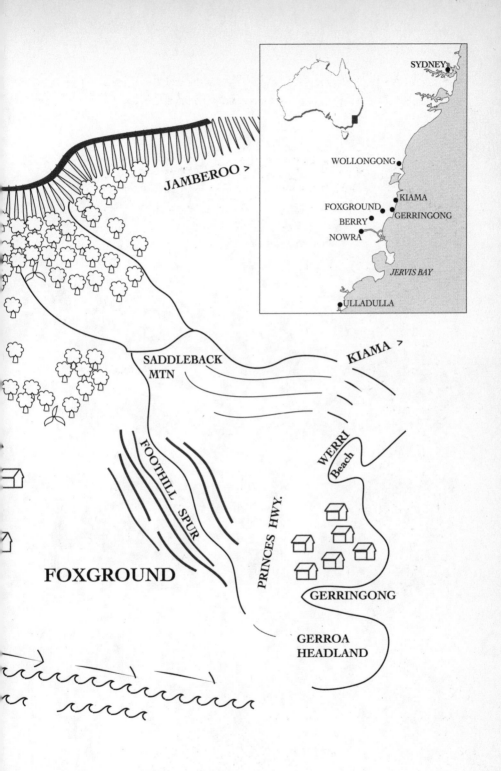

SYDNEY

WOLLONGONG

KIAMA

FOXGROUND

GERRINGONG

BERRY

NOWRA

JERVIS BAY

ULLADULLA

JAMBEROO >

SADDLEBACK
MTN

KIAMA >

WERRI

Beach

FOOTHILL SPUR

PRINCES HWY.

FOXGROUND

GERRINGONG

GERROA
HEADLAND

Map of the property showing the key features

Prologue

This is a memoir of five decades when I revelled in tending a gentle empire. I liked to think of myself as the careful care-taker – a facilitator, which I once accidentally changed to *felicitator*, a Freudian slip that stuck. During that time I nurtured kids (four going on dozens) along with an anarchic spouse, farm and domestic animals, plus injured or orphaned wildlife. My domain included scores of city visitors nostalgic for old-fashioned good times, as well as Australians from older, more traditional cultures, my arms stretching ever wider to gather in all comers to our old dairy farm high above the Shoalhaven on the New South Wales south coast.

Our property, Glenrock, at Foxground, is a magic place of rainforest, creeks and waterfalls, pure mountain air. We made it a wildlife refuge, intending to keep it our very private hideaway. Instead it became Wild Country Park, a place of refreshment and inspiration for more than a quarter of a million people.

Our aim was to create an 'island' of relatively uncleared bush amidst the farm and grazing lands, where we could bring back and help to breed up native wildlife which had been hunted and pushed out from their original homes. As the story of what we were trying to do spread, the flow of inmates to our rainforest ark grew, involving us in more work, expense and anguish than we could ever have imagined. Our place became a depot for creatures in need. All sorts of lost, run-over, orphaned Australian animals and birds were brought to us, there being no formal organisations

to take them in those days apart from zoos, which soon became full
to overflowing. We looked after our guests and gradually released
them back into the wild on the property and beyond.

During the 1960s we lived an idyll, growing our own food,
embracing old-time methods and tending the hobby that turned
into a life's work – the rehabilitation of displaced native fauna so
we could release them to live free. The process was taxing, funny,
poignant, occasionally dangerous. We called it 'phasing them back
to nature'.

There were few precedents when we began. As our experience
grew and wisdom replaced our naivety, we were proud to share our
knowlege, believing that personal example is the best teacher. Our
views were out of step with the majority at the start, and in some
quarters still are. Writers and photographers by trade, and later
film-makers, we documented the growing up of our country and
tried to nudge it in directions we believed were healthy, a process
parallel to parenting our kids. The embedded story shows how our
campaigns and notions, our follies and fancies, reflected changes
generally, but also how they – and we – evolved. An evangelist for
change, I learned that change can be expensive. And painful.

So, is this an animal story? Yes and no. A 'woman's story'? You
might well think so but I wouldn't have said that. For much of my
adult life I was one female among a big cast of males and thought
I was one of the fellas too, until finally I understood that society
didn't see me the way I saw myself. Revelation. My memoir is as
much about knocking the corners off ideals as about doing what
I did. It should appeal to everyone who has ever dreamed of
dropping out, living off the land in small cosy communities where
people matter more than mathematics. It may also enlighten those
with warm and fuzzy notions of trading in the poodles for some
kangaroos and a wombat.

A wombat? Did someone say, 'Now that is what I'd *really*
love!'? Well, I suggest you read on before committing yourself.
Anyone wishing for a wombat or a kangaroo or koala, or any of
Australia's unique, primitive wildlife, needs to understand what's
involved. And needs to ask themselves if they're truly prepared to
take on the job. In fairness to themselves as well as to the animals.

You can't treat wild animals as you do domestic ones. They
aren't that adaptable. Dogs and cats and horses have been bred to

fit in with their owners' routines, to adjust to their personalities even. But with wild creatures, adjustments have to come almost entirely from the humans. To try and domesticate a wild animal is to do it a terrible disservice. We may call them our pets but, in the true sense of the word, they cannot be that. So in our family, although we gave our charges names or continued to call them by the titles they arrived with from other carers, we were always mindful of their needs and instincts as we shepherded them toward a free and natural life, among their own kind.

After living with both wild and tame animals for many years, I believe we became closely attuned to them without, I hope, spoiling them. We had to alter our own behaviour a lot. We learned much and changed our ideas and illusions about 'nature' and nature's children, including ourselves. Over time I developed ways of caring for animals which, after a few distressing failures, work. My keyword is respect. Try to see things from where the animal stands. What does *it* want to do? Use that as a starting point for what *you* want it to do. Use the same technique with people and you won't go far wrong.

This story is about humans and animals both. While trying to explain the behaviours of Gidgea the grey kangaroo and William the wilful wombat, yarns are also spun about their Foxground friends, among whom are Freya and Saxon and the rest of our Friesian cows. Jim – Lucky Jim – the fine blue-heeler dog and his wives, Laika and Brownie, are a big part of the story. In it also are Blind Bruce and Big Joe and Thalos, would-be kangaroo patriarchs who met sticky ends. So is Tootsie the red-necked wallaby, Horace and Monica and other eagles, Stripes the glider possum and many many more. Including wombats. Yes, plenty of wombats. And last but also first among the friends of Gidgea and William are the Carter family – Jeff and Mare, Goth, Van, Thor and Karen. We tried to peel the plastic off modern life, to find a peaceful and meaningful existence in the country. And as part of that, to set a good example along the way.

1

Grays Point, 1954–1961

Our wildlife story begins with our first kangaroo, Hanogi. She came to live with us when we were still city-dwellers, more or less, in a little half-formed suburb on the shores of Port Hacking, south of Sydney. I like to reflect on our seven years at Grays Point, because they signal the way we were – the way we all were – and the influences that made us what we became.

Four years previously, very early one rosy Sydney summer morning, I disembarked at Woolloomooloo wharf, fresh out of college, an American fugitive, fleeing from many things but especially an ultra-civilised upbringing in Pasadena, California. You know: where millionaires went to die. I was itchy-footed by nature, a legacy of my legendary but ever absent father, Beriah Magoffin Thompson, who was first a naval commander and then an overseas agent of the Roosevelt government. Daddy was a T-man (US Treasury roving negotiator and investigator) and stories of his world travels made me yearn for an adventurous life far from the rigid disciplines of my childhood alone with Mother.

Born of decent Missouri farmers, she, Adeline Leota Tussey, ran away young to Hollywood with her sister, Ruby Ramona, who became a writer, an opera singer, wife of a Hollywood stuntman and Indianapolis racing driver. She died before middle age of breast cancer. My mother became an actress in silent movies, then a divorcee after unwisely marrying a man who was later sent to jail. Even though she worked hard to present a respectable front, there hung about her a whiff of the flapper: roach-smoking and gin in silver flasks, Chanel Number 5 mingling with fresh corsages on fox furs. Her snapshot albums show pretty women in cloche hats, with silken legs and names recognisable still from old film credits.

Next she married my father and entered a heady sociable milieu as an officer's wife. My first year was spent following the US fleet up and down the west coast, mother at the wheel of a natty cab-riolet, me and my bassinet in the rumble seat. Babyhood was spent in Kentucky living well on an officers' post; as a toddler I gazed down on snowdrifts from our Washington DC hotel apartment, bemused as Mama and Papa swanned off to Army–Navy football games and the President's Birthday Ball where FDR and Eleanor presided.

By my fourth birthday, the glamour had ended. My mother packed us off to southern California, her marriage to Daddy finished. The secrets and lies of why remained hidden for decades. A pity. I believed it was my fault, because I was a sickly kid and needed a warm dry climate. Mother set us up in a solid gold neigh-bourhood among the palm trees and orange groves, big house, fine furniture, all financed by Daddy's generous alimony. She traded on past successes, which ingrained in me a mistrust of snobs and a desire to know and to speak the truth. Romantic, naive, intensely patriotic, now also super conformist, Mother determined to continue riding the high society bus and I was her ticket. To save me from her own indiscretions, her lusts and flings, never admitted – an even greater pity – she held me on a tight leash, steel fingers in fine white gloves, grooming me relentlessly as a virgin princess. Given education, impeccable wardrobe, polite manners, I inched through my teens malnourished by a past rich in secondhand memories and a present bland, lonely and totally correct. I dreaded my future: a sacrificial bride for some upper-class neighbours' son. Poor mother, she never realised her dreams. But I did.

My aspirations leant toward a frontier life and they weren't so unusual, given that California was the outer limit for would-be pioneers who journeyed as far west as they could till they baulked at the Pacific Ocean. I kept on going. My goal, typical of my social class, was the Sorbonne with my five best friends from college, members of a writing fraternity, Sigma Tau Delta. United by a love of literature, yearning after bohemian experience and unrepressed sex, we worked and saved hard for our big adventure. In 1949, as quickly and cheaply as possible we sailed for London, but when the one Australian in our group grew ill and had to return home to Sydney, we all accompanied her. Kings Cross, she assured us, was just like the Left Bank.

When I landed in Australia more by accident than design, I felt myself a refugee from my native land of plenty. Marinated in idealism, like many American kids of that post-war era, I had left disgusted by the hypocrisy of racial and religious persecution, sickened by galloping consumerism, frightened by McCarthyism. Well bred and well fed, I hungered for austerity, for freedom and challenge. The Sydney I came to in 1950 beguiled me from the first sun-spangled morning when the vivid green of the Domain lawns, the lap-lap of harbour waters ensnared my heart. They haven't let go yet.

Sydney was bursting with migrants and what I saw then as opportunities, apart from a desperate housing shortage and a White Australia policy I hadn't yet heard about. Here, if you paused to window-shop, the owner of the business came out and offered you a job. In Darlinghurst I found what I had hoped to find in Montmartre, and settled in to work at a variety of jobs, to enjoy, to live. After a year or so, I returned to California at Mother's urgent summons, hoping our differences would be reconciled by my having become, while overseas, a fellow adult. No way. She was so angry with me for my defection that normal relations between us were impossible. Feeling guilty, disappointed yet also peeved, I moved north, following once more my five college chums and our new friends from Australia who had followed their dreams by moving to the States. Again I was smitten, this time by that other elegant, bohemian harbour city, San Francisco. I found satisfying jobs in the social work industry, as a statistician in first the YWCA and then a private adoption agency. I shared digs with some of my friends from the American–Australian group, lived frugally but wildly well, saved money, learned heaps, grew. Then in 1953 I returned to my first love. Flying back into Sydney set my heart doing flip-flops, and so it does even today.

Funnily enough, my American travel companions and all but one Sydney friend opted to live in the States. He and I were the only ones who returned to live Down Under and ironically, of our American group, I had been the only one who did not use the ten pound migrant fare offer. I paid my own way, a principle which remains strong in me.

After the frightening witch hunts being conducted by the McCarthyites in California, Sydney seemed peaceful and full of promise. In my four years since graduation from college I'd had jobs in bakeries, as GPO phonogram operator, as a barmaid and as an office worker. I decided this time to seek employment leading toward my chosen career as a writer. Thus I fetched up at a small independent publishing house near Central Railway and there encountered my destiny. Jeffrey Robert Carter. Roamer, iconoclast, bushman from Bendigo, Victoria, he had laboured his way around most of eastern Australia and now was editor of *Outdoors and Fishing* magazine, where we met.

An only child, like me, Jeff had fled from a domineering mother and an ultra-conservative household, having decided by the age of nine that his parents knew less than he did and marched to a drumbeat he rejected totally. Although he lived at home until age seventeen, he kept his own counsel. His mother doted on him. His father, as was normal in the 1930s–1940s, found little time for kids. Both parents worked, a difference between our backgrounds. The Depression had affected the Carters badly and forever. Where Mother and I had been cushioned from unemployment and suffering by my father's government salary, Jeff's parents, Doris and Percy, had had to fight their way to the financial security they knew after World War II. They enshrined hard work, the Menzies liberal government and frugality, even when not appropriate. The left-wing politics of their only son, his wanderlust and his courtship and parenting practices first puzzled, then angered and finally disappointed them.

After eight years of working his way around the countryside, filled with ideas and plans and much practical skill, Jeff was a facinating lunch companion. I didn't see him as a suitor, because he was married. What I didn't know, at first, was that he was estranged from his wife, whom he had married too young and hastily, thus aborting his teenage years and setting his itchy feet upon a road which never ended. He never did, never would tire of seeing what was beyond the next hill. By the time he was eighteen, Jeff was the father of Karen; by twenty-two, of Thor.

When Jeff explained what had transpired between their mother Dorothea and him, the dramas and defections that had ruptured their marriage, I began to view him differently. I softened enough to accept his invitations to come out bush with his good friend, Eric Worrell, an author and one of Australia's leading herpetologists. Jeff had no car but he had his camera, with which he took pictures for books and magazine articles of Eric at work. Eric used to drive to the riverlands in western New South Wales in his utility – a Holden because it was Australian made – catch snakes all weekend, then return to Sydney with a deadly cargo in special boxes in the back. At home, he would milk the reptiles of their venom, dry it and send it to the Commonwealth Serum Laboratories to be made into anti-toxins.

I have to admit, it was a dramatic introduction to country Australia and its wildlife, especially its less popular species. We would drive late into a Friday night, along roads which today are freeways but then were single-lane, pot-holed, often untarred obstacle courses, singing rollicking versions of 'Waltzing Matilda' and 'The Road to Gundagai'. Both Jeff and Eric were passionately patriotic about native flora and fauna and on those long, dark journeys they indoctrinated me with their principles, which has done me no harm since then.

Once we reached Eric's destination he and Jeff would build a huge fire, because it was freezing at night in winter, and we would stand around warming ourselves while sipping mouth-burning raw rum from metal mugs. Then Eric bedded down on the front seat of his ute leaving Jeff and me to climb into a strong canvas swag for sleep but mainly talk. And love-making. We did a lot of that. And in between I learned much about Jeff's background. His schooling at Melbourne Boys' High where he imbibed some of his radical philosophies. His flirtation with Communism when he joined the Eureka Youth League. His daydreams of being part of the Spanish Civil War, and the nights spent stumping about downtown Melbourne dressed in a trenchcoat, lugging his portable typewriter, Hemingway style, longing to meet, to woo, girls he was too shy to approach. I heard about his running away with Dorothea on the back of her motorbike and all their bizarre adventures until Karen's birth brought him down to earth and he tried for security, combining agriculture on a small holding with journalism. And then their marriage came unstuck. Continuing to live on his little farmlet in Sydney's Sutherland Shire, he was still labouring at his two favourite jobs – writing and raising goats and chickens – and trying to find a way forward. His passion and fervid plans kept me warm on those cold windy riverbanks. Searching out tiger snakes, blacks and king browns by day (and never, ever, showing I was scared) sent me home on Sunday nights alight with new experience. Kings Cross began to seem tame and, indeed, Jeff wanted me out of my terrace room and into his neck of the woods, which was south of Sydney.

But still I adored life in the Cross in the early fifties, the relaxed, artistic residents, many of whom were refugees from European cultures with a taste for the good things of life. I could stroll out at nights after work, shop for the sort of delicatessen fare which was common in the States but exotic in Australia, drop by a coffee shop and chat with dancers and writers and actors . . . it was San Francisco all over again and if there was crime back then, it did not threaten those promenading beneath the plane trees. Jeff feared he would lose me there. He conjured up the idea of a little boatshed on the Georges River. That sounded good, so I agreed to look for accommodation in the sparse To Let columns of the Saturday paper. Which is how we found the little Grays Point shack. Boatsheds, it turned out, were scarce and ferociously expensive. When it was time for me to move, Jeff announced he had decided to join me. He felt he had to live with me.

He had formed the conviction that I was the perfect partner for his grand plan. Which was to escape the nine-to-five routine, the fetters of acquisitive society, and make his living photographing and writing about outback people, self-reliant citizens beyond city constraints. He recognised in me a person who could complement his dreams, an accomplice in schemes which seemed to meld with my yen for simplicity, for hardship even. He talked me into putting aside misgivings about his domestic past and set up house with him in the little fibro cottage at Grays Point.

I was vulnerable to Jeff's arguments. Never having known a father to scoop me up and swing me high, hug me and pet me, tickle and kiss me, his strong masculine dynamism, his warmth and passion were irresible, his blueprint for the future, ditto. Not a person to give up once committed to an action, Jeff told me he would never turn back to what he had left, whether we were together or not. I believed him. My mother had never trained me to be independent. She schooled me to obey and I was biddable, a follower. So I caved in and agreed to give it a try.

Grays Point was a rocky spine covered in bush and like all others, our block was steep and long, stretching from the road down to the waterfront. At the foot of our property, just above muddy mangrove flats, was a sandstone cave, the roof blackened by smoke from thousands of campfires, the floor deeply littered with bones and shells and carbon. That Aboriginal kitchen midden on our land was a bonus, a link with times past, but also a mystery, a worry. Where had those fisherfolk gone? It was just the beginning of many things I would touch which previously I had only read about.

When we moved there, Grays Point had only one road, untarred, ending at a ramshackle boatshed hiring rowboats to weekend fishermen. The two-room wooden school was next to the community hall, ugly and unpainted but a source of pride to the local citizens who had built it themselves for meetings and weekend family dances. Next to that was the tiny fibro shop, which was post office, newsagency, grocers and – most important, surrounded as we were by the Royal National Park – bushfire headquarters. The shop had Grays Point's sole telephone. Private homes had none.

The house we rented and later bought was also an unlovely fibro box, half way down to the waterfront. It had been someone's fishing shack and nothing had been done to beautify it. We rectified that, in our low cost, bohemian style. At first we painted the walls and window panes in black and white squares and spatter-painted the old floor lino like a crazy rainbow. Having gotten that out of our systems, we settled for all white with black trim, against which our red-checked tablecloth looked great. That little cottage, three rooms and two verandahs, seemed the perfect hide-away for a pair of freelance writers with a common goal.

From the beginning Jeff and I shared a vision of a 'free and natural life' for ourselves and our children. This meant

side-stepping the narrow mores of our time and, instead, express-
ing love and new ideas openly, singing in tune with nature, ranging
out into the hinterland to touch what Jeff believed was the real
Australia. We chose Grays Point as our base not only because it
was affordable but also because it seemed closer to our ideal than
more fashionable suburbs with grid-like streets, houses lined up
like soldiers behind front fences penning barbered, soulless
gardens. Grays Point homes sprang up any old where, tucked
away among tall eucalypts, ribbon grass and tangled scrub.

Life at the Point, although more raffish than other suburbs,
was typical of those post-war years when life was conformist yet
chaotic, goods and services were in short supply, bureaucracy
ruled but people were optimistic because the fighting was over and
work abounded. They saved, scrounged, lived rough while
building their own homes.

Our nearest neighbours and early gurus were Peg and Wal,
tucked away in the scrub in their hand-built house, and on the other
side, Pop and Nanny Amos. Four self-sufficient elders, gems of
people – wise and calmly satisfied with their lives. The first couple
were old residents. Wally was a respected foreman on the Sutherland Council, a wise survivor of World Wars I and II, passionate
for the Common Man and what he had to contend with. Sometimes
on summer nights when Peg and Wal sat beside a little campfire
outside their rough unelectrified abode, Jeff and I would eaves-
drop without shame, wishing we had a tape-recorder, as their
voices, roughened by cigarettes and raw spirits, brought us through
the leafy distance Wal's eloquent answers to Peggy's questions
about how the world worked.

The Amoses were less introspective but just as admirable. When
they reached the age of retirement, they moved from the city and
bought a small solid cottage beside our block, planting an orchard
and vegetable gardens where everything grew. Everything
thrived. When the tide was right, they clambered down their steep
sandstone steps to launch their little wooden boat moored at the
edge of the mangroves. We would hear snatches of their conversation, the squeaking of their oarlocks as they rowed out into
deeper water where they could catch fish for tea. Saturday afternoons they watched the wrestling on television and Nanny roared
encouragement to the combatants as if she were at the stadium.

Sundays their grown children came for lunch, the grandchildren clattering and singing out as they raced their parents down the steep path from the road. Laughter, wholesome food with lots of onions and mixed herbs, and loving kindness were what emanated from the Amos household and luckily, some of it rubbed off onto us. We spent several Christmases with them and their clan, when every table in the house was laid end to end, there were balloons and crackers, and the food went on forever. The dignity of their self-sufficient and unassuming dynasty set me a model for rich family life.

Younger and distressing were the occupants of the only other dwellings within sound and sight of ours. Beyond Amoses', a middle-aged couple nurtured Pekingese dogs and a sway-backed horse that the husband had taught to drink beer out of the bottle. He badgered Jeff to take its picture and boasted of how he used his position as a strapper to nobble racehorses. His wife had a voice that could blister paint, bringing to me through the trees profanities I had not heard before. 'Rough as guts' was an apt description for that woman, but also hypocrite; she had the hide to talk against me at the shop because she spied me through the trees one hot midday hanging out washing in the nude.

The neighbours on Peg and Wal's side were far worse. It was a house of violence. Twice. The first residents were young and the bloke seemed permanently furious. Embittered when his wife left him, he drove his motorbike into a tree. After his death, the block was bought by a sour English ex-serviceman with a sad pale Italian wife he had impulsively married at the end of the War. They had two thin sallow children, whose screams and whimpers sometimes broke our lovely night silence, drowning out frog songs and the rustles of owls, the chatter of possums and occasionally the crashing of deer, feral in the National Park, who swam across the estuary to sample our small vegetable patch. At weekends, the disaffected Pom laboured to enlarge a bald scar on his block, which threatened to intrude across our boundary line. He cut down every tree and scraped the earth clean of vegetation, as if to eradicate this Australian nightmare in which he found himself and somehow start over. I found him dreadfully disturbing but he and the Pekingese harridan set me a powerful example. It taught one valuable lesson: put plenty of physical distance between your home and your neighbours' – in case they turn nasty or mad.

Those early years at Grays Point were intensely instructive. Not only was I learning how to conduct myself away from my mother's rule, I was also studying avidly this new culture which sometimes had little similarity to my own except a common language. Even that required attention, to avoid giving offence. Many of the friends we made then remained friends for life. We all worked hard during the week, but at weekends played light-hearted games of deck tennis beneath the gum trees, shared the odd flagon of plonk and occasionally hosted folk music bonfires. Our mates were mainly musicians, writers, artists or social historians, and not all lived locally. Grays Point was a pleasant place to visit, even in those rough old days.

The locals were a cheerfully unified bunch, perhaps because The Point was isolated by awkward geography and the fact that few people owned cars then. Most were trade-unionists, mainly labourers, all battlers and quite a few were left-leaning, if not actual Communists. One couple who did belong to that beleaguered party were journalist Rupert Lockwood and his wife Betty. He became a famous – some would say infamous – participant in an alleged spy scandal. We admired them and their children for sticking to their principles, and they introduced me to revolutionary politics by lending us their recordings of Irish rebel songs. From catchy jigs and haunting modal melodies, I imbibed the spirit and the despair of the Easter Uprising. I loved to watch Betty chair meetings at the hall, inspired by her intelligence, fairness and sense of democratic process. Committed open-handedly to the wellbeing of the community, her quiet feminism did not deter her from being a 'good' wife and mother by the lights of those times.

Our first year at Grays Point, Jeff and I travelled to Sydney by train to jobs, working and saving hard. When we moved to Grays Point, we had no car and no money. Jeff had given all his capital and his property to his first family. Fair enough. We were young and strong and would work hard to build up capital from scratch. Our furniture was packing cases and rickety cane chairs from the Tip. I loved that! A rackety little bus which ran only three times a day, except Sunday when there was no service, ferried us all to the railway station, at Sutherland. You dared not miss the bus.

Grays Pointers used to sprint up their rocky paths to the road, bags and briefcases flying, the women flinging off their old shoes at the last moment to be retrieved that evening and slipping on a good pair before mounting the steep step, all out of breath, greeted by friendly chiacks from the crowd. The Drunks' Bus was what they called the one on Friday nights because it stopped outside the pub and blew the horn until everyone tumbled out and climbed aboard, singing and joyful. On Saturday nights when there was no dance at the hall, a special Picture bus ran. Although from our house we could hear the thump of the band, the merry shouts of the dancers, we didn't attend the frolics in the hall, despite repeated invitations, because Jeff was very shy of social gatherings and a non-dancer, to my secret disappointment. We went to the Sutherland movie house, however, sitting on cracked wooden chairs that pinched your bottom, nursing children on our laps.

Yes, we did have children, who were wanted but not planned. As happened in those days. It was a few months after moving to the Point that we began to host visits from Jeff's older children, Karen and Thor. I vowed to never, ever stand between them and their father but to encourage them to spend as much time with him, with us, as possible. Indeed, Nanny Amos later told me she had never met anyone who put as much thought and consideration into another woman's children – an opinion which signalled some cultural difference I hadn't yet grasped. On an early visit to Grays Point, four-year-old Thor suddenly said to me: 'You took away our father'. What could I reply to that? I began to see that I would never justify myself to those children, without further hurting them. Never could I tell them what I knew about their parents' estrangement. So I would have to wear that prickly robe. My discomfort increased when Jeff's mother, Doris, journeyed up from Melbourne to inspect me. In her eyes, and the eyes of the Melbourne Carter clan, I was the Other Woman. And would be for some time.

There were times in those early days when I felt so uncomfortable with my position that I began to think the best thing I could do, for my peace of mind and theirs, was to leave the relationship, despite all its pulls and bonuses. The hitch was, I became pregnant – as one did in those days, contraception or not. Jeff urged me to stay with him. He said: 'There has been so much hurt already caused by this. Don't compound it. What we have together is too good to let go.'

So I stayed, vowing to try and make it up to all concerned. And thus we set about to create the 'perfect partnership'.

Our son Goth was born fourteen months after we came to Grays Point, then two years later, Vandal. I was seven months' pregnant with Van when the bushfire came through. By bad luck, both Harry Amos and Jeff had gone to the city on business. I left little Goth with Nanny on her front verandah while I carried boxes of Jeff's negatives, our only valuable asset, awkwardly down to the waterfront, and covered them with damp sacks. When that was done, we stood together, hearing the flames roaring nearer, trees exploding and crashing down, smoke all around us, and just as I turned to Nanny and said: 'It's going to get us,' we heard the fire-fighters coming, leaping like giants over rocks, their heavy boots thudding on the ground. 'She'll be right, Missus,' they shouted to us, and somehow they saved our homes. Afterwards, we made them cups of tea and stood around, sweaty and streaked with ash, thanking our lucky stars.

I could go on and on about Grays Point, our neighbours and friends there, and our enemies, because it explains the sort of people we were. And the sort of people we became. At the end of our first year together, Jeff was able to realise his dream. He resigned from the magazine and never worked in formal employment or for anyone else again. At my urging, he let his hair and beard grow. Short back and sides were no longer required in his new lifestyle. Four years later, we were still using makeshift furniture, but we owned a camping vehicle which accommodated our two little boys, plus Karen and Thor at weekends and on school holidays. Jeff built a canvas canopy with side curtains over the back of the Peugeot utility he chose for his first car (because Peugeot had won the Redex Trial the previous year). He always bought the best he could afford in equipment – cameras, vehicles, hi fi – trading up in quality as we became more prosperous. Other things could wait. He was quite happy with our makeshift household, scrounged or bought cheaply. And on trips, camping was good enough for him. He preferred it in fact because it put us close to whatever he wanted to photograph, and it kept him away from the sort of social situations he could not handle, including hotels or guesthouses. So I learned to cook outdoors. Nappies were washed in mountain streams, hung out to dry on barbed wire fences. The first couple of years, Goth and Vandal were easy to travel with on journalistic assignments, up and down the coast, into the forests to meet timber-getters and charcoal burners, onto tobacco farms and hop gardens. People welcomed our visits, because we tried to be unassuming, friendly, helpful and they warmed to Goth and Van, the little nomads. We covered the shooting events at the Melbourne Olympic Games in 1956, while staying with Jeff's parents. Jeff wrote about and photographed the Snowy Mountains scheme and its workers. When travelling with the children was too slow and cumbersome, I stayed at home with them, writing pulp fiction and minding the fort – a small business we named, prophetically, Kangaroo Press Service – while Jeff ventured out alone.

It was on one of his trips that he acquired the orphan kangaroo who profoundly affected our future direction.

There had been animals in our lives at Grays Point from the beginning, and our attitudes to them were pretty standard at first. Which means, a bit silly. The previous tenant of our house had been a cat-collecting recluse. The place reeked of cats and many still slept among the foundation stones and prowled the surrounding bush. Our aggressive young neighbour used them for target practice, shooting out his side window, which unnerved me. We adopted one beautiful tabby kitten we named Baptiste, after the hero of 'Les Enfants du Paradis', and we adored him until he too was shot. Next we took home a beautiful black cocker spaniel we found in the Cronulla sandhills, tall, pale, pristine, where we used to take the four children to play. Now they are gone, sad to say, sold off, spirited away, as if they never existed. Anyway, this cocker spaniel we named Thurber because he looked so much like those mournful cartoon dogs. Thurber, we discovered, had disgusting habits. He had bonded with humans when very young and now wanted to mate with everyone he met. Which is probably why such a gentle, handsome dog was abandoned at the beach. We took him back there, feeling guilty, and left him for the next gullible dog-lover (or Thurber fan) to take home.

Our next dog was another stray, a border-collie cross, one of those sweet-faced sheep herders, black with caramel eye-brows and a white chest. She looked exactly like the Russian space dog in the news then, the first animal to orbit the earth alive. The space dog's name was Laika. That's what we named our dog. Laika.

It was between Thurber and Laika that we received Hanogi, the little red 'roo who sowed the seeds for much of what this book is about. She took us beyond the realm of domestic pets into the tricky unknown country of wild creatures. We had no idea what a challenge we were accepting.

2

Hanogi, our first kangaroo

As was his habit now that he was well and truly freelance, about every six weeks Jeff went away gathering magazine stories beyond the ranges, finding places and people the average city journo didn't cover. This trip, in 1959, he had been to western New South Wales. Well past midnight I heard his footsteps coming down our steep bush track, and his special whistle (the up-tempo version of 'The Toreador Song' from the movie *Carmen Jones*).

I jumped out of bed and hurried to unlock the door. Joy! I hadn't expected him back until the next day. He enfolded me in a robust homecoming embrace, smelling of whiskers and campfire smoke and the dust of outback roads. Then he looked at me with a get-ready-for-the-big-surprise twinkle and rummaged in his camera bag.

From the folds of his jumper, up popped two long ears. They swivelled inquisitively. Out came a delicate face, with two huge almond eyes staring at me brightly, and a velvety nose a-twitch with nervous enquiry.

'Oh no,' I said, utterly captured.

I reached out to stroke the little creature but it ducked fearfully back into the bag, burrowing deep into the sweater for safety.

'Wherever did you get it?

'Near Tibooburra,' Jeff said. 'I met up with some professional 'roo shooters and did a story on them. They said I could take one of the joeys. Usually they just bash them over the head or leave them for eagles or dingoes to finish off.'

The little orphan poked its head out of the bag again, jittery as a butterfly yet strangely trusting. It stared all around and uttered a little chattering sound, a bit like a cat's sneeze.

'I guess she wants some milk,' Jeff said. 'And I wouldn't mind a cup of tea. I've been driving since dawn.'

I quickly pumped up the primus and boiled a billy. Jeff asked me for some of the water. He reached deep into his camera bag and extracted a hot-water bottle, handing it over to be refilled.

'Lucky I had it with me,' he said. 'It kept my sleeping bag a bit cosier, until they gave me the joey. Night winds on the western plains are freezing.' Then he reached into his jacket pocket and brought out a tobacco tin and a can of evaporated milk. Carefully he mixed milk with boiled water, fifty-fifty, explaining how the shooters had taught him to feed the youngster by gently pressing its nose into the warm mixture.

'Once it got hungry, it learned to lap in no time. The shooters say they always use a tobacco tin – it's just the right shape and easy to clean with boiling water.'

The question was obvious: 'How do kangaroo shooters know so much about saving joeys' lives?'

Jeff shrugged. 'Country people often rear up a young one as a pet for their kids, but they don't like them in hundreds, eating grass they want for livestock.'

The little newcomer uttered a strong 'Chut-chut-chut' that clearly meant: 'Where's the grub?'

Jeff put down his cup of tea and prepared to feed the baby.

'Wait,' I said. 'We must show the boys.'

Jeff thought it a shame to wake them as they could see the kangaroo in the morning, but something made me insist. I had a feeling we would all want to remember the night our first joey came to stay. So we took the camera bag out to the side verandah where Goth's little bed stood next to Van's cot. Dropping the side I scooped him up, all snug and drowsy in his sleep sack, and sat with him beside his brother.

'Wake up, fellas. See what Dad has brought from out west!'

So we went through the magic again. The astonishing ears

poking out of the bag first, then the big eyes and soft questing nose. 'Chut-chut-chut', cried our guest.

'It's hungry,' chirped Goth. The boys goggled, thrilled as I was.

Jeff lifted the baby out of his bag, still wrapped in the sweater. We had our first glimpse of limp velvet tail and great gangly legs before Jeff jackknifed them back into the folds of wool, settling the bundle on his lap. Then, very gently, he held the tobacco tin under the 'roo's mouth and with his forefinger pushed down on its nose until its lips were submerged. The joey began to lap. Noisily.

The boys grinned at us and we grinned at each other. Such a glow of delight bound us that we forgot for a while that it was two o'clock on a shivery winter morning.

'Right,' said Jeff when the joey had licked up the final drop and buried its head back into the warm swaddling. It was bundled back into the bag, on top of the hot water bottle. Then Van was laid in his cot, Goth snuggled down again and Jeff and I went off to bed, with the camera bag on the floor beside us.

Next morning was the first of hundreds when our wakening minds were greeted by 'Chut-chut-chut'. It was an urgent little call that could not be ignored. Had the mother kangaroo been still alive, the joey would simply have sucked on a teat at the bottom of her pouch and satisfied all its needs at once. Loneliness, fear, hunger. Chut-chut-chut. We had to do our best to provide.

We stoked up our little wood stove, as was our winter morning custom, and put the billy on, adding an extra quantity of water this time because there was that hot-water bottle to fill as well as tea to make. A pot of porridge went on the back of the stove to simmer.

Goth and Van were clamouring to see the baby, who was singing out for attention as well. So we brought them all in before the fire, the boys still in pyjamas and dressing gowns, and gave the orphan her breakfast. I can still recall the joy within the stove's circle of warmth as we watched her whiskers bead with milk and listened to her velvet lips lapping up every last drop with surprising efficiency.

Jeff and I were excited not only for ourselves but because we felt this was something special for our little boys to experience. We felt it was a link with native Australia which was undervalued in those days. It did not seem odd that we were filling the joey's stomach first. Nor did we realise that we had commenced a routine which would go on for months and months (and later, for years and years).

When the boys were dressed and tucking into their por-ridge – Van in his highchair and Goth at his little table – Jeff asked me to devise fresh bedding for the kangaroo. He wanted his camera case back. He'd been told that country people hung orphan joeys in a sack near the wood stove and thought we might do the same.

I volunteered my clothespeg bag and found some spare woollies to insulate it. Threadbare nappies and worn baby sheets would serve as linings. Within minutes we were in business, mothering the marsupial way, a system of reproduction different from all others in the animal world, and uniquely Australian.

'Now watch this,' Jeff said. He removed the little 'roo from her sweater wrapping and set her carefully on newspaper in front of the stove. It was our first full look at her and the boys stared at her soft wispy fur, long hind feet on which she stood unsteadily, using her tail for balance, her neat front paws – almost little hands – which she carried demurely against her chest.

We had little time to satisfy our curiosity, however. Warmth was vital to a pouch baby, Jeff told us seriously. He held the peg bag in front of the little 'roo and by gently touching her on the top of her head and at the base of her tail, he induced her to somersault into the opening. Goth and Van crowed with surprise and amuse-ment. Jeff then banged a nail into the woodwork behind the stove and hung the bag on it. The shape of the animal inside was discernible, her body bowed, her limbs folded like an umbrella. She seemed quite comfortable.

With that accomplished, the normal routine of the day took over. Jeff went to his darkroom to develop the photos he had taken on his trip. The little boys played with toys until it was warm enough to venture outdoors. And I gathered up clothes for the day's laundry. Jeff's jumper which had bedded the 'roo went on the pile. I wasn't yet aware of it, but I would be increasing my daily washing almost as much as if we had borne another human child.

By mid-morning Jeff was back with sheets of contact proofs for us to see, still wet from the fixer. He wanted to show us how the kangaroo skin industry worked.

I had seen kangaroos in small groups, coy amongst mulga scrub or fleeing fast from the sound of our motor, when I accompanied him out bush. It was a huge thrill for an American to glimpse such unique animals in the wild. Jeff's pictures showed piles of carcasses. They showed men with skinning knives, blood staining their clothes. They showed a claypan filled with salted pelts neatly pegged out to dry in the sun.

The boys stared at the pictures, round-eyed. 'Why do they shoot them, Dad?' Goth wanted to know.

Jeff tried to explain in simple terms the industry he had travelled far to do a story on. It was a business, as well as a blood sport, which helped graziers to rid their land of animals competing with sheep and cattle for the native herbage. The government encouraged it. Kangaroo skins added to the rural export product, along with meat and wool.

In those days Jeff was a moderate conservationist, acknowledging that in places where bores had been put down for livestock, the unusual water source caused 'roos to breed up to higher than normal numbers. But he was concerned about total clearing away of native species. And he questioned the use of marginal lands for grazing which, in drought times, often resulted in erosion and destruction of native pastures. It was not a view commonly held then. Few people saw value in preserving natural habitat. Land was something to exploit. Jeff favoured setting aside some unprofitable outback properties as sanctuaries where the natural ecosystem could prevail. Then controlled culling of kangaroos could continue without wiping them out.

Jeff would put his concerns across subtly in his article. He had too much respect for the hardy outback people he met to offend them, whether they were graziers or bore-sinkers, drovers or stockmen, mineral prospectors or fencing contractors. Or professional shooters. He sang their praises in magazine stories and later in books. And if he sometimes questioned the value of their actions from a national heritage point of view, he still gave them credit for stamina and initiative, which he reckoned was being lost by city dwellers.

By adopting one little orphan into our home, he felt we were somehow getting closer to a 'real Australia', an ethos from beyond the bitumen.

'What shall we call it, Dad?' Goth wanted to know. 'Is it a girl?' When Jeff said it was, both boys piped: 'Call it Miss Hanogi!' Miss Hanogi. An unlikely name? Not for movie buffs like us. It seemed perfectly logical. For weeks we'd been saying it over and over in the sweet drawl used by Marlon Brando in *Sayonara*, the film we had all watched at the drive-in. The story's setting and its dainty heroine were Japanese. Brando played an occupying US soldier from the deep south. 'Miz Ha-NO-gi?'

Luckily the little 'roo had come into a home in nursery mode. Goth was four, Van was eighteen months. Hanogi fitted into a routine geared to nurturing the very young. Like all marsupials, she had left the birth canal in a primitive state. Her foetal development occurred within the pouch. Now fully formed but unable to maintain body heat or eat grass, she would need at least six months of care and protection.

Her drinks of milk coincided with morning juice and afternoon Ovaltine, learning times and playing times, naps and baths. Toilet training and daily hygiene. Cuddlesome affection. We used to sit on the couch and lay Hanogi across our laps, grooming her fur while we explored her parts, taking care she didn't get cold. Her back legs had three distinct sections – a meaty haunch, a lean muscular lower leg and a long bony foot. That foot consisted of one thick toe ending in a strong straight nail. After we borrowed reference books from the library, we understood why she belonged to the Macropod family – big foot, get it? – and we looked for her tiny fur-combs on the side of each back foot, two curving nails joined by a flap of skin, with which she would groom herself later.

Her front paws had five distinct 'fingers', covered with hair on the top and with a soft grainy pad underneath. She liked to hold one of our fingers while she drank but because she had no opposable thumb, she clenched all five digits. Considering this, Goth and Van gained insights into their own dexterity.

It was a learning experience for us all. The boys liked to gently fondle Hanogi's long tail. It was already muscular and served as her balancing pole, functioning almost like a third leg when she stood. Her fur, dense but not yet long, had reddish tinges like bricks, the colour of the Australian inland. Underneath, it was bluey grey. And on her muzzle were pretty black and white streaks. Hair extended only halfway down her nose – a characteristic of red kangaroos, we learned from the books. Other types had totally furred or completely bare noses.

What with observing Hanogi's progress toward independence and assisting Goth and Van in their growing up, that winter passed very quickly. Goth, the chatterbox, quick and curious, seemed to learn a new word a day. Van, the strong silent type, became mobile and spent less time in his playpen. When he moved out, Hanogi moved in. We lined its sides with chicken wire, its floor with newspapers, and encouraged her to stand in it once the room was warm. We put shoots of grass under her nose to tempt her to chew, taught her to drink her milk from a dish standing on the floor, and stroked her gently to induce her to pass water before somersaulting back into her peg-bag pouch.

While Van disdained his bottle and mastered drinking from a cup, Goth practised eating with a fork rather than a spoon and insisted on cutting his food with his own little knife. Van rejected the highchair and joined his brother at the small table. Hanogi began to nibble chopped apple, brown bread and rolled oats. Her daily intake of solid foods increased and you could see her growing. You could see them all growing.

When the cold weather began to mellow, the boys spent mornings playing outdoors. If the sun shone really warmly, I encouraged Hanogi to be outside too. At first it was only for a few minutes, lest she become chilled. We'd put her playpen in a sheltered corner where grass grew. She began to nibble at it and to lick dirt she scratched loose with her front claws. The books didn't tell us why.

If a bird flew low overhead or a dog barked across the river, Hanogi became instantly alert, heaving back onto her tail, ears flaring. Agitated, she would chatter and hop about in a panicky fashion until we came to hold out her bag so she could somersault gratefully inside. Within a month, however, she had grown used to our back garden and seemed to crave more space than the playpen allowed. 'Let her out,' begged Goth and Van. 'We want to see her hop.'

Unrestrained at last one sunny morning, Hanogi stood poised, ears swivelling like radar dishes, velvet nose quaffing the air. Then she leapt sideways and took off. In seconds she was out of sight. Frightened for her, we all began to run. Our yard was nothing more than a clearing in the bush. No fences had we – it wasn't that sort of place. Development was still patchy, with cottages placed haphazardly under trees along the hillsides. Bracken, ribbon grass and yellow daisies grew knee high. Little Hanogi might easily lose herself.

We need not have panicked, however. She came flying back at the same top speed she had left us and stood trembling, sides heaving. I rushed to pick her up and felt her heart thudding against her delicate ribcage. When I set her down again, ready to grab her if she seemed inclined to take off, she simply put her head down and began to graze. We concluded she had just wanted to stretch her legs. And that became her daily pattern. When first we released her outdoors, she would listen, sniff, then leap sideways and accelerate away. Round the house she flew, stretching out her thin legs, bounding over obstacles. Once, twice around she went, then returned to graze quietly near the boys' play area.

Goth had built a little cubby in the fork of a wattle tree. 'Goth's House' read a hand-lettered sign. I used to carry out toy boxes, the small chairs and table, and set them up beneath the tree. With the kangaroo grazing nearby, it looked like a scene from Winnie-the-Pooh. Beneath the Angophora, with the estuary glinting far below, life seemed peaceful but my ears were tuned for the sounds of trouble. Not only for the crash of an overturned tricycle or the piping argument which sometimes ended in blows and tears, but also for the urgent chatter of an alarmed joey and the thump of her back feet on the earth as she prepared to flee.

'Mum!' the boys would shout, and I would rush out to scoop her up and cuddle her until she was calm again.

Dogs were our big worry. Without fences, they went about freely. We circulated the news amongst the neighbours and at the shop that dogs were unwelcome round our place. Jeff actually fired his rifle over the heads of two grinning mutts who wanted to establish a permanent route across our land. They changed tack. However, we realised a fenced area for Hanogi was the only answer.

She needed to be outdoors more and more. Milk no longer satisfied her, she wanted lots of grass as well. Doubled in size, her fur thicker, she outgrew the peg bag and now slept stretched out on her side on a mat placed, by special pleading, beside the boys' beds. They were awakened each morning by Hanogi reaching up on tiptoes to pat their faces, sniffing and chattering and clearly saying: Come on, chaps, it's another day! So Jeff bought chicken wire and cut a few saplings to construct a run for Hanogi. The fence was two metres high. During the day when we were about, she still grazed free around the house. But when we went shopping, we put her in her yard. We thought she would be safe there.

Alas, we were wrong.

One afternoon we returned from an outing to find Hanogi's yard empty. The wire was bent where she had gone over it. Something must have come and frightened her terribly. We all began to search, calling her name and chut-chut-chutting, but there was no sign of her. Jeff went to the houses of our neighbours. They had heard and seen nothing. I went up to the shop, social hub of our little community, but neither storekeepers nor patrons knew anything of our missing kangaroo.

Maybe she'll come back by herself, we told ourselves, and periodically went outdoors to call her as daylight faded and frogs and owls awakened round our house. We were a miserable little family at dinner that night. All our ears were tuned to the bush outside. We went to bed hoping we would hear the chut-chut-chut signalling Hanogi's return. More hours were spent listening than sleeping, but dawn brought us the realisation that our dear little 'roo was indeed gone.

We searched for the next two days. Thinking she might have dashed so far away that she had lost our scent, we drove around in the car, calling. Nothing.

Maybe someone took her in, we thought. I penned a notice and took it up to the shop. On the way home, on impulse, I called next door at the little school. It was recess and the headmaster was outside supervising the kids at play. I told him our story and he promised to quiz the pupils when they went back into class.

And that was how we finally learned what had happened to Hanogi. It was all so innocent, just a series of pure accidents which ended tragically.

One of the pupils reported sorrowfully that his father had run over the little kangaroo. It had bounded out of the bush, down near the boatshed, straight into the side of his car. He had picked her up,

badly injured, and driven to a veterinary surgery. When he called
back next day, he was told she had died.

But how had she come to be so far from home? That was also
revealed at the school. Two little girls had gone collecting for the
Brownies with their dog trotting beside them. When they tripped
down our path, it barked at Hanogi from outside the wire until,
terrified, Hanogi flung herself against it again and again, finally
managing to clear the top and dash away, the excited pooch in
pursuit. They went far before the dog gave up the chase. It went
home. Hanogi did not.

We felt angry, frustrated, yet unable in fairness to lay any blame.
The girls were distressed at what their dog had done. And the man
who had run over her was very upset. He refused to let us pay the
vet's bill and mourned with us that no more would there be a little
red kangaroo in our bit of bush.

The pall from Hanogi's death hung over our house for a long
time. We remembered distinctly the joy of her coming. Just as
distinctly, we recalled the pain of her going. Never again, we said.
We'll never rear another kangaroo. The risk of losing it is too
great. We'll never take on another one.

But, of course, we did.

3

Glenrock Farm, 1962

By the time our second kangaroo arrived, our situation had changed drastically. For a start, we had moved from Port Hacking to the New South Wales south coast. When Grays Point seemed set to follow its more upmarket neighbours into tree clearing, road making and the dreaded subdivision (dicing up bush into building blocks), we began to look for another home, further out.

We had hoped to buy an old farm in the Jamberoo area south of Wollongong, having come to love it through our friendship with Howard and Ivy Judd, rangers of Minnamurra Falls Reserve, which was at the head of Jamberoo Valley. When we first met them, in 1955, the Judds were living about a mile below the waterfalls, in a hewn slab cottage adjoining the park. They lived like pioneers, their tiny home overhung with grapevines, shaded by a giant camellia tree. Everything was small and handmade. Howard built them a generator by soldering tiny cups onto a bicycle wheel; it turned with water pumped from the creek running past their front door. The contraption was only strong enough to power baby globes, so their household appliances were primitive. Light came from kerosene or pressure lamps. Their radio was a crystal set built by Howard into a child's suitcase. Ivy cooked on a primus stove or the big wood range which also heated water for the bath and laundry. Clothes were washed in a tub with wooden paddles turned by hand, another Howard invention.

We had met them by accident, seeking shelter from bad weather on one of our journalistic trips. I was very pregnant with Goth and although the first night we insisted on camping in their paddock, as was our habit, from then on they urged us to stay in the house. We liked one another at once, forming a friendship that was life-lasting, and Jeff sensed in them a good story that wanted telling.

Howard understood, when no one else seemed to, that to preserve the rainforest, the surrounding bush must also be kept as shelter against drying winds. He lobbied the Kiama Council, which controlled the Reserve in those days, as well as local service clubs, seeking protection from land-clearers. His voice and Ivy's sounded small amid the clamour for 'development', but they were undaunted.

Along with hosting the park for visitors each day, the Judds grew their own food. Ivy put great faith in the healing properties of fresh produce, especially vegetables steamed lightly in a pressure cooker, plus the good cheer brought by a nice hot cup of tea. In her low little kitchen, which was also living and dining room, she managed to turn out big fluffy scones and bottles and bottles of rich jams and pickles, always pressing on us jars to take home. I can still picture her pumping her primus vigorously while Howard spoke about his latest botanic investigations. Using an old-fashioned microscope, he had identified and classified the rich flora of the hidden rainforest reserve, bringing it to the attention of university scholars and earning him an invitation to join the international Linnaeus Society.

The Judds welcomed visitors to the falls with the same warm hospitality they extended at home. I can still conjure Howard's long face, smiling then serious beneath a ranger's hat he wore squarely on his head because it gave him the 'official' appearance he needed so that people would hark his messages about protecting the reserve.

To educate visitors to the reserve, Howard patiently recorded the residents of the forest on a tape which he played for people through a simple loudspeaker above the fern board, his old-fashioned parson's voice intoning the name of each bird before its call. He built the handsome log information board and mounted samples of ferns and leaves on it. The Judds' vision was to use only materials appropriate to the park and this created a rustic environment for people who came to walk the quiet rainforest tracks to the falls. Using tree trunks and river stones, Howard built a kiosk and picnic area. Later, when the reserve gained in popularity, Howard resisted the Council's offers to build larger amenities of concrete. At considerable discomfort to themselves, he and Ivy did without electricity for years until the Council agreed to put the wires underground, out of sight.

The Judds' principles, their passion, their good humour and friendliness inspired Jeff and me to write about their work many times. We dubbed them 'The Keepers of the Forest'. Their story appeared in magazines like *Walkabout*, *The Women's Weekly* and *People*, and later became a chapter in a book Jeff titled *Stout Hearts and Leathery Hands*. The publicity attracted an ever widening public and reinforced Howard's petitions to the Council. We became their publicists. They became our inspiration!

The valley matched our ideal of a free and natural life. Each time we drove through it on our way up to the Judds' magic forest domain, daydreams were spun. Here, or there, would be a perfect little niche for us. Naive as we were, we imagined that any property with rustic sheds and an old farmhouse needing paint would be going cheap. We didn't understand that surrounding the quaint wooden dairies and muddy yards was improved pasture, green and weedless, watered by small clean streams. Jamberoo was prime dairy land. The price on the rare farm which came up for sale staggered us and, disappointed, we would retreat home to our hideaway on Sydney's fringe. When Jeff's parents retired and moved from Melbourne to Grays Point to be near us, we settled back and put our dreams on hold.

Then a Gerringong real estate agent whom Jeff had approached during our searching days rang to say he had the perfect property for us. He was so lyrically certain we would like it that we decided to treat it as a picnic outing to our favourite part of the world. That day changed our lives forever.

The name of the valley he took us to was Foxground, named for the native fruit bats, or flying foxes, that roosted there. It was a few miles further south than Jamberoo but its situation, nestled beneath the coastal mountains, was very similar. Turning inland off the Princes Highway, we immediately felt comfortable as we drove past dairy farms crisscrossed by streams, traditional wooden buildings, huge old fig trees and cabbage tree palms. After two miles the tarred road ended and we began to climb between trees which in places mingled overhead to form green tunnels. Small creek crossings had to be forded slowly, but they were a plus to our way of thinking. Excitement began to build, though we reminded each other we weren't really in the market to buy, not then.

We crossed a wooden bridge over a sizeable stream, then the road rose steeply until paddocks appeared on either side of us. First we saw, on the right, a graceless cottage, just an unpainted fibro square next to a bare boulder as large as itself – momentary disappointment. And then, on the left, we saw *It*, a perfect old south coast farmhouse with a white picket fence topping a stone wall encrusted with lichen. The two-storey dwelling snuggled among trees and flowering shrubs.

We stepped from the car into air so fresh you could taste it, and silence punctuated only by bird calls and distant running water. An elderly man, stooped, grey, diffident, came to greet us. The vendor. What did we want to look at first? The house? Or the land?

I looked hopefully toward a little wooden gate into the front garden, but the men prevailed and we set off up the back to explore the property, crossing several small streams on stepping stones. The farm covered 105 acres, less than half of which had been cleared. The rest was hillside forest. Small paddocks fenced for grazing were divided by five creeks. Growing along their steep banks was subtropical rainforest, the same as in Minnamurra Falls Reserve. The canopy included red cedar, lilly-pilly, coachwood, the trees looped with vines, the humus busy with delicate ferns that tickled our ankles or clung to rocks and tree trunks. The boundary fences were old stone walls, like those for which Jamberoo was famous. Our excitement neared the boil, but there was still more to come.

'You mightn't have time to visit the waterfall,' ventured the owner, implying that we, like he, had walked enough. 'They get a lot of rain in these parts,' he murmured, as if he felt we should be warned. 'Makes it kind of humid. Some people can't take humidity. Saps the energy . . .'

We assured him we were unfazed and, leaving him to limp back to the house, we followed the agent up the road. About 100 yards above the farmhouse, where an old plough perched atop a huge boulder, he led us into the forest. Once our eyes grew accustomed to the dim light, we saw a narrow animal pad and followed it downward, hugging the hillside between tall rainforest trees, toward the glint and gurgle of silvery water. We emerged onto the slanting face of a huge rock ledge. A stream raced quickly downward over it and plunged into a big pool. Lianes and tree ferns shaded it but dappled sun on the water showed it to be very deep.

'At the far side, it spills over a rock lip and falls a hundred feet to the lower creek,' the agent explained.

Oh, no! That was almost as tall as the Minnamurra Falls. To think that one could *buy* a waterfall! The agent said casually, 'Oh, there's several on this place. This one is the biggest.'

We walked back awed into silence. Below us, rust-red iron roofs clustered like a child's toy farm on the ridge between two of the creeks. The old buildings squatted among ancient fruit trees. Beyond, we could see the spartan fibro cottage next to its giant boulder, part of the property, an extra dwelling thrown in for free.

In shock, we entered the broad back gate next to a small stone dairy. The agent mentioned that water and electricity were connected to the dairy, despite its air of decrepitude. 'Perfect for a darkroom, Jeff,' he said encouragingly. Adjoining were open barns and sheds built of bush poles and thick wooden slabs. In one hung long crosscut saws – two-man saws – which had shaped those slabs from living trees a century before. In the same shed stood a forge with huge leather bellows and an anvil. The former long-term owner had been the local blacksmith. Under his warped work-benches was a treasury of old iron and handmade implements.

The back yard was a maze of poultry runs and bird aviaries between old citrus trees and a small vegetable patch. Waiting for us on the tiny back verandah sat the man's wife. Pallid like her husband, her bearing spoke of depression and worry. Beside her on a cane lounge rested her enormous cat, fluffy and smug. Each day, she told us fondly, it laid in her lap a bird caught in the garden. Beside the back door leaned a rifle. 'Loaded,' the owner confided to Jeff, man to man. 'I keep it handy. We get foxes and tiger cats after the chooks here.'

Speechless, we entered the house through the kitchen. It was like stepping back forty years. The ceilings were low and the rooms small. A big stone hearth had been boarded over but looked accessible. There was a walk-in pantry and a small dining room facing onto the back garden.

The slab kitchen had originally been separate, in case of fire, but now was joined to the rest of the dwelling by a low verandah, at the end of which was, as an afterthought, the bathroom. It was just big enough for a claw-foot tub, a chip heater and a tiny hand basin. No toilet. That was outdoors, at the end of a stone pathway.

There were small steps between the rooms, evidence of how the house had grown according to the needs and whims of its owners. I found that endearing. There was a small room in the centre of the house, next door to the bathroom, which would do for a guest room. Off the central hallway, steep hand-hewn stairs led to twin rooms beneath the eaves, unlined except for newspapers pasted onto bare boards. These attics had low doors, handmade, the adze marks plain on their unpainted wood. Our boys would love these for bedrooms, I thought.

The two main rooms downstairs were so small their old-fashioned furniture filled them. One was the master bedroom, the other the lounge, with another stone fireplace, also covered. Both rooms had old-style domed windows and solid wooden doors, complete with huge iron keys, opening onto the front verandah which faced the road. Two big jacarandas stood guard over the front garden and beyond was forest, birdsong and that murmuring creek below. Heavenly.

When we emerged from our tour of inspection, it took all our concentration for Jeff and me to remain coherent. With amazing restraint, we muttered we'd have to go home and talk it over with Jeff's parents. We'd need to bring them down for a look, but, oh yes, we were very interested.

What we didn't learn until later was how relieved the sad couple were to find us. No one else wanted to buy the place. As a farm, it had been established by hand and by horse but was now considered too steep for new-style mechanised agricultural methods. And no one, in those days, would have bought Glenrock as a dwelling or a weekender. It was ten minutes drive to the beach and Nowra, the nearest sizeable town, was eighteen miles south.

Only people like us, with a love for old things, a yen for self-sufficiency and the ability to work from home, would want such a place. Such a paradise. The desperation of the owners was reflected in the price. They had bought the farm too late in life and, after only a few years, the man had suffered a heart attack doing battle with lantana and blackberry. Now they desperately wanted to get back to city living.

That day was one of the high spots of our life. We talked nonstop on the drive back to Grays Point and when we called to pick up Goth and Van at Jeff's parents' house, they listened, stunned, as we raved on and on about what we had seen. Never ever again could we find such a property at so affordable a price. Doris and Percy were surprised at this sudden new impetus, but agreed that they would drive down with us on the weekend and give their advice.

As it happened, Jeff's Uncle Gordon arrived to visit them and he came along too. He and his wife (Doris's sister) made money speculating in property and were much admired by Jeff's more cautious parents. They would heed his opinion.

Luckily, he agreed it was a jewel of a property. The price was low for the acreage and its natural attributes. It would need hard work to maintain, but at 31 and 33 respectively, Jeff and I felt keen for outdoor work. With the power and telephone connected, a school bus calling nearby, plenty of fresh mountain water, rich volcanic soil, rainforest, and only two hours drive from Sydney, it seemed perfect for us. Not only Uncle Gordon but also Jeff's parents agreed it was too good to pass up.

While Goth and Van were poking excitedly among the old tools and fascinating bits of metal in the blacksmith's shed, we went to speak to the owners. They couldn't believe their good luck. Neither could we.

We put our place on the market at Grays Point and as quickly as possible we sold it. The Amos family were the only close neighbours I felt sad to be leaving. Most of our other good friends assured us they'd be coming to visit us on the farm. During the intervening months, Jeff travelled down with his dad to work on the farmhouse – not to modernise it, just to make a few basic renovations to match our dreams. Percy Carter was a jack of all trades and he welcomed a chance to practise his skills.

Upstairs, the dinky attic rooms had to be stripped of their newspaper coats and lined with masonite before Goth and Van could sleep there. As Jeff scraped away layer upon layer of yellowed newsprint, up came World War II, the Depression, pioneer airman Kingsford-Smith's takeoff from the local Seven Mile Beach for an epic flight to New Zealand (laden with extra fuel, his plane needed a very long runway to become airborne), then the Diggers' return from World War I, and Federation! The earliest date was 1879. Our new home had already lived a long life.

Downstairs, the men replaced the old floor coverings with new lino and painted the thick slab walls of the kitchen and side verandah a sparkling white. They uncovered the two fireplaces and installed in the kitchen a second-hand Metters 'Canberra' wood stove purchased from Nowra's auction rooms.

We bought some nice old furniture there, including a brass bedstead. It was funny. Many locals were getting rid of their old things, trading up to maple veneer and laminex with chrome while old leather sofas and marble washstands went cheap or were left out in the weather for chooks to roost on. We were thought eccentric for reversing the trend.

Beguiled by romantic notions about old-fashioned technology, I loved cooking on a stove and bathing in water heated by wood and couldn't wait to use the aged copper in the tiny laundry which faced onto the side garden. It was a lovely, fragrant place of old, overgrown wygelias, May bush and agapanthus, overshadowed by mature oaks and a white cedar tree, under which was a huge boulder, crowned rather mysteriously by rock orchids.

I mastered the wood cooker and the bathroom chip heater, which roared like a hurricane when alight, but the old laundry copper gave me trouble from the start. It smoked! I used to retreat with eyes streaming and stinging, then plunge back in, cursing as my little fires spluttered out yet again. I learned that sap-filled coral tree was not good tinder and finally understood that the old flue was blocked and rusted beyond salvation. I persevered, yearning for the steam off clothes boiling in suds of Sunlight soap. I knew it made clothes *really clean*. Drying on a line outside in dappled sunshine and pure Foxground air would complete the production: baskets of washing smelling sweet like Grandma's used to.

While work within the farmhouse continued in the first weeks after we all moved to the farm, we camped in the little cottage. It looked mean on the outside, standing square in the centre of an open paddock, baldly unpainted, with neither garden nor tree to soften it, only that giant bare boulder for company. But inside it had charm. Its simple country furniture kept us comfortable those first busy weeks and most of it is still being used today.

The cottage, we quickly learned, had a life of its own. Two families had been coming there to holiday for years. They were friends of the blacksmith and one, a Sydney plumber, had helped instal the property's water supply, a simple line of buried pipes that used gravity to bring fresh mountain stream water from above the waterfall. The other, an academic, was a keen bushwalker and naturalist. They showed us how cottage tenants, while adding to our income, could be rich sources of information about Glenrock Farm, its flora and fauna. Particularly the bird life. It was birds, not marsupials, which prompted us to make the place a Wildlife Refuge.

Three bird encounters influenced our thinking from the outset. The first involved the improvements at the farmhouse. Replacing the old floor coverings meant taking up layer upon layer of worn linoleum, under which was another feast of historic newspapers. The new lino was heavy duty – reflecting our optimism that we would live in the house forever – and of a strong, honest blue. As Jeff and his dad swept the trimmings out the back door, they were seized and carted off by bower birds for their courtship mounds. One of these had been boldly positioned quite near the house during its brief vacancy, so that when we moved in, I was startled to see this vivid display of blue lino chips spread out around a U-shaped structure of twigs. Guess where?

I mentioned that the toilet was located at the end of a rough stone and concrete path leading from the kitchen door. The simple boxy building was screened by a giant privet and faced onto a grove of bulbs and shrubs, a playground for birds so pleasant that the little handmade wooden door was usually left propped open. This is where the bowerbirds built a bower, so that using the toilet included witnessing a display of courtship song and dance.

Their song sounds a bit like a buzz saw and the male's routine involves a fussy rearrangement of decor, mainly blue. Why blue?

The bird book did not explain but I noticed that the eyes of mature bowerbirds are blue and wondered if that acted to filter out other colours. What we did learn was that the shiny black males are mature, but of the other birds, green with brownish wing tips, not all are females. Young males start life green but later acquire the plumage which has won them the title 'satin birds' from old-timers. If the male bird can woo a female with his song, dance and decorative bower arrangements, they mate in the bower and fly off to nest in a tree. Then another male takes over and the whole process begins again. Those first weeks, we all sat longer than necessary in the toilet, quietly fascinated by the performances out front.

The second bird experience also occurred early. Just outside the verandah windows, I spied the most exquisite honey-eater I had ever seen supping from an old fuchsia bush beside the house. As it hovered close to my eyes, made confident by the glass separating us, it drank from pink and mauve blossoms like hanging Japanese lanterns, and I marvelled at its intricate markings – rich caramel, chalky white, outlined in blackest black. Stopped in mid-task, I watched and thought, we *own* this beauty's home – what a favoured country is Australia, with species still intact that people in other places can only find in books or zoos. I rushed for Neville Cayley's classic *What Bird Is That?* and learned I was watching an eastern spinebill. A feeling began that day which persisted and would never leave me: that what we had bought was not just a farm, not just relict rainforest, but a sacred trust.

The third episode of our definitive bird experiences happened very, very early on a warm Easter morning, our first at Foxground. We were still in bed when the thump of boots resonated down the garden path and a cheery voice called: 'Anybody about?'

We rose to see, near our back door, a stranger wearing a hunting vest, bandolier and other paraphernalia, and carrying a high-powered rifle. He introduced himself confidently as someone who annually visited the property for an Easter shoot. He was just doing us, the new owners, the courtesy of making himself known before he went up the back to blast away. His quarry? Wonga pigeons.

We were appalled. Under the guidance of Howard and Ivy Judd, and also the bird-watching tenant of our cottage, we had taken numerous strolls in search of birds on lists they had given us. Among these were several species of pigeon. We could hear them daily cooing in the bush, but sighting them was difficult. The scarcest but also the most beautiful we had only glimpsed in the farthest reaches of forest. These were the big wongas, their plump breasts of rich bluey grey necklaced by vivid white bands. They made, we had been informed, delicious eating and thus had almost been shot out. Intensely shy, they strut and bob among the leaf litter searching for seeds and insects, until an approaching enemy spooks them into lift-off, which they do with a heavy sound like a horse blowing.

To the surprise of our visitor, we told him hunting wonga or any other pigeons on Glenrock Farm was now finished. He grew indignant. He had been coming here for years, the blacksmith had been a mate of his, he was careful not to shoot near cows . . . Adamant and unashamed, we ushered him, spluttering, back to his car and off the property. As we recovered from the shock over breakfast, Jeff's anger grew. The man had boasted of a whistle which would call the wongas close to him. 'With a big rifle like his, he'd blow them into bits at that range,' Jeff growled.

Now shooting was not something he shied from. Jeff's people came from Bendigo, in Victoria. Leisure time was spent in the bush, hunting and trapping and fishing. Young Jeffrey learned well from his father and uncles. *Outdoors and Fishing*, the magazine he edited in Sydney before turning freelance, was devoted to angling and gun sport. At Foxground, hunting rabbits would keep numbers low on our property while providing fresh meat for our table. But shooting birds was something else.

We were told that some European migrants shot them to eat, as was their custom in their homelands before moving to New South Wales. Not just pigeons or – *horreurs!* – lyrebirds, but little wee songbirds. We found that distasteful and when shots from nearby properties rang over the tree-tops, we became increasingly uneasy. Port Kembla, with its Yugoslav and Italian steelworkers, was only half an hour's drive away. Foxground's bird life drew them like a magnet.

Howard, our mentor from Minnamurra Falls, offered a suggestion. Why not apply to make our farm a Wildlife Refuge? This was a new government initiative which aimed not to inhibit agriculture but merely to protect native habitat on properties – wetlands, small stands of trees, catchments, creek banks, and so on. Its purpose was to slow the total clearing or draining of 'scrub'. We could see its value as a deterrent to shooters who, like our Easter visitor, were not of a mind to take 'no' for an answer. A feeling prevailed then that hunting was a sort of freedom owed to any red-blooded Australian, even on private land. We wanted some sort of official signage which warned of legal penalties for shooting on Glenrock Farm.

We also wanted to protect the rainforest on our place. Every week huge timber jinkers ground up the road which ran through our place to vacant lands above. They returned laden with logs, exhausts popping like gunfire as their engines strained to hold their great loads. In the 1960s, most small towns of the Illawarra and Shoalhaven still had a sawmill. Harvesting native trees was a respectable local industry. We accepted that but wanted to preserve the cedars and coachwoods and other lovely species on our place as a pool of what used to be – *should be* – growing here.

Not only saving trees preoccupied us. We discovered that someone was parking a truck near our bottom bridge and sneaking up the big creek, stripping off staghorns and bird's nest ferns to sell. Even bush iris and small ferns like maidenhair were in danger. It was not considered stealing to pluck native plants from the roadside for transplanting into one's own garden, rather it was another right of red-blooded Aussies, mostly women. Respectable suburban housewives thought nothing of pillaging the bush.

So before the year was out, we submitted an application to have our property declared a Wildlife Refuge. It proved to be a long and tedious process. We discovered that everyone has rights over your land – the Electricity Commission, the Department of Mines, the Water Board, Main Roads, the Council and so on. We had to canvass them all. But we persevered. It would be over a year before we could establish that no one had any plans for our land except us. Then and only then would we receive a registration certificate and official Wildlife Refuge signs.

Meanwhile, we studied the flora and fauna on our place avidly, adding to our lists of wondrous birds and plants. It was our spare-time research project and passionate hobby, involving many bushwalks and the collection of discrete samples to compare against puzzling and often inadequate reference books. Our early bird list included Lewin honey-eaters, whip birds, yellow robins, blue wrens, firetail finches, grey thrushes plus brown, bronze-wing and wonga pigeons. The elusive Superb Lyrebird was our most coveted sighting, so rare that usually we had to content ourselves with finding one of its long curving tail feathers. Our fervent hope was that with the property legally protected and in our caring hands, the threatened species would build up and our lists would grow.

Even though our main impetus was agriculture during the early years, we began our rescue operations fairly soon. It was birds that started us off. Most of our patients were victims of window glass. The sickening thud of a bird in full flight colliding with a window-pane was a not infrequent sound in our bird-rich garden. The impact never failed to bring us to peer out, dreading what might lie below. Sometimes birds merely glanced off and kept flying. More usually, the victim woud fall to the ground stunned. In the early days we used to run out, collect the casualty and stretcher it indoors, frantically thinking: first aid? Placing it in a box of straw or soft rags, we would massage its breast if it were gasping and offer drinks of water, most of which were ignored.

We had to acknowledge that our Red Cross technique was not saving many lives. In fact the treatment seemed to cause the birds as much trauma as the original accident had done. So we progressed to quietly collecting the bird and putting it in a safe place in the garden, in touch with the earth and its natural envi-ronment but out of the way of dogs and other pedestrians. This was so much more successful that we evolved into method C, which is simply to leave the bird where it lies, call the dogs indoors and warn away passers-by. Given time to rest undisturbed, many birds can find the strength to rise and fly away. It might take them all day, but by nightfall they will be gone. Those less fortunate and more critically injured will also be 'gone' by dark. My own conclu-sion is that human contact harms wild birds more than it aids them. Handling little or not at all is best. Yet the urge to help, the fascination with peeping at the victim, is hard to resist.

I remember the first time a bird bashed into our window so hard that the old pane broke and tinkled to the floor inside. I rushed over to find a beautiful brown pigeon teetering on the windowsill. Slowly it began to sag forward like a person fainting. My first impulse was to steady it. The counter-impulse was to not touch the bird at all, lest I add to its shock. Thus I stood still and watched the pigeon slowly keel over and fall. It was dead before it hit the floor. Telling the story to a friend living in Jamberoo, I learned that fast-flying birds broke his windows too. One actually crashed through, kept flying, and crashed out a second window on the opposite side of the room. It was a kookaburra. A very strong and lucky one.

A solution might have been to curtain our windows which, in certain lights, gave the impression that our house was a through-way. However, in the Carter home, curtains were anathema. Jeff had grown up in an upholstered household where every orifice was covered with three layers of material. It strongly influenced his ideas about home decorating.

The first bird that actually stayed in our house was a baby mudlark, which most locals call a peewee. Goth found it on the ground beneath the tall oak tree at Foxground's school bus stop. Apparently it had been blown out of a nest and there was no way to put it back. Left there it would surely have been gobbled by a fox or dog or domestic cat. So Goth claimed it and named it after his favourite teacher.

Rodney J Watson's new nest was on a hot-water bottle inside a deep box lined with cloth. Goth offered him an eye-dropper of water. He turned aside at first but after a while he surprised us by opening his beak. When the fluid was squirted down his throat he closed his beak and swallowed. The secret was to come at him from above, as his mother would have done.

The next thing was to find him some food. Luckily worms were plentiful in our damp garden soil. Jeff laid down the law from the start: 'Now listen, Goth, this bird must be your responsibility. So you keep up the supply of worms, right?'

'Yes, Dad.'

And dig worms he did, lots of them, building a supply in a tin of earth. There were dramas when the worms crawled up the side and escaped but we found a better container so that problem went away.

Getting Rodney to take the worms was tricky but Goth perse-vered, with plenty of advice from the rest of us. He introduced the food from on high, holding the worm with tweezers. After one or two failures, Rodney got the hang of it. As soon as he spotted the dangling worm suspended above him, he opened up and down it went – except when the worm got caught sideways, with its head writhing out one side of Rodney's mouth and its tail lashing the other. We all held our breaths until Rodney learned to give a shake and a snap and gulp the dinner down.

He was no trouble, that Rodney J Watson. In fact he was a very sweet creature. He slept in Goth's attic bedroom and when he grew older, he used to walk about on the desk while Goth did his homework or built his models. He dropped a few calling cards but Goth kept a box of tissues handy and he emptied his own waste-basket. The bird liked to sit on Goth's shoulder, watching everything that went on. 'Peep,' he used to say, 'Peep?', and rub his beak against Goth's collar.

One weekend Goth wanted to sleep overnight at his friend's home down in the valley. He asked us if Rodney could stay in our room, so he wouldn't be lonely. Which was how we came to have Rodney's box at the foot of our brass bed. During the dark hours, I wakened to hear Rodney sort of cooing to himself.

'Are you all right, Rod?' I asked softly.

A drowsy 'Peep' was his answer.

Next morning I was awakened by a louder, insistent 'PEEP' close to my ear, Rodney had hopped out by himself and was strut-ting about on the floor under our bed. I got into my robe and offered him my hand, held flat with the palm up. He stepped onto it confidently. After a minute or two, he sank gratefully and pressed his downy breast against my warm skin. He was cold.

Rodney J was a trusting pet. When his feathers came, they formed a crisp black and white pattern I never thought until getting Rodney that I would have the chance to examine closely. As he grew, his appetite increased. Goth had no hope of keeping up the worm supply, not unless he gave up school and stayed home alto-gether, a plan he favoured but which was vetoed by his parents. So Jeff and I had to work the nine to four o'clock shift, shovelling into the garden earth. Rodney was walking about by now and he would stand beside the digger, peeping like a steaming kettle.

'Here, get in and dig a few for yourself,' Jeff used to say. But Rodney wasn't ready for that yet. He sat about in the garden, perched on low branches where we placed him, hoping he would begin to learn to fly. All in good time. First there was this giant hunger to keep satisfied.

One day we had a visit from an old school chum of Jeff's. Hyam was a scientist with the CSIRO (the Commonwealth Scientific and Industrial Research Organisation). We were always pleased to see him at the farm because part of his research involved agricultural animals and he was a good source of information. Walking him from the gate toward the house, we were accompanied by Rodney, peeping urgently between our feet. 'Just a minute, mate,' Jeff had to say. 'Before we go inside for a cup of tea, I've got to dig a few worms.'

And so it went through the day. We couldn't sit down to lunch until Rodney had been fed again. Lingering over coffee and conversation, we had to get up and find more worms. The air was rarely free of his summonses.

At last, Jeff's old friend began to laugh. 'I reckoned you'd become successful, Carter. Independent, self-employed, living free of the rat race? But I find you enslaved. Enslaved by a bloody bird!'

We could see the funny side. And took seriously his parting advice concerning diseases transmittable to humans by birds. We kept our hands washed from then on and told Goth the bird should not sleep in his room any more. Which was okay, because Rodney was capable of sleeping outdoors now. Our only worry was snakes and other nocturnal predators. So we compromised by building Rodney a night perch on the front verandah. We had wired it in so that it was secure.

When at last Rodney learned to fly and left us, we felt it was a job well done. He was the first bird we successfully rescued and gave back to nature. But he was not the last.

4

Turning back the clock

We felt pretty pleased with ourselves when finally we learned from the Parks and Wildlife Department that we had become 'Glenrock Wildlife Refuge – number 159'. We hurried to Sydney to collect our signs and Jeff nailed them up in the most conspicuous places. The public thoroughfare that ran diagonally across our 105 acres was narrow, unsealed and infrequently graded, but we wanted to inform the rare motorists who used it that they were passing through a special place. The signs signalled that the Carters' property was a different ball game to the rest of Foxground. All around us, land-holders were clearing. We intended that our farm remain an island of sanctuary in the midst of 'development'.

People in those days held attitudes about the country that I felt ranged from the naive to the cavalier. For example, one day a woman alone motored up and pulled in beside our gate. I came out to greet her, as was my custom – a legacy of both my mother's hospitable manners and the welcome we almost always received when we travelled out beyond gates and grids on journalistic assignments – but found she wanted nothing more than a chat, a small reward for having ventured so far off the main road. She may have been having a holiday but I was not; I had work to do. Yet I lingered with her, too polite to say so. To avoid asking her in, I walked with her to the edge of the road near her vehicle and began to answer her questions about the many sorts of trees growing down the gully there. Suddenly she spied a vivid pink blossom peeking out of the long grass. 'Oh, how lovely!' she exclaimed and reached down. Before I could stop her, she had picked it. Something in my face must have tweaked her conscience. 'I shouldn't have done that, should I?' No, she shouldn't. It was a rare native bulb which throws up one bloom infrequently. But what could we do about it? The damage was done.

Another day, a carload of Sunday motorists rolled up, parked and proceeded to climb the fence into our orchard. They began picking apples and peaches. Something in me resented that. My own sense of privacy, of private property, was strong. 'Can't you see this is someone's property?' I demanded. 'How would you like it if I entered your garden and picked your roses?'

Befuddled but without apology they departed, taking with them, after some fumbling, the fruit they had in their hands. I nursed my outrage like a sore tooth until calm returned. I conceded they might have thought the trees did not belong to our house, which stands on the opposite side of the track. In any case, the garden was well-tended and clearly belonged to someone. Just because they were not in sight was no excuse to steal their produce. Not in my book, anyway.

I felt guilty after confronting those people, yet I resented their ethics. Or lack of them. The last straw came one day when we were out and someone pulled up near the bottom bridge to dump several boxes of wastepaper. I saw from their tyre tracks that they had then turned around and departed from Foxground. Their only interest in it and our property had been as a convenient place to carry out a chore they could have performed at home. It would have been so easy for them to burn their refuse in their incinerator, but they had chosen the lazier option, which was to dispose of it in a country lane. In those years, the bush used to be full of people's rubbish. Old mattresses, broken beds and chairs, boxes of tins and bottles. It was a nasty practice – which thankfully does not exist now – and it outraged me then to contemplate the disdain for nature such people exhibited. How arrogant to think that motorists driving past would have to look at that mess, instead of a nice green roadside, pristine in itself. I have to confess that I went through those discarded envelopes and circulars until I was sure of the address of the dumper. Then next time I went to Sydney, I stopped by their house – which, as I suspected, was immaculate – and popped the boxes over their front fence. It was the only time I did such a thing, but I hoped it would make someone think.

Of course, I felt guilty about my reactions and wondered if I was being too stroppy. Debating moral issues was my practice, often when I was home alone. Then when Jeff turned up, I laid them out before him, in intricate detail. He had no such qualms, of course. A very direct thinker, Jeff. First the thought, then the action, then on to the next thing. Our differences were profound and mainly (I later found out) gender based, but there were also cultural dissimilarities between us, family influences which made us see the tasks ahead from different perspectives. His own was an anarchic view of the world. Do it yourself. Do it now. My forte was tact, and trying to see the other person's viewpoint. I was sunny where he was taciturn. His shyness was compounded by a disinclination to suffer fools gladly. Fortunately, our differences dovetailed into an attractive whole, or so our friends led us to believe.

Our circle grew and continued to grow when we moved to the farm. Jeff's old school chums, our Grays Point friends, the cottage tenants, journalist mates, they all liked to visit Glenrock and they brought their friends, who always turned out to be interesting and congenial. And apparently they found us the same. I encouraged their visits because I saw that, as writers, we needed stimulation from outside our new world of agriculture in an obscure valley.

From the start, Jeff read everything he could find about small-scale agriculture and, with the single-minded dedication that was his style, he devised a careful plan by which we would grow our own food and sell any surplus to supplement our earnings from freelance journalism. He approached the bank and arranged a loan which would buy us time, machinery and livestock to get his program working.

We still keep that brave four-year scheme in our files. It makes us smile, recalling the faith we had in our ability and energy, which at the time felt bottomless. We had no doubts we would take to and master the ancient art of farming. Both of us had rural grandparents whose lifestyles appealed to us more than the city suburbs where our upwardly mobile parents had strived to plant us. Although from opposite sides of the world, Jeff and I had a common mistrust of their philosophies, which were basically similar. Our folks had clambered up the social ladder out of peasantry. We yearned to reverse that direction. And in so doing, we felt we would be creating a better life for our children, the same motive which, ironically, had driven our parents to reject life on the land.

My grandparents were farmers. By the time I knew them, they had fetched up in a semi-rural backwater of southern California. Grandma kept a milking cow, chickens and ducks, and grew fruit and vegetables which she made into memorable jars of pickles and jams. My childhood notion was that somehow, Grandmother's lifestyle was cosier than my upbringing in the suburb of a small affluent city.

Jeff's grandma grew vegetables too. As a boy, he stayed with her while his mother and father went to work, and he often visited his Uncle Norm, a soldier-settler who had received land in Victoria's western district after serving in World War I. His uncle's attempts to carve a homestead from wilderness created a yen in young Jeffrey to do the same.

He had already tried agriculture on the five-acre holding he established on Sydney's outskirts before we met. He ran poultry, dairy goats and grew vegetables. His plan for Foxground was more ambitious. It involved the purchase of calves to be reared and sold as replacement heifers to dairymen in our district. He also planted an orchard of young fruit trees – peach, apricot, fig and plum – around a big new market garden. I saw that Jeff had a very sure touch with vegetable growing, and in no time it looked a picture.

He contacted the local agronomist, who was willing to come out and assess our property. The fellow warned against weeds encroaching into our paddocks – blackberry, lantana, tussock and bracken – and told Jeff how sprays would minimise backbreaking work with brush-hook and mattock. He also advised how to improve our pasture with grass seeds and superphosphate. He was not encouraging about all the hard work involved on a steep property like ours and was clearly puzzled that Jeff seemed undaunted by the tasks ahead. In fact, Jeff was eager to get started. So was I. And so were our kids. Goth was now seven years old, Van was five, just ready to start school at Berry. Thor and Karen, Jeff's children from his first marriage, were twelve and fourteen. They lived with their mother in Sydney but came down for school holidays to join in the adventure. Helping to plant and later to pick fresh beans and corn, pulling baby carrots to eat as a snack, digging new potatoes – the simple pleasures of life which we loved providing for our youngsters.

As Jeff tilled the earth for his trees and vegies, he often called us to look; our soil was so rich and friable it was like a treasure hunt. Sometimes he, or the boys looking for fishing bait, turned up giant worms as long as your arm. Others were fat, pale pink, finger-thick; when touched, jets along their bodies shot out fluid like a garden sprinkler. The locals called them 'giant squirter worms'. Jeff photographed them and wrote about them for *Pix* and *People* magazines. The earth was full of fat buttery larvae, attracting a squad of assorted birds which strutted behind Jeff as he gardened. It was all grist for our journalistic mill, which we could not afford to abandon. My magazine articles went to *Country*, *The Women's Weekly* and *Woman's Day*, and we both contributed to *Walkabout*.

After reinforcing the old yards and sheds, we bought hens and some newborn calves. Jeff considered himself expert with poultry but cattle were a new ball game. We studied our neighbours down in the valley hungrily, and tried to emulate them. There were nine working dairy farms at Foxground in the 1960s and two families became our special mentors. Both were generous with advice and they sold us calves and fresh milk.

Every second day we drove down with our new one-gallon can and while absorbing the fragrance and techniques of milking time, we asked questions and learned. One of the farmers, Jim Waite, was a progressive. He had been a milk vendor prior to buying his farm and he was the innovator in Foxground. He built a stud of well-bred Friesian cows using scientific breeding principles and extensive herd recording; he dosed his cattle with the newest veterinary drugs, milked by fast machines and cultivated his paddocks with modern equipment.

The other farm, next door, was worked by the Conroy family. They milked Jerseys and Ayrshires and espoused traditional farming, which they had down to a fine art, stubbornly resisting costly new trends. Good enough for them were salts of mollasses, Stockholm Tar poultices, an old gasoline chaff-cutter and a vintage Ferguson tractor.

Between the two of them, we witnessed a debate about new versus old methodologies and were able to strike our own balance. Generally, in the beginning, Jeff leaned toward the Waites' theories of new-ag, but we paid careful attention to the Conroys' advice too. From the scientific Waites we bought calves out of Jim's registered Friesians. I started a herd book and we chose names for our 'stud' – Freya, Helga, Thoragird, Saxon and Kirsten. Frith. Jeff still fancied Scandinavian or Anglo-Saxon names, like the children's.

It was the traditional Conroys who showed us how to stick our hands into warm milk mixture so the calves would suck our fingers until they got the hang of drinking. Dick Conroy and his son Phil came up and helped Jeff build rough feeding bails where the calves' heads could be locked in place while they drank. This reduced the risk of kicked-over buckets and wasted milk formula, which was expensive to buy. The dairy farmers, of course, had surplus milk for feeding their calves but we had to buy bags of Denkavit and mixed it twice daily, hygienically and carefully.

Jim Waite taught us how to inject our growing youngsters against pneumonia and red-water fever. On his advice, we bought syringes and medicines from the local chemist, who in those days stocked almost as many veterinary remedies as human ones.

'Whatever do you want with that expensive rubbish?' queried the Conroys. 'All you need is a vinegar bottle and about a quarter cup of Epsom salts. You could add a drop of sugar, to make it taste better . . .'

We innoculated against blackleg and spontaneous abortion, but when the time came for tuberculosis testing, we had to call in the local vet, George Borys. He was a cheerful Ukrainian, built like a bull himself, who tolerated our innocent notions and helped us on many occasions. His clients included influential cattle breeders and winners at the Royal Show where he served as an honorary vet, but he was never too busy to call at the Carters', his smallest but eventually his most unusual clients.

From the beginning, we interested him. When he learned Jeff

and I wrote stories for magazines about life on Glenrock Farm to supplement our income, he was intrigued. One day, he called in while photos were being taken and roared with mirth. 'By jingoes, Jeffie, you grow the potatoes, then you take their picture. You sell the photo, you sell the potatoes and what is left, you eat! You are a pluddy beauty, mate!'

Down in the valley they must have laughed at our earnest industry. We would roll up to buy milk, or eggs when our hens didn't lay enough, or to borrow some tool, and out would come our latest puzzlers. Like how to tell when our heifers were ready to bear calves, and what semen we should ask for at the Artificial Insemination Centre. Scientific Jim Waite opened his studbook and coded us into his breeding program. Tassie Brazabon the Third was the bull whose seed we would require.

Ascertaining exactly when the animals were ready to be inseminated was more difficult. There are certain aspects of farming that come only with experience. 'Look for the ones that are bulling,' we were told. How could we? We didn't own a bull. 'No, they takes to jumping on each other,' Dick Conroy's wife, Eva, explained after an embarrassed pause. 'Oh. Well, which one needs the service – the jumper or the jumped?' In the end, we got the hang of it.

After eighteen months of diligent work, Jeff invited the district agronomist back to view our paddock improvement program. We had done as he said, growing brown and lean in the process. Enthusiastically we beat back jungle encroaching on our new clover and ryegrass. We revelled in sessions of bracken bashing or tussock digging. Friends visiting from the city were recruited and we all worked up terrific sweats, returning virtuously exhausted to the cool shade of the farmhouse for home-grown feasts. Big dishes of fresh corn on the cob, running with butter. The blue platter heaped with fried rabbit legs. Mounds of sliced beefsteak tomatoes, a bowl of crisp green beans sprinkled with pepper and crispy bacon. Freshly dug potatoes mashed with local cream. And big fat loaves of country bakehouse bread.

We thought we had struck it rich but the agronomist said our efforts were not enough. We must do more if we hoped to raise the productivity of the farm. Jeff had been spreading superphosphate by hand, striding over the hillsides with a sack on his back, his arm swinging rhythmically, trying to reach all the crags and crannies where cattle might graze. The expert suggested we hire the new pilot in the district who was fertilising and spraying from his aircraft. Young and earnest, he fixed Jeff with a face-the-facts expression. 'It might not be worth it on your place. After all, you're only subsistence farming here.'

At the time, we were offended. Now, I wonder why. Then, we felt goaded to try harder, victims of local enthusiasm for Increased Production, the bywords preoccupying local newspapers and conversations whenever farmers gathered, whether buying supplies at the Berry Rural Co-op, strolling round the showground during the agricultural competitions, or simply chatting at Foxground crossroads waiting for the mail. Progress and New Methods were what talk was about.

So Jeff put in an order for the plane to aerially superphosphate our paddocks. A few days later, the peace of the valley was disturbed by the motor of a low circling aircraft belching clouds of white powder over our foothill land. We became the first in Foxground to have this done, a feather in the caps of the new chums (but also another entry in the debits column of my farm ledger).

By the time our heifers were due to calve, we felt satisfied with our efforts to improve the farm and entered a period of anxious watchfulness. We had been advised that when a heifer began 'springing', we should lock her in the yard. Otherwise she would go bush to have her calf, hiding in some awkward place where we could not help her should anything go wrong. What could go wrong? We weren't sure. As for recognising 'springing', we had no confidence at all since none of the farmers we spoke to could describe it to us succinctly. When the udders of our maidens began to swell, we put them in and out of pens. Too soon. Now I can recognise a springing beast at 50 yards, but then it was different.

Finally we saw that Freya was definitely ready to drop her offspring. We yarded her and nervously gathered about, clucking and watching for 'bad signs'. We had quizzed all our neighbours about this business. They hinted darkly at complications they had experienced but when we tried to pin them down to say how a complicated birth looked, or a natural one, reticence overcame them. With pressing, I got Jim Waite to estimate how long a normal labour took. Once the feet or nose emerged, if more than twenty-five minutes passed without progress, then human assistance might be required. What we'd need to do in that eventuality was fairly graphically explained. The Conroys told us to make ready the twine off a hay bale, a bucket of hot water, chaff bags and old towels. We added an alarm clock, so we could time proceedings.

Poor Freya. Never was a new mother attended by so many midwives. So many inexperienced, anxious midwives. Probably she was doing fine but when the calf had not emerged at twenty-nine minutes past time, we rushed in to tie hay bands around the little protruding pink hooves and began to haul away. Jeff and Goth were on the pulling end while Van and I reassured a very surprised Freya. She stared round at her rear end as her calf popped out like a cork from a bottle and skidded across the yard towed by Jeff and Goth on their backsides!

That birth was a fine thing for us to share. The first hour was pure magic. Freya nudged her little wet bundle with her nose and began to lick it. Afterbirth in her mouth would stimulate her milk to begin flowing, or rather, the colostrom which puts the newborn into digestive mode. After cleaning her baby, she urged it to stand up. We were transfixed as the little calf struggled onto its shaky legs, all knobs, its tail flicking busily, encouraged by the soft throaty 'moo' of its mother. Never would we forget that time together, nor tire of watching the birth drama.

It was probably significant that Helga, the next heifer to calve, slipped away to the top of the farm long before she was due and stayed there until the deed was done. We had to search her out, helped by the keen nose of our new cattle pup, Jim, a well-bred blue heeler and gift from Jeff's mother. When we spied her deep in a thicket, she looked decidedly cross at being disturbed and mooed warningly for us to keep our distance. She had had no trouble producing a healthy calf, without the aid of baling twine or alarm clocks, and we had so much difficulty yarding the rest of the herd before their time came that we reckoned the heifers passed the word around: keep away from those crazy Carters until your babe is born.

Oh, we made some silly mistakes in those early days but we had some of the best times of our lives. Of our original eleven calves, we successfully reared nine. One died of starvation the first winter. She literally wasted away. We hadn't known that kikuyu grass loses its nourishment during the cold months. Our ignorance was revealed when the Conroys drove up on their tractor and, without reproach, dumped bales of hay in front of our hollow-ribbed herd. The heifers ate ravenously and after that we bought hay until the spring growth came. It was too late for poor little Saxon, however. She was already too far gone. She contracted pneumonia and died.

Another day we sat for hours on the steep hillside across the creek from our house patting a dying Amanda, keeping flies off her with a household insect spray-gun. She, too, was probably a victim of our inexperience. We felt our failure acutely and were almost as sorry to lose her as we would have been to lose a family member.

Looking back, I reckon our average of success wasn't too bad. One thing farming teaches you is how to take death in your stride. When Frith slipped off a steep path above the waterfall and injured herself so badly that Jeff had to shoot her, we were initiated into one of the harder tasks of self-sufficiency.

We told ourselves we must be objective about our animals. You could grow fond of them as you nurtured them but you must remember why they were being raised. One day they would have to leave the green paddocks, their family and friends, for the dairy or the saleyard. We decided the way to accept losing them was to give them the best life possible during their growing and reproductive time at Glenrock. The realistic attitudes we forced upon ourselves then stood us in good stead for later, when we took on the real work of Glenrock Farm – the care of injured and orphaned native creatures for release back into the wild.

It was for me a very happy time. Very satisfying. My misgivings about Jeff's former family were under control now that Thor and his sister felt comfortable visiting the farm and coming away with us on trips when appropriate. Their mother, Dorothea, seemed to be making her own life, and that helped too. It felt so good to me to be part of a big and growing mob, presiding over an open house, after my sequestered single-parent upbringing. People found us an attractive whole unit and it reinforced our faith in what we were doing.

Part of the charm of our partnership was that we loved one

another with passion, with humour, with inspired excitement. It was another strength of our union. We never masked our fondness, as was the custom then; if anything, we flaunted it as an example we both believed should be seen. Love is catching. We even hung a string of Greek goat bells on the post of our brass bed. When we made love, they rang. Years later, when they understood, our sons told us they used to wonder what Mum and Dad did to ring those bells so often. We believed affection honestly expressed was one of life's most precious lubricants. We wanted to share ours around.

We felt proud to be a Wildlife Refuge. We spread the word quietly when we spoke with neighbours down in the valley. A wider broadcast of our ideas occurred in the magazine articles Jeff and I wrote. Although the bulk of Jeff's stories originated in inland Australia, he, and I, often wrote about happenings on the property. His regular 'Wild Country' column in *People* was perfect for nature tales. Some were poignant, many were funny.

There was one about a young possum brought to us to rear. It had been blown out of a tall tree and there was no way it could be put back. Many suburban residents wanted to be rid of possums – too noisy at night, chattering and playing on roofs, or inside them. Possums like to squeeze under the eaves and build nests in ceilings. This is a potential fire danger and also stains where the animals urinate. In the city, a small industry flourishes around expert possum trappers.

Anyway, this little sweetheart came in a shoebox with holes punched in the lid. We decided to name her Tuppy, and made her a cosier bed and kept her indoors, safe from night predators. She woke up at sundown and her bright little eyes peeping up at us expectantly more than paid for the trouble of feeding her. Our standard mix of oats and dried fruits was popular enough, but having read that possums eat green shoots, I raided the garden and hand-held tender leaflets while she daintly nibbled them down. New rose shoots were her favourites. She grabbed them with her quite agile front paws and devoured them.

Later I found that possums' partiality for roses is another reason they are not welcome in gardens. However, we preferred to risk a few plants so the animal population round our house would grow. Having read that possums do a good job by spreading pollen, I decided to let nature find a balance, and in fact we didn't lose our flowers. The trick was not getting stuck on growing something which was irresistible. What could survive did.

When the time came for the possum to try living outside, we rejoiced for her. She passed from our sight for a day or two, a night or two, and then just on dusk, her usual handfeeding time, we heard something clomping on the roof above the kitchen. A possum's tread sounds loud and heavy on corrugated iron. We went out and saw her peering expectantly down at us from beside the chimney. What to do?

Returning indoors to ponder the best course of action – did we want to encourage her to live in the house again or should we persevere with 'phasing her back to nature'? – we heard overhead an incredible racket. She was climbing the chimney. She was coming inside that way. But she chose the wrong access – she tried to climb down the flue pipe!

Action stations! All hands to the pump! Jeff issued instructions like Captain Bligh, boys flew to fetch tools, ropes, et cetera. We knew we hadn't cleaned the flue since installing it, and from inside the metal tube at the back of the stove we could hear a terrible hawking and gasping.

Jeff wrenched the long pipe off the stove and out of the chimney – quite a feat of strength – and laid it on the hearth. Goth and Van helped him hurriedly disjoint it and they shook each section. Out of one dropped a black, gritty, choking little animal. We quickly gathered her up in a towel and brushed the soot off her as best as we could. When her bulbous pink nose appeared from beneath the grime we felt relieved, but her eyelashes were all tangled in smuts and her breathing sounded like someone needing a good dose of Vicks.

That night we kept her indoors again with no qualms. But gradually we encouraged her to sleep outdoors and eventually lost sight of her until one day Van spied her grey back wedged between the chimney and an angle of the roof. There she slept for the next months until wintry weather drove her to seek a more sheltered bedroom.

Possums are marsupials. The babies spend about five months in their mother's pouch, then ride about clinging to her shoulders as soon as their fur is long enough to protect them from chilling. All four feet have long curving nails, good for climbing and holding.

Since they had managed to survive well in towns, common old garden brushtails or ringtails did not have much mystique. Except to us.

Right under our noses, however, we were harbouring a totally uncommon animal – the antechinus, or marsupial mouse. We were no strangers to mice inside Glenrock farmhouse. Because it was already 100 years old, there were shrinkage cracks between floorboards and walls. In some rooms, like the pantry, ancient woodwork could be gnawed through to gain access. Since we were generally 'soft' on animals, we didn't try too hard to get rid of them, until their messes and their bold foraging while we were present prompted a spate of trapping.

I will never forget the day I decided the constant chattering behind the wood stove, the brazen scampering round the kitchen, through the pantry, onto the sink, should stop. No one but me was at home, so I set a mousetrap. Within minutes, it went off. I saw I had caught not an ordinary house mouse but an antechinus. I extracted the still warm little body and, because the animal was so beautiful, I laid it on a sheet of newspaper to show the boys when they returned from school. The trap was set again and I returned to my typewriting, which I was doing on the kitchen table that day so I could boil up some jam. Snap! Another small furry corpse went onto the newspaper. The pelts of those antechini were luxuriant and so richly coloured you could have made a pretty little fur scarf of them. I set the trap again and again. The animals were so intent on their own activities in our kitchen, they had no sense of danger.

It was my first chance to examine marsupial mice up close and still. Their noses are very long, their carnivorous teeth needle sharp, eyes like shiny black beads. Within half an hour I had five small bodies on my newsprint morgue. Fortunately, none of them were females with pouch babies or my remorse would have been unbearable. I later learned that when marsupial mice become active within a house, they are males seeking to mate. They scamper about boldly, chattering and fighting, and in between other pursuits gobble up flies and cockroaches and other kitchen pests. Once they impregnate a female, they die almost at once.

As I watched the bloom fade off them, I felt wretched and showed them to my sons with misgivings. We talked about the pros and cons of eliminating native animals which became a nuisance within our domain, the house, and maintaining an honourable balance of nature outdoors. We agreed never again to set killing traps for antechini but always to catch them in deathless traps and take them away, across wide creeks, and release them to relocate as best they could.

Most of our visitors, of course, did not sympathise with our attitudes. Many were, in fact, shocked by our casual explanations that since we lived so far from anyone else, our mice were 'clean'. They fed only on our own compost and table scraps (or insects), so that they were not likely to be carrying disease as urban mice might. We felt superior to city visitors, with their fear of all rodent-like creatures which in some cases was phobic.

One weekend when the house was full of guests preparing one of the all-in spontaneous parties we specialised in, a woman went to fetch cutlery and screamed. Blasé as usual, we came to see what had frightened her. 'There are mice in the drawer and one is eating the other,' she babbled.

Even while dogmatically pooh-poohing this report, I pulled open the drawer and saw that what she said was true. A mouse with an unusually long snout was chewing its way through another, smaller one. Well, yuk! I quickly banged the drawer hard and washed the cutlery.

Next day, investigating the zoology texts, I learned about the antechini invading our kitchen. They are carnivores, feeding mainly on insects but also on other meat, such as the innocent house mouse in the drawer. That they are also marsupials had already won them a place in my hall of fame.

As usual, we retreated into our 'well, aren't you *lucky* to have sighted such a rare Australian mammal' mode. Which I, in fact, believed; but I'm not sure our guests felt the same.

5

The blacksmith and family

One morning during the 1963 school holidays, we received a surprise gift. A car drove up, swung around and parked outside our gate. Most drivers who got as far as our place were slow and tentative, if not downright panicky, but this woman radiated confidence. She was tall and fit, and so were her three offspring who hopped smartly from the vehicle. 'Coo-ee,' she called over the gate. 'Mind if I take the kids for a bit of bushwalk?'

We liked her at once and began to direct her onto tracks they might take but she cut us short. 'We'll find our way, thanks,' she said and off they strode.

I watched them open the first Bogan gate, then returned to my tasks, puzzling. Three hours later when they returned, my curiosity was satisfied. She was Valda Staples, daughter of the blacksmith. She had grown up on the property and liked to keep her children in touch with it. 'Hope you don't mind. I heard Glenrock had changed hands again.'

Mind? We were delighted. I invited them in and Valda said she'd appreciate a cup of tea but her kids wanted to show Goth and Van how to slide on chaff bags down slippery rock slopes above the waterfall into the deep, icy pool. Our lads set off enthusiastically with their junior visitors while we took Valda into the kitchen. Sitting round the table, we kept the tea flowing as she opened windows on what was to become *our* past as well as her own.

During the 1930s Depression when she was just a toddler, Valda's parents had moved to Foxground from Sydney where he had been a farrier. 'Dad said: "If we're going to starve, we might as well do it in the country. At least a man has a chance to grow a bit of tucker and live off the land." Dad set up his blacksmith outfit in the shed and made all the implements we needed. I was the only child so whatever he did, I was his offsider. Mum called me Dad's Little Mate.'

Her strong face glowed with the pleasure of remembering. 'It was Dad built the dairy. He added to the barns, using stone and timber off the place. Some of the slabs were cut in the last century. He could show you the sawpit, up the mountain opposite the house.'

They kept cows, a few sheep, a pig or two and, of course, poultry. 'He was a great one for birds. He had peacocks, ducks, geese, the entire yard was full of aviaries. He trapped finches in the bush and bred them for sale. People used to come from all over to see Dad's birds.'

Horses were his first love. And hers. Foxground was all horses when they came. She learned to ride before she could walk properly and always helped Dad cart their cream cans down to the butter factory at the crossroads. Later she rode her horse to the little timber schoolhouse nearby. 'It looks derelict now but there were twenty pupils in my day.

'There were three butter factories in the valley at the turn of the century but only one was left by our time,' Valda told us. 'I remember the two churches at the crossroads. One was burnt down by accident, the other by boys getting back at the pastor who chided them.'

When she reached her teens, she was allowed to drive their cattle out to the saleyard on the main road, swinging her stock-whip. 'The highway was still narrow and rough in places,' she recalled. 'An old bus took us to high school in Nowra, wheezing and stuttering up and down all those hills. If you wanted anything in Kiama, it was easier to go by horse over Saddleback Mountain.

'The mail was delivered along that ridge. A fellow would bring it on horseback and leave it in a hollow tree. The trail was called the Zig Zag. Dad and I kept it open for years. He could show you where it is, even though it must be well overgrown by now. He always rode Valleywood, his stallion.

'It was Valleywood who safely carried Dad up the mountain one terrible stormy night during World War II, when an army plane crashed into the cliffs above our farm. Dad saw that all had perished, then rode back down to inform the authorities.'

Mentioning the war stirred other memories. 'Once a platoon of cavalry rode through on their way to conduct a survival exercise on the plateau, what they now call Barren Ground Faunal Reserve. It was just wild heath then. Every afternoon following school, my job was to ride my horse up to our top paddocks and bring the cows down for Dad to milk. Up on the cliffs, I heard the soldiers yahooing. I waved to them,' she giggled. 'I thought they were just being friendly. Next day, they were at it again, but they seemed a bit frantic. Dad twigged they must have lost their way down, so we rode up and rescued them.' Valda roared laughing.

'I knew every inch of the mountainsides,' she said, which was just as well because sometimes she had to ride out to find her father. 'Once when he went missing, I rode all over the place till I found him stuck up a tree. He'd been sawing it through and it snapped back, pinning him.'

After she freed him, Dad made her promise not to tell her Mum. 'She's always saying not to get off working places on me own,' he'd said. 'If she hears about this, it'll give fuel to her arguments.'

Valda admitted he was a bit of a legend in the district, her dad. People came to get their horses shod and stayed to listen to his yarns. 'They all wanted to see his flying fox. He built it across the waterfall, hauling the cable up on his back over loose rocks, through the big trees, palms, the lantana and thorny vines. Wait-awhile was the worst. When it hooks you, it won't let go.

'Up on the flat, Dad cleared and ploughed a paddock, then planted crops. After harvest, he launched his bales of fodder off a platform he built and down a wire he'd anchored at the bottom to a ploughshare stuck in a boulder. I'd be waiting there to unhook them. Then I'd sing out, "She's right, Dad" and down would zoom another.'

Her memories of this land we now called ours were so vivid, it was easy to visualise the life they'd led. The family used to sleep on the open verandahs. 'If it stormed, Dad would throw horse rugs over us. Otherwise, we enjoyed watching the stars and feeling fresh air on our faces all night long. We grew our own food and of course there was always plenty of milk.

'When I grew up, I learned to drive Dad's car. The road was different then, it went through the paddocks. There were seven gates and five creeks and many's the wild night I wore a bushcoat over a pretty frock so I could attend a ball. After the butter factory, I took off the rough gear and changed into my party shoes. One night I forgot them and had to dance in bare feet. You couldn't waltz in gumboots.' She roared laughing again. 'By the time I got back through those gates and creeks, I'd be mud to my waist. I really felt like Cinderella then!'

She rose and cooeed out the kitchen door. Kids came spilling out of the bush, trotting down the hill wet-haired and frisky as pups, gleaming with that special cleanness you get from cold creek water.

Feeling guilty, I asked Valda why she hadn't taken over the farm. She dimpled. 'Dad would have liked that. It's why he built the cottage. But I fell for a Sydney chap. We have a place fronting the Georges River, so I'm still surrounded by bush. And my going probably tipped the scales toward them selling the farm. Mum had put up with isolation and hard work for all the years with good will, but she didn't drive and never would. She put her foot down and said they must retire, buy a little place on the beach where Dad could fish and she would be closer to civilisation. So they let the place go but the buyers didn't last long.

'I'll bring Dad over to meet you before we go back to Sydney,' she promised. 'Dad'll be pleased to hear someone has bought the place who can manage it.'

Her words were like a benediction. As we walked out to her car, she commented on the garden as if she was mentioning old friends. Each shrub was known to her. Clearly there was a story attached to them all. Knowledgeable as she seemed about horticulture, she said her mum was the real expert. 'She'll tell you if she comes up with Dad. She'll show you the well.' The well? 'Everything had to be hand-watered when they first came here. Even the water for the kitchen came in by bucket. That was Mrs Henry's system.'

Mrs Who? Our curiosity flared afresh but Valda demurred. She'd spent longer than she intended. Best leave the rest of the story to her parents. They left us enriched, presented with a living past on which to graft our lives at Glenrock. We waited eagerly for their next visit.

About ten days later, Valda returned with her father. She was such a robust woman, the type you see at gymkhanas mastering big horses, it was a surprise to find her dad was small. Small but dynamic. Ernie Staples was a leprechaun of a man, wiry, skin like wrinkled leather, knots of muscles on arms and legs that were never still. A kind of blue fire crackled from his eyes, indicating the energy fizzing within him. Like his daughter, he was a prolific raconteur. She let him go, listening avidly, his tales a familiar, beloved catechism.

'Now, Valleywood,' he started off. The horse figured in everything he liked to recall about Glenrock. Soon after moving to Foxground, he'd spotted the young stallion grazing in a paddock and fronted up to the owner, asking to buy him. Money was pretty tight then but he made an honest offer.

The owner tried to fob Ernie off with other horses. 'No, I'll take the big fellow or nothing,' said Ernie. At last the breeder, with a mean twinkle, agreed. 'You can buy him if you can get a bridle on him and take him home.'

'I could see that fellow was banking on me to fail,' recalled the blacksmith. His chest puffed up, his shoulders squared just thinking about it.

He mastered the spirited horse and convinced him they would be mates forever. They were. 'It nearly broke me heart when he died,' said the blacksmith. 'Up on the Zig Zag, it was. He was trying to haul something for me, trying like a champion as always. His big old heart must have give out. I don't mind telling you, I shed a tear when I seen him lying there.'

(I don't mind telling you I shed one too, hearing the story.)

Well, that Valleywood. 'He won his share of ribbons at the shows. And sired some of the best horses this district ever knew. Yet he was a worker.' A great help to a small man working alone in a big forest.

'He was that sure-footed. The night the bomber crashed on the mountain during the war, it was amazing how he got us up to the wreck. It was black as sin, the wind was roaring, trees were crashing onto the track . . . There was nothing left of the poor devils in the plane, of course. She'd driven herself full throttle into the cliff.

'The plane burned. Even in all that rain, she burned for hours. I rode down again and took the news out. Next day the farm was crawling with air force johnnies. They wanted a big enquiry. They were going to collect all the wreckage and take it away, to check it for sabotage.

'Trouble was, there were stickybeaks turning up from everywhere. It was amazing who did hoof it up to the wreck. Old ladies, cripples . . . and every one of them souvenired a little piece of plane. In the finish, the air force men waited down at the bottom gate and took the stuff off them as they headed home.'

The blacksmith smiled. ''Course, I salted away me own mementoes, hid them deep in scrub until things quietened down. Only things a man could make use of. You may have noticed me bridge across the creek? Made it from an engine cowling, filled in with stones.' His eyes sparkled. 'I did turn up a machine gun later. Must have got flung quite a distance from the crash. I shoved it back out of sight in the bush. Later on, I couldn't find the blessed thing.'

He directed his beam at Goth and Van. 'I always meant to go back and take a proper look. Me grandsons tried to find her but never had any luck. Now, you fellows want to keep your eyes open, if ever you're scratching around up there . . .'

I could see Ernie knew he was planting seeds that day and it was a generous gift. Lost machine guns are the stuff legends grow around. And expeditions. Many brave parties of boys have searched the jungle beneath the escarpment since then but, so far, only torn bits of metal have been found. The search goes on.

He spoke of other treasures to be discovered in the rainforest. Bush orchids, spraying down in creamy cascades. Giant tree ferns. Huge green bird's nest ferns, staghorns, elkhorns. Ernie's passion had been relocating them round his garden, on top of the boulders. 'You could earn big money selling ferns, Jeff,' the blacksmith told us seriously.

'This is fast-growing country,' he said. 'It'll grow over the top of you if you stand still. Took us all our time, clearing this farm and keeping it clean. That hillside across the creek now, that's an example. Had it clean as a whistle over there and look at it now, in just a few short years. Lantana creeping back. Grass disappearing under rubbish – you want to keep it cleared, Jeff. You can graze an extra beast or two, if you keep them little clearings open.'

He described how Valda and her mother had planted kikuyu, after he had felled trees and led Valleywood to drag away the rubbish. They laid the grass runners in little trenches along the steep hillside, weighting them down with stones and covering them with earth carried up in buckets.

'There was no soil there,' the blacksmith recalled. 'It's all rocky scree. Bit of a treacherous hillside, Jeff. You'll hear a landslip, from time to time. But we established those little paddocks there. The wife used to go across every day and bucket water up from the creek until the kikuyu took hold.'

Jeff assured him that he and the boys were maintaining his handiwork, spending hours with brush-hook and saw to keep open the narrow hill-hugging tracks between small steep clearings. It was here that Frith had slipped over the edge and lost her life. Ernie nodded sympathetically about that, and smiled to hear about the time Goth and Van had gotten lost over there, during our first weeks on the farm. They had taken one of the many animal pads up from the creek and, being small, they were able to follow it into tunnels beneath the thicket. Before they knew it, they were immersed in lantana, unable to see which way to go.

We heard their little voices calling to us from across the creek but could not see them. 'Keep shouting,' Jeff called. He and Thor took ropes and tools and followed the sound of their voices. Being bigger, they had to go on top of the lantana, striding like giants, their legs breaking through in places, until they could cut a hole into the boys' prickly prison and lift them out. I can still picture them trudging back up to the house in the twilight, scratched, tired but triumphant. Ernie and Valda understood the scene and reassured the lads that such adventures were natural on a property like Glenrock. The stuff of heroes. We felt proud that we were already building our own small myths.

As we talked, we walked, following him up the track toward the waterfall. At the ploughshare in the rock, we paused to hear again the story of the famous flying fox.

'Now, there's a pity,' the blacksmith concluded. 'I had them paddocks up top all established. Look at it now. All that effort, gone to waste.'

Ernie was well past sixty. On his brown sinewy legs were scars from a recent horrific motor accident. It didn't seem to have slowed him down. We were hard pressed to match his pace as he retraced the boundaries of his former kingdom. You could imagine the ring of his axe, the creak and squeal as a tree swayed and broke loose, pulling down vines and a shower of leaves. Valleywood's whinny seemed to reappear, a ghostly echo, amongst the voices of whipbirds and cicadas and the incessant coo-coo-coo of wood pigeons.

'They make good eating, you know, Jeff, them pigeons. Used to be brush turkeys too, but they seemed to have got cleared out. And the lyrebirds! Well, they are that good of mimics that you wouldn't pick between a real axe and their imitation of it. Often-times I've been caught. "Who the devil is that?" I've asked meself when I heard hammering or sawing down a gully. One of the wretches even copied me own whistle when I called up the dogs.

'I used to tether them under that old coral tree out near the cattle crush,' he told us. 'That's where the chickens roosted. It was a scheme of mine to try and keep the foxes and tiger cats from cleaning them out. Each evening I'd scatter grain at the base of the tree. After the fowls had had their feed, they'd hop up and settle in the branches for the night. And do you know, I've often spotted lyrebirds among the chooks? They'd come up out of the gully, quiet as anything, and scratch about like strong little hens.'

Ernie and Valda led us onward, up hills and across creeks. 'You'll want to see the old saw-pit where they used to cut timber with them big two-man saws? It's a bit hard to get to but another day, I'll show you. A landslip has partly filled it in. Better if we head up this way. There's big stone walls hiding in the woods up the back. Near covered over by regrowth. It's a shame.'

The stone walls, a hallmark of the Illawarra district, were built, according to legend, by one man, Thomas Newing. From Wales, he and his family contracted to build fences for farmers using stones they cleared from their paddocks. The method, called dry stone walling, was traditional from the old country. Two parallel lines of rocks would be laid, wide at the bottom and converging at the top. The centre would be filled with rubble. No mortar was used and a row of capping stones was placed on top.

'Pity so many of the old walls are being dismantled,' mused the blacksmith. 'Farmers reckon the rabbits hide in them. I used to keep rabbits down on my place with traps and me old shotgun. There's traps of mine still hanging in the shed, Jeff. You want to use them.' Jeff assured him we already had.

As Ernie talked, we accepted that his ideas typified the era when bush was a force to be conquered and turned to use – wildlife ditto. Our own philosophy was heading in another direction, but we listened keenly to what he said. We had much to learn and the blacksmith was an enthusiastic teacher.

He led the way up into the shadowy forest at the back of the farm. 'This was all cleared, Jeff. This is regrowth. I kept pigs up here. It's a pity. Them pioneers worked mighty hard to clear the jungle and establish their little places.'

The first settlers came from over Saddleback, he told us. 'Them early days, it was only ship transport out of Gerringong and Kiama. The way south was too rough. The cow-cockies followed cedar-getters who lived rough, slept dirty and hauled out a wealth of lovely timber with bullocks. Within a few years, the big brush was all cleared away. Only the odd cabbage tree palm or native fig was left, to show it used to be jungle and so was rich ground.

'A lot of the flying foxes got cleared out in them days. The valley was named after them. They're still about only in lesser numbers. They're devils for eating your fruit. Have you been troubled with them, Jeff?'

Jeff admitted our orchard had been visited, the evening sky alive with the flapping of their big leathery wings. We were still debating whether the expense of putting nets over our fruit trees, the trouble of it, would be worth while. Hanging empty tins on strings tied to the branches was our antidote thus far, and not very successful.

'Hoddle was the government surveyor, back donkey's years. He established a route leading from Moss Vale, on the tableland, across the Barren Ground and down to the coast. Cattle, pack-horses, even bullock carts of wool and butter and stores used Hoddle's track for years. It was all cobbled, you know, Jeff. You scratch away the leaves and rubbish sometime and you'll find cobblestones. That track is still good today, but nobody uses it. They go by the highway instead.' He shook his head over the weakness of modern folk scared of the bush and prepared to let it beat them.

As we headed back down toward the house, he continued: 'It wasn't just dairy stuff they took out of Foxground, them early days. They used their corn to distil spirits. Used to put the liquor under the butter in their packsaddle bags. Sold it in Kiama. There's remains of an old still in the creek just below the farmhouse, if you scratch about. (We did. And found some interesting old bottles in a cave beneath the overhang.)

'Oh, you could live off this land, no worries, Jeff,' the blacksmith assured us. 'A man would never have to spend a penny if he was short. Make your own tools. Hoes, scythes, pitchforks – you don't want to go buying stuff, Jeff, not with the price of things today. There's plenty of iron lying about and the forge is all set up for you.'

We paused to open a gate, the blacksmith's own handiwork, and admired the view. Behind us, shadows were settling down over wooded mountains; before us, grass and trees and distant farms rolled away to meet the sea. Humans seemed tiny in relation to the setting. Yet beside us stood the little blacksmith, in the winter of his life, still fired by an urge to tame the bush. Although our ideas even then did not match with his about that, we were anointed with the spirit of his undertakings and felt inspired to make of Glenrock someplace worthy of its brave beginnings.

'Now Mrs Henry, she was a woman of the old school. I bought the place off her,' Ernie said, as Valda tucked him into her car. 'We haven't spoke of her yet, Jeff. I'll come back and bring the wife. We'll talk about Mrs Henry next time.'

When he returned, months later, the blacksmith brought us a present. It was a concrete birdbath for our back garden. He had moulded it round a ploughshare. 'I always meant to make one before we moved away, Jeff. I know the mob of birds that get about here.' His gift told us we were accepted onto the property. 'Ernie's drinker', we would call it, a monument to the blacksmith and his family, and it would stand forever on its pedestal outside the back door giving refreshment to wrens and finches, bower birds and magpies, parrots and honey-eaters.

He also brought his wife, as promised. Elsie Staples was a perfect match for her husband. Small but strong and peppery. In a pretty afternoon frock, grey hair curling modishly around her face, she looked such a lady, you'd never guess the hard farming life she'd led. Well, that was all behind her and good riddance, she told me plainly.

'I didn't mind doing it but I'd had enough,' she said.

The blacksmith began edging toward the gate. 'You tell Mrs Carter about the garden, Else,' he instructed. 'I want to take Jeff up and show him the way to the Zig Zag.'

This division of activities was clearly more suited to Ernie's style and his generation than having me doggedly tag along as I had done on his previous visit. Valda was all right, she was an honorary son, but I was different. I had looked forward to seeing the Zig Zag but didn't argue. I also wanted to hear Mrs Staples' reflections. Like her husband, she told a vivid story.

When she had first moved to Glenrock from Sydney, it seemed like the end of the world, she said. The garden was so overgrown you had to go down on your hands and knees to get in the front door. The entrance had become a tunnel through flowering shrubs and bulbs grown rampant.

Mrs Henry, from whom the Staples had bought the property, had been famous as a gardener. Her fingers were the greenest green. She never went anywhere without bringing back a pinch of this, a cutting of that. It was said she even hopped off a train once, when it paused at a siding, to pluck something she spotted growing beside the line. Everything she planted grew.

From Elsie Staples I learned that the mystery tree in the side garden – twisted corky trunk with pea-like flowers of brightest crimson – was Mrs Henry's Japanese fire-wheel tree, brought as a seedling from Queensland. Against the house nearby were two robust camellias she had nurtured; one had white flowers, the other, tall as a small tree, had pink flowers with sports striped like candy-canes, a *C. macarthurii*. The big jacarandas shading the front garden had begun life as her seed pods.

The garden had once been a showplace. People used to drive up in sulkies from all over the district to view it. Mr Henry was shy and used to hide down the paddock when visitors came, but his wife was gregarious and would serve them tea and scones baked in a camp oven stood in coals on the open hearth. Her afternoon teas were a legend also.

Mrs Henry had come to Glenrock as a bride, moving into the house built for her by her family. They were Jarmans, a family which had settled early and widely in the Shoalhaven and along Saddleback. The little farmhouse was simple in the beginning. Built in the last half of the previous century, it was not even lined until the 1920s. By 1930, when the Staples bought the place, Mrs Henry had been a widow for many years. 'Poor old soul, she couldn't look after the place any longer.' The blacksmith moved the old lady's possessions himself to a little cottage further down the valley. She used to enjoy coming back for a visit. Liked to see what was being done to her old home.

'There was never a wall round the house in her day,' Elsie Staples told me. 'Ernie built that, one time while I was away. Oh, I got fed up with rain and the cattle getting in all the time. Stormed off to me sister's. When I returned, Ernie had the garden all nicely enclosed for me.'

A giant fig tree grew in the side garden. Its goliath limbs spread above the house and possums used them as springboards to jump on the iron roof at night. 'The commotion was something terrible.' Fearing the tree might break some stormy night and crush them as it fell, the blacksmith began to remove it, limb by giant limb. 'When Mrs Henry saw what he was doing, she lifted her apron to her old eyes and cried.'

She was also shocked by the thinning out of her garden, which had become a solid tangle round the house. To provide a safe area where Valda could play as a toddler, Elsie regretfully ripped out beautiful plants which she tossed down the gully opposite the house. Some of them took root, bringing up lillies and gladioli and roses rambling among the natives.

The house had no running water in the 1930s. There was a little well in the garden. It supplied water for plants, animals, humans. A bucket did the lot.

The blacksmith's wife smiled at our improvements. They, too, had added on and updated. The kitchen was separate in those days, a precaution against fire. Its slab walls, six inches thick, had been sawn in the pit up the hill, from trees grown on the property. It was Ernie who had joined the kitchen to the house by building the side verandah. Valda slept there while her parents slept on the long front verandah. Both were unwired, open to the elements. Mosquitoes? Never seemed to worry them.

The outside laundry was also the blacksmith's installation, she told me. 'That copper was never put in properly,' she stated flatly. 'It smoked, would not draw and should be replaced.' The bathroom, however, had nothing wrong with it. The blacksmith had built it and installed the bath and chip heater himself. Those *were* the improvements, in their day.

The dining room was Ernie's addition. She seemed surprised that we had enlarged it by about four feet and made it our bedroom. She did not relate to our passion for making things bigger, although she did allow that our knocking out the wall between the tiny living room and master bedroom resulted in a more comfortable lounge. Had we noticed the lining boards? They were cedar, put up in 1926.

The walk-in pantry, that was one of the blacksmith's innovations. We had added more shelves. I showed her, proud of my rows of preserved fruits and vegetables. Elsie complimented me on my efforts, although we both knew mine would never win prizes at the shows as hers had done.

She was pleased to see that we were making good use of the huge apples from the old tree in the orchard. Did we know its name? It was called maiden's blush, because of the red streaks striping the plump green cheeks of the fruit – fruit as big as melons. It exploded into sweet snowdrifts when stewed.

Blackberries were not the only wild fruit to make jam from, she told me. Native raspberries made lovely jelly and pies. They tasted pallid when eaten raw but cooked with sugar they became intensely flavoursome and fragrant, lending vivid pink to pears or apples.

She sighed, remembering the mountains of scones she had baked in the old wood oven, topping them with her preserves and fresh cream. She'd had her share of visitors over the years. Nephew Jim and his friends used to come down for a bit of work and a bit of sport. They'd bring her rabbits to cook, yabbies they'd caught in the creek – eels, too, and perch. They'd all fetch up round the kitchen table, yarning, while she prepared the food.

I was pleased to tell her the tradition was being carried on. Our friends from the city were happy to visit us, drawn by fresh country air, mountain water, a bit of outdoor work and lots of home-grown produce. Almost every weekend we had a houseful, sleeping in the spare room, on the verandahs, in the lounge. This was why Jeff planned to enlarge the kitchen.

That perplexed her but she said if we did move the little marble sink her husband had installed, we'd find an old scar beneath the kitchen cupboard. It was a bullet hole, fired in error by one of her nephew's mates when he was cleaning his gun. Nearly took off the leg of her treadle sewing machine which used to sit under the window. Nearly took off the leg of her nephew's mate, in fact. He lost a toe in the accident.

Which reminded her of her husband's foot injury. 'The silly beggar near cut off his toe while chopping wood. He stuck it back on and wrapped it with rag inside his boot. The smell! Gangrene. Doctor said it was a miracle he didn't lose his leg. It's a wonder he didn't break his neck, some of the things he got up to. I can't convince him to take things easier, even now. He always charges at any task like a bull at a gate.'

'Well, Else, that's how we got things done,' Ernie reminded her, returning just then from his walk with Jeff. Jeff looked pooped but Ernie was still fresh.

Elsie Staples sighed again. She supposed so. Well, she wasn't sorry it was behind them. The mud and the humidity, the bush mice and rats and possums that chewed their way through weak spots in the flooring or wormed into the ceiling under the eaves. The mildew that covered everything with fuzz during rainy times. No, she'd done her share, they both had. At their time of life, they wanted a bit of comfort.

Where they lived now, their house fronted onto Seven Mile Beach. Ernie had his little fishing boat pulled up on the front lawn and a tidy vegetable garden round the back. The house was a joy, carpet on the floors now there were no muddy boots tracking through, pretty curtains and a few frills. Just down the street was a little shop where she could buy what she needed.

'We've earned our retirement,' she said firmly, as they prepared to leave.

The blacksmith's retirement was being spent working as a handyman at the government bull farm. 'Well, I couldn't just sit around, Jeff. I'd go bonkers if I did.' He paused outside the shed where smoke was billowing into the yard. Inside we heard the whoomf-whoomf of the bellows being pumped, the clink of hot metal hammered on the anvil, the sizzle as glowing iron was plunged into a water bucket. It was our boys, happily hard at work.

The blacksmith smiled. He almost purred. 'That's the ticket, Jeff. Let the lads learn what it's all about. Then they'll never want for anything. They'll not be running to the shops to buy that expensive rubbish, like the johnnies do today.

'I tell you what, Jeff, I miss me old forge, where we're living now . . .'

6

Thalos, our second kangaroo

What the blacksmith and his family gave us was the gift of continuity on our land. Because there had been only two long-term owners before us, and because the Staples were such graphic raconteurs, their history and what they told us of the Jarman–Henry connection became part of our own history, a seamless graft which I found tremendously strengthening.

We received another important gift which began a subtle shift in our focus. Teenaged Thor visited a cattle property in northern New South Wales with a schoolmate. The lads were taken on a kangaroo shoot and told they could bring home a joey to rear. Thor was thrilled, knowing his could reside at Foxground.

Thor named his orphan Thalos, inspired by recent studies of Greek history. The joey was a male grey, about six months old, which is to say that he was less than two feet tall and that his fur was still short and growing. He arrived in a hessian bag, looking a bit scraggy, with a mild case of diarrhoea.

Bedding him warmly was the immediate problem. Jeff prepared a box of hay, Goth and Van filled hot-water bottles, I dug out old jumpers and blanket ends to swaddle the baby in, and we suspended his bag, papoose-style, from a hook near the kitchen stove, so it dangled down into the nest of warm straw. Then we rushed out to buy some tins of infant milk formula. He had been drinking condensed milk and water but this time we opted for a vitamin-fortified drink, such as we used in our calf-rearing program. Nothing but the best for our new little 'roo!

I have to say at this point that I will record feeding as it happened, not as it should be. In those days, as far as we knew, no milk formulas existed for native animals. People like us worked in the dark, trying this, trying that, sharing information with other experimenters. It would be fifteen or twenty years before demand brought onto the market milk drinks for marsupials and books on how to rear them.

Since Thalos had already been taught to lap, we thought it would be a retrograde step to offer him a feeding bottle, a decision we had cause to regret later. Instead, we chose for him a shallow bowl which could be sterilised after each feed. At least four times daily he would be served a warm brew of one part Lactogen and two parts boiled water. As he grew older, the milk component would be strengthened.

It was a cold, rainy spring. The stove had to be kept alight round the clock until the weather warmed up. For those next few months, there were no quibbles about whose turn it was to get in wood, however. We all wanted Thalos to thrive. Night after night we took it in turns to rise from bed to stoke the fire and replenish the hot-water bottles. Each morning we were awakened by the chattering cry that signalled a hungry little 'roo. No need for an alarm clock – Thalos called to us at dawn. Gladly we responded. The whole household focused around the new baby.

Every day there was laundry to be done for him, as mild attacks of the runs came and went. Usually these followed our enthusiasm for seeing him hop about after his meals. We thought he must have wanted exercise but his body heat was quickly lost and the result of that was diarrhoea. Elimination became the barometer of his state of health, which the entire family studied and debated. We were like amateur mechanics trying to tune an unfamiliar engine by small adjustments – his food, handling, exposure to the elements. Too much? Too little? We just couldn't seem to get the mixture exactly right.

On colder days we scarcely unswaddled him at all, but we picked him up as often as possible, in his bag, because in his natural environment he would still have been in his mother's pouch, close to her heartbeat. There was no shortage of nurses for

Thalos. When the boys came home from school, or when visitors called, someone always wanted to hold the joey. He made such a cute bundle wrapped in his bunny rug, his body bowed in a perfect U, with long bony hind feet and tail stuck up at one end, his delicate face at the other. His backbone and hips seemed very loosely jointed, to enable him to concertina into pouch positions.

He made an armful for Goth and Van, but they loved to hold him, sitting very still, gently stroking him along the line of his fragile jaw. This was his sensitive spot, like a cat's. He didn't like being patted on the head or back, but touch him under the chin and he would lean against your fingers, almost purring.

At first there were squabbles about whose turn it was to snuggle the 'roo, so a roster system was agreed to. While the boys were away at school, Jeff and I had work to do so we nursed him when we had lunch or a coffee break. Without meaning to, we conditioned him to love hot coffee or tea. Just to smell it on someone's breath was enough to start him quivering. He would reach out to clutch at a cup or sniff the lips that smelled of the sweet milky brew. Visitors found this alarming. They thought Thalos was trying to claw them or bite. A ridiculous notion, once you understand the gentle nature of a joey.

But there was a biter in the camp who posed a danger to Thalos. This was Jim, the blue cattle dog. When we first moved to the farm, Jeff's mother presented him with this well-bred blue heeler puppy. She reckoned that if Jeff was to be a successful cattle breeder, he would need a herding dog. The Queensland heelers are famous for their yen to work, determination, intelligence, faithfulness to a master and spirited courage. Jim had all those qualities.

We named him for two favourite Jims in our lives just then – one was Lucky Jim from the Kingsley Amis novel of the same name, and the other was Little Jim (Jim Knees) from *The Goon Show*. Poignancy leavened with humour. To that mixture Jim the pup added his own special characteristics. He was utterly irrepressible. From the beginning, he had the strongest 'ego' I have ever seen in a canine.

We already had Laika. She had come with us from Grays Point. She was sweet, wagsome, willing. Her own border collie/kelpie lineage fitted her for farm life. But by the time we received her, she was past training for real work. She accompanied us everywhere we went, obeyed us, but tended to keep on the outskirts of the action.

Jim, however, was always at the centre of things. He circled it, jumped up on it, took it in his mouth, lifted his leg on it. All the while he watched our faces, especially Jeff's, waiting for instructions. He was eager to learn, desperate to please. During his first six months at the farm he was an utter nuisance. He chewed things, dug things up, gobbled things down. Nothing was left unscarred by his sharp little teeth, his frantic little paws. We forgave his puppy mischief because of his quality. Neighbouring farmers eyed him covetously. Everyone admired his vitality, his neat lines.

Jeff was proud of Jim and keen to teach him to round up cattle. A desire to do this had been bred into him. Time and again he would circle our small mob, nipping the heels of stragglers, to head them in the direction he thought we wanted. (Which was not always the right direction but the fault was ours for giving confusing orders.) If a beast kicked him, he would go back and try harder.

Goth and Van, and Thor when he was staying with us for the weekend, raced with him, wrestled him, encouraged him to play tug-of-war with bits of rope, old socks, leather straps. He carried off their toys and chewed them to bits. They scolded and at once forgave him.

Laika permitted him to take out his excessive energy on her when no one else was available. She acted like an indulgent aunt as he chewed her ears, pulled her tail, jumped all over her body. Only in the matter of food did she stand firmly against him. If Jim came anywhere near her bowl, she would curl her lip into a nasty snarl quite unlike her usual pretty smile, and Jim would never dare touch her dinner. In all other matters, however, he was the dominant one.

When Thalos joined the household, Jim found it hard to share the stage. He strutted about stiff-legged and alert, clearly jealous. If we carried Thalos, Jim tried to jump up. His presence made Thalos very nervous. Goth and Van took turns to pat and mollify Jim while the other held the 'roo. This solved two jealousy problems by helping both lads feel they were doing something important. Our daily task was schooling the dogs not to harm the kangaroo, because eventually Thalos would be moving around freely.

As the weather improved we carried Thalos out into the garden, trying to induce him to urinate and defecate outdoors. We also hoped he would nibble grass, believing that his digestion would work better if he were eating natural food. He was a terribly selective feeder, however. We used to kneel over him, to screen him from draughts, and push stuff under his nose that we thought would tempt him. Half an hour's encouragement might result in one little leaf chewed, or two or three blades of grass consumed. Dry leaves interested him the most and we guessed he needed some roughage.

Thalos was very nervous outdoors and this distracted him from eating. His fur rippled with apprehension and his ears swivelled constantly. If we moved apart from him, he chattered anxiously and hopped after us. It was weeks before he gained enough confidence to graze a small patch of lawn adjacent to the back door while we kept an eye on him through the kitchen window, calling out encouragement. Loud machinery noises terrified him. A motor mower, the tractor or a timber jinker grinding down the road laden with logs – all would set him off. He'd rear back on his heels, chattering desperately, and if we didn't rush to reassure him, he would bolt blindly around the garden. The slightest wind springing up meant he had to be scooped up, swaddled and popped into his bag.

Poultry worried him. Each afternoon we let out the chooks so they could pick and scratch for insects among the flowerbeds, which were so long-established that little could damage them. We loved to watch the hens took-tooking over garden and paddock, led by the proud white rooster. They would dash toward a tidbit discovered by their leader and a brief melee would occur as those at the top pecked crankily at the less dominant ones. Thalos was not amused. Whenever a chicken came into his field of vision, he would startle, shivering and chattering and readying himself to fly. The hens, silly creatures that they were, used to press in, craning from every angle, scolding and clucking while the rooster strutted around them shaking his comb and wattles. They seemed to sense that here was someone they could get the better of. If we didn't intercede, Thalos would jump aside in alarm. This unsettled the rooster badly but Thalos was too scared to notice. Nor did he seem able to 'notice' anything much. He appeared to operate on an instinctual level, his focal point just beyond his nose.

If we tried to shoo the chooks away from Thalos, Jim would grow excited. If we didn't watch him, he would herd the flock round and round the yard, winding them up into choruses of soprano alarm. This roused Laika's latent instincts and she would come stalking from another direction. To avoid pandemonium, we had to quickly separate all parties. Once the chickens had been shooed from the scene, Jim needed praise for his obedience, Laika required reassurance that she had not disgraced herself and Thalos had to be beguiled to commence browsing again.

Although Thalos was wary of poultry, the dogs seemed to fascinate him. He was drawn to approach them, lacked the sense to avoid them. This kept us on our mettle. Each time we heard a warning growl from Laika or Jim, we had to come running. Laika knew she must not harm him. If he entered her orbit, she would slide away and watch him from a distance, with something like disgust at his stupid, innocently provocative ways. Jim was the real danger. Backing off was not in his nature.

Once we were in the kitchen when we heard Jim growl just outside the door. To our horror, we caught Thalos actually sniffing at Jim's face, slender forepaws stretching out to clutch his jowls. Poor Jim snapped, like any red-blooded heeler should. 'Jim!' we shouted.

Thalos reared back, trembling. Two tiny dots of blood welled from teeth marks on his nose. We had to spank Jim, on principle, but really our sympathies lay with him. He was so ashamed for rising to the bait and clearly puzzled about how he could have been tricked into doing wrong when he was trying to mind his own business. For the next few weeks, we followed Thalos around, making sure he kept away from Jim.

Thalos's most aggressive enemies were animals we did not equate with danger – our heifers. Normally cows are shy. They can become tame if milked every day, although not many enjoy being touched by humans. They subtly drift out of reach.

One day the heifers were grazing just outside our backyard gate. From behind its mesh Thalos surveyed the warm-breathed monsters with his usual nervous indecision. Suddenly he squeezed himself underneath and before we could stop him, he hopped straight into the midst of the herd. We expected his arrival to spook the mob away. To our amazement, the docile dairies turned into a frenzied, vindictive gang. They wheeled and stamped. They tried to kick Thalos. They wanted to trample him to death.

Thalos brayed in alarm, but he hadn't the wit to flee. He kept heading into the centre of the melee. We all ran out calling to Thalos, but he didn't respond. Just as he went down under a barrage of flailing hooves, Jeff dashed in and scooped him up. He carried the frail little bundle of limp fur back inside the gate. We were sure he'd been kicked and broken, positive he'd be dead or dying. Jeff held him close while I looked for blood or fractures. Goth and Van hovered beside us, touching their little pet compassionately. Laika whimpered and circled in the background and even Jim seemed concerned.

Miraculously, we found no damage to Thalos. He was conscious and not apparently agitated. Jeff lowered him carefully onto the grass, ready to catch him if he looked about to topple. He did not. He simply put his nose down and began to nibble grass. If Thalos seemed unaffected by his experience, we were totally shaken. We adjourned inside to administer first aid to ourselves. Only after sweet drinks and cookies and many retellings of the near disaster did we regain composure.

From that day on, we took great care to separate Thalos from the cattle. Which is not to say he always stayed inside the house garden. We began to introduce him to the farm. So Van took him on fishing expeditions down to the creek and we took him blackberry picking or to work in our orchard garden. Always we used his name, hoping he would learn to come when called, as he would have done if his mother were still alive, and we did our best to imitate her chatter: 'Chut-chut-chut'.

Whether by training or by instinct, Thalos was always prepared to return to the house when we were. A proud procession we made, dirt farmers laden with buckets of fruit and veg, a perky blue cattle dog at the front and a little grey kangaroo hopping at the rear. After these excursions we'd search both the dogs and the joey for ticks. Some of these bloodsuckers can be toxic to animals or humans. Our neighbours down in the valley all told at least one sad tale of a valued worker or friend dead because of tick-poisoning. They warned that immunity comes gradually. Mother animals groom their young constantly to remove the tiny parasites and by their second year, resistance is building; by the third, immunity should be firmly in place. So daily we went down on our hands and knees to search the fur of our pets.

It was not hard to find ticks on Jim. His flecked grey hair was short. With Laika it was more difficult, since her black coat was long and shaggy. Luckily, its density kept her free of parasites except on her belly and inner ears, where her skin was exposed. Being older, she also probably had some immunity.

Thalos groomed himself daily, using his front claws and dual hind toe as a comb. The one place he could not reach, of course, was just where the little devils chose to lodge – around his eyes. Extracting them took a lot of patience. Kangaroos have a long stiff fringe of eyelashes along their upper lid, and long antennae-like eyebrows. All of these had to be folded aside. While one person restrained Thalos's long hind legs and braced his body against their lap, another of us would grasp his slender front wrists, immo-bilising them. Then a third person could probe those layers of fringes and try to grasp any ticks with tweezers.

Thalos loved a cuddle but this three-on-one wrestling was some-thing else. He used to chitter and struggle mightily. Often we were tempted to give up on a tiny white mite embedded in his lid rather than risk puncturing his eye with tweezers. After a day the tick would engorge with blood and present a bigger target for removal, so once or twice we weakened, not liking to distress him. Our compassion cost him dearly.

One day Thalos appeared listless, standing dejectedly, his head drooping, chin almost on the floor. Within an hour or two, he began to sway. When he moved, he was unsteady on his legs. These were classic symptoms of the onset of tick paralysis. Quickly Jeff stuffed him into his pouch, which he had all but outgrown, and drove him to Berry, where our ebullient Ukrain-ian vet lived, his surgery adjoining the house.

Jeff was away for ages. The boys and I waited, pessimism building as the hours ticked away. When at last we heard the Land Rover coming up the road, we were prepared for the worst. In walked Jeff, carrying a groggy Thalos, weak and unable to stand but still alive. George Borys had injected him with antitoxin and then insisted that Jeff stop to play chess with him!

We bedded Thalos warmly in his box with hot-water bottles packed all around him. He looked very ill. The entire family hovered close, worried and caring. Every few hours we offered Thalos warm drinks of Lactogen, laced with glucose and coffee to tempt his appetite. He licked feebly but consumed very little nourishment.

All through the night we took turns to get up and offer him warm sweet drinks. Just before dawn I was awakened by a faint 'Chut-chut-chut' from the kitchen. 'Did you hear that?' I nudged Jeff into wakefulness.

My ears were not the only ones cocked for that hopeful sound. Goth and Van came tumbling down from their attic. 'He looks better,' they shouted.

We made him a drink and Thalos lapped with something like vigour. A little while later I returned from outside chores to find Thalos standing on the kitchen floor with Vandal beaming beside him. Our little 'roo was on the mend.

After that narrow escape we searched him diligently for ticks and removed every single one as soon as we found it. Whether because of our attention or because the injection began to build resistance in him, Thalos was never adversely affected again. In fact, he put on a spurt of growth. Over the next four months his fur became thicker, perhaps in anticipation of the approaching winter. And his appetite became almost insatiable.

Trying to interest Thalos in food other than milk – because Lactogen did not totally agree with him – we had introduced him to brown bread, rolled oats, wheatmeal biscuits, grated carrot and banana. Now he daily fronted up for tidbits. Bread was his favourite. With his great bursts of hunger, he craved it more and more. We kept our bread in a big tin. Thalos learned to nuzzle off the lid. He enjoyed chewing up the paper wrapping almost as much as the contents.

Trying to cut sandwiches with the 'roo in the kitchen became almost impossible. He would stand on his hind toes and tail tip so he could stretch out his front paws and grab at things on the table or sinktop. Once Thalos caught the scent of food he fancied, he would not give up until he got it. Scolding had no effect. His eyes

became opaque and very dark. There was no expression of understanding in them, as there was with Jim or Laika. Thalos was just
a simple series of strong urges. Try to thwart him and there was
trouble. In the end, the only way we could eat a peaceful meal in our
kitchen was to evict Thalos altogether.

There is only one way to pick up a kangaroo. You grasp him at
the butt of the tail with one hand. With the other, you grasp him
under the arms, around the chest. Lift. Walk. The trick is to set
him down carefully so that his tail and hind feet can form an
unshakeable tripod. It would be dangerous to let the delicate
forelegs touch ground first, supporting his weight.

Thalos didn't like being removed from the kitchen. He soon
came to appreciate the routine and would hop into the bedroom
or down the hall to avoid being caught. Before he became too
excited, the only thing to do was grab him by the tail and pull him
into position for picking up. Speed and determination were essential. After capturing his tail, it was vital never to let go; he must
never believe that escape was possible. He didn't like this much
and chattered indignantly.

Once ousted, Thalos would hop up and down on the back
verandah, complaining. Clearly he hated being separated from
his family. Not to mention all that lovely fragrant food! If anyone
opened the door, Thalos would push back inside, evading knees
and hands trying to block his path. It was simpler to use a different door and go around the house rather than run Thalos's
gauntlet.

We worried lest our dear 'roo become traumatised by being
barred. I hatched an idea that I thought might solve the problem.
For some time I'd been thinking how quaint it would look if our
back door were cut in two. While the bottom half could remain
closed, keeping animals in or out, the top half could be open,
giving a nice breezy view of our back garden. The kitchen door
had become our main entrance, as happens in all country homes.
The kitchen was family room as well as dining room and general
meeting place.

Jeff loved the idea and performed surgery on the wooden planks.
When he had finished, we had a charming stable door, or Dutch
door, in keeping with our clean blue and white colour scheme. It
enabled Thalos to chatter to us while we ate, until he grew weary

from standing on his tiptoes, peering over the edge. Then he would subside onto his heels and stand with his nose pressed to the crack of the aperture, breathing in the smells of our meal.

Sometimes Thalos sucked the hem of a raincoat hanging on the back verandah. This sucking habit came on him after he had been with us for several months. There were lessons in it.

Long-standing friends had come to visit us for a week. Their teenaged daughter was flushed with maternal longing and became fascinated by Thalos. For hours she would sit beside him on the grass, gently working her fingers through his soft fur. When he allowed it, she took him on her lap to cuddle. She loved giving him his dinner.

She begged and begged to try him with one of the baby bottles we used for calves. Hating to disappoint her, I agreed. (Lesson number one.) Thalos took to it at once. She was so thrilled that it seemed harmless enough to let her continue, but after she departed, Thalos was a changed character. His instinct to suck had been roused, and although we returned to our practice of serving his milk in a dish, he still wanted to suck. When he was tired or upset he would fasten his long lips and palate onto the collar or hem of a shirt, or a trouser cuff. He was like a baby with a dummy. A big baby.

He looked quite pitiful and we wondered if we had deprived him by making him lap. After checking our reference books, however, we learned that in the wild, Thalos would normally continue to suck milk from his mother even after he left her pouch. (Lesson two.) For six months he would stick his head back inside to drink from one of her teats, even if she had a second tiny infant sucking on another. Incredibly, we read, different strengths and sorts of milk would be produced by a mother kangaroo at the same time, suited to the developmental stages of her two offspring.

We tried to cuddle Thalos more. He was still a very nervous, dependent young animal. In the evenings, Goth or Van held Thalos on their laps. During the day when they were off at school, however, Jeff and I had less time for pampering. To augment our farm income, we had to contribute articles to magazines. We had converted the old dairy to an office by enclosing the open front. Filing cabinets and our two desks stood where the bails used to be. The adjoining cream separating room became Jeff's darkroom.

With stories to write and photos to print and caption, we often found ourselves hurrying across the back yard, dodging Thalos.

Our busyness during the day caused Thalos to seek out the dogs for company. They tolerated him better now that he was older and, while not actually playing together, they could all lie in the same quarter of the garden, drawing comfort from each other.

Any visitor who arrived while we were at work found himself welcomed effusively by the animals. Laika would smile and wag, Jim would jump up again and again, and Thalos would fasten onto some corner of their clothing. This caused alarm at first. Visitors thought the 'roo was trying to bite them until it was explained that he was just a lonely little orphan. Without exception, they submitted gladly after that. I have seen guests stand in one spot for a quarter of an hour, taking in the clear mountain air and admiring the tree-filled surrounds, rather than deprive Thalos of his bit of human company, his portion of cloth to suck.

The solution seemed obvious. What Thalos needed was companions of his own kind. These he would never find in the bush surrounding the farm. All our explorations had shown the area to be barren of kangaroos. We assumed the species had been shot out years before, along with koalas. There were a few wild wallabies still about, very shy, but no kangaroos. We set about to rectify that.

Jeff visited his old friend, Eric Worrell. Along with the Judds of Jamberoo, Eric was a strong and enduring influence on our thinking. Earlier than us, he saw the advantage of being outside the urban hurly-burly. At his home near Gosford, as far north of Sydney as we were south, he created a sanctuary he called the Australian Reptile Park. Jeff helped Eric to publicise his work and Eric helped us in many aspects of ours.

Not only was he the country's leading reptile expert, Eric championed all Australian wildlife, particularly those species unpopular with humans. Dingoes, wombats, emus, lizards, crocodiles and the many members of the kangaroo family sheltered within his safety net. Eric's mission was to convince the public that *every* creature plays a part in the plant and animal ecosystem, which in Australia is so delicately balanced by harsh climate and difficult geography. He wrote articles and books, appeared on radio and television, spoke to schools and service clubs.

The principal work of his park was to extract venom from poisonous snakes so that it could be dried and made into antivenin by the Commonwealth Serum Laboratories. The park also served as the official holding station in that district for wildlife in need of care. Jeff learned that Eric had an embarrassing surplus of orphan kangaroos. When Jeff asked if he could take one home, Eric replied: 'Take three.'

While Eric arranged the paperwork for the transfer, Jeff rang to tell us what was happening. I rushed to inform Goth and Vandal. 'Dad is bringing home three more joeys!' They were thrilled. *I* was thrilled. Then I began to reflect. What was I getting into? After more than a year looking after Thalos in much the same way as a human child, I was enjoying freedom from daily nappy washing and frequent milk drinks. Particularly sweet was unbroken sleep at night. Now I was about to commit myself to triplets. 'You must be crazy,' I told myself.

'But what about Thalos?' my better self argued. How else would he find companionship of his own kind? Not only company but also a chance to mate and populate our area with his offspring?

Thankfully, my better self won the argument and when Jeff arrived home I rushed out with the boys, jostling each other to see what he had brought. In the ute we found three sugar bags, their tops tied with string. Goth was given one to carry, taking care to support the tail and hind elbows. Van was bursting to carry the second bag so, despite his smallness, he was allowed. Jeff brought the third while I rushed ahead to open doors and keep the two dogs and Thalos out of the house until the new arrivals could settle.

When released, the joeys set off almost at once to explore. The kitchen, our bedroom, the back hallway leading to the bathroom – nothing escaped their attention. While we watched in quiet fascination, they nosed into every corner, insinuating themselves beneath chairs and under the bed, so that we were sure someone would get stuck. But they just kept moving, until they had sniffed over every inch of their new domain. They 'walked' precisely, with front paws flat on the floor, balancing on their tail as their hind feet were drawn forward in unison.

As they went, they dropped a few calling cards. 'Steamers', the boys called them. This was another reason I was happy when Thalos grew old enough to live outdoors. There is no way you can house-train a kangaroo. As with most of their functions, they are very simple and direct about defecation. When they feel the urge to do it, they simply relax their sphincter muscle and out pops a chain of pellets, usually bound together in a sort of dark green sausage. There is nothing you can do but sweep them away in a dustpan and wash the floor often. The droppings of an eight-month-old joey are not very big or smelly but now, I thought, there will be three of them. Two more joeys than we'd ever had before.

'Panic not,' Jeff urged. He explained how young animals were cared for at the Australian Reptile Park. There, an entire room was devoted to creatures needing warmth and confinement. Small pens had been built in tiers with pull-out trays underneath containing sand or sawdust for daily emptying. Heaters installed around the walls at head height kept the temperature at a constant 28 degrees. The curator at Eric Worrell's park was thus able to care for multiple patients simultaneously, which she was often called upon to do. We could not spare an entire room for joey keeping but Jeff thought he could build a sort of heated cupboard on our sheltered front verandah where the three orphans could be cosily enclosed. So with that optimistic plan in mind, we invited in first Thalos and then the dogs to meet the newcomers.

Thalos quivered all over, excited at confronting three of his own species. He sniffed them rather aggressively and tried to pat them with his front paws.

Two of them were females. One was fluffy grey like Thalos himself. Her face was very pretty. The male was similar. The other female was different. She was taller, her fur was shorter and her face was long. She had a wound in her hip the size of a coin from the bullet that had killed her mother while she was in the pouch.

'Let's have no more exotic names,' Jeff proposed. 'Let's start off with the most Australian we can think of.'

'Waltzing Matilda?' Van piped up.

'Beauty,' Jeff agreed.

'What about Opal for the pretty one?' Goth offered. Jeff had recently travelled to Coober Pedy to write a story about the opal miners there. He brought back some stones for our rock collection which intrigued the boys. Although they were not valuable specimens, they showed a little of the fire and colour which made the Australian gem worth more than gold at that time.

'Good one,' Jeff said. 'Mathilda and Opal. That'll do for the girls. Now, how about Mulga Mick for the male? You couldn't get more Australian than that.'

So the names were decided, beginning a new tradition.

Jim, our jealous cattle dog, was not pleased to find he and Laika were now outnumbered by marsupials. He circled round and round the three, alternately wagging his tail and curling his lip. He kept bumping into Thalos, who chattered nervously. Suddenly the kitchen seemed too full of animals. Keeping a firm hold on Jim's collar, Jeff warned him succinctly not to touch the new arrivals. Then he picked Thalos up firmly by the butt of the tail and evicted them both. Laika followed.

Mathilda, Opal and Mick came down off their haunches, their hair settled back from bristling alarm to velvety down, and their dark eyes became moist and soft again. Their homecoming had been completed.

Within a day, Jeff and I built the Carter version of a joey incubator. We called it the kangararium. It was about seven feet long, three feet wide and four feet six inches high. The front was solid boards for two feet. The upper half was made of flyscreen frames which lifted up on hinges. This would facilitate cleaning and would allow fresh air in when required. Over the screen windows I tacked roll-up canvas curtains to keep out draughts and retain warmth inside at night.

On the floor we laid an electric blanket, with several chaff bags underneath to prevent heat from escaping downward. On top of the blanket we laid plastic sheeting and covered it with two inches of sawdust. Jeff installed a small bar-heater in the roof of the cupboard, angled downward but out of reach of the joeys. He put a thermometer inside the pen and a large bowl of water in a non-tippable frame. He had been warned that it was necessary to induce humidity, like that in the marsupial pouch, lest the joeys become dehydrated by the heater. This could be very dangerous.

When we introduced the three orphans into their new home, they settled at once, standing contentedly in front of the heater and preening themselves by its glow. For the next four months the heater and the electric blanket would be kept on constantly. This doubled our winter electricity bill but the system worked so well that we had no qualms about the extra expense.

Never had we seen such blossoming joeys, which we attributed to constant warmth and companionship. Their fur looked thick and fluffy and they never showed a hint of the diarrhoea which had plagued Hanogi and Thalos. In fact their droppings were small and dry, disappearing into the sawdust underfoot. Their urine also dried in minutes. Daily I raked over the sawdust and sieved out the droppings. Once a week I removed the joeys into the warm kitchen while I shovelled out the sawdust, made sure the electric blanket was dry, replaced any bags that had become soiled and put in fresh bedding. It was a very good, low maintenance system.

We all agreed the orphans should be bottle-fed. The sight of Thalos pathetically sucking cloth when he felt tired or lonely was something we didn't want to duplicate. Or triplicate! But here again, Jeff had brought back a good idea from Eric Worrell's park. The marsupials curator, a Finnish woman named Raija Krauss, had invented a special device which was more suited to kangaroo mouths than the pet-feeders sold for puppies or kittens. Her invention used a normal screw-lid infant bottle, with its inbuilt mechanism for letting air in as milk is sucked out. This eliminates the wind which can cause distress to a bottle-fed joey. The accompanying human teat was too fat and short for the slender jaws of a kangaroo, however. Since young marsupials clamp onto their mother's nipple for many months, it becomes super-elongated, reaching back to the baby's glottis.

Raija inserted a length of firm plastic tubing into the centre of the human teat. Over this she stretched the soft bladder of a fountain pen. We kept our local newsagent busy and puzzled ordering replacement bladders, but the system worked fine. Our only worry was that the joeys might suck the rubber tube down their throats and we kept ever vigilant. Later on, when ballpoints came on the market and it became difficult to buy fountain pen ink sacs any longer, we performed many experiments with catheter tubing, bicycle valve rubber, even fingers from small-sized rubber gloves. None of these worked as well. Eventually, a Kangaroo Protection Committee member in Sydney moulded a special latex joey teat. They were scarce at first but as demand grew, they became obtainable through veterinarians.

It wasn't much trouble rearing multiple babies because Goth

and Van were always keen to help feed them. When the boys were at school, Jeff and I simply took turns. If they were hungry for milk, the joeys stretched onto their tiptoes, trying to climb out of their pen. It took dexterity to extract two, leaving a ravenous third 'chutting' and hopping from one end to the other until his turn came.

Cuddling is an important element in the rearing of marsupial babies. We had learned this for ourselves and seen it reinforced by the staff at Eric Worrell's park. We needed a lot of willing hands and laps to sit with an armful of joey wrapped in a bunny rug while stroking Thalos and Jim, and rubbing Laika's broad back by foot. Visitors were pressed into the act and this became part of a visit to the Carters'.

Happily, Opal, Mathilda and Mulga Mick were such good company for one another that they did not need as much human companionship as a joey on its own. They used to stretch out beneath the heater on the warm sawdust, within touch of each other. After three months I found I could give at least some of the four or five daily feeds while they remained standing in the kangararium. I held a bottle in each hand and if no one was available to hold the third, I sometimes gripped it between my knees. This kept all three slurping contently together.

By the time the worst of the winter cold had passed, the animals had grown so much that the cupboard was becoming crowded. We decided to let the trio sample sunshine and green shoots outside in the garden. To keep them warm I made three simple jackets from a disused woollen jumper, fastening them at the front with big safety pins.

Mulga Mick was usually first out of the box, closely followed by Opal. Mathilda was not so nimble because of her bullet wound. It had healed over, after daily dressing for quite a long time, but there remained a scar and a weakness in her haunch which we hoped would disappear with exercise.

As soon as the 'roos were let through the screen verandah door and stood with their feet upon real living earth, they stayed very still – ears swivelling, fur a-ripple – until they were satisfied there was no danger. Then they gave the same joyous sideways leap we had observed in the other joeys and took off around the house. Sometimes Opal was the leader, at other times it would be Mick or even Mathilda. It was an energetic caravan once it got moving.

No sooner would the last one hop out of sight than the first would come bounding past on another lap. At first Thalos stood and watched with amazement. During the winter, he had been allowed into our kitchen for only a few hours each evening. The rest of his time was spent grazing the lawn or sheltering in the blacksmith barn where he slept in a nest of hay. Now he was emerging from a winter lethargy like the rest of us and he began to join in the morning hop-athon, thumping his hind feet down hard to announce that he was king of the herd.

Had we not restrained Jim, he would have joined in as well. We had to snap the leash onto his collar and tether him to the lemon tree. As each 'roo bounded past he would dance and bark while Laika, sitting nearby, smiled and wagged and looked a bit apprehensive about all this noise and movement in the garden.

Thalos looked forward to the new morning routine. We would awaken to find his face pressed against the big window of our bedroom, ears swivelling to hear us when we stirred, uttering the occasional 'chut' to hurry us along. As soon as we went into the kitchen to brew breakfast, he transferred himself to the front verandah door, literally hopping from one leg to the other in anticipation. Often it would be Goth and Van, still in pyjamas, who rushed to open the kangararium and let out Opal, Mulga Mick and Mathilda. They would cluck, answered outdoors by Thalos, until the screen door was opened and the around-the-house laps could begin. The boys' barracking, plus the dogs' yelping, drowned out for a while the din of birds proclaiming the morning. It was a good way to begin a day.

While the boys, now spruce in school uniforms, ate their cereal and toast, the marsupials settled to graze the lawn. 'Goodbye, Rooies, goodbye,' called the lads as they climbed into my old 1928 Essex tourer in which I ran them down to the bus. Its big open wheels and low gearing were perfect for hilly Foxground. By the time I chuffed back home and parked beneath the oak tree, the kangaroos and the dogs would be stretched out, resting together companionably. The sight was a triumph.

As summer warmed around us, the three younger 'roos joined Thalos in sleeping outside the house. Eating plenty of grass, they only came to the kitchen door for bottles of milk at breakfast and

dinner times. Thalos always fronted up with them, demanding
tidbits and a pat. He was spoiled, Thalos; if unacknowleged he
would pursue you, clutching and scolding. Jim was equally
demanding. Crossing the yard to the back door often meant
running a gauntlet. We decided to open the gate between the
garden and the half-acre paddock below the house which faced
onto the creek. It had been rested, since the current batch of calves
had grown into heifers and been put up into the back paddocks.

The kangaroos appreciated access to more, longer grass but
always gravitated back to the house yard by late afternoon. Once
they were safely inside the garden, we shut the gate. To foster this
homing urge, we called them and rattled feed buckets and dishes
as the shadows lengthened. We were learning that wildlife can
respond to a repeated command, issued always in the same tone
of voice, almost as well as domestic animals, provided food is
offered consistently. Food is the only key for conditioning wild
creatures.

One day Vandal, ever the sharp-eyed bushman, thought he saw
Thalos mate with Mathilda down in the calf paddock. We hoped
he was right and that it would be the same with Opal. The idea of
joeys in the girls' pouches was very exciting.

Mulga Mick was still too young to mate. But he was old enough
to spar with Thalos. I was alarmed by their behaviour. Each would
rear back on his tail and kick at the other's belly, growling. At first
Mick was shaky, nearly toppling sideways, and his barks were
mere adolescent squeaks, but he soon strengthened to the game
which Thalos enjoyed as much as he. Taller than Mick and
stronger, Thalos had an advantage which he seldom pressed. A
telephone call to Eric Worrell confirmed it was all part of a
learning process, not serious.

Where I found their jousts a worry, Jeff and the boys responded
like fans at a prize fight. Their own masculinity was roused by the
daily contests and they always stopped to watch the gladiators.
Thalos, being older, was the dominant male but Mick, the young
contender, enjoyed much encouragement from the bystanders.
One day he might want to seriously challenge Thalos.

Before that could happen, Thalos began to wander further
afield. Van reported he had squeezed out under a gap in the fence.
Fortunately the heifers were nowhere in sight. We coaxed him

back into the home province and fixed the fence. Next day he had found a way out again. After several such escapes and returns, we decided to let him go, to take his chance in the wide world. Perhaps there were other kangaroos he could smell, although we had never sighted any, nor heard reports that the species still existed in Foxground.

As we watched him hopping confidently up the road past the waterfall track, we all felt pangs of loss. We all hoped he was big enough to cope on his own. We all prayed he would find his way back soon.

7

Under Fox Ground

I have to mention the record and the book which slipped into our lives like stones into a pond and lodged there. It might seem trivial to combine red-blooded productive friends, *real* people, with ephemeral characters from literature, yet that was how it happened with us. They are all melded together, building blocks of our Foxground experience.

We listened to a lot of gramophone records, instinctively resisting television for as long as we could. Beginning with the folk songs which had captured us at Grays Point – Pete Seeger and his sister Peggy, those mournful Irish singers, Spanish flamenco, Miriam Makeba – we progressed through jazz to Bob Dylan and The Beatles. Lovely to listen to, good background for our children, we thought. Ditto the spoken word which, along with music, filled our house and preoccupied our thoughts, sloughing off bits into our vernacular. The humour of Stan Freburg seduced us first, then *The Goon Show*. Ah, the Goons. They shaped my two sons' minds and once saved my life – but that's another story.

The recording most relative to our early Foxground impressions was a BBC production of *Under Milk Wood*, a play for voices by the poet Dylan Thomas. I mail-ordered it through the Mary Martin Bookshop after reading about it in their newsletter. The play celebrates village life, exposing human foibles through gossip. Lying together on the floor in the evenings, we listened to the rich plum-sauce tones of Richard Burton and the Welsh cast until we knew the characters so well that we would slide into sleep and dream them, waking smooth as silk to take up the story consciously again. Willy Nilly, the Postman who steamed open the mail; philosophical Blind Captain Cat; Nogood Boyo, the idler; rhyming Reverend Eli Jenkins; the two Mrs Dai Breads, wives of the baker; milky Polly Garter, hanging washing in her breezy back yard where nothing grew but babies; Mrs Butcher Beynon's little treasure Lily Small, who might well have echoed a repressed Mary Letty Thompson when she wished to 'sin 'til I blow up!' Ah, how easily in our imaginations the residents of Milk Wood meshed with our new neighbours down in Foxground valley. 'Under Fox Ground,' Jeff liked to intone affectionately. And of course, once we got to know them better, we realised they were nothing like as yeasty and poetic as Dylan Thomas's characters.

Our earliest and nearest neighbours were a big family who rented the farmhouse at the bottom of our property. The 150-acre farm on which the house stood stretched all along our border and down the road some, its owner living elsewhere but using the land as a dry run for his dairy cattle and a horse or two. The farmhouse was small, basic and had stood empty for some years until the family spied it and moved in just before we did. There were seven children to start with and this number increased to thirteen during their stay in Foxground.

As soon as we arrived the four boys, aged five through nine, trudged up the hill to commence what became a daily ritual of visiting, scouting through our possessions, asking us questions, volunteering news (they seemed surprisingly well-informed about the district, for reasons we later understood) and ingratiating themselves into our household. They were bright little tykes, blond-haired with big teeth and broad grins, and open sunny names like Kerry and Buckie and Andrew, except for the second eldest, who had a thin rat-like face and a truly mean disposition. Kenneth. Clearly they were fairly poor, told us they always slept two or more to a bed, and Dad was often away for months at a time. It was a while before we learned that during these absences he was in jail. By this time I had taken them to my heart and urged them up to our table, fetching them to and from the school bus stop, or at least their cases and the smallest

amongst them when there were too many to squash in beside
Goth and Van.

Our lads shared their rooms and toys and enjoyed the company
at first – those kids already knew more about our property, its
caves and crannies and views, than we did. If anyone slipped into
the creek or fell among mud, I sent them home in dry clothes
which usually I told them they could keep. It was the matter of
Goth's and Van's money-boxes which began to tarnish my open-
hearted attitude and presented us all with a dilemma. Into these
tin replicas of a Commonwealth Bank building clanked weekly
pocket money plus largesse from their grandparents, who doted
on saving – never countenanced spending – money. My own
philosophy was that the best way to understand the value of
money was to earn it by doing chores, then spend some but not all
and decide whether what you bought lasted or brought long-term
pleasure. It was during the monthly shake-out of coins that we saw
our neighbours' treachery. And their wiliness. Those neighbour
lads had been sneaking up to the bedroom, extracting two-shilling
pieces and substituting pence, which were about the same size.

Next came the mystery of our petrol, which was delivered
monthly and pumped into a big tank near our back gate. When I
went to fill up my old Essex car, there was not enough fuel. At first
we thought the carrier, Billy Gill, had made a mistake or was
robbing us, both almost unthinkable because he was also livestock carter, footballer and a respected son of the district. Asking
around, we learned that everyone else in the valley had lost petrol
at night until they put a padlock on their tank and tied up a dog
nearby. We followed suit but were saddened by the news that
other things had gone missing from farmhouses while the owners
were out – preserves from the pantries, loaves of bread from bins,
sheets and towels from linen closets. The fact was that the family
living next door to us were notorious thieves! Even the smallest
of their kids helped, learning early to be boosted up and squeezed
through open windows to give their brothers, sisters and father
access.

Foxground houses which had not locked their doors in years
commenced to do so. We followed suit. Actually, we lost little by
comparison with other neighbours and this was probably the
result of our acceptance of the children into our family routine.

The worst they ever did to us came under the heading of 'understandable boyish curiosity'. One day when we returned from a trip to Sydney, we found the record player on and the turntable still revolving. Checking further, we found muddy shoe-prints, greasy fingermarks, an empty peanut butter jar and Jeff's expensive telephoto lens out of its case and damaged. Probably they had mistaken it for a telescope. This was too much. Jeff marched down the hill to confront the parents but found only a fresh-faced 'girl' who turned out to be the mother of the brood and wife of Ronald, who was away serving time again. She heard Jeff out and insisted the lads involved must cart firewood for us for a week, as reparation. 'I don't want to be visiting my kids in prison later,' she stated with feeling.

Democratically, I continued to transport the children to and from the bus stop and tried to remain friendly to them, but they were informed that ours was no longer open house. This hurt me and I fretted about the wrongs being done to those likeable youngsters by their parent's criminal habits. My neighbours down the valley did not share my misgivings. They banned the family from the start and felt vindicated as more and more often the police car prowled up our quiet road and searched their house for contraband. Eventually they became involved in major crimes. Ronald was put away for a long stretch and the mother and her by now baker's dozen of offspring were evicted from the property for long-term non-payment of rent. I felt truly sorrowful but I was alone in that sentiment.

How out of step with the locals I was can best be illustrated by our Christmas parties. In those days, the place to mix socially was at Rotary meetings, the Red Cross, or one of the church fellowship groups in Berry or Gerringong, differentiated according to gender – Presbyterian Ladies' Group; Baptist Men's Fellowship, and so on. But Jeff was no joiner and was too often away on his journalistic trips for consistent attendance at anything, even if he'd had a mind to. I scrupulously attended Parents and Citizens meetings at Berry, which were not segregated; in fact many fathers came, taking the lead in activities requiring muscle or equipment – erecting the stage at the School of Arts for student concerts and prize-givings, mowing the playing field, et cetera. I took my turn at tuckshop duties and tidying the school garden, but apart from

that, my socialising took place at Glenrock, usually at the
weekends, when visitors from Sydney or Canberra rolled up to
stay and eat and enjoy. So I felt inspired to stage an open house
for locals at Christmas time, some carry-over from American
customs stuck in my psyche.

It urged me to share our hospitality with neighbours down in
the valley, who made Goth and Van welcome on their farms and
who generously advised us about our agricultural aspirations. The
school bus was the social cement for Foxground youngsters, the
whole valley was their playground. Ours was the last inhabited
property on Foxground road, a track to nowhere beyond
Glenrock farmhouse, a sort of nether kingdom above 'normal'
rural life – and it tickled me to imagine the neighbours driving that
mile or so up the roller-coaster track for a jolly yuletide get-
together. Another of my romantic notions, my vanities, which over
time could land me in trouble.

So I prepared a smorgasbord of festive food, laid on beer and
wine along with fruit juice, and arranged all the spare chairs in the
living room, then waited with munificent good spirits for the
guests to arrive. The farmhouse was a beacon on the dark forested
ridge; I turned on all the lights, upstairs and down, including a
coloured string along the front verandah; in the lounge our live
Christmas tree winked and sparkled, exuding piney fragrance.

When the trucks and muddy sedans began to roll up, Jeff and
I went forth to the gate to welcome the arrivals. Kids spilled out
first and our boys took them in tow, to play the outdoor games
we'd planned. No worries about them having a good time. The
grown-ups were a different matter.

'Evening, Jeff,' the men said gruffly into the darkness, shaking
hands seriously but avoiding eye contact. For me, a duck of the head
and a mumbled, 'Mrs Carter?' The men said, 'Looks like a bit of rain
about . . . well, we can do with it.' They led their women onward and
inward. Diffident, dressed more formally than normal, hair slicked
back or freshly permed, we scarcely recognised them as they
trooped through our kitchen and up the hall to the lounge. There
the women sat upon the chairs, tugging at their skirts to cover their
knees – the era of the mini was upon us and Foxground madams
had raised their hems, apparently a bit more than they felt comfortable with – while the men passed through, out onto the verandah.

Most accepted a beer but drank it slowly, almost reluctantly, their ruddy faces oddly green or blue beneath the coloured lights. Outside the children ran and shrieked and partied freely. But indoors, the women sat frozen. Shyness? Disapproval? We had a big Bob Dylan poster tacked on our wall. Who was he, they wondered discreetly. Was it one of Mr Carter's photos? All refused any sort of alcohol, grudgingly took fruit juice ('Just a small one, thanks'), so stilted in their attempts at polite conversation, it occurred to me there might be undercurrents I had not accounted for – jealousies, religious differences, who could know?

The men talked farming fluently enough, their voices rumbling beyond the open windows, their dress boots making the old verandah floorboards crack and groan. Their wives spoke of nothing much at all, the children raced round as usual; somehow I convinced the parents to nibble a piece of cake or a Christmas cookie and then let the kids loose on the rest. After a decent interval, the guests trooped out again. When their thank-yous and farewells had faded back down the road, I was left with masses of uneaten food, undrunk grog and a feeling of disappointment. Why had the gathering not caught alight, as our other parties did?

Three times we staged this fiasco. The third year, I excelled myself with the catering. Among scones with jam and cream and oblongs of fruit cake, which I had by then learned was standard fare, I provided a magnificent punch which I intended to spike with alcohol ever so subtly, in the hope that it might do the trick. I put it on the big blue platter, in a hollowed-out watermelon with slabs of fresh pineapple, strawberries and orange rings afloat inside. It made the buffet table so pretty. Everyone commented on it. But nobody would accept a drop of my punch. Nobody.

That was my final attempt. Blow it, I thought, too much effort for no gain.

Years later, I met one of those Christmas guests in the street at Berry. Our children had all grown up and gone, they had moved from Foxground valley. 'Do you remember,' she said, 'those gorgeous Christmas parties you and Jeff used to put on? We were only speaking the other day about that punch you made in the watermelon! Trying to remember how you did it.'

Perhaps we were ahead of our time, in Foxground. Not perhaps, definitely. During the 1960s, country people shied away from innovation. Exoticism frightened and offended them. I remember one tuckshop session when women cutting sandwiches began talking about Italian food. *The Women's Weekly* had published a recipe for bolognese sauce. One woman said, 'I tried making it, but hubby said: "What's this muck? I'm not eating that!"'

The rest nodded sympathetically. 'My husband wouldn't touch it, so what's the use of cooking it?' they said.

I've never forgotten that day – a revelation to me of just how conservative our neighbours were. Pasta was no stranger in our kitchen or those of our Sydney friends; eating at Italian, French or Chinese restaurants was normal and Elizabeth David's *French Country Cooking* had become a culinary bible. Not so in our district.

That fear of foreignness extended to a family in the valley who had bought a rundown farm on the 'dry side' of the road, where water would always be a problem. The Bentosiks had migrated from Central Europe, their faces broad and Slavic, ditto their two fair-haired children, and all four had the gaunt look of hardship. How that family laboured to make a go of their miserable dairy farm! It was pitiful to watch them, out in all weathers, the woman alongside her husband, she dressed in black with a kerchief over her hair, the kids barefoot and skinny. Whenever I mentioned them to our Australian neighbours, the reply was always the same: 'They're *bred* to it.'

How wrong they were. I learned the family's real circumstances while collecting our mail.

The Foxground post was delivered by car to a tiny tin shed at the crossroads, where the school bus turned around. Inside was a little locked room with a lift-up window opening onto a dusty foyer so small it could only accommodate one person at a time. The 'mail lady' walked across the road from her farmhouse a few minutes before the car was due and you could buy stamps through the window across a rough counter. She would gather in your letters along with those that had already been posted through a hand-chiselled slot in the door, and put them into a blue sailcloth bag sewn, we were told, by prisoners in jail. She tied this bag up with string sealed by lead clamped with a special tool. While she prepared this you chatted with whoever had walked or driven a tractor, or even ridden a horse, to the post office. Once the roadside mailman had arrived, handed over the blue bag of incoming letters, accepted the bag of outgoing and driven off again, you chatted some more while the mail lady undid the new bag and sorted the contents. Those not picked up in person were put into crude wooden pigeon holes in the weeny foyer for later collection.

I first met Mrs Bentosik when she walked up the road from their farm to catch the mail lady in action. Her mission, it turned out, was to collect in person the Child Endowment. She told me in halting English that her husband would take it and keep it for the farm bills otherwise. She needed it to buy clothes or school supplies for their two children. The amount involved was a pittance but it was the only money that woman ever handled. My heart went out to her. And stayed with her as her confidence in me grew and she told me their story over periodic cups of coffee at my home.

They had met in a displaced persons camp at the end of the war. She said several men wanted to marry her, all strangers, but the one she chose was Polish, like herself. As a teenager, she had been conscripted by German soldiers and taken far away to work on a farm. That stint of forced labour was her only agricultural experience. Her husband was no more skilled but both were willing and when they fetched up in Australia, they took advantage of a scheme to put New Australians, as they were called then, onto the land, signing up for a mortgage they did not have sufficient English to comprehend. It had monstrously harsh terms and they were labouring their lives away paying high interest without ever paying off any principal. They only understood their mistake when their son grew old enough and educated enough to read their contract.

The magnitude of their enslavement on the property by the bank poisoned their marital relationship. When I began chatting with her, Mrs Bentosik said her husband had not spoken to her for two years. Their suffering was intense. So the picture the locals had of peasant farmers toiling stoically side by side in the fields was a false one. But when I tried to put it into everyday terms to the Australian farmers' wives, they remained indifferent. The Polish family was just too foreign to inspire sympathy.

Poor devils. At least we were not that odd. So long as we farmed, or tried to in our small fashion, they related to us all right. Our family values looked sound. Our politics they knew little about. Our lack of church affiliation probably caused some tut-tutting, but overall we were treated well, like amusing pets at the high end of the valley, benign clowns who wrote stories for *The Weekly* and *Post* which made them feel included and a bit special. Our real schism was in the nature conservation field, but at that time, we, or I, did not realise what a deep gulf that would be to cross.

What set me apart from them were my American terms of reference, which I tried hard to hide within a carefully constructed Australian mask – another of my vanities to believe assimilation would be that simple – and also my Yankee education. Because I had studied zoology and anthropology at college, I viewed with awe the native species of Australia – animal, vegetable, mineral or human. Treated with indifference or even contempt by folks born here or transplanted from England, Foxground's rich wildlife was to me treasure, for study and nurture. When I raved about it, the locals heard me out and then, with British reticence, declined to discuss it.

I worked hard at emulating their behaviour in order to blend in, for my children's sake as well as my own. This was helped by my taking on the job of relief mail lady when she went away on annual holidays. I learned the mysteries of postal forms and the lead-clamping machine, and I drove the routes from Gerringong post office delivering to roadside mailboxes. They numbered about one hundred and fifty, but oddly enough, the surnames on the letters were mainly three – Sharp, Miller, Hindmarsh – closely followed by Campbell and Noble. The reason for this was that they were second and third generation farmers from the original landholders, who had bred big families and sub-divided, selling to neighbours' sons or to brothers or cousins. Hard-working, upright citizens. If you could get hold of a Gerringong telephone directory from those years, you would see what I mean.

Foxground was included in that slim volume. And our telephone calls went through an exchange operating from a house at Toolijooa, where a farmer's wife connected all telephonic traffic. Local numbers had only three digits. When you placed your call, you might be informed that 'Una's not at home today, she's gone to her daughter's. Would you like me to try there?' Or, 'Fred won't be back until tomorrow. Shall I tell him you were wanting him?'

I studied the locals avidly, as if they were the Welsh natives of

Milk Wood, and acquired a set of manners which seemed to win their confidence. To some degree, I fitted in.

There were also other spectres in our early life at Glenrock whom I felt I knew better than the locals. They came from an influential book I bought through Mary Martin's mail-order service. It was *Green Mountains* by Bernard O'Reilly, and we read it nonstop one rainy Saturday. It rained a lot those first years. Eighty inches and more. (That's over two thousand millimetres.) Rain meant getting out with hoe, mattock and shovel and clearing the drains lest the track erode. We tended not just the drains beside our immediate drive but all along the mile down to the post office corner. Unwary travellers regularly became bogged in the creeks crossing that road and turned up at our door, soaked, seeking help. Going down to dig/push/tow them out was a wet weather task never shunned. It was all part of country helpfulness.

During the rainy months our back verandah held four pairs of boots in ascending sizes, plus a few spares for visitors. Above them on pegs hung our rain coats and hats. There were often double sets of damp clothes hanging there too – easier to slip on while the rain held than continually dirtying fresh garments. We emulated our dairy farming neighbours, going out willingly in all weathers, returning wet, muddy, sometimes chilled, but proud of ourselves for never shirking outdoor maintenance and never, ever, showing fastidious disgust – as some of our house guests did – when thick gobs of red clay coated our boot soles and smeared our legs. *We* felt proud.

So it was one of those early rainy weekends when I suggested to Goth, Van and Thor that we begin reading *Green Mountains*. It had been reviewed as a truthful adventure of human courage, set in wild country behind what later became the Gold Coast. We tucked up on the front verandah, all piling onto the big saggy bed which lived out there and where sometimes the boys or overflow visitors slept.

Green Mountains was Bernard O'Reilly's autobiography. He was a bushman living with his family on an isolated farm high up in mountains where mists rose and descended like curtains onto rainforest slopes and gullies that sounded so much like our own situation that we slipped at once into the story.

As rain dripped steadily outside, just a few feet away beyond the flyscreen, sometimes quickening into such a racket on the iron roof overhead that I had to shout to be heard, I read to them how one day the flight from Sydney to Brisbane did not arrive. In those days planes were still small enough and flew low enough to be aural and visual punctuation points in the day. Regular as clockwork. So regular you checked your watch by them.

Over the wireless, distorted by extra static from violent electrical storms, news flashed about the missing plane. All day searches were made along the coast, on the assumption that the pilot had been blown off course east over the sea. No debris was sighted, nor did anyone report hearing a crash. By next morning, the entire nation was alert to the tragedy. Reports, speculation and promises of assistance filled the radio air waves. Searching intensified. On board the plane was a son of the Proud family, Sydney's leading jewellers. His father offered a big reward for anyone finding the wreckage.

It wasn't monetary gain that magnetised young Bernard – he wasn't that worldly a chap – but an obsessive niggle that something was not right. Mountain folk *feel* their climate; they read the winds and changing temperatures. The last time the plane had been heard by one of the remote farmers south of the O'Reillys' place, it was inland of its normal course. Bernard reasoned that the pilot might have flown west to try and dodge the bad weather. Thus the plane could have fallen completely outside the search area, into their own neck of the woods.

He dashed outside and climbed to a vantage point he knew, the only spot where one could see a panorama of that steep, dense landscape, if only the mist would rise long enough for him to get one clear view.

O'Reilly was a devout person. Prayer was part of his daily existence and he wrote of his faith openly, a natural element in his communication. As he strained to see through the fog filling the valleys like whipped cream, the clouds thinned and swirled briefly, parted by a fine finger of sunlight. It showed Bernard what he needed to know, what he was expecting. On a distant peak he saw one freshly broken, burned tree! Only a bushman of his experience would have noticed it, or understood its significance.

He dashed back to the house, informed his parents, grabbed up rope and his canvas bag, and set off. Driven by what he had seen, he took the most direct route, scrambling up slopes then sliding down, using the sure-footedness of his mountain boyhood to carry him forward, using all his bush sense to make sure his direction was true.

Back at Foxground, engulfed by rain, surrounded by tall dripping trees and high cliffs, we four read on, completely engaged. Pausing to prepare a snack, we took it back to the big bed, snuggling under blankets as the temperature dropped and breezes splattered us with raindrops. It did not occur to us to move indoors; the exposed verandah was utterly appropriate to the story. When my voice faltered, Thor took over, then Goth. Even Van wanted a brief turn, elementary as his reading skills were. All day we read.

O'Reilly did find the crashed plane. Miraculously three men had survived, including the jeweller's son. He and another chap were injured but were struggling to keep alive with the fortitude common in those days. The third had set off in what he hoped would be the right direction to try and find help. Making the two as comfortable as possible, Bernard hurried after him, realising that speed was vital. He almost despaired as he pondered the task of mounting a rescue in that huge country where no road ran. But his sense of duty drove him onwards, choosing the most direct route possible toward where he knew there would be people with a telephone. Again it was his faith that sustained him. Then he came upon the body of the third survivor, sitting dead at the bottom of a cliff with his back against a rock, his shattered ankle in the icy stream, holding in his hand the pocket watch inscribed to him by his father. Bernard paused to remark his valour. He had been a city fella, no bushman. But he had done his best.

Then onward, to raise the alarm. As the men of the district rallied tools and ropes, the women prepared food for the rescue parties which set off at once, led by Bernard. It did not occur to him to rest. He retraced the path of his marathon journey. As some raced upward with blankets and bandages, other men cut a track for bringing out the two survivors and the bodies of the other victims.

It was nightfall by the time we finished the book. Sharing it all in one sitting, on such a day, in those surroundings, drove the powerful story into our lives as if we ourselves had lived it.

Bernard O'Reilly's green mountains matched our own. Forever after, when we bushwalked, climbed or searched the creekbeds, that story sustained us. Inspired us. It was not just the adventure of what O'Reilly had done, it was his philosophy while doing it. Far stronger than any moral lecture were those old-fashioned virtues, which I felt so gratified to have laid before our sons without them even noticing.

8

Wally, Jodie and Wallaby Hill

Wallaby Hill was what we called the mountain-side facing our house across the creek, where the lads got lost that time, and where the blacksmith planted his tiny precipitous paddocks. The reason we called it that was because it was the one place we occasionally spied the wild macropods we were sure still survived at Foxground.

Each morning, the first rays of sun gilded that steep slope in a cheerful yellow, spreading downward from top to bottom, highlighting our stone wall boundary and the trees and thickets like a romantic stereoscopic slide show. Now and then a wallaby would emerge from the undergrowth to soak up an early morning sunbath, sitting trimly on its tail, cleaning its fur. Van's sharp bushman's eyes would spot it from upstairs, then Goth would pipe the news and we'd all go out to see from the side garden. A good way to start a day.

The wariness of wallabies prevented us from ever getting close enough for a good look. No doubt that quality was what saved them from the fate of other marsupials. On rare occasions we might encounter one up the back of the property, but it always saw us first and bounded smartly into the undergrowth. We thought them intriguing animals and longed to see more.

One day a man in Berry telephoned, at the behest of Georgie Borys, the vet. His widowed mother had a back yard wallaby that had lived with her since it was young. Having been reared in the house, it was now sleeping in the fowl shed. Trouble was, his mother had got on in years until her home was too much for her. The one deterrent to her moving into a flat was what to do with her pet. Could we take it?

When we agreed, the old lady asked her son to bring her to inspect our place. I walked them carefully round the garden, explaining our practices with wildlife. I pointed out Wallaby Hill and suggested that in time her animal might gravitate over there and thus be reunited with its own kind. She commented on the good condition of Opal, Mathilda and Mick (and their apparent truce with the dogs) and all the birds in the flowering shrubs, then said she would like her pet to live with us. Its name was Jodie.

The son brought the wallaby, unaccompanied by his mother. She had been upset at the parting, he said. Tears had flowed. We could well understand.

Jodie was fully grown, having lived in the Berry back yard for five years or more. Her coat was thick, a dusky chocolate brown. She had a faint white stripe along her jaw and her long tail was tipped in white. That tail was longer and slimmer than the 'roos', and Jodie's forearms were much shorter than theirs. She was also stocky and only half their size. But it was not just her appearance that was different. Her personality was the opposite of theirs. Very positive in all her movements and reactions, we were surprised by how composed she seemed compared to her nervy kangaroo cousins.

Jodie was fussy. She would not let us touch her, yet she regarded us without fear and seemed to settle easily into our garden. I was alarmed to see her snatch off bites of my favourite shrubs and to try and distract her I rushed out with a dish of goodies – rolled oats, bread, sliced apple, carrot and so on. She regarded me intently with dark beady eyes then hopped to the dish and, without hesitation, began selecting what she liked. She whipped up a piece of apple, holding it firmly in her front paws and chewed it vigorously. All the time she ate, she watched me, watching her, unafraid but warning me to keep my distance. When she found the few raisins I had mixed with the oats, she was delighted. She scratched the other things out of the dish, impatient to uncover them. She gobbled them up and sat back on her tail, staring at me as if to say: 'More.'

The chickens were out for an afternoon browse. With excited gabbles, they dashed forward to pick up the scattered oats and bread. Jodie puffed herself up indignantly and rushed at them, scaring them off. No stranger to chooks was Jodie.

Later on, when I filled a dish for the hens with poultry pellets and wheat, we learned Jodie liked them as well. She really enjoyed eating. As soon as the poultry bowl touched the lawn, the chickens were dispersed by a leaping form with long tail and glaring black eyes. The fowls simply had to wait until Jodie had eaten her fill. The strutting and scolding of the roosters impressed her not. She took no nonsense from them and had them under her orders from the start.

The dogs soon got her message too. Jim strutted up and walked around her, stiff-legged, trying to convince her how tough he was. She rippled her fur but stood her ground, glaring at him with those hard little eyes. Since we were standing by, to mediate or chastise if necessary, Jim decided to pretend he wasn't interested. Laika watched his retreat and wagged. She always seemed able to understand any situation, Laika, although she rarely took the initiative.

Jodie was very clean. She sat neatly on her tail beneath a bush and licked and scratched until her fur shone. She had a fur-comb toe, like the kangaroos, and she used it with precision. Her belly coat was pale, a contrast to the rich mahogany of her back, making her handsome if a bit intimidating.

I made her a bed in our laundry, which faced onto the garden and was entered from outside the house. Putting layers of feed-sacks onto the concrete floor I covered them with an old woollen overcoat, adding a pillow against the wall for Jodie to lean on.

'I do hope she'll be comfortable,' I fretted as night approached.

'An animal that's spent the last five years sleeping in a fowl house won't be expecting frills,' Jeff reminded me succinctly.

As often happens, he was correct. Jodie chose to sleep out of doors, under the fuchsia bushes. The nights were fairly mild then. She never did use the laundry, except to hop in for a short stay if it rained really hard. Mainly she preferred to shelter under the foundations where there was a gap of about eighteen inches. Our house had been built on huge logs laid on living rock. Near the laundry, the rock dropped away and stone piers supported the side verandah, creating a cave-like space which suited Jodie well.

Although she was standoffish, it was good having Jodie around. She was a different kind of marsupial to get acquainted with. We consulted the reference books and learned that Pelsart, the Dutch explorer who was shipwrecked off the West Australian coast in 1629, recorded seeing a strange hopping animal which was probably a Dama wallaby. In 1770, Captain Cook's party discovered a larger wallaby at Cooktown which they called by the Aboriginal name: *kangaru*. The scientific name later became *Wallabia cangaru*; the animal is popularly known today as a whip-tail wallaby.

It was some years before the differences between wallabies and kangaroos were sorted out. Zoologists finally agreed to the following classification: the entire family was called *Macropodea*, or big foot, and the animals were divided into types according to the size of that foot. Those with hind feet measuring less than 6 inches from heel to toe (not including the nail) would be classed as small wallabies. Those with a hind foot measuring 6 to 10 inches would be true wallabies, such as the red-necked, agile and swamp wallabies (Jodie was one of the latter). Animals with hind feet exceeding 10 inches would be kangaroos and wallaroos.

Our next phase of learning brought us back to the real world. A young man rang to ask if we could possibly accept his pet wallaby. He had found it while on a hunting trip in the bush and from the first night it had slept with him in his sleeping bag. He wanted to keep it but had been offered a scholarship overseas. His mother told him he'd better find a home for it, along with his snakes in bottles and his mineral specimens. Apparently she didn't fancy sleeping with it herself.

Here young Vandal came into his own. He had recently been given a baby rabbit for a pet by the Conroys, who had found it in their nets when they went ferreting. The fluffy mite spent its first day at our place riding inside Van's jacket, tucked in next to his chest. No doubt it welcomed that dark moist place against the racing, thrilled heart . . . a good place to forget its fearful eviction from the family burrow.

By evening, it had become quite used to Van's smell and his hot, tender hands. He took it out and showed us how quietly it sat, nose twitching, little pink-veined ears lying confidently down over its back. Van offered it milk in a jar lid, pressing its jittery nose into the warm liquid. The rabbit lapped. Will I ever forget Van's expression? It was an exquisite moment of achievement – a reward for understanding and patience and applied technique – and the smile welled up from deep inside our seven-year-old until it warmed us all.

When it was time for Goth and Van to go upstairs, of course the baby bunny went too. Downstairs in the kitchen, Jeff and I could hear giggles swelling into gales of laughter as the bunny hopped about, delicate as an insect, the boys thumping and bumping after it, rooting it from under a bed, from behind a desk.

'Take it easy up there,' Jeff called. 'Be gentle with that young animal. Better make it bedtime.'

We heard the winding up of boyish affairs, then as we went up to make our goodnights, a sudden silence. We intended to bring the little rabbit downstairs to sleep in its box of straw beside the fireplace.

'Where is it?' I asked.

Suddenly, the giggles burst forth again. Goth was leaning out of his bed so he could peep through the door into Van's room, where his younger brother impishly peeled back his bedclothes to reveal the little grey form bundled into his pillowcase.

'Oh, fair go, it'll leave pellets in your bed,' we said.

'They're only tiny ones.'.

'And make water.'

More laughter. 'It's already done that,' Goth chirped. 'In the lid of the train set.'

'Well . . .'

'Oh, please, Mum. Dad? Please let it sleep with me?'

How could you resist it? Tenderness radiated from the bedrooms beneath the eaves. Of course we relented. And went downstairs loving the thought of Van snugging down with his warm little bunny.

Next morning when Jeff and I got up very early, both boys were still in bed. Van was usually awake first but when he slept, he slept soundly. Goth was a light sleeper but he'd cultivated the habit of reading quietly in bed. I knocked on the stairs to say good morning and in a few minutes went up to root them out. Goth hopped up and we both went into Vandal's room. 'How's the baby?' we wanted to know.

Van rummaged under the covers. His sleep-blurred face cleared. 'Oh, no!'

In his hands he held a limp grey body. The tiny rabbit was dead. Van had smothered it in the night while he slept.

'Oh, Vandal . . .' Goth's high voice vibrated with sympathy.

Van had a touching way of crying. He used to duck his head, then big tears would well out and splash down his chest. He kept silent, the opposite of his voluble brother. Jeff came upstairs and we all sat on Van's bed for a while. What could you say?

Later there was a funeral and a burial. Van rose to the occasion but he was soberly contemplative for quite some time. He had been taught a hard lesson at a young age. Typical of him, he learned it well.

So we were happy to receive Wally, another young animal in need of warmth and comfort. We had no qualms that Van would night-nurse him perfectly.   .

Wally was a different personality to Jodie. Wearing a collar to which a leash could be attached, he was quite people oriented, or at least young human male oriented. He was used to going on bushwalks with his former benefactor and he transferred his trust to Van very quickly. We began to appreciate the hardiness and adaptability of wallabies. They seemed markedly more able to cope with change than kangaroos.

The first encounter between Wally and Jodie was dynamic. They stood off from one another, stretching out their noses the better to sniff each other's scent. Ears swivelled, fur bristled. Then Jodie uttered a distinctly antagonistic bark. Wally shot off in the opposite direction. He dashed around the house, coming to a halt in the front garden. We approached him gradually, stretching out hands that held the favourite biscuits his former owner had left with us, speaking his name quietly. He allowed himself to be reassured but wasn't yet ready to be touched.

We left him to potter about outside but kept an eye on him through the windows lest he tried to leap over the gate. The chooks came took-tooking past. Wally stood up in alarm, fur bristling. He had obviously never encountered poultry before. Van rushed out to offer another biscuit. Wally calmed down but he never really liked the chickens. And the feeling was reciprocal.

He did grow to like their pellets, but he never dined when they were present, as Jodie did. As for sharing her meals, there was no question of that. She laid back her ears and growled at him, just like a dog. Wally kept a respectful distance from her. If his feeding dish was set down within her sight, she would leave her own dish and hop across to his. He would vacate the spot at once, totally dominated by this irritable animal old enough to be his mother . . . or even his grandmother.

Yet we had hopes they would grow used to each other. And, when Wally became old enough, that they might mate. Wally-and-Jodie watching became our favourite sport. We spent much time peering out the windows overlooking the side garden, which was Jodie's main camp. Gradually Wally began to infiltrate her territory.

While the nights were warm, we encouraged Wally to begin staying outside the house. Van had done his duty but Wally was growing bigger and older and we all thought it was time he became more independent. By moonlight we watched his shadowy form bend, browsing the lawn. Not far away would be the bigger silhouette of Jodie. Gradually, gradually, Wally closed the gap.

After a dewy night their thick coats would be beaded with silver. Rain never seemed to bother them, repelled by their dense fur. Most days, now, they lay within sight of each other under branches drooping with flowers – a pretty picture. If the dogs raced past or the chooks paraded by, they raised their heads but did not bother to rise. They even began to feed near one another but always from separate dishes – and nothing would deter Jodie from reaching across and stealing some tidbit she fancied on Wal's plate.

The seasons turned around. Wally grew bigger. And bolder. He began to approach Jodie more positively. When she batted at him with a paw, he didn't shy away. If she hopped from him, he followed doggedly. The wallaby watchers were thrilled to catch the pair in a sweet attitude one day. Lying side by side, Jodie yawned, stretched and reached across to nibble a mite behind Wally's ear. Was it a motherly gesture? Or could it be love?

When Wally was seen to stand behind Jodie and pat at her flanks in a persistent sort of way, her spinsterish nature reasserted itself. She hopped crossly aside.

The apparent courtship continued and our hopes rose. But it didn't quite 'click'. Was Wally a slightly different species to Jodie?

We rushed for the books and tried to interpret what we read. Could it be that Wally was a rock wallaby, a petrogale? They lived around Jenolan Caves, which is where the young man had found Wal.

Meanwhile, Wally's restlessness prompted him to push more persistently into the shrubbery along the boundary of the garden. At last he found a place he could squeeze out. One morning, we found him missing. We had by now acquired some flair for finding animal escape routes. We found the hole under the wire. Jeff's first impulse was to block it up. But what if Wally wanted to return? Or better, what if Jodie followed him out? We debated the subject for days.

Wally did return. Then he left again. This time Jodie followed. But she came back smartly. She was a more domesticated wallaby than he was. However, she eventually went back out and gradually both wallabies visited our garden less and less. Each evening we left out their dishes of food. Next morning, we sometimes found them empty, other times not. Were they still living close by? Or was a possum eating their meals?

Van decided to track them and solve the mystery. He rose very early one morning, hung the weighty pair of field glasses round his neck, and sneaked across to Wallaby Hill. He spotted two animals lying close together. Under magnification, he saw without doubt they were Wally and Jodie.

'They've made a home across the creek,' he reported proudly at breakfast. 'By the way they're lying together, I reckon they've probably mated.'

Months later, we saw through the field glasses that he was right. Jodie definitely had a drooping pouch. And later still, we saw her with a little one at foot, nuggety and so much stronger and neater than a lanky kangaroo joey. We felt triumphant with what had transpired. Jodie and Wally had been successfully staged back to nature.

9

The Boys' Museum

Foxground was our passion, our hobby, our recreation. Seeking information about its natural and human heritage, we went to Sydney to consult the experts.

We started at the Mining Museum near the Harbour Bridge. Rock collecting had long been a hobby of mine. Despite a paucity of knowlege, and the puzzlement of Jeff, I often picked up interesting looking stones on our journalistic safaris through the outback. With the help of books and the advice of several friends trained in earth sciences, I tried to identify what I brought back home.

My interest was taken up by Goth and Van. Like most children, they were natural collectors. I fostered their curiosity about the world around them and encouraged their playmates as well. For some of them, the prime interest was money. To find gold or diamonds, kids will shift a ton of dirt. However, the trick is to implant the notion that all rocks can be interesting, because rocks are the clues to prehistory as well as the geography of a region. Which is usually the reason, along with climate, that it has been settled. Or left unsettled.

We had been told that Foxground sits amid ancient volcanoes. This explains the rich red soil, the basalt quarried since the early 1800s for building blocks and road base, and the coal underlying the Illawarra cliffs, part of seams bedded in Permian times. In our creeks could be found petrified wood, a modest spectrum of quartzes and specks of alluvial gold. The lads had great fun wading, foraging, splashing; Van was especially good at finding crystals ranging from pure glassy quartz through amethyst to red and yellow jasper. To understand more about our growing collection, we combed the geological museum.

Then we went to the technology museum at Ultimo. Goth and Van had been there before and loved the working models of engines, especially the old steam models, but now their interest was expanded after finding relics of early machines and devices on Foxground farms. Up in the bush they uncovered rusting cogs, horse hames – even Ernie Staples' old roller made from a heavy log bound in iron; it was like discovering treasure and had us spinning daydreams of early times.

Our final stop was the natural history museum near Hyde Park. We paced intently around the exhibits, calling out when we found something of relevance to our Foxground experiences. In one section were stuffed birds we'd been hearing in the bush but found hard to sight; we stared at them, so we'd recognise their size and plumage as they flashed among the trees. Next were marsupials. We stared at them too. Elsewhere we pondered collections of Aboriginal artefacts; some matched our souvenirs from travels in Central Australia. We ploughed on until our heads grew giddy and our feet nearly melted off our legs.

Our marathon museums day sent us home aware that we were wealthy, rich in natural history and old-time relics right on our own property. It set off Goth's imagination. Inventing things and trying to build his own gadgets were his prime sources of amusement, for which he had plenty of scope and materials, living where he did. So when Goth disappeared into his room to work at his desk, we weren't surprised. Next morning he came down bursting with plans he did not want to tell us about until he'd talked with his mates on the school bus.

A real social club was the bus which took youngsters eleven miles from Foxground to Berry Primary School and then continued a further nine miles to the high school at Bomaderry. An elderly bus, slow to move off, crotchety climbing hills, skittish going down. Sometimes we heard hair-raising snippets, like 'the time the brakes failed on Rumbles' Hill' or 'when the tyre fell off in Tindall's Lane'. During rainy times, getting bogged was normal – the kids hopped off to push, revelling in the muddy challenge and hoping the creeks would rise high enough to cancel school for a day or two. So the bus-ride was an experience in itself and took almost an hour each way.

Following our excursion to Sydney, the bus was enlivened further by Goth's Great Idea.

'Let's start a museum,' he proposed.

He had it all worked out and unfurled what he'd stayed up late in his attic to produce. It was a dummy constitution for his creation, which would be a co-operative effort, run on democratic principles. Goth's Foxground friends took to his idea at once. And when Goth explained it to us that afternoon after school, so did we.

The lads wanted to meet at our place after class next day to consolidate their plans. Again, Goth worked late at his desk, meticulously copying his constitution onto a large sheet of cardboard. It was a marvellous document.

THE CONSTITUTION OF THE BOYS' MUSEUM

One: Three officers should be elected – President, Secretary and Treasurer.

Two: Elections should be held every month.

Three: Each boy must purchase a share valued at 20 cents.

Four: Each shareholder must do an equal part of work, or else sell their share back.

Five: Admission will be charged – 10 cents child, 20 cents adult.

Six: Profit will be divided equally among shareholders.

Seven: Ten percent of profit will be given to Berry School.

Eight: The museum will open Sundays, 2–5 pm.

Eight boys put their signatures on the Constitution, committing themselves seriously to its tenets. There were three sets of brothers – Nicholas and Simon Kale, David and Peter Cullen, Goth and Vandal Carter, plus David Binks and David Waite. Their average age was nine, with the eldest boy being twelve years old and the youngest seven. Goth, the founder, was eleven. It was a very exciting proposition.

Each lad nominated what he could contribute. The Binks family collected fossils, many of which were uncovered while ploughing their fields. The Cullen family collected and polished gemstones as a hobby. David Waite had great-uncles and aunts who had left souvenirs of India and the Great War. Two-thirds of the exhibits were made up of our own collectables, which provided a nucleus for the museum's five sections: Rocks, Fossils, Natural History, Aboriginal Artefacts, Relics of Olden Days.

Goth nominated our blacksmith barn as the site of the museum. With its anvil, working bellows and farrier's tools, old horse shoes and harness wear, it was a natural. When Jeff and I agreed to Goth's idea, it never occurred to us that we would lose the use of our shed – along with our weekend privacy – for many years ahead. At the time, we could only applaud the project and felt very proud of Goth for thinking of it. I was appointed museum advisor. My first duty was to supply cookies and fresh lemonade to toast the enterprise, then drive the boys back to their homes in the valley. Thus was established a long-lasting routine.

The following Saturday was the first of many working bees to put the old shed in order. It had to be cleared of junk, but not too much was actually discarded. Most was found suitable for the Relics of Olden Days section, after a dust-off, a coat of blacking or a rub with polish. Talk about dust! The barn had an earth floor which had been trodden for a century into fine powder.

The roof was tin laid upon saplings; the unlined ceiling was festooned with cobwebs. The walls were thick rough slabs, pit-sawn on the property using huge two-man saws with handles of whittled pegs; these became prime exhibits. Gaps in the walls had been filled with scraps of tin.

It wasn't glamorous, our old barn, but it was perfect for a museum and it bespoke the primitive methods of its construction and the work that had gone on within. Windows along the sides had no glass, nor was there a door, just a wide gap between huge corner posts into which iron hitching rings had been screwed. You could easily conjure horses tethered there, snorting and stamping.

The boys were very keen to build their own display shelves. I saw no reason to discourage their industry, although they were not yet skilled at carpentry. They used old planks and bits of wood and the result was rough but totally honest.

Painting was what everyone thought he was good at. As I recall,

1962, our first year living in Glenrock farmhouse, with the 1928
Essex Tourer, in which I ran the boys to and from the school bus.
It handled the unsealed serpentine road with ease and kept us in
the mood for turning back the clock. L–R.: Van, Goth, Mare,
Laika, Jeff.

The Carter family at orphan kangaroo feeding time. L–R.: Van with Opal, Goth with Mulga Mick and Mare with Mathilda.

An orphan joey wearing her 'going outdoors' jumper. Warmth is vital to young marsupials, which normally rely on the shelter of their mother's body and the heat of her pouch to sustain them during childhood.

JEFF CARTER

Mare weighs an orphan who tipped the scales at less than a kilo. Trying to hand-rear orphan joeys is tricky. They lack their mother's milk which is biologically correct for nurturing them, and they need constant warmth.

JEFF CARTER

Jeff with Horace the wedge-tail eagle. Found in the outback as a baby and hand-reared in a flat in Sydney, Horace was passed on to the Carters to be trained to hunt and live free before being released at Foxground.

The editing suite of Jeff Carter Films in a refurbished barn on Glenrock farm. Karen Carter and Roger Whittaker at work on the *Wild Country* documentary movies, helped by Gidgea the kangaroo.

L–R: Mare, Jeff and Van, with a python which wandered into the farmhouse kitchen during the filming of *Wild Animal Farm* and found itself a movie star.

In 1978 I initiated the Bush Detective program at Wild Country Park, to help school excursions come to grips with rainforest ecology and show them how to meet free-living native animals. As soon as they arrived I prepared the pupils for discovery, tuning in their senses to the sounds and smells of our environment, as well as its sights. Today we meet those kids, now grown up with families of their own, who remember and would love to do it it all again.

the Carters provided some of the paint. And the brushes. It was amazing how different the old building looked inside after several coats of whitewash. We all knocked off and just stared at our handiwork. Then we scuffed into the dust any paint splashed on the 'floor'.

That was just the beginning, of course. Exhibits were assembled in our lounge room and on the verandah, according to the section they belonged to. Some things needed to be mounted on cardboard or bedded on pieces of velvet or leather, usually scavenged from the Carters' cupboards. Labels had to be handwritten. The boys asked me to purchase pens and glue and fine white card to produce the best job. They worked in industrious silences broken by excla-mations when something went wrong. The dictionary and our reference books were thumbed earnestly to make sure spelling and information were correct. What energy flowed from those eight lads, what ideas followed by action. Preparations went on for weeks, after school and on Saturdays. It reinforced my belief that boys can move mountains when motivated.

From the start, everything was conducted democratically. Suggestions were put, discussed, voted upon. The procedure was recorded in a book of minutes. It is a priceless volume. The treas-urer laboriously recorded into a simple ledger the purchases made with their foundation fund plus a small loan from the Carters. Receipts had to be kept. Sums needed doing. Those boys grappled with new concepts of book-keeping – accountability, loans, interest, outgoings and income yet to come. When the workers grew tired, or debate became heated, the 'advisor' produced refreshments. Some meetings took place in the living room but whenever the weather was fine, we met underneath the old lemon tree in the back garden near the museum. That tree supplied fruit for gallons and gallons of lemonade for the boys.

When the day came for the opening, there were fifty guests, mainly parents and other family members plus neighbours. I am sure no one expected to see such a good job, such an interesting collection, so many slicked-up and proud lads. The guest of honor was the headmaster of Berry Primary School. If ever there was a Mr Chips, Reg Griffiths must have been patterned in his mould. Nothing was too much trouble for him if the welfare of the kids and his school were at stake. Speaking before cutting a ribbon the boys had tied across the entrance, he rose magnificently to the occasion. 'There is too little of this sort of thing being done to give children something to do which interests and teaches at the same time. Adults as well as children will be interested in this museum. I've already spoken to people in Berry who would like to donate items to it. I think this could lead to something big.' All his prophesies came true.

The opening was covered by the local newspaper, the *Berry Register* (incorporating the *Kangaroo Valley Chronicle* and the *Shellharbour Light*). This alerted a television station to send a journalist and cameraman. Once out, the news spread. The boys placed a few modest advertisements in the local press but mainly it was word of mouth. Visitors were impressed by what the lads had achieved and the way they presented it.

At first there were four boys rostered for each Sunday. They liked to conduct people around their exhibits personally. One lad sat out front, at an ancient, lift-lid school desk, complete with inkwell. He collected the money and explained the museum, inviting people to sign a visitors' book. Guests then progressed through the sections, escorted by a guide. Each boy had a favourite section about which he could wax most freely, but they agreed to take it in turns so they would all become familiar with all their exhibits.

Most people conversed with the lads, especially old-timers. The museum triggered recollections which they shared with the boys; often they could explain some function or history of an exhibit, so that the boys learned from their guests. Many wandered outside enriched; reluctant to leave, they stayed to enjoy the clear air, the view of the mountains so close around, sometimes to chat with other visitors in a similar mood. A bonus was the young kangaroos in the paddock below the house. I kept an eye on proceedings and when children or overseas visitors stood mooning at the fence, I led them through the gate quietly and showed them how to approach the animals. I had stale bread on hand and if someone wanted to take a snapshot, a crust held out and an encouraging word enabled them to get close. My first concern was always the 'roos and I was never backward about fending off visitors who were pushy or too noisy. Thus the animals grew accustomed to strangers and became an asset on Sunday afternoons.

A number of visitors wanted to donate things to the museum. In many cases they had been longing to find a home for interesting relics, but local historical societies were not prevalent then, or at least did not have storage premises. So within its first few months, the collection began to swell.

A south coast authority on Aboriginal culture gave the museum artefacts from his big collection. He also donated a surveyor's peg from the Berry estate, and vintage bottles. A scholar of Berry gave the lads a pocket sundial, a short-handled miner's shovel plus huge, wonderful books, bound in leather and handwritten in the finest, formal penmanship. They were journals of the Berry School of Arts for 1898 and contained inspiring essays by citizens of the district who felt strongly about affairs of the day.

A timber-getter sent them a full bullock yoke with chains. Friends of ours who had lived in New Guinea presented us with a cassowary feather headdress, a money belt rich in pig tails, plus two long black bows made of palm wood which no one was strong enough to bend. Comparing the arrows and spears from New Guinea with spears made by Northern Territory Aboriginals gave the lads valuable lessons in anthropology and comparative cultures; their new insights were passed on to museum visitors.

Lapidary was popular then. Members of rock clubs visited the museum, took back news of the boys' collection and soon mail began to arrive – letters of congratulations along with intriguing parcels of geological specimens, labelled and described. Since gem hounds travel far in their quests, through their donations the boys' vision of the world widened out. Copper, bauxite, sapphires, and fool's gold joined our local minerals. Letters were read aloud at the meeting, maps were produced to find where the rocks had come from, and thank-you notes were voted on and relegated to the secretary to write and send, assisted by the advisor. The extra work for the scribe of the month (and the advisor) was well outweighed by the kudos of receiving mail from Sydney and beyond.

At each monthly meeting there was fresh news to impart. The confidence of the shyer boys grew measurably. Everything was recorded in the minutes, sometimes curtly, often in naive detail, depending on the age and eloquence of the secretary that month. For example: 'During the week Goth was sick and had a few ideas . . .' and 'We aleckted new officers'.

Goth's original concept of revolving duties among the members worked well. The chaps began to take the democratic process in their stride, even those tasks which did not naturally suit their personalities, and vied to move and second a motion.

Goth or Simon were always ready to take the president's chair, followed soon by Nicholas. Their confidence inspired David Waite and David Cullen to take their turn. Finally, the quieter, more tongue-tied Van and Peter and Binksie learned to chair a meeting, patiently assisted by their peers. Although I doubt they really ever liked the position, they learned the satisfaction of shouldering their duties and the boys as a group came to understand the strengths and weaknesses of their friends and be tolerant of them. Rosters were shaped to team shy boys with talkative ones.

The least loved job was that of treasurer. The fun part was sharing up the money. The boys knelt on the carpet with pools of coins, dividing them into piles, but before the money could disappear into their hot stubby fingers, the treasurer had to record the process. That was the head-scratching part. Cross-outs and erasures, and the occasional swearword, would follow. Ever puzzled by leftover amounts, they had to use maths, including percentages. However, the rewards of keeping good simple books were many, not the least of which was pride in seeing how much they were earning. Their ledger told them their museum was growing. A monthly pleasure was donating to their school its share, and Mr Griffiths made time at the school assembly for the presentations.

During Education Week he announced that the National Trust had learned of the Boys' Musem and was commending it. The boys were asked to supply details for the Trust newsletter and, following that, they were invited to join the Museums Association, becoming its youngest members.

By the end of their first year they had welcomed over 1000 visitors and doubled their exhibits. Their Annual Report records that they now had a sign, made by one of their fathers, erected on the corner of Foxground Road, as well as a bank savings account, a petty cash fund and a new member, Glenn Askew (cousin of the Kales) who had just moved to the valley from England.

They went on bushwalks with their advisor, had picnics, and an excursion to Minnamurra Falls, plus the fossil cliffs at Kiama. Fast dissolving was the gaucherie of the more sequestered farm boys. They blossomed in confidence and broadened their interests. As their proficiency with the public grew, rostered teams were made smaller in order to space out their weekends on duty.

They all fronted up to host an excursion of sixty school children plus a dozen adults. The nine lads guided the youngsters in groups around their museum, gave talks about local history and demonstrated Aboriginal clack-stick rhythms. Each group was conducted on a bushwalk past the kangaroos and down along the creek to the waterfall. Later, the boys served afternoon tea, dispensing buckets of fresh lemonade squeezed by themselves, plus cakes donated by their mothers. They had waived their usual entrance fee for the school children, but the accompanying adults were so impressed they passed the hat among themselves and left a sizeable donation.

Of course, not everything went smoothly all the time. Since the shed was open on two sides, regular problems were dust and wind-blown debris, plus rat and mouse droppings. Some of the boys grumbled from time to time about the need for repetitious and on-going maintenance but overall they faced up to the task at hand. The Boys' Museum taught valuable character lessons, along with social and business skills.

It should be said here that although the basic tenets of the constitution came from Goth, the spirit of co-operation and of donating to good causes was common in our 1960s country area. In Berry, service clubs and church fellowship groups rallied to help when something needed doing. This might range from mowing the oval at the showground, which doubled as the town's rugby ground, to repairing seats in the park or fences at the public school. When a fire took the house and the lives of three children and their father, the town closed around the widow and the remaining kids until a new home was built using donated labour, money and materials.

Once when a Sydney motorcycle club settled on the Berry pub as a fun spot for weekend devilry, they blocked the footpath and roadway, chiacking maidens and matrons alike and interfering with traffic. The men of the district formed themselves into a militia and backed the local policeman to warn off the intruders. The thought of those reserved, sun-bleached farmers brandishing axe handles at the invaders tickles me still.

Down in Foxground valley, the spirit of co-operation was the same. At hay-making and other harvests, neighbours helped each other. The kids loved to pitch in. When storms brought down trees and creeks rose to block drains, it was accepted that the local farmers would form a repair crew, calling the council only as a last resort. So it was not an uncommon set of ethics which drove the Boys' Museum. And kept me at my task as its advisor.

After it had been going for several years, was on all the tourist maps and had contributed much both to Berry School and also to the lads' development, one of their mothers liked to tell me: 'Oh, we all think it's wonderful what you do, but we ask ourselves how you find the time?'

This always left me flummoxed, because in fact I was quite busy with farm and journalistic business. I longed to say: 'It's because I don't play tennis in the afternoons or attend Red Cross tea parties like the other women of this district. The museum is my recreation, my hobby, my social contact, my contribution to the boys. And sometimes it is a bit of a chore.' But I never said that. And somehow I fitted it all in, and enjoyed doing so, most of the time.

By the museum's third birthday, the boys had over one hundred fine specimens in their Rocks and Fossils sections. Among their Relics of Olden Days was a human yoke (used to carry water), a glass-windowed ballot box used in the 1908 referendum, Mrs Potts' irons, a moustache cup, a cabbage tree hat, letters with pre-Federation stamps, medals and insignia from many wars and battle fronts, handmade milking stools and bottles of curious shapes and colours evoking memories of castor oil, ink and ginger beer.

The wonderful constitution which hung on the museum wall faded with exposure to light and had to be recopied and signed again. A few of the snakes and animal embryos in bottles grew smelly and needed topping up – or turfing out. Rats gnawed some of the delicate birds' egg collection. The shark's eggs dried out. And, of course, the labels needed redoing often as wind and mice and busy-fingered visitors mixed them up, smudged them or carried them right away.

Finally, the museum began to falter as first one then another family moved away. The remaining boys grew into teenagers and their studies became more demanding. Also, their interests changed. Even Vandal resigned. Finally there were only Goth and Glenn left to run things. And in late high school, they could no longer spare the time. So we put ads in the newspapers to let people know that after six years the Boys' Museum was closing. And it did.

Although we didn't know it at the time, having it on our property for so long influenced our creation of Wild Country Park a few years later. Our friendship with the Judds at Minnamurra Falls unwittingly nudged us in that direction also. Thanks partly to our magazine articles, the falls were attracting an increasing number of visitors. This placed quite some stress on Howard, not only to keep the paths open and tidy and to replace the heavy plank bridges across the stream after flooding rains, but also to sniff out the ladies who liked to steal a little fern or two from beside the track, hoping to transplant them in their gardens at home. Howard knew all his plants and when one or more went missing, he became very agitated. He could spot a likely fern thief at twenty paces and took to asking older women to turn out their pocketbooks. Ivy worried about his state of mind and suggested they take a little holiday.

The only people Howard felt he could trust to protect the reserve as he did were us, and since we were self-employed and made our own working schedules, we were available, with some forward planning, to stand in as rangers of Minnamurra. The experience would be valuable for our own youngsters, we felt, as well as helping our old friends. Along with learning about the rainforest, they would be exposed to Howard's growing collection of yesteryear tools and household implements, which he dreamed of housing in an old slab hut. What other people threw away, Howard gathered up. He was a passionate preserver of artefacts as well as the environment, and his ideas inspired us.

So it was that on several occasions we stood in for the Judds while Howard and Ivy sneaked away down the coast for rest and recreation. Only during the quietest times of the year, mind. Our offspring were allowed to take the week off from school, a practical learning experience for them, we felt, superior to classroom instruction.

There were aspects of the experience which provided a surprising lesson for Jeff and me, too. We had never before dealt in a cash business, having been first salaried employees and then freelance in a profession where the standard method of remuneration was by cheque, three months (or longer) after delivering the job. So staffing the little log kiosk was quite a change and quite a revelation.

'Just put the money into the teapot under the counter,' Ivy said as they departed. 'That's all we do.'

The kiosk sold only packets of crisps, a few lollies and drinks kept not very cold in a kerosene fridge. Without electricity connected, the Judds could not stock ice creams. But they had a primus stove, kettle, and all the paraphernalia for serving tea on trays. People used to take their refreshments to the tables Howard had built overlooking the creek. By the time they had walked for two hours to reach the waterfalls and returned, they were well ready for 'a nice cup of tea', Ivy's universal panacea. The kiosk also stocked a small range of stickers, postcards and spoons.

Our experience was the same as the Judds'. People might drive up smartly, park in a rush and hurry across the first footbridge onto the track leading up toward the falls, but by the time they returned, their pace was leisurely, their faces were relaxed and they were in a chatty mood. Thus they hung about, reading Howard's fern board and the copy of one of Jeff's articles about the place which the Judds had framed and hung on the wall. A great tonic was Minnamurra Falls Reserve, both to visit and to work at.

In the evening, after locking up, we drove back down to the little cottage to dine and sleep, relaxed and pleased with ourselves. The first night I thought we had better take the money teapot with us, for safekeeping. After eating our meal, we all sat around the table and by the light of pressure lamps we counted into piles the coins which filled it. Amazingly, that humble teapot held quite a tidy sum! Along with the entrance fee, which went to the Council and was kept in a cigar box, there was serious money coming in. All in cash! We had fun counting every night and the experience influenced our thinking, although the result of that would not be apparent for a few years yet.

10

Blue Belle and Big Joe

osting the Boys' Museum in our back yard on Sunday afternoons plus our stints minding Minnamurra Falls Reserve schooled us in handling strangers. One Saturday, a dusty old station wagon drove up and parked. The driver was a cocky little bloke, wiry, seared by the sun. His wife sat in the car but there was no way the kids would stay put; they erupted through windows as well as doors.

Across the back gate, which Jeff was careful not to open, their old man had Jeff by the ear. He said how he enjoyed reading Jeff's magazine articles about outback travels, how he and his family went bush whenever they could. The kids by this time were crowding his heels. Sizing up our back yard with quick hungry eyes, they flicked the chain off its hasp and would have surged through the gate had we not held it firmly closed.

More taciturn by nature than I, Jeff often surprised me – embarrassed me, even – with his reticence. 'We can't ask you in today,' he said. 'There's wet paint in the shed there, and some animals we don't want let out.'

'No worries,' replied the man, waving his wild tribe aside. One spotted the path down to our rubbish tip across the way, hidden among trees, and they all went whooping down there. 'What I come for, Jeff, we've got this kangaroo. We found it out bush, the kids reared it up, took it to bed, rode it like a horse, taught it to box . . . trouble is, she's getting a bit too big for the back yard. We thought youse might like her.'

I was distracted by yells of discovery coming from our gully, but gathered the visitor wanted to sell his animal. Jeff ignored his heavy hints about money and said we would simply care for the, 'roo and release it after it had acclimatised. He mentioned that what we were more interested in was a male to mate with the females we already had.

'Well, I could get you one, next time we go out,' persisted the man. 'All I'd want for it would be a bit of money for expenses . . .'

Jeff declined firmly, explaining it was strictly against the law to traffic in native fauna unless licensed to do so. He began to edge the chap back from our gate. It was not easy. 'I see you've got an old blacksmith bellows in your shed,' he said, peering past us into the gloom where Goth and Van were working industriously. 'What're the lads doing in there?'

I explained that they had a museum with some of their friends.

'Well now, I could help youse with that!' our visitor exclaimed. He knew of bottle dumps behind remote bush pubs, old tools and furniture on abandoned properties, mineral specimens they'd picked up around Broken Hill. 'We love fossicking. Trouble is, the cost of petrol, Jeff. A man'd be going out there more often, if he had a bit more cash . . .'

I felt a bit guilty as I followed Jeff's example and walked him firmly to his car. 'Where's them kids?' he demanded. His wife jumped and pointed over the bank beyond.

'Your children are in our rubbish dump,' I informed him sweetly.

'*Youse kids!* Get yourselves up here quick!'

They swarmed back up the steep slope, covered in mud and dragging old motor tyres, broken teapots, three-legged chairs. They grinned like wolves at their father.

'Put that stuff back,' he ordered.

I sized up their trophies quickly and assessed their value to us as nil, so, feeling mean, I said, 'Oh, that's all right, they can keep it.'

After they and their junk were bullied back into the car, the family drove off with cheery waves.

'Isn't he a type?' Jeff said. 'With any luck, that's the last we'll see of them.'

It wasn't. A week or so later, they arrived again. 'You remember that 'roo you wanted off us? Well, here she is!'

A melee followed as the kids burst from the car dragging their kangaroo with them.

'Where do you want her?'

'Where should we put her?'

'Shall we take her in the house for youse?'

Jeff headed the boisterous procession across the back yard to the paddock where Opal and the others lived, while I planted myself firmly in front of the Boys' Museum.

With cheerful shouts and shoves, the kids consigned their 'roo to her new home and then tore on down toward Opal, Mick and Mathilda, who took fright and scattered. They could not escape the devil tribe, however. The girls were mauling Opal, trying to look inside her pouch, while the boys had Mick bailed up, urging him to spar with them.

Something in me snapped. 'Hey, *youse kids*! Cut it out!'

My bellow astonished me and actually caught the attention of their father, who took up the shout and ordered the youngsters away from our animals.

'Whacko, there's a creek down there,' one shouted. Through the long grass they swarmed and climbed up the wire fence like monkeys. This time it was Jeff who roared. In quick time he rounded them up and marched them back outside our gate. He was slow to lose patience but when he did, he made no bones about it.

Our little visitor was tenacious, however. He had things on his mind. After ordering his brood back into the car, he began to offer propositions. They involved everything from scouting travel information for Jeff's writing to rounding up emus and more 'roos in the wild. This last was his pet subject. He'd take a motorbike out with him, tie it to the roof of his car. It'd be better than running the animals down on foot. How about birds? Would we like some wild budgerigars, maybe even an eagle or a dingo pup? He could trap one easy, bring it back in a cage.

'I wouldn't charge you for me time, Jeff. No, we love the experience of getting out in them places. All we need is a way to pay for our petrol and a bit of tucker.'

Jeff refused all his offers. The man was a dreamer, a schemer, an ebullient sort of rogue you could almost admire for refusing to be stuck in a rut. However, we didn't approve of his attitudes and wanted nothing to do with his proposals.

We would not have accepted his kangaroo, but he insisted. When he understood there was no way we would buy it, he admitted he had to get rid of it. It was a problem in the neighbourhood where he lived. Instead of him doing us a favour, as he'd originally implied, it was the other way around.

So that was how Blue Belle came to live with us. The name was our own because although she was a red kangaroo, females of the species have soft blueish fur instead of the short russet pelt of the males. She had a pretty face, reminiscent of Hanogi, and I fancied there was sadness in her expression. Can kangaroos express emotions in their faces? Or was I just projecting what she'd been through with the wild bunch? In any case, Belle was hard to approach at first, very nervous. We just let her find her way, making sure she had plenty to eat and drink. The peace and quiet of our place would heal her, if possible.

The other kangaroos gave her a wide berth and this seemed to suit her. She kept her head down, grazing the lush grass and starting violently at the slightest noise or intrusion into her space. Being a different species ensured her solitude.

The kangaroo paddock, as we now called it, was being populated too slowly for our liking. The gender mix was wrong. Thalos had only succeeded in impregnating Opal before he disappeared. For weeks and weeks we stared at her in profile, trying to convince ourselves that her tummy contained a little bulge. At last the bulge moved, independent of Opal herself, and we were elated. Once when Jeff took the bucket of pellets down to feed the 'roos, he caught Opal cleaning out her pocket and glimpsed her infant inside. It was still translucent!

Six months passed before we saw a little face peeping out. Van spotted it. By then, Opal's pouch was stretched, drooping with the weight of the baby which looked to be unfurred. Soon we could see it was covered with fine grey hairs. Its eyes bugged out, its nose was pink and naked. Sometimes its lanky legs or tail protruded. The feet were long and soft, almost wet looking, their skin new and shiny.

Opal was a petite animal and her year-old infant seemed almost as big as herself before we were rewarded with the sight of it standing on the earth beside her. Mathilda hovered near, like a covetous aunt. It seemed her mating with Thalos had not taken but she dwelt on Opal's child and Opal permitted this. On the sunniest days, Opal would lie in the grass beside her joey, her legs barricading it from the world and her front paws resting protectively on the baby's shoulder. If we attempted to approach, she stood up hastily and the joey somersaulted back inside her pouch. We respected Opal's reluctance to let us come close, but we couldn't stop peeking at the baby from a distance. She was a jewel, our first-born. We named her Potch, after the rock in which opals occur.

With Thalos gone roaming, Opal, Mathilda and Mick looked small and vulnerable in their half-acre paddock which at the top adjoined our backyard. We wanted more kangaroos. Mick was a year away from fathering joeys and we still weren't sure if Thalos' mating with Mathilda had taken, so Jeff rang Eric Worrell to see if his Park had a population problem. They did. At once, we set off for Gosford.

Having established himself as a protector of Australian wildlife, Eric, his family and staff were kept busy by people seeking advice or a haven for all manner of injured or orphaned native species. Eric's task was to channel the dependents back into the bush. People like ourselves with an isolated property and a passionate yet realistic yen for wildlife were required.

We left Gosford with two female grey kangaroos secure within chaff bags, only their heads sticking out. The animals lay in the back of our utility, bedded on a pad of sponge rubber. I rode with them, stroking them and speaking softly to keep them calm. Amusing myself along the way, I thought up names for the new-comers, Sheila and Doreen from the writings of Banjo Paterson seemed to fit.

It was a five-hour drive back to Foxground. We arrived at dusk. Goth and Van had walked home from the school bus stop and were waiting to open the gate for us, followed by Jim and Laika, yapping and wagging. 'Get those dogs back in the house,' their father ordered testily and the boys obeyed, then returned to watch him gently lift out the larger, older animal, Doreen. Carefully Jeff untied the neck of her bag and instructed us to slowly peel it off her while he supported her round the chest. When her shoulders, her back, her haunches were exposed and her tall was straightened out behind her, Jeff delicately removed his hands.

We all kept still, very still, to see what she would do. Doreen was half-grown. Her thick fur rippled with nervousness as she sniffed the strange smells of our garden. She stared at us, her eyes dark with apprehension, then she bounded off.

'Let her go, let her find her way,' counselled Jeff. We followed cautiously as Doreen hopped round the garden, skidding to a stop at the picket fence, then hopping at a tangent through flower beds bordering the house. She was panicky, finding nothing familiar to reassure her.

'Perhaps you'd better go round and block her path before she gets up too much momentum,' Jeff whispered. Goth and Vandal complied instantly, circling the house like shadows, gliding softly like bush boys with a minimum of gesture and no speech. Doreen came upon them and skidded again to a halt.

She looked at them. Looked back at us. Her fur was standing out, rigid and you could almost see her heart banging in her chest as her ears swivelled frantically. Suddenly she gave a mighty bound that took her over the front pickets. We watched her streak for the forest through the fading light. And that was the last we saw of Doreen for a long, long time.

We all felt totally consternated. What had we done wrong? We agreed we should carry Shella indoors and liberate her on the front verandah. So the dogs had to be ordered out of the house and into the garage where they were again locked in. Jim began to bark hysterically. 'Will somebody shut up that damn dog?' Jeff ordered, his patience beginning to fray.

'I'll stay with him, Dad,' Goth offered, an admirable sacrifice for a lad who never liked to miss out on anything.

With silence restored, Jeff hefted Sheila and we went, in procession, into the farmhouse. Sheila was a bit younger than Doreen, more lethargic, and she reacted less anxiously to her release from the bag. After sniffing fresh air through the fly-wire door, she put her head down and began to nose about the floor.

'Shall I get her a drink of water?' whispered Van.

It was a good suggestion. Sheila drank strongly. Then she continued her slow promenade, investigating every bit of the porch which probably retained faint scents of the other kangaroos. Moving very slowly, we offered her a dish of oats, chopped apple and carrot but she passed it over and continued to prowl.

We left her to it, closing the door into the house. Calling in Goth and the dogs, we sat at the kitchen table for a catching up of news and a post mortem on the loss of Doreen.

'Maybe she'll find her way back to make friends with Opal and Mathilda,' Goth suggested.

'Maybe she'll find Thalos,' Van speculated further. 'Maybe they'll come hopping back together.'

On that optimistic thought, we went to peep at Sheila. She seemed quite unperturbed. 'We had better keep her in until morning,' Jeff suggested. 'By then, she'll have this place well and truly into her nostrils.'

With that decided, I fetched armfuls of newspaper and began quietly spreading them out on the verandah floor.

'Don't stir her up,' Jeff warned sternly.

But I persisted quietly, strong in an intuition that Sheila would not panic. My efforts would make tomorrow's clean-up less arduous and would also block any drafts which might waft up through cracks in the old floorboards. I was acquiring a feeling for animal wellbeing.

After we had eaten supper and the boys were ready for bed, we took out a dish of warm milk, mixed to the formula used at Eric's Reptile Park. We left it in Sheila's path and quietly withdrew. The boys retired upstairs and Jeff and I sat together in the kitchen, reading the day's mail over a peaceful cup of tea and suddenly it felt as if we'd put in a long day. We imagined the boys would be tired too, having had to hoof it the last steep mile home from the school bus, but upstairs we could hear them talking earnestly.

At last, Van sang out, 'Dad, can I come down? I need to go to the toilet'.

Jeff and I looked at each other. This was unusual but of course we agreed. As a slightly sheepish little boy in pyjamas sidled through the kitchen and out the back door, Goth trilled, with just a hint of a giggle, 'Dad, I need to go, too'.

When Goth had flitted out into the night, we heard the toilet door bang, a burst of subdued laughter, then the thud of bare feet on the path leading round the house. A minute or two later, two young detectives returned to report that they had peeked through the screen door of the verandah and seen Sheila lying down.

'She's drunk her milk,' they announced triumphantly and then skipped back upstairs before their subterfuge could bring a reprimand.

Lucky they were quick, else they'd have noticed their parents smiling together over their ingenuity.

Sheila settled in at Glenrock Farm as good as gold. When we let her off the front verandah, she grazed placidly within the garden. In no time, she grew used to the dogs, winning their tolerance if not their active friendship. She began to gravitate to the fence separating the kangaroo paddock from the garden and often lay with her back against the wire. Before long we noticed her sniffing Opal through the mesh.

We opened the gate to let them get properly acquainted. At first, Mathilda and Mick came into the garden to size Sheila up properly, smelling her from end to end, clucking and patting tentatively at her back. She tolerated this nervously and there was no drama. She seemed content to let the three residents lead the way and she tagged along after them.

We left the verandah door propped open for a few nights, in case Sheila wanted to come inside, but she had been used to sleeping outdoors at the Reptile Park and she obviously preferred the company of her own kind to ours, even though she would always be the outrider of their convoy. Our herd was slowly growing.

When the school holidays came around, Thor went to visit his friend's property in New England again and returned with another orphan joey for us to rear. This one was much younger than Thalos or the other three had been when they arrived. The poor little creature weighed scarcely a kilo. Her eyes bugged out, her nose was almost hairless and pink from having been pressed continuously against her mother's teat. The fur of this mite was no denser than velvet on her back and almost non-existent on her pale tummy. She looked a pitiful little skeleton, peeping fearfully out of a wheat-sack.

'Shall we call her Hanogi Two?' I asked and immediately regretted it, sensing that name might bring bad luck. Despite my misgivings the others liked the idea, so I set myself the task of trying to save the life of Hanogi's namesake.

It was an uphill fight from the start. She arrived with diarrhoea which we attributed to the shock of her mother's death plus getting cold while in transit to Foxground. We made her the warmest nest we could devise and put a little charcoal in her milk mixture. This was an old-fashioned remedy recommended by the Conroys and other farmer neighbours.

Hanogi was too young and frail for the kangararium. She needed to be swaddled all the time. Were her mother still alive, she would not have left the pouch for some months yet. Frequent gentle cuddles should help her. But she arrived at a very busy season. The vegetable crop was a bumper one, the back verandah was daily lined with buckets of produce to bottle or make into pickles. Jeff was putting together a book about his outback travels, so he was extra busy, too. There didn't seem enough hours in the days and nights to accomplish all we'd set ourselves to do. Often I begrudged the time to sit nursing Hanogi until I saw her pinched little face and felt the frailty of her long skinny legs and my patience returned. She was the most vulnerable of all our charges.

Her diarrhoea persisted, which meant daily washing of bunny rugs and bag-liners. Washing meant boiling. I sterilised all her linens and her bottles. And rang Worrell's Reptile Park for advice. Was told that sometimes a 24-hour fast would rest the gut and clear up the problem. So I cut out milk from her formula and fed her only boiled water, glucose and vitamins.

Every few days I wrapped her in a big handkerchief and laid her on the scales I used for my jam-making. She rarely gained an ounce and now she began to lose weight. Her skull wobbled on her tiny neck and her head needed to be supported. She was limp as a rag doll.

Maybe she was lonely, we thought. Goth and Van gave her a nurse after school, sitting patiently at the big kitchen table in their blue and grey uniforms, tenderly holding the little parcelled up invalid while they polished off an afternoon tea of fresh farm milk, bread and home-made preserves. Unlike her predecessors, Hanogi Two showed no interest in what they were eating. Balefully she regarded them with sad, bug-eyes, then ducked her head back into her covers.

When they were at school, I carried her outside as I pegged up the washing or watered the lawn. Thinking she might miss being in motion as her mother moved along with her in the pouch, I tied her sack to the bib of my apron, hoping this would encourage her.

I doubt if it did, but at least I then had two hands free for my work.

I even crouched on the lawn, lifting her head out of the bag with my finger, encouraging her to sniff the grass, maybe even take a bite. Both Jeff and I had faith in the healthful properties of natural food. When Hanogi did not respond, I picked tender tufts and tried to push them into her mouth. That was futile, so I force-fed her pinches of earth, hoping it would set her digestion into gear. Nothing helped.

A feeling of dread grew. Daily I watched her fading. Surely there must be something I could do to give her strength. I hovered beside her, letting my other tasks go, willing her to improve. Not until her last minutes did I give up hope. Then we all had to accept that she was lost to us.

A lingering bereavement fell upon us. We vowed never to use the name Hanogi again. Over and over, we puzzled about what had gone wrong. Still only learners in the marsupial mothering game, we suspected she had been a lost cause from the start, too young and too ill for saving. Did we actually cause her more suffering than she deserved by attempting the impossible? We chewed upon her post mortem for weeks.

Then something happened to take our mind off Hanogi Two. It was the annual visit of the Ambulance Man.

In those days, the District Ambulance Service was staffed by a special breed of person. They were decent, compassionate, old-fashioned gentlemen who knew everyone in the district and performed their duties for very low pay. The Service relied on subscriptions to keep going. Each year you paid dues into the Ambulance fund and this entitled you to a ride in the wagon should you need it.

Few folks ever required an ambulance ride, but you subscribed just the same, to keep the system operating. The Ambulance man who called for your money was assured of a warm welcome, and his unhurried visits were as much a social call as a money-collecting exercise. In our area, Harold Clark of Berry was the collector and he was a particularly genial person who enjoyed a good chat. He always brought to it news from right around the district.

This time, Mr Clark had something extra on his mind when he sat down to a cup of tea and fresh scones in our kitchen. He wanted to ask us a favour.

The Clarks had a kangaroo in their backyard. She was fully grown, about five years old, a female. They called her Chutt. Although they loved her dearly, they believed she needed more space and company of her own kind. Also, Harold said his wife was unwell. Caring for Chutt was becoming a burden. Would we give her a home on Glenrock Wildlife Refuge?

Our family talked it over. We agreed that accepting adult 'roos was a quicker method of expanding our herd than breeding, and should be less trouble than rearing orphan babies. Ha ha ha. Another naive theory to be tested.

Chutt did not arrive in the ambulance, as we hoped. Harold and his wife brought her in the family sedan, which proved a bit of a struggle. Mrs Clark was very anxious about Chutt's well-being and came prepared to stay with her for some hours until she settled in.

We decided to release her straight into the half-acre paddock where the fences were higher and she would have access from the start to the other four 'roos. After a little while, we left Mr and Mrs Clark sitting in the middle of that big grassy slope, facing the creek, watching Chutt. After some nervous exploration, she seemed to settle. When evening shadows spread down around their shoulders, the Clarks tiptoed back up into our yard. Within seconds, Chutt bounded up to the fence and was chattering at them through the wire.

Mrs Clark was all for going through the process again but her husband urged her gently into their car. 'She'll just have to get used to it here, dear,' he kept saying. It was like leaving a child on the first day at school.

They had brought her feeding bowl and generous supplies of what she ate. The question was where to put it, so the other four would not get it. There was quite a bit of to-ing and fro-ing until bedtime, as we fed the others, then followed Chutt along the fence-line and back with her dish of tucker. She was quite stirred up and Van observed that she always faced the direction she had come from, toward Berry, holding her head in an alert way as if receiving signals from home. Nothing we did seemed to calm her and we realised that here was a down-side of taking adult animals. They had already bonded to their previous carers and saw no reason to bond to us. Frustrated and concerned, we left her outside in the dark. When Harold Clark rang to enquire, we tried to sound reassuring but when he admitted his wife was fretting, we hoped they would decide to take Chutt back.

That did not happen, however. Next morning, she was still hopping back and forth along the southern boundary of the 'roo paddock. The other animals eyed her curiously but as she totally avoided them, they left her on her own. We kept her food bowl full and spent a lot of time getting her to take bread from our fingers as she used to do from the Clarks. Periodically, she would lift her head and listen, or sniff the air, one couldn't tell which, and then commence the fence-pacing again.

She was a worry, Chutt. Gradually Harold's telephone calls decreased, but whenever I saw Mrs Clark in Berry, I wished I hadn't. I knew I must reassure her, but did not want to actually lie about how Chutt was behaving. By the end of the first month, she seemed to have accepted her new home and even her neighbours Opal and the rest, but she still looked homesick and periodically took up that obsessive patrol along the southern boundary.

One day when we were out, she disappeared. I checked the fences and found where she'd cleared the wire, bending it in her flight. A little tuft of grey fur was all she left behind.

I hurried to telephone neighbours down the valley. Nobody had seen Chutt but they all promised to watch out for her. Jeff and I jumped in the Land Rover and drove around, looking and calling. We found nothing. There was ten miles of hilly country between us and Berry. Most of it was settled but there were fences, cattle, farm dogs, and of course, roads. What chance had Chutt of making it home, we asked ourselves?

Mortified, I rang the Clarks that night and told them the bad news. They said they'd keep their eyes peeled for her. As Ambulance man for the district, Harold knew every farm and he said he'd ring around and put people on the alert in case she turned up. He was very kind, not blaming us for her escape, but I felt we had disappointed him.

Goth and Van kept saying Chutt might have gone up the back to find Thalos and Doreen. Secretly, I doubted that. But I still hoped Thalos would return, alone or in company, and rejoin Opal and Mathilda and Mick.

No one lived on the several hundred acres between our back

boundary and the foot of the escarpment. It was owned by three burly brothers from Berry who ran cattle and sheep on old abandoned paddocks up there. With big machines they put in dams and graded tracks, ripped and cleared and harrowed, strung fences to enclose their livestock. They had been timber-getters on the north coast before moving to our district and they harvested trees up the back, hauling them down through our farm on big noisy semi-trailers. Once or twice we caught them felling cedars inside our top boundary and had to warn them off that practice. Trouble was, the trees were gone. There was nothing we could do to put them back.

Ours was a love–hate relationship. The brothers welcomed shooters onto their dry runs, men as tough and dangerous looking as themselves who ground up our rough track late on Friday nights, headlamps raking the bush, then banged away at rabbits and foxes all weekend, returning on Sunday afternoons unshaven and dirty. The road that ran diagonally through our land had two gates across it to enclose our cows. Sometimes the visitors failed to shut our gates. Other times, the brothers left the back one open to give their cattle a feed of our grass.

I always felt mildly at siege when the brothers came through, although we formed a grudging admiration for their land management up the back. Their earthmoving did not cause erosion and in places stopped it. It was annoying though that someone always had to go up, or down, and check that they'd shut the gates behind them. Once they drove a wide grader up to their land and to make it fit through, they removed our back gate altogether. They promised to replace it later, but never did.

The brothers were men of few words. However, if Jeff came out of his office in the dairy when they were passing and leaned on our gate, they'd pull up for a terse yarn. Jeff asked the brothers to keep their eyes peeled for the missing kangaroos and they said they would. On their way back home, they stopped, big engine idling, and spoke briefly with Jeff. They'd spotted a dead 'roo way up on the far paddock.

Next afternoon, Jeff and Van set off up the back. They said they were going hunting for rabbits, which they often did, stalking silently through the dusk and returning with bunny carcases strung from their belts, a fine feed for the dogs and ourselves. Goth did not accompany them on these forays, preferring to draw and build his contraptions – billy carts, beach racers, grass sleds with bedsheet sails. I was no hunter, either. A seeker, an observer, yes, but not a killer. Besides, I had chickens to feed and lock up for the night, fires to build in the house, dinner to prepare. But Goth and I both knew the purpose of this particular expedition and we waited for their return, keen to know if the corpse belonged to Thalos, or Doreen, or even Chutt.

It was past dark when we heard boots tramping down the track, with Jim and Laika running ahead to announce their return. They had found the dead kangaroo, they said. It was unmistakably Thalos.

He had been dead a week or more, shot. Just popped off from a distance by some hunter – probably one of the bunch who periodically came over the mountain from the Jamberoo side. We would hear their firing distantly, and the yelps of their dogs which occasionally became separated from them and chased all over the high lands, baying and harassing wallabies and livestock, until their masters returned to whistle them up the following weekend.

How they, or anyone, could have been so thoughtless – so careless – as to shoot a kangaroo, one of the few remaining within miles, was beyond me. Surely they guessed it would be someone's pet?

Anger filled us, but also sadness. Poor little Thalos. No more would he wrap his lips around our clothes and suck. Not for him the pleasure of siring a huge dynasty with Opal, Mathilda and other females.

So filled with enthusiasm was I for Australia's disappearing natives and our plans to bring them back that I failed to appreciate how other people could feel differently. When I began to glimpse what we were up against, my resolve strengthened to change the common opinion. However, it was many years before I accepted how firmly entrenched was the mistrust of, the aversion to, wildlife.

We were eager to see more joeys produced but, now that we knew Thalos was gone for good and with Mick still too young to mate, we needed a mature male. Nature provided an answer. Early one Saturday morning, Van came racing into our bedroom to awaken us with startling news.

'Dad, there's a big kangaroo outside the fence!'

We got up, very excited, and went out to see. Sure enough, a large buck was going up and down the fence-line, clearly wanting in to the one-acre paddock. He looked enormous next to Mathilda and Sheila, who had come across to touch noses with the visitor through the wire. Mick followed and even Blue Belle looked interested.

We mounted one of the spontaneous campaigns at which we were becoming proficient. Goth was to sneak down quietly inside the paddock, crawling through the long grass to avoid alarming the animals, and open the fence where we had a bogan gate. Then we would go out and surround the visiting 'roo, advancing slowly to drive him into the paddock.

It was a good plan. But unfortunately it didn't quite succeed. As soon as we opened our back door, the buck sat back on his haunches, swivelling his ears in alarm. Alert, he detected us moving across the back yard and retreated up the hill toward thick bush.

'Oh well, he'll probably return,' we said philosophically, and went indoors to get some breakfast.

That weekend we were expecting a visit from Athol and Ayleen, our best friends from Sydney. They were both writers and Athol was also a photographer, like Jeff. They had just arrived, late in the afternoon, and we were seated round the kitchen table sipping tea and exchanging news when Goth and Van charged in.

'The big buck is back,' they reported.

Sure enough, it was as before. We sprang into Plan A again while Athol and Ayleen watched excitedly through the kitchen window. Again, the visiting 'roo was wary and retreated.

'He'll be back tonight, for sure,' Jeff said. 'We'll have another go, first thing in the morning. I'll load my cameras, so we might get a few photos as well.'

And so at dawn, when Van came again to whisper: 'He's here, Dad,' we were expecting the summons and sprang into action, being as quiet and economical in our movements as we could. Jeff and Van slipped out the front door while Goth slithered as far as the gate. He couldn't get it open. Grass and vines had grown through it, entwining with the wire mesh. He signalled the problem in a stage whisper. However, the big buck wasn't so worried by us this time. Or maybe he was keener to get in with the females. He roamed about on the slope beyond the fence, clucking. Mathilda and Sheila seemed to dither, while Belle sat back on her tail alarmed and Mulga Mick became agitated. He uttered a little cough. The visitor clucked louder.

Jeff hurried to get his cameras and, telling us to stay still inside our yard, he slipped out through the back gate and circled like a commando until we saw him appear on the hillside behind the kangaroo. He began snapping photos as fast as possible, expecting it to hop away. Instead, it advanced on Jeff. While Jeff clicked away, the buck came right up to him. At the last minute, Jeff lowered his camera and ducked as the animal swiped at the camera with a well-muscled forearm. Jeff went backwards and the 'roo followed him.

My heart began to pound. 'Look out, Dad,' piped Goth. The animal pursued Jeff, trying to grab him from behind. Jeff turned round and the buck reared back on its tail and aimed a kick with powerful hind feet. Jeff danced sideways and avoided the blow easily.

We who were watching became heated. Roused by our shouts, Athol came out and was astounded to see Jeff being pursued round the hillside by a huge kangaroo which grunted challengingly and stood up every few feet to try and kick. Athol became excited too. He shouted facetious encouragement, but I was fretting. 'Carter, do you need a hand?' Athol called.

'No, I can manage him,' Jeff shouted back, somewhat breathlessly. 'Try and get a few pictures.'

Athol dashed for his camera. For the next ten minutes he photographed an amazing series of passes on the hillside. Jeff was the matador, the kangaroo was the bull. Or was it the other way around? The point was, Jeff was able to keep out of his reach, dancing and weaving like the boxer he'd once been. Only when Athol had shot all his film did Jeff abandon his sport and come in for breakfast. I loaded the table with cereal and kept hot toast coming while a postmortem was held on the extraordinary happening. It was agreed that the visitor must have been reared by a human; probably it was someone's pet which had gotten away, drawn to our place by the scent of the females.

The buck hung about on the hillside making clicking sounds through the fence at the 'roos inside. When the sun rose, he lay down under a tree, propped on an elbow and watched the ladies, who also lay down nearby, on the opposite side of the wire.

'Well, looks like we've got our male kangaroo. All we have to do is get him inside the paddock,' Jeff said, restoked with energy.

It was decided to cut the wire and rejoin it later. While we were making our plan – Plan B – Goth and Van fronted up with another newsflash. The big 'roo was on his feet and moving off. We all rushed outside and watched the big buck hop up the hill in a stately but determined manner. Something in his bearing told us he wouldn't return. We watched until he went out of sight. So much for Plan B.

At least we had the photos in Athol's and Jeff's cameras. They disappeared into the darkroom, the old cream-separating room in the dairy, windowless and cool, and with plenty of running water. When they emerged with contact proofs and a few sample prints, we postmortemed all over again. The buck looked almost as tall as Jeff when he stood on his hind feet. His forearms were as thick as Jeff's. He looked dangerous.

'There was really no problem,' Jeff assured us. 'I'm fast on my feet and my reach was longer than his. I could push him away. With my arm straight, he couldn't touch me.'

The photographic account of the contest told a different story. It was an extraordinary series of pictures. Jeff decided to use them for his weekly 'Wild Country' column in *People* magazine and tell the story of our mystery weekend drop-in.

The sequel came shortly after the article was published. Our telephone rang and it was farmer Alcock from Gerringong, seven miles distant. 'I see you had a visit from our Joe,' he said. 'We wondered where he'd got to. He went missing for three days. Then he turned up back at the farm and has settled ever since.'

The caller related Joe's story. He had arrived in a cornflakes box as an orphan. He'd been reared in the house like a human baby. The little girls of the family used to push him around in a doll's pram. Later their brothers would wrestle with him and they taught him to spar. That would explain why he had no qualms about coming up to Jeff and engaging him in playful combat.

Mr Alcock continued, 'We think Joe is a bit bored, now that the kids have grown and gone out to work. That must be why he jumped the fence. But Foxground seems a long way to travel. He would have had to cross the highway, and all.'

'Well, we might see him here again,' Jeff concluded. 'We've got four lonely females. A visit from Joe is just what they need.'

As Jeff predicted, Big Joe did return to our farm. And this time he came to stay. The circumstances were different than we had imagined, however.

Harold Alcock rang. He was upset. Big Joe had attacked someone and was now under a police restraining order. The incident had occurred the previous day, when a young veterinarian arrived to innoculate the farm's cattle. He was freshly graduated from university and had just started employment with the local vet. Alcock's was his first field assignment. Dressed in bright new overalls, shining with purpose, he drove into the yard and got out of his car, medical bag in hand. At once, the six-foot kangaroo appeared and began kicking the tripe out of him.

The young vet went down, his overalls in tatters, two ribs broken. His yells for help roused the farmer and put Big Joe to flight. As Mr Alcock opened the kitchen door to go out, Joe hopped in, very agitated. A melee ensued; chairs were knocked over, milk jug went flying and the farmer received several hearty thumps from his rampaging pet.

Mrs Alcock came running, wielding a broom. Between the two of them, they managed to hunt Big Joe outside and into the chicken coop. Then they hurried to aid the young vet, who ended up in hospital on his special day.

The local copper came to view the scene of the crime. He knew the family well and had often given a friendly cuddle to the 'roo when he was still known as Little Joe. The seeds of the trouble had been sown then. When Joe was a youngster, he was the prime companion of the farmer's growing sons. It was they who taught him to 'box'.

A terrible misconception was rife then about boxing kangaroos. It was spread by showmen who exploited the animals' normal instinct to spar with their fellows, in order to provide a spectacle, a contest between man and beast. As so often happens in such cases, the strongest, most aggressive animals – be they bulls or lions or buck kangaroos – were no real match for organised humans. The cruel and often bloody competitions began to lose favour with audiences at circuses and carnivals. But the myth persisted that kangaroos enjoy sparring matches with men.

In the case of the Gerringong family, their 'roo's habit of wrestling with boys in their farm clothes continued after the lads had grown and gone out to work. On washdays, when the overalls were hung on the rotary clothesline to dry, a lonely Joe would attack the laundry. He would stand on his tail and drop-kick, sending the clothes spinning. As the overalls came around again, up Joe would go, lashing out with his hind feet. It was a truly funny routine, one which the family saw no reason to discourage until the innocent game put a young vet in hospital.

Sympathetic though he was toward the family and their pet, the policeman knew his duty. He informed them Big Joe was too dangerous to remain loose around the farm. He was too tame to release into the wild. It looked as though a bullet would be the only solution.

'Just let me ring Jeff Carter,' the farmer said. 'He's got special yards and fences up on his place, way back in the hills where nobody lives close by. And he's got female 'roos that'd keep our Joe content for the rest of his days. He's only bored, that's his trouble.'

So the proposition was put to us over the telephone. Would we reprieve Joe by giving him a home?

Jeff agreed. With Thalos gone – gone forever – we needed a mature buck to mate with our females. And Jeff thought he knew how to manage Big Joe. He set about concocting a plan for transporting the big buck from Gerringong to Foxground.

We rang our friendly vet in Berry and asked if he could provide a tranquillising injection for an animal about the weight of a man. George Borys said he could and became interested in the project. For extra muscle, he would bring his teenage son, Stefan, who was already six feet tall.

As luck would have it, another strongman and his family were staying at the farm for a few days. Keith Finlay was editor of *People* magazine, which published many of Jeff's feature articles plus his weekly column. Keith had been a champion swimmer. He kept very fit. His fourteen-year-old son, Kim, a surfboard rider, was a replica of his old man.

The expedition was shaping up nicely. But first Jeff had to construct a suitable place to put Joe once he arrived. He rushed out to the farmers' cooperative store at Berry and bought pig wire and eight foot steel posts. Then he and the boys strengthed and heightened a big yard outside our dairy. This yard adjoined the kangaroos' paddock. The Finlays helped.

When all was ready, George Borys was sent for. Then he and his son joined Goth and Van and our two house guests in the Land Rover. The party set off for Gerringong in a spirit of adventure, leaving the ladies Carter and Finlay at home to hear the saga later.

They told us Joe looked very large in the chicken coop. He wasn't happy about being kept there. He barked and roared, kicking at the wire. None of the men was game to front up to him, so farmer Alcock led the charge, despite two strapped ribs cracked in the affray a day or two earlier. He put a headlock on his big kangaroo, then the other men wrestled him to the ground so the vet could inject him in the hip.

They sat on him until the tranquilliser worked. The dose was big enough for two men, the vet said. Nonetheless, it took all their concentration to keep Joe down.

At last he became groggy. He never became totally unconscious, but was docile enough to be lifted and carried out to the Land Rover. When he was bedded in the back, held down by the chaps, Jeff headed quickly for Foxground.

Throughout the journey, he received anxious bulletins from the back of the vehicle.

'Think he's waking up, Dad.'

'No, keep going, Jeff, he's just turning over.'

'Dad, he wants to get up!'

'No, it's okay, Jeff, he's settled back again.'

No one felt comfortable with a lively Big Joe in a Land Rover full of people! However, they got him to Glenrock safely and carried him into his new yard. Then very briskly they left him and came out, locking the gate behind them. Within half an hour Joe was on his feet, drinking water and showing interest in eating pellets. He had arrived.

We kept close watch on Joe to make sure he settled in. The kids wanted to peek at him frequently but we warned them to be silent and keep out of sight behind the shed wall. It was in nobody's interest to excite him.

An amazing animal, was Joe. When he stood up to stretch,

he was as tall as Jeff. His forearms were as muscular as a weight-lifter's, his front paws almost as big as human hands, with inch-long nails like iron. The central toenail on each hind foot was over two inches long and hard as ebony.

Fortunately, Joe seemed content to be back at our place. There was plenty of grass in his yard beneath the old pear trees. He sniffed the fresh bush air appreciatively and touched noses through the wire with the kangaroos living in the paddock next door. When we reckoned it was safe to do so, we let them come into Joe's yard to get acquainted.

At first we let in only Mathilda, Opal, Potch and Sheila. They shivered at being close to Big Joe but he clucked and patted them so gently that they soon became confident with him. Belle was blatantly disinterested at first, and Mulga Mick was clearly put out at being separated from the other 'roos. After a while we let him visit Big Joe's yard along with the females and stood by in case of trouble. There were no problems, not at first.

Big Joe mated with Opal and Sheila easily. Potch was still too young and Mathilda was reluctant. She had injured her hip, the same leg which had suffered the gunshot wound in her infancy, and she moved with a distinct limp. Whenever Joe approached her, she moved steadily away from him. He followed, clucking and patting at her rump, but she kept just out of his grasp. We didn't know if this was because her oestrus cycle was not ready or because of her disability.

Mulga Mick seemed keen to sniff Joe out and to be sniffed. He was more than two years old now and we guessed that soon he would also want to mate with the females. When he began to stand up to Joe and bark provocatively, we thought it was the beginning of a challenge. Since Mick was only a third the height of Joe and very slender by comparison, we kept a close watch on them.

Joe tolerated Mick surprisingly well. In an almost bemused manner, he let Mick rear back on his tail and slam his hind feet into Joe's ribs. It was a pretty shaky drop-kick, but Joe didn't turn a hair. He simply grunted and lifted his chin to dodge Mick's flailing front paws. Mick repeated the attacks and began to find his balance after each kick. We planned how to dash in and rescue Mick if Joe turned nasty and began to retaliate, but he didn't. He seemed to realise the smaller, younger buck was no threat to him.

Their jousts became regular encounters, usually just before dusk. As soon as we heard Mick's treble challenge answered by Joe's deeper grunt, we came running. When we saw it was not a serious fight, we stayed to watch because it was a good spectacle, one that particularly fascinated Jeff and the boys and any male visitors. They identified with the testosterone-charged atmosphere. We concluded that Joe was instructing Mick in the manly arts.

It was always the young 'roo who shaped up first. On his toes, he hopped and danced in and out, just like a boxer, while issuing his sharp adolescent bark. Joe would reply in his rich, lower voice. He, too, would rear back and sometimes he would kick out at Mick in retaliation. But his full strength was not in it, this was obvious. Had it been, Mick would have gone sailing like a football over the fence and into the next paddock.

Mick put all his energy into his boots, however. You could hear his hind feet slamming into Joe's barrel-like torso. Once in a while his blow would hurt and then Joe's bark took on a new warning note, but he never lost his temper. As both males grew hot, they dribbled saliva onto their inside forearms where the fur was sparse. This was a cooling mechanism, since kangaroos do not sweat.

After they had danced and weaved and kicked up and down the yard for a while and both were panting, their arms dark with spit, Joe would come down on his heels again and drop an arm good-naturedly around Mick's neck as if to say, 'Come on, little buddy, let's take a break.' Then they would loll in each other's embrace, like two friendly gladiators, before moving off together, grazing side by side.

We began to recognise another bulge in Opal's pouch. I wanted to believe the joey was Thalos's, a delayed gift before he departed. We had read that females can carry an embryo in their bodies until the time is suitable for it to be born. However, the father was probably Big Joe bcause soon after we noticed Sheila also had a joey in her pouch. Poor Mathilda, everybody said. We hoped she would stop walking away from Joe soon.

He seemed fairly settled at our place those first few months. True, he did become agitated every so often. Then his eyes would darken and become as opaque as black beads. His fur stuck out and rippled at any stimulus. Whenever one of us went in to give him pellets or fresh water, he was tetchy and inclined to stand up aggressively. We figured it might be the phases of the moon and gave him a wide berth during these two-or three-day periods of aggression.

Twice Joe jumped over the fence and had to be lured back. This involved all of us, circling and coaxing, offering bribes of bread and dishes of pellets, all the while watching that we didn't let ourselves be cornered against a fence. None of us totally trusted Joe – wise instinct, as it turned out.

We instructed our boys to keep their friends out of Joe's yard, and to never enter it themselves if we were not at home. Once we returned after an outing to find Van and his mate from down the valley, Ian Conroy, bubbling with boyish triumph. Their football had gone into Joe's yard and they had retrieved it.

Mindful of our warning, respectful of the taboo, they explained how they had lured Joe to the other extreme of the yard by putting bread through the fence for him to chew on. While he was busy, they had crept as silent as shadows into his yard to pick up their ball, then ran as swift as the breeze back out through the gate. Since both were experienced farm boys, and since they had thought their campaign through so carefully, we let it pass with a caution. Jeff and I understood that it was not only adolescent Mulga Mick who needed to flirt with danger and learn how to deal with it.

Each time Joe escaped, Jeff raised the height of the fence. It was now over seven feet tall. During Joe's challenging phases, Jeff also began the precaution of carrying a hoe when he went in with feed, figuring he could push Joe out of reach until the food and water chores were completed.

One day Jeff let himself out the gate and was just about to latch it when Joe slammed into it with a gigantic drop-kick. The kick lifted the gate off its hinges and Jeff found himself holding it in his hands like a shield between him and Joe. Needless to say, he dropped it back onto its spindles quickly, slid the bolt home and then bolstered the gate with his body as Joe kicked it peevishly several more times. The gate was reinforced without delay.

In between these brief flare-ups, however, Joe was good as gold. He suffered us regally as we tended his requirements. With dignity he welcomed his harem and the visits of his protégé, Mick. The rest of the time, he lay on his elbow in the shade of the pear tree, king of all he surveyed. We believed we had fitted him into our scheme, thus saving his life and providing a sire for our kangaroo herd. We thought we could handle Big Joe.

We were only fooling ourselves, however.

One morning after Goth and Van had gone to school, Jeff went out to feed the 'roos while I tidied up the kitchen after breakfast. It was one of those still mornings, rich in birdsong, when the air has been washed clean by overnight showers and the cliffs rising out of the forest above our farm stood vivid against clear blue sky. Vaguely wondering why Jeff was taking so long, I went out to empty the compost bucket. As the back door gave its habitual bang, I heard faintly the oddest cry from the direction of Joe's yard.

I dropped the bucket and ran. When I opened the gate and went into the yard, I couldn't believe what I was seeing. Jeff and Joe were locked in a terrible embrace, collapsed off balance against the chicken-yard fence, which sagged under their combined weight. Jeff's clothes were shredded and hanging off him. There was blood all over his face and his arms. He seemed barely conscious as he croaked, 'Get this bastard off me. He's killing me!'

Jeff's breath was grating horribly in his throat. He had Joe grasped by the wrists to keep those terrible claws from raking his face further. Jeff's body was turned desperately aside, protecting his belly from Joe's lethal hind toes. The animal was clearly regathering its strength and it panted hoarsely. Any second, Joe would regain his wind and explode into kicking action again.

What to do? What to *do*! Into my racing mind, a trivial thought: I've got my damned thongs on! What good can I do without boots?

I did the only thing that seemed feasible, given that my strength was as nothing compared to Joe's. I picked up his tail as close to the butt as I could and lifted. My notion was to destroy his tripod of strength. To a degree, it worked.

Joe began to move but he was off-balance. 'Hang on,' Jeff croaked. 'For Christ's sake, don't let go!'

We were both dragged across the yard as Joe tried furiously to shake us off. Desperate, we clung on. When we reached the opposite fence, we all three crashed into it and fell, facing the wire. Jeff contrived to land on top of Joe's shoulders, while I dropped onto his flank and lay with all my weight pressing him against the earth.

We all lay panting, getting our wind back. My mind was racing again, trying to think of a solution. It would be only a matter of seconds before Joe would start to struggle. Next time we would not be able to contain him.

I noticed that one of his hind toes had stuck through the pig mesh. If I could just secure it there . . . I reached up and unwound a tie-wire from the fence. With shaking fingers I twisted the wire around Joe's foot, hopefully binding it to the fence.

I muttered to Jeff what I was doing and he seemed to approve. I searched for another tie-wire within reach and managed to secure the other hind foot. Underneath us, Joe was heaving and uttering horrible, angry barks. We were both convinced that if he tried hard enough, nothing would hold him. But we hoped he might not realise this.

Jeff said: 'Run as quick as you can and get the rifle.'

This I did, while Jeff lay a few seconds longer, pinning Joe's shoulders, trying to summon enough strength to get himself up and running. When he managed to do this, we both expected Joe to burst free and get after us, like a demon of uncontrollable strength. But in fact we had temporarily immobilised him.

Jeff shot him cleanly through the head where he lay.

With blood running from slashes to his forehead and cheeks, his bleeding shoulders laid bare and only tatters of clothing left on him, he looked a wreck. But he was still on his feet.

'Have you got enough strength left for me to take a photo?' I asked.

He nodded. 'Go and get a camera,' he croaked.

In our family, we always remember the reporters' creed: as the boat sinks beneath you, as your plane plunges out of the sky, keep shooting. You may be finished, but your photos could make history.

So I photographed my battered mate. Then he began to shake. I helped him into the house where he went into shock. I sponged off his body where Joe's footprints were etched in red. For the next fortnight, layer after layer of bruising would rise to the surface. One of the scratching claws had come within a fraction of removing his eye – the standard tactic of fighting bucks. What was left of Jeff's clothing went into the rubbish bin.

After some nourishment and a nap, he began to feel more like himself, apart from being terribly stiff and deeply sore. We conducted a little postmortem on the event and concluded we had been incredibly lucky.

Jeff realised he had kidded himself, thinking he could manage the animal. Big Joe had only been playing when he attacked people on previous occasions. Once Joe was serious, no man would be a match for him. Jeff recalled how he had fallen down again and again under Joe's kicks. He had tried to run away but Joe was too fast for him. He had tried lying doggo, hoping Joe would lose interest, but the buck stomped all over him, would not let him alone until Jeff staggered up and engaged him, one on one, in the terrible embrace in which I'd found them. Jeff said he honestly believed he was done for; he had not meant to call me, thinking there would be nothing I could do against Big Joe, but the cry for help had been involuntary.

I shuddered to think of the children who visited our place. What if one of them had gone in with Big Joe? And what of Van and Connie that day? They were braver than they realised.

Why had Joe turned so nasty this time? We asked ourselves this repeatedly, until Jeff figured out a probable explanation. He had been wearing his old yard jumper, in which he often carried round the female 'roos. Their smell would have been strong on Jeff's clothing and this must have been why Joe suddenly saw him as a rival.

Before Goth and Van were due home from school, there was one thing we agreed we must do. I drove Jeff to Gerringong. We wanted farmer Alcock and his wife to see what Joe had done, so they would know that shooting him was inevitable.

They were completely understanding and terribly sorry that Jeff had suffered such a frightening experience. We left them to return to Foxground in time to pick up the boys as they got off the school bus. It was a cautionary tale we had to tell them – a lesson for us all.

Later, talking to old-timers round the district, we learned that what happened with Big Joe had been repeated elsewhere. The consensus was: never keep a fully grown buck as a pet. They become too dangerous. They always turn mean and, having no fear of humans, they ultimately vent their frustrations against a person, which results in them being condemned to death.

We vowed that we would never let this happen again. We would encourage bucks to go bush once they were old enough. And if their fate was the same as Thalos's, at least they'd be spared the even worse end of poor Big Joe.

Jeff and I had become a pretty efficient team by this time. Working the farm, *en famille* with the kids, outback on journalistic jobs, we knew how to cooperate and functioned like a well-oiled unit. Jeff was in charge of the dynamic planning and the tempo of the operation, but I expanded any project in ways which enhanced it artistically and humanely. Almost nothing was too intricate for my mind, while Jeff liked to deal simply with things. Deal and move on. Ever in my mind were images of the family, our friends both at Foxground and in Sydney, and in the countryside where I kept up correspondence with many of the people we had met while doing a story about their lives.

On long trips I used to try out ideas on Jeff, concocting theses based on what I'd been reading or on our encounters with new people and new environments, which was easy while covering the great distances of the Australian backblocks. I read aloud books like *The Red and The Black* and Patrick White's *The Tree of Man* and then set about analysing them. Sometimes Jeff would take part in my musings but often he listened and simply drove. At least I thought he listened. Later I suspected he shut off and concentrated on the task at hand. But at least my conversations – my monologues – helped keep him awake at the wheel. There was no question of my driving, not for years. Jeff's style was to do it all himself. And maybe he was right. Millions and millions of miles he drove, starting at dawn and finishing late into the night, and he never had an accident.

A mishap or two, yes. One occurred early in his freelancing career, out past Broken Hill on a station track where no traffic passed regularly. He had traded up from the Peugeot, which was stylish but expensive to maintain in those days, to a Holden station wagon, following Eric Worrell's lead by buying Australian product. However, on this occasion the vehicle had bogged in deep sand. It took Jeff all day under a hot sun to dig himself free. Chastened, he returned home with two firm resolutions. One, he would buy a four-wheel-drive vehicle and two, he would no longer travel out into remote areas alone.

Thus commenced our series of Land Rovers, and also my accompanying him several times a year on his longer trips. Once Jeff's parents retired and moved to Grays Point, they did not mind caring for Goth and Van for periods of ten days to two or three weeks, even a month, during our absences. The arrangement presented me with a dilemma. I did not enjoy being separated from our boys. Likewise, the doings of home, family, friends were ever in my mind and I ran through them like rosary beads as I sat beside Jeff over the long miles. Often at dusk we would pass rural houses where, as lights came on in windows and the smoke of dinner cooking and bath water heating rose above the roofs, I used to shed tears, lonely for my lads, our animals, the responsibilities and routines of our warm and loving homeplace which had given me what I had lacked in my childhood.

I kept my face averted, sensing Jeff would not appreciate my homesickness. I was glad that he relied on me, that he felt stronger and more whole with me beside him. The notion that he would take anyone else on those trips would have been a worry, had there been any prospect of it. As it happened, our kids were not yet old enough for the assistance he required and our male friends all worked at jobs which left them unavailable for the sort of expeditions undertaken by J Carter. Indeed, even then we knew that he was becoming a role model for his male readers who had neither the courage nor the freedom of movement that he enjoyed. I knew that it was my attitude to his career that permitted it to continue as it did, and so I put my own misgivings aside and took pride in accompanying him to places I would never have had the courage for without him.

Thus during my twenties and thirties, we built through our writings the myth of Jeff and Mare Carter, which one *Wheels* magazine cartoonist satirised into Jeff and Hoss Carter. I rode beside him *In The Tracks of the Cattle* and *In The Steps of The Explorers*, which became magazine articles and then two books published by Angus & Robertson. He researched the stock routes and also explorers' journals in the Mitchell Library before undertaking those journeys, and they made exciting projects. We formed life-lasting friendships with drovers, prospectors, the keepers of the Wild Dog Fence, all remote and resourceful people in lonely locations. *National Geographic* magazine asked him to produce hundreds of colour transparencies for their publication about Central Australia and this introduced me to the nation's heartland, which I still think of as my second home. When my mother decided to visit us unexpectedly, she had to wait with Doris and Percy at Grays Point until we had returned from Arnhem Land, another *National Geographic* assignment. (She didn't take to Australia, nor to our humble but, I thought, idyllic homelife and she stormed back to California suffering further disappointment with her wayward only daughter which persisted for years more.)

I had complete confidence in Jeff's abilities to carry off the complicated assignments he set himself. And I schooled myself to be as much help as possible. Jeff was born red and green deficient, a partial colour-blindness which might have handicapped a less determined photographer. I advised about hues which otherwise would have escaped his notice (and incidentally never wore reds or greens but always chose other earth colours, plus yellows and blues), and carried equipment, trudging back to the vehicle for more film or whatever he lacked. Gifted with the sort of personality people warm to, I smoothed his path socially (no effort and great fun for me) and also learned how to quickly create 'home' on the sheltered creekbeds Jeff chose for our campsites. We slept together as one wherever we landed and that was lovely for me, invigorating for him. On his fortieth birthday, we were in the Kimberleys. I had hidden some secret packages among our supplies and actually persuaded him to take an afternoon off to celebrate. The champagne I had brought never properly chilled in the tepid water of the Fitzroy but the tinned fruit cake looked festive under its porcupine coat of candles and the books I brought on improving your sex life gave us both a good laugh. Plus a few new ideas.

Of course, Jeff took pictures not only of his subjects but also of us covering them and this was more grist for his journalistic mill. He lived life through his lenses. Photography gave him vicarious encounters with people and places he could not comfortably cope with in those days. When the title *I Am A Camera* appeared in print, I thought it utterly apt for J Carter. My involvement with people and places was actual and I often longed for more time to pursue, to enjoy. But Jeff, once having captured his interests inside his camera, was ready to be off. To be on the move was what he liked best.

That and coming back home to our family, including the animals. Then he was into the darkroom, pounding his typewriter, immersed in the long and expensive process of turning where he'd been into good stories.

11

Snakes, indoors and out

In our rainforest paradise, reptiles were a fairly visible part of the animal community, which is not surprising given the large population of birds and small mammals. It was Eric Worrell who introduced me to wild snakes in the early 1950s when Jeff and I accompanied him on trips to the Darling and Murray rivers where he collected reptiles on behalf of the Commonwealth Serum Laboratories. Our friend taught me the important role reptiles play in any habitat. The trips also began my love affair with the Australian inland, very strange country for a girl from California.

I learned to control my fear on those safaris where the purpose was to *find* snakes, not avoid them. With lizards peeping out of his pockets and a sack of poisonous snakes over his back, Eric was so matter-of-fact as he handled potential killers that he inspired me to wear a brave front. So I was luckier than most novices when we moved to Foxground, arriving with a respectful tolerance for reptiles which was shared by the Carter offspring. Our farmer neighbours were surprised at our conservationist philosophy. They would go to any length and put themselves in some danger to kill a snake. Not just the rare serpent that turned up near their house but those in the fields and even in the remote bush. To neglect to despatch it was seen as an abrogation of a duty ages old. We often saw dead bodies draped triumphantly on the barbed wire fences along the roadside. Whether they were meant as a warning to other reptiles or a trophy for humans to applaud was something we could not fathom. Motorists made a point of running over snakes – red bellied blacksnakes, browns, tigers or whatever. We were the only folks we knew who dodged them.

The one snake farmers did admire was the one most often seen. The carpet snake, or diamond python, is a non-poisonous constrictor, useful for catching rodents which forever raid storehouses of grain. Unlike venomous species, pythons are slow to move out of the way of humans. Farmers often pick one up in the bush and bring it home as a mouse-catcher. The blacksmith told us he kept a big one in the little feed room adjoining his shed. Even Valda, his matter-of-fact bushy daughter, admitted to being startled when she went in for chicken feed and found it coiled comfortably on top of the sacks, staring at her.

A python was what we heard gliding within our ceiling, accompanied by squeaking from the mice which nested there. Talk about the call of the wild! Sometimes we'd sit in the living room and hear a drama going on overhead far more poignant than anything on television. Slither, slither, slither, shriek! When Jeff had new electric wiring put in, he found inside the lining boards several shed skins among the leaves and chewed paper of the rodents' nests. One skin was seven feet long, with a circumference as big as my arm.

In summer Goth and Van might look out the windows of their attic bedrooms and see a carpet snake stretched out on the iron roof, warming itself after emerging from under the eaves, its intricate pattern of scales highlighted by the sun. Rarely seen were the mice that scampered in and out regularly, but the sounds of their chasing and courting and fighting and tending their babies was ever present. The warm salty smell of their nests and the danger of fire within the weatherboard building was a worry we learned to live with. Although we tried to block off the gaps beneath the corrugated iron, our efforts were never completely effective so our ceiling was clearly a long-standing habitat for rats and mice and a happy hunting ground for pythons.

Although rodents regularly found ways into the actual house, making messes in the pantry and nests in cupboards, snakes rarely penetrated beyond the wall cavities. The first time I saw one indoors was when I danced into the bathroom and found a big python twined around the taps above the hand basin.

I danced straight back out again, like a character in one of those silent movies when the film was run in reverse.

'There's a good photo to be taken in the bathroom,' I informed my mate casually, trying not to go squeaky in the voice.

He came with his cameras and shot a sequence of pictures he would use in both magazine stories and books. 'Just go and stand in the picture,' he instructed.

As always, I obeyed and while he was absorbed in his art, I had a long, close look at a diamond python. It was watching me too. Which helped me master the involuntary shudder threatening to unsettle all my logic. Its eyes were taking me in, assessing whether or not I was a threat. The snake was ready to move off, as was I, but while I stood quite still, and while Jeff moved with his customary photographer's stealth, the creature stayed in place. It had simply come in the open window for a drink. And stayed to rest a while in our quaint little blue and white, old-fashioned washroom.

Another day I found a different, bigger python in the kitchen, stretched out casually along the plate rack behind the sink. This was during a dry spell so I reckoned thirst, once again, might have been the motive for entry. After filming the snake Jeff picked it up by the tail, slowly and carefully disengaging it from the crockery. It coiled around his forearm and began to climb toward his shoulder. Still holding its tail, he walked outdoors and put it down on the lawn. Thalos happened to be lying on the grass nearby and as the snake crawled past his nose and literally over his legs, Thalos paid it not one bit of notice. Which suggested to us that kangaroos don't see pythons as any sort of threat.

It could be a threat to a small unattended animal such as a joey, however, and we took great care to guard the orphans in our care following a ghastly event which occurred on our front verandah. One of our neighbours down in the valley was going away on holiday. Having heard we were good with animals, she asked if we would keep and feed her galah during her absence. It had belonged to her grandmother and thus knew her family for three generations – a very precious pet.

We were happy to oblige – it was just one more of many mouths to feed and water – so we stood its cage on the verandah near the kangararium, thinking it would be safe but happily exposed to balmy fresh air and a view of the trees through the flyscreens which enclosed the area. All was well for two weeks. On the morning the lass was due back to pick up her bird, I tripped happily out with its last breakfast at our place and received a terrible shock.

Inside the cage was a python. Its middle was swollen by a lump as big as your fist, there were literally pink feathers round its mouth and the bird had disappeared. The snake looked at me. I looked at it. The story was all too clear. I saw where the snake had entered by pushing under a loose section of wire mesh and then squeezed through the bars of the cage to get in. It was now too fat to get out.

I called the family balefully and we agonised over what to do. What could we do? We took the cage outside and left the door propped open. The snake decamped in its own good time. When the lass arrived, there was nothing for it but to tell the truth. I still feel shamed.

Living in an environment where reptiles play an active part, one of the most interesting things I witnessed was how pythons hunt, kill and eat. On at least three separate occasions, I was able to watch the entire process. The first time, I didn't understand what was going on.

One afternoon, I heard little birds scolding in the garden, an incessant chirping which usually means a snake is about. Around the lemon tree outside our kitchen door I found a whole congress of agitated finches piping and hopping above a diamond python which was making its way through the leafy foliage. In the dappled sunlight, its camouflage was immaculate.

The snake seemed totally absorbed in what it was doing and ignored the birds – and me – completely. Running from one low branch of the tree to another was a pole we had placed for Rodney J Watson, Goth's mudlark, to use on launching exercises. The snake positioned itself above the pole. Wrapping its tail around an upper branch, it lowered its head until it just touched the pole. Then the snake retracted its body, forming a figure S above the pole. After several trial runs it froze in this position and became almost invisible. The green and yellow design on its skin blended with the leaves and sunlight. The subtle curve of its body melded into the tracery of branches.

And so it remained for the rest of the day. The family and I kept peeping at it, speculating about its purpose until well into the evening. In the warm moonlight, its disguise was perfect. Then we realised what it was doing. Rats, mice and even possums used that pole to pass from the house to the garden. No doubt the snake could smell their trails and was waiting for an evening meal to gallop along, heedless of danger, until a fatal strike.

To leave the ambush in place did not present us with a dilemma. We were all convinced that non-intervention was best, even though it gave us frissons to guess what would ensue. Stoically we went inside to dine and did not see the end of that particular drama. But not long after, another such set-up occurred inside the Boys' Museum. This time a python positioned itself along a shelf among antique bottles. It lay as still as the wood and glass in grey-green shadows, waiting for the mice which ran along that ledge, their regular route. They plagued the feed room next door, scampered about leaving droppings among the museum exhibits, and often chewed or carried away the exhibit labels. The snake was lying in wait for its dinner. This time we were able to witness what occurred and Jeff actually took some pictures, although the light was too poor for clarity.

When a mouse ran along the shelf near the snake, it struck, snapping a coil around the little body. The strike was amazingly quick, given that pythons are usually such languid movers. The mouse twisted, looking for escape. The snake held it round its middle, using a loop just below its own head – what would have been its shoulders, if snakes had shoulders – and almost looked as if it were cuddling the tiny torso, until a wave of muscular contraction rippled along its body and crushed the poor little mouse to death. Then it began to eat.

You've probably seen photos of snakes with their jaws unhinged as they swallow down some prey. We had looked at them often, in magazines like *National Geographic*. But it is different when you observe the real event close up. The jaws come agape as if they are broken. Then the furry body, which moments ago was supple and alive, begins to move slowly, very slowly out of sight by means of muscle contractions in the snake's throat. It is an incredible system. The differences between snakes and animals with legs and grasping paws or hands become eerily obvious.

My third chance to observe the process occurred outside our

office next to the old dairy. There was a clump of vines and mint
growing against the stone foundations and under this was a tunnel
where mice had dug through the old mud mortar giving them
sweet access to typing paper, photographic negatives, correspondence from our wastebaskets – all the nesting material a colony of
mice could wish for. One afternoon, I noticed a diamond snake
lying in the shadow of the greenery.

As I watched, it allowed a mouse to run across its body twice.
In, then out its hole. Third time unlucky. With that amazingly fast
movement, a coil encircled and held the mouse. Although revolted
by what I knew would follow, I made myself watch. If I prided
myself on becoming a bushie and an observer of wildlife, then I
must take the bad with the good.

What follows a reptilian feast is also interesting. The bones and
fur not digested are regurgitated. After the snake itself has gone,
the resulting mound of white detritus tells the story of what has
happened, and is sometimes a welcome warning that one is about.
It looks quite arresting to watch the violent muscular contractions
the snake goes through to rid itself of indigestible material.

One day we had city visitors who were real greenhorns, bless
them, and what they had already seen of our country lifestyle had
made them eager to return to their concrete stamping ground.
Before they left, I served them hot tea with scones, homemade jam
and fresh farm cream to settle their nerves. Seated secure and
comfy in our blue and white farm kitchen, their faces suddenly
turned horrified again. They were facing the little window next to
our fireplace. Framed within its old-fashioned panes was a big
diamond snake just outside. It was hanging by its tail from a bit
of conduit, writhing and heaving in an alarming manner.

'Oh dear, it must be sick,' said the visitors, curiosity overcoming
their revulsion (the snake was, after all, safely outside the window,
which was closed).

As if to verify their diagnosis, the snake opened its mouth extra
wide and out poured a conglomeration of white matter, detritus
from an earlier meal. Our visitors lost interest in their afternoon
tea. Despite our explanation that what they had witnessed was a
normal occurrence but one which they were *extremely lucky* to
have seen, they up and left, never to return.

Most of our guests had more stamina, however. Whether

renting our holiday cottage or weekending with us in the house, they professed avid curiosity. Wildlife was what they had come to see and they were prepared to tramp miles in almost any weather to see it. Most visitors were apprehensive about encountering snakes, of course, and a few reckoned they had when probably they hadn't.

We tried to convince them that intermittent rustles in the bushes were almost certainly skinks, which are common and not a menace. Snakes move with a continuous slide. On the rare occasions when that is heard, it is prudent to mind where you step.

Jeff was always sceptical about reports of snakes, discounting them as imagination. There were a few genuine sightings, however. One poor friend tried to rouse our interest in a blacksnake she said she had seen amongst our rose bushes in the front garden. Jeff was disdainful to the point of rudeness and even I reassured her that she probably must have seen the tail of a lizard. A week or so later, I noticed a big blacksnake crawling among the roses. A whopper. At my approach, it calmly went up the stone wall and left the garden, crossing the road and heading down the gully toward the creek. Just as if it used that route every day. It probably did!

Now, we had a couple of rules to guard against treading on a snake, which we passed on to all our visitors: walk heavily and never step into long grass or undergrowth where you can't see what is there. Venomous snakes – in our area, anyhow – tend to keep out of the way of humans. They will go to any lengths to avoid you, in fact. But if caught short, they will hide themselves and then keep very still until you pass. Lacking ears, they 'hear' by feeling vibrations along the ground.

Our second rule was to always wear boots or shoes when going into the paddock. Never thongs. Vandal used to flaunt that one until he trod on the tail of a big blacksnake out near the chicken's pen. Yes, he was wearing thongs. Luckily the snake was too intent on getting away to bite. Van was equally busy trying to head off in the opposite direction. He said there seemed an awful eternity before he could shift his balance from the foot pinning the snake and get going. After that, he was better at remembering to leave his thongs on the back verandah and slip on his boots when heading for long grass.

That chicken pen was where I once surprised a hidden black-snake. The memory still makes me feel slightly sick. One of our hens was sitting on eggs. The lads were at school, Jeff was not at home, and I couldn't resist tiptoeing up to the chicken house to see if there was cheep-cheeping under the hen. All was silence, however, and she eyed me crossly. I left her to her job. When I returned in an hour for another peek, I saw the mother had left the clutch unattended for a few minutes. It looked as if there were fewer eggs than last time I had seen them. Sometimes one rolled out by accident or by some system of the hen's to cull her clutch. Curious, I lifted the nesting box to look underneath. To my horror, there was a blacksnake coiled up beneath it.

Quickly I lowered the box and left the hen house. With relief, I saw the hen returning to sit. When I calmed down, I knew she would have no way of protecting her eggs or hatchlings. The vision of a black head sliding out from under that box and questing beneath her feathers kept playing in my mind like a horror film. Equally revolting was the thought of how cosy the snake must feel curled beneath the hen's warm nest. Being cold blooded, warmth is essential for them.

What to do? Should I wait for Jeff to come home? It would be after dark by then, too late. Would I leave it at least until the boys returned from school? What? And expose them to getting bitten? Do and say nothing, and let nature take its course? The dilemma filled my next hour. I knew I wasn't brave enough to kill the snake with a hoe or shovel as the men would have, but I couldn't leave the mother hen in such peril. At least I could remove the nesting box to a safer site. So I put on trousers and thick socks, got the brush hook and, feeling very shaky, returned to the chicken house. I gave myself a pep talk, grasped the nesting box as near to the top as possible and lifted. The hen gabbled at me angrily. The space beneath her nest was empty. The snake had gone.

Although I wasn't willing to abandon our baby chicks to preda-tion, I tried not to interfere among the native population. We accepted that the quest for food resulted daily in murder outside our garden fence. Within, the same rules had to apply if we were serious about our principles, which were tilting more and more toward letting 'nature' balance its own books. However, there was one time when my resolve slipped.

One quiet spring day around noon, when Goth and Van were at school and Jeff was away, I heard the alarm piping of little birds. Following the sound, I came out the back door and round the house to the chimney where, in a crack between its stone blocks, a clump of tiny daisies grew. There was a blue wrens' nest hidden within.

Blue wrens are everybody's favourites, because of the males' vivid indigo markings, the cheeky uplifted tails of both genders, and their reeling musical song. Their intricate, dome-shaped nests have a side entrance, and I had been aware of this one for a few days, lucky enough on my way to the toilet to hear the clamour of babies as mother or father brought them insects. This ruckus had nothing to do with feeding, however. This was danger.

Sure enough, at the base of the chimney was a young diamond snake, svelte, about five feet long. Its head roved about, sensor tongue questing, then it began to glide up the stone wall toward the daisies while the parent birds peeped and piped futilely overhead.

This time I reacted instinctively. To hell with principles. Grabbing the hose coiled nearby, I turned the tap on full and directed a stream of water at the snake. It recoiled sideways for a moment, swaying to try and avoid the shower. Neither hurt nor even annoyed, it was clearly puzzled by the horizontal rain. However, it was reluctant to abandon its hunt. I came closer, screwed down the sprinkler head to its finest jet and really peppered that reptile. It ignored the hose jet and pushed on up the wall, its nose probing among the clump of flowers for its quarry. My maternal instinct was right out of control now, so I did what I had never done before. I picked up the snake by its tail and, holding it at arm's length, shoulder high, carried it across the garden, putting it down in the big rockery in the corner. It quickly crawled forward and disappeared among the plants. Within a minute, the birds had quietened. I knew I could not protect them always, had only saved the babies this time by chance, but I hoped they were nearly old enough to fly and thus might escape before the snake returned for another try.

Our little outdoor toilet was the scene of several snake encounters. It was just a few yards from the house, set amongst citrus trees, hydrangeas and bulbs, a pleasant place to sit and rest, cogitate and, sometimes, to read. I kept a little wooden box there on the floor to hold copies of newspapers and magazines for the pleasure of family and visitors alike. One day Goth took up a *Sydney Morning Herald* and uncovered a fat blacksnake dozing amongst the media. It was a race to see who could leave the building first.

One warm evening I tripped outside and down the little path, not looking where I was walking. Yes, I had broken Rule Two and was wearing thongs, since it was only a few steps from the house. In a way Rule One as well, because my attention was distracted. My mind dwelt on where I was going to sit. This was because a frog had taken up residence in the crease round the top of the toilet bowl. A most unpleasant place to settle, I would have thought, but nonetheless, there he sometimes was. If you didn't watch out for him, he would get washed into the maelstrom when you flushed, clutching desperately at the porcelain sides with his little suckered feet. It gave one a dreadful feeling, so I tried to scout before I sat, and if he was there, lift him out with a stick.

So, concentrating on this, I failed to see a young blacksnake stretched across the doorsill, as straight and motionless as a crack in the wood. I must have stepped right over it. The frog was absent so I sat down and then noticed the snake. It was frozen, very aware of my presence, watching to see what I would do. He was only a baby but I didn't fancy letting him nip my bare toe. I was hurriedly winding up my business when one of the dogs came sniffing and wagging down the path, just to share the balmy moonlight with me. His arrival activated the snake. I kicked out at the dog, shedding a thong, then made one of those extraordinary leaps seen only in fairy tales or comic books – or when jumping over snakes in the toilet doorway.

No harm done, but it reminded me to be more watchful in future. Goth had a similar experience one moonlit night when he nearly trod on a reptile stretched across the path to the toilet. Like me, he had just nipped out for a quick one before bed. It was only a carpet python but it prompted formation of Rule Three. Never go outside at night during the warm months without a torch or turning on the spotlight above the back door.

It was red-bellied blacksnakes that put me off Wallaby Hill. One afternoon in jam-making season, I climbed the steep slope and scrambled over the stone wall which separates our property from the one next door. The land was unoccupied, a disused dry run, and its paddocks had gone back, gradually filling with tussocks and big clumps of blackberry bushes. I headed for the area where last year the fruit had been growing thickest, swinging my bucket and musing on how good life feels with the sun warming your back and nothing to hear but birds and wind rustling the tree-tops, when my attention was caught by the sight of tails withdrawing into the tussocks. Not just one or two, but dozens of them. Every darned tussock seemed to have a blacksnake hiding in it. Yikes!

I skipped back to the wall, dodging those tussocks with an agility not usual for me. Like will-o'-the-wisp, I jumped, hopped, literally flew across that ground. As I clambered back over the boundary wall my brain was picturing reptiles hiding within its crevices, and recalling cautionary advice about taking care when stepping over a log (or stone wall) lest something lurks on the opposite side. Totally paranoid by now, I recall uttering one of those expedient prayers that bubble up surprisingly in times of crisis. 'Please, just get me out of this and I'll never come over here again.'

I never did. But I didn't talk much about the reason for my aversion, nor my rout that day. Without seeing what I saw, the family would have said I'd gone silly, imagining more than was there. Jeff, as I said, was always sceptical about snake sightings. Except his own. He often saw blacksnakes and occasionally a brown when he went brush-hooking or shifting the cattle up the back of the property. He just let them go their own way.

Eric Worrell always said the majority of people who get bitten are those trying to catch or kill. Given an opportunity to escape, reptiles will take that option, in our area at least. However, it is worth pondering what their chosen direction might be, and going the opposite way. If the snake keeps coming toward you, it will probably be because you are standing near its home where, perhaps, it has eggs or babies. It will not be coming to attack you, as such, if you leave it alone. Snakes don't eat people and biting them is more trouble than it is worth, two bits of logic which most people don't consider when they see a snake. Backwards or sideways is the best way to go – and mind where you step.

One of Jeff's favourite snake sightings occurred when he heard a weird, wild shriek coming from a huge clump of blackberries. He got down on his hands and knees to peer inside. A really big python was throttling the life out of a rabbit kitten. Jeff did not interfere.

His least happy encounter was inside our office. One hot summer midday, he left the door open to catch a breeze and was kneeling on the floor studying maps when Jim encountered a brown snake just outside. Jim barked and charged, chasing it through the door. That snake was hot, it was cranky, and very active. Jeff stamped heavily on the cement floor, thinking to deter it from penetrating further, which usually works but this time Jim was blocking its retreat. Jeff shouted fiercely and sent Jim packing. The snake turned to Jeff, who leapt onto a workbench. The snake followed, slipping up the flat surface as smoothly as butter and faster than Jeff could accommodate. He scrambled across a filing cabinet and jumped for the door. While he went to get a shovel, he saw the snake glide outside and head off, still moving quickly and aggressively. Jeff shut the office door. Forget about fresh air.

Jeff's scepticism about other people's snake encounters could be annoying sometimes. Like the night I danced out across the grass to our back gate. It was full moon and everything had that enchanted silvery look. Dew sparkled like rhinestones on the lawn. It was about two o'clock in the morning and I was in my nightie with bare feet, having woken from sleep with an impulse to see if friends had arrived safely down at the cottage. If so, I should be able to see moonlight glinting on their car. Craning, I realised I needed a wee so I pulled up my nightie and squatted down. Near me, I heard a distinct *huff*.

There was a death adder, poised close to my bare feet in the striking position. Adders are quite distinctive, with broad heads and a weeny upright tip on their fat tails. I took this in, also recalling that adders are nocturnal, and saw that the snake was between me and the grain shed, where it might well have been 'caught short' on a mouse hunt by my sudden quiet arrival. One of those big intakes of information within a few seconds.

Light and quick as a fairy, I dropped my nightgown and danced back indoors. Then I made yet another resolution about torches and footgear. *Then* I wondered if I had been dreaming. Back in bed, I pondered it. No, what I had seen was real. My dew-damp tootsies validated it.

Next morning, Jeff pooh-poohed my experience. There weren't any adders in our district, he stated. Only after I asked some of the long-term farmers did I learn that adders had been seen, but rarely, usually only at night.

Jeff was equally adamant that since tiger snakes thrived in the dry regions, there would be none in subtropically humid Foxground. For some time farmers had been saying that they were sighting tigers in their paddocks and attributed that to the big, bad bushfire which had burned out the heathland on the escarpment behind us. Having moved down from their natural habitat to escape the flames, some tiger snakes stayed on. Jeff remained sceptical until the day one came boiling out from under his vehicle parked just outside our gate. It nearly crawled over Jeff's boot before shooting away down the gully. Jeff grudgingly changed his tune after that.

They reckon it was a tiger snake that bit the little boy at Barren Ground Reserve. It is a hanging swamp, the watershed for our creeks and others feeding the Shoalhaven River system and a perfect habitat of heathland flora and fauna, including two rare birds – the ground parrot and the bristlebird. Part of the National Parks and Wildlife chain of sanctuaries, Barren Ground is staffed by a ranger and visited by many student groups as well as other people keen on birds and wildflowers.

The lad was part of a school excursion, but he was mucking about. Playing chasings, the boy leapt blindly into a thick clump of bush to avoid being tagged. A venomous snake was hiding there and it bit him. Sad to say, before he could be transported the long distance to Kiama hospital, he died.

So remember the rules. Not only look before you leap but don't leap at all unless you can see where you are stepping. That poor snake was doing its best to avoid those people. It just wasn't given the chance it deserved to escape them.

Interestingly enough, that one child is the only fatality I ever heard about in our district, where people have been bush workers for generations. All farmers spin yarns about near-misses and most families have one or two tales to tell about snakes behind the fridge or wrapped around the dunny. But actual snakebites are rare.

One of our bulls was bitten while scrambling up a gully. We found him dead with not a mark on him, except for a big black bruise on his chest. Neighbours looked it up in their home veterinary manual and said it sounded like snakebite. The gully was a shortcut from the creek where we often saw a big red-bellied blacksnake sunning itself. It was just bad luck that our big robust beast trod on it.

Some years on, a teenage lad was bitten at Wild Country Park. We had a few harrowing escapes there, but I'll save them for later.

12

William, our first wombat

A lady rang who had read an article of mine in the *Women's Weekly* about our kangaroos. She wondered if we would like a try at a different sort of marsupial. She wanted to give us a wombat.

Well, she didn't really want to part with it. It had lived with her family for about a year. Before that, it had been reared by a friend who'd found it in the pouch of its dead mother. The baby had been only four inches long. Now the wombat was adolescent, totally people-oriented, a much loved household member.

The reason the caller had to find it a new home was the arrival of another baby, a human one. This created a conflict of interest in their house. The human child wasn't fussy, but the wombat was jealous of the intruder who also drank milk, cried to be picked up and slept in places nature had clearly intended for wombats. The wombat kept trying to evict the new baby from its nursery furniture!

Her story sounded fun and we decided to accept the wombat. The afternoon it arrived, I saw it was clearly a strong favourite of the woman and her ten-year-old daughter. Before they even came indoors, they began listing its escapades with such affection and good humour that they seemed to be saying, 'For two pins, we'd give up the baby and keep the wombat.'

The wombat's name was William. He was asleep upside down

in the daughter's arms while the lady held her infant. When the girl passed the animal to me, it woke up and tried to bite me. Here's a test, I thought. I recalled reading that you must win the first battle with a new animal or all is lost. So I grasped the wombat very firmly around his stubby front legs and, although he struggled mightily, I did not give in. After a minute or two, the wombat relaxed and went back to sleep. The woman and her daughter smiled.

'He likes you,' they said.

He was a solid little character, as nuggety as a baby rhinoceros and much more bristly than a kangaroo. His paws and anvil-shaped nose seemed gross in comparison to the delicate animals we were used to. William was heavy as well. 'He weighs thirty pounds,' his owners told me proudly. 'But of course, he's not full-grown yet.' No wonder I was beginning to wilt.

'Oh, put him down,' they urged. 'He'll be all right.'

As I turned him over and set him carefully on the grass, William woke up again. He stood on three legs like a statue, his front paw raised, his fat triangles of ears pricked, his battering ram nose lifted slightly as if to catch the smells of this new place and filter them through the intelligence system in his gross little skull. Then he lowered his head and began to eat grass. It seemed a promising beginning. He ate steadily and without concern for anything but consuming as many blades as possible, a stolid little mowing machine. How different from the nervy kangaroos we were used to.

We stood chatting beside him in the back yard while William steadily cropped the lawn around our feet. His owners had dozens of amusing William stories to relate. All centred on destruction. They used verbs like bash, batter, tip up, knock down. It occurred to me we might be taking on a batch of problems. But I was already too intrigued to quit.

Suddenly, William flattened out and waggled his bony backside provocatively at the daughter. 'Oh oh,' she chortled and began to skip around the yard. William followed. One minute he was a stolid, lumpish grass-gutser, the next he was a fast-moving, coquettish leaper. Yes, he leapt. He reared back on his stubby hind legs and projected himself forward almost his whole length, landing on his short front paws. It was an amazing action. The wombat looked about as articulated as a stone. Yet he was agile as could be!

As the daughter squealed and galloped, her mother laughed, ready to dodge the little grey body charging about our back lawn.

'It's his romping hour,' she said indulgently.

Encumbered as she was with her infant, it seemed only sensible for her to move toward the gate, out of reach of the hijinks. I opened it for her, then shut it quickly behind her as William charged up and crashed into the metal and wire. It shook under my hand like a mini earthquake.

The next minute I found myself sidestepping, hopping and whooping, until I reached down and grabbed William firmly round his barrel body and swung him up into my arms. I turned him on his back and he subsided with a huge sigh.

I felt proud of myself. I must have a real aptitude for wombats, I thought. As I congratulated myself, the daughter slipped out the gate. Farewells were brief. With an alacrity I couldn't fail to notice, the donors of William drove away.

As they left, Jeff arrived with Goth and Vandal, whom he had picked up at the school bus stop. 'Look, look, we've got a wombat,' I greeted them.

They crowded round to see and thus began what might be called our Wombat Period. It lasted fifteen years. And long after that.

The first few days we underwent a crash course in wombat management. Note the adjective. Left alone with him, we carried Will indoors and, putting him down on the kitchen floor, offered him some of the food his owners had left for him. It was kibbled dog food. William began to crunch his way through it with no sign of nervousness. That seemed a good sign.

When he had eaten his fill, he toddled across to the nearest pair of feet, sank down with a loud sigh and went to sleep. Well, he'll be no trouble, we thought. Wrong.

As soon as the owner of the feet got up and moved off, William awakened and trotted after them. He would not settle until he had a pair of feet to snuggle between.

It was the hour for chores. Jeff needed to attend to the cattle, I had chooks to feed and the 'roos, Goth and Van had homework. Who could spare the time to stand, or sit, with the wombat? It was the first of many hundreds of times that question would be posed in our household.

We answered it then as we answered it forever after. Someone rearranged their activity to fit in with the animal. One of the lads brought his school assignment down to the kitchen table and did it while the wombat squatted between his feet. When my outdoor work was completed and I came in to prepare dinner, I inherited the wombat. It was difficult moving from sink to fridge to stove with an anxious creature dogging your footsteps. If I moved too quickly, William uttered a funny little 'meep'. Or put his front paw on my foot, as if to pin me down to one spot.

When Jeff came indoors for the evening, he took over the job of wombat minding. Seated in his customary spot at the head of the kitchen table before the fireplace, William settled between his big boots, utterly content. Jeff read the paper, we chatted, I prepared and served the meal, Goth and Van came in and sat at the table, William slumbered unconcerned. As long as the boots stayed put, he dozed, oblivious. But once Jeff moved off the spot, William became instantly awake and ready to follow.

We were totally captivated by our new furry friend. When he stood up, he looked so funny from behind. His little legs were bandy and his hind feet turned in. This pigeon-toed stance was accentuated by the shape of his narrow back feet, which were quite different from his front ones. Also, his tail seemed a vestigial relic of some once useful, now redundant appendage. It was hairless, round and smooth, about as long as the last segment of my baby finger.

After dinner we adjourned to the living room. William came too. Jeff put on a record – we were engrossed in Beatles enthusiasm then – and the boys and I seated ourselves on the couch to listen. Next minute, William leapt up beside us. What a feat! This animal, the size and shape of a watermelon and apparently no more agile than one, managed to catapult itself up twice its own height. It was the equivalent of a fat person making a standing jump of twelve or fourteen feet. Upwards.

Once beside us, William systematically went the length of the couch, rooting out the cushions and raking them off onto the floor. It was no trouble to him to walk across our laps or push behind our backs. When he had tidied up the sofa, he settled down to sleep with his head on Goth's knee.

After an hour or so of music, we returned to the kitchen for our bedtime cocoa, standard evening routine. No need to lift William onto the floor. He awakened with a start and leapt like a porcupine diving off a cliff. Plonk. He landed on his feet and galloped after us down the hall. Slipping away to bed was going to be a problem, we could see. How much of a problem we never imagined. Ever optimistic, and totally capitivated by William despite his compulsive ways, we knew we'd figure out a system.

Our first idea was to bank cushions round William and then for each of us in turn to sneak quietly out of the kitchen while he slept. The last person would turn off the light and leave William on his own. One by one we departed, silent, systematic as a well-drilled squad of fighter pilots.

Within five minutes, William was awake and pounding up and down the length of the house, searching for us with such plaintive 'meeping' that we all gathered again to soothe our boy and make a new plan.

Jeff had removed his boots and was now in bedroom slippers. I got the empty boots and gestured to Van, between whose feet William was now sleeping. Gently he withdrew first one foot and then the other, while I substituted the empty boots. Between them, William continued to slumber. Stage One of Plan Two completed. O-kay.

Goth, the jokester, picked up two orange draught-stoppers and stuck one in each boot. They looked like a pair of knock-kneed legs in orange stockings. We thought we had invented a perfect wombat minder.

Stifling giggles, we tiptoed off to bed again, this time leaving the kitchen light on but shutting the doors leading off the side verandah to the front of the house and the door to our bedroom. Unfortunately I did not quite secure our bedroom door, which was warped. Will burst it open with no trouble. Jeff and I lay rigid in the dark, hoping William would not realise that we were there, high above him in our old brass bed. For a minute, William stood still, apparently listening and sniffing the air. Then we heard him trot out of the bedroom. His claws clicked across the kitchen lino. More silence. Then he click-clicked back, entered the bedroom and, without a pause, jumped up onto our bed!

Another extraordinary leap! We put on the bedside light, got up, carried him out, went throught the boots routine again. When

William nodded off, we returned to our bedroom, shutting the sticky door tightly. We were just settling down when we heard a terrible thudding and scratching outside our door, interspersed with screams of obvious anger. Wearily we rose to formulate Plan Three.

We did not solve the problem that night. We simply grew so weary as the hours passed that we locked ourselves in our bedroom and put up with the commotion William was making in the back part of the house. We slept through it, in the finish.

We awakened at first light, however. Only the usual morning symphony of birds and insects could be heard. The house had become silent. Maybe William had settled down well.

He was settled, all right, trapped amongst the chaos of our bathroom. He had tipped over the chair, screwed up the rug, dragged towels off the racks and upended the laundry basket. Having chewing its wicker lid and rim to shreds, William burrowed into the contents and fell asleep. Debris jammed the door shut, making William a prisoner of terry towelling and soiled clothes.

Along the verandah leading to the bathroom was chaos also. Everything that could be turned over had been. Magazines dragged off shelves had been chewed, a wastebasket ditto. The entire back part of the house looked a wreck.

I left the scene as we found it until Goth and Van came down, otherwise they would never have believed it possible. They thought it was a great joke, of course, but Jeff was not amused. While he drank a cup of tea, he considered the problem. This gave William what he'd been wanting – a pair of feet to sleep between. He sank down in innocent content.

'Bring me my boots,' Jeff ordered grimly.

Van obliged his father. Jeff tiptoed away as Van positioned the boots on either side of Will and patted him gently to keep him asleep. In a few moments, Jeff returned from outside with hammer, three-inch nails and planks. He began to nail them across the doorway leading from the kitchen to the side verandah. The hammering sounded like gunshots but Will slept undisturbed, soothed by Van's presence.

When we first moved in, Jeff took away the door which used to close off the kitchen from that verandah and the rest of the farmhouse. 'We'll never need a door there,' he said at the time. Now we had a barrier about kneehigh.

'But, Dad, how are *we* going to get in and out of the kitchen?' Goth asked with just a hint of impishness.

'We'll just have to step over,' Jeff said firmly.

'I hope we don't forget,' Van said dubiously.

'It's only for a week or so until William gets used to the place. Then he can stay outside at night,' Jeff replied testily. 'We won't forget.'

So guess who forgot first and tripped over the barricade? Its creator, running to answer the telephone. But that's another story.

That first morning, we took William outside. He ate some grass, then he stepped delicately into a bush and stayed there secretively for about three minutes.

'I think he's going to the toilet,' Van reported.

It was information I was pleased to receive. His owners had assured me William would not urinate or defecate in the house. With all the other sorts of mess he was capable of making, it would have been too much had they been wrong. I returned to the house to clean up the debris.

With his morning business completed, William came out full of play. He waggled his rump invitingly at the lads. The next moment, he was chasing them round and round the back yard. They loved it and so did he. When he couldn't keep up with them, he leapt across the distance separating them, to narrow the gap.

If he couldn't quite catch them, neither could they stop running. They dodged around the house. William followed. You could hear their footsteps pounding over the grass. Round they all went, once, twice, until finally Goth and Van dived in the screen door of the kitchen, exhausted by running and laughing. I looked out the window and saw William poised at the door, his head cocked, ears up and listening. He looked bereft. I moved to open the door for him, but there was no need. Up went his stubby front paw and, very efficiently, he raked at the screen door. It flew open and he scampered inside.

'Oh no!' Goth and Van said.

But William wanted only to sleep. They banked him round with cushions and one of the towels he'd screwed up in the bathroom. Thus he slumbered for a while lulled, I suppose, by our voices, our comings and goings in the kitchen as we got on with our morning routines.

It was a Saturday. The members of the Foxground Boys' Museum began to arrive for their meeting. They were delighted by the wombat. It was recorded in their minute book how he overshadowed their business that day. As they sat round the table, William went from chair to chair and stood on his hind legs, trying to clamber up. The boys giggled. Finding one chair vacant, William efficiently raked off its cushion onto the floor. He began to hammer it with his nose. Bonk, bonk, bonk. The boys hooted with laughter. Then William wrapped his stubby legs around the pillow and clutched it to his belly, rocking with it. More laughter as boys twinkled at each other knowingly. I suggested they wind up their meeting and take the animal outside.

Outdoors, William had plenty of willing feet to chase. It was obvious the boys responded to this young animal's warrior-play. Like their reaction to jousting kangaroos, it excited their own instincts. One problem was Jim. He regarded the wombat with real distaste. Perhaps it was William's smell. Or maybe because he walked on four feet instead of hopping on two. Jim tried to keep out of the newcomer's orbit but William was willing to be friends. Or rather, he didn't bother to deviate from a chosen path just because it happened to cross Jim's. We hovered about, warning the dogs not to mix it with the wombat. Jim retreated further, but it didn't sit well with him to do so. He sulked.

Laika, as usual, simply kept out of William's road. When she did encounter him, she quickened her step, ears and tail lowered. She wanted nothing to do with him. Neither did the chickens. They scattered as he lumbered across the yard. The kangaroos likewise.

That evening, as on most Saturday nights, we went to the pictures at Gerringong. They were screened in a solid little town hall which sat on the main street overlooking the ocean. It was elegant at night, a spotlight illuminating the shire coat of arms above the door. Inside, the lighted foyer beamed an invitation to neighbourliness as well as entertainment. Movie-goers drove from as far away as Jamberoo, which also ran a picture bus, small and rattly, for youngsters and folks reluctant to drive over the mountain at night.

When the south-easterly blew off the sea, it was a struggle to mount those town hall steps but once inside, it was cheerful and cosy. You bought your tickets from Councillor Waghorn, who held the cinema franchise, quickly exchanged greetings with his wife at the door to the hall where temporary chairs were set up each week, then you were escorted to a seat by their daughter, if required. It was a family show.

Not everyone was as keen on the actual films as we were. It was the outing that mattered for many. Screenings always included a cartoon and at least one 'action' movie to please the farm kids out for a weekly play-up. Dialogue didn't interest them and they shouted, hooted and booed through it, much to our disgust. Less raucous but more intrusive was their boredom if the companion feature was a love story or a drama. They chatted and threw lollies across the rows, until Mrs Waghorn came with her flash-light, warning and occasionally evicting.

During intermission, everyone trekked up the street to the shop, which stayed open late to accommodate a rush for lollies, ice creams, hot pies and sausage rolls. The shop belonged to another established Gerringong family, who lived in an adjoining house. Dim and spartan by day, the shop was transformed on Saturday nights as picture-goers clamoured for a turn at the milkbar counter, eager to get back before the second feature began. Significant money changed hands at the shop on Saturday evenings.

When we returned from the pictures that night, the silence within the house was palpable. As we unlocked the kitchen door and went inside, we sensed a frightened presence, poised in some dark corner, listening, trying to assess what danger was coming for it.

'William?' we called.

'It's all right, Will, it's only us –'

The held breath was released and in a rush William came galloping from our bedroom, anxiously meeping, his claws scrabbling across the lino until he literally leapt into Van's arms. Goth and Jeff crowded round to pat him and speak soothingly – part of our conditioning program to help him associate us with safety – while I followed Will's trail into our bedroom. We had left the door closed when we went out, and in front of it. I had made a temporary barricade of cardboard cartons, piling in everything of weight I could find – ten pounds of potatoes, a Sydney telephone book and so on.

The cartons had been shoved aside, tipped up and rummaged in. Among the debris were several half-chewed potatoes and a well-chewed phone book. The bedroom door had been burst open, more a fluke than any special skill of William's, I guessed, and inside was a horrible sight. Somehow William had overturned the heavy nightstand beside the bed. Books, tissues, lamp, doily, all lay mangled together on the floor. The table had an opening cupboard at the bottom. This was agape and William had raked out the papers inside, which I had been storing for future reference. They were chewed and crumpled so badly that they were fit only for the wastebasket. Well, that was one quick way to clean out a chaotic cupboard!

We bedded William carefully in the kitchen, amongst boots and cushions. After his busy night during our absence, he seemed ready for a sleep. We felt the same so, leaving the mess for tomorrow, we secured the bedroom door, hoping fervently Will would not disturb our rest that night. Those early days, we assumed William's body clock would have adjusted to human time. Wrong. As often happened, until we learned more.

In fact, he did not scratch at our door. We all awakened refreshed and entered the quiet kitchen believing that the worst was over. We were wrong. Actually, the worst was still to come. Although our wombat was innocently asleep on his nest of cushions, he had been up, and busy, during the dark hours.

In the pantry, flour, rice and sugar mingled with their chewed packets on the floor. They had been stored in metal bread bins which I thought would be wombat-proof, having removed other more obviously vulnerable items from the lower shelves. That was an early lesson. Almost nothing on earth is wombat-proof, if the animal wants to get in. Other lessons would follow.

'Right,' said Jeff grimly. He stormed out and returned with more planks and heavy nails. Bang, bang, bang, up went another barricade, across the pantry doorsill this time. The kitchen was becoming an obstacle course.

Clearly William's most pressing need was for human company. Soon, we hoped, he would switch to his own kind. But for now, he would not, could not leave us alone. That afternoon being Sunday, he found plenty of minders. The visitors to the Boys' Museum received a bonus, a carefully supervised cuddle of

William. The boys were thrilled to have him to show, their guests were equally thrilled with what was, for many, their first and, for the rest, their closest look at a live wombat.

After tea when we were alone *en famille* again, we adjourned to the living room for music time. Jeff was holding William on his lap. He began to jig to the beat and William loved it! He sat like a fat furry Buddha, bouncing up and down on Jeff's knees. A jazz bear.

Jeff got up and began to dance. He held William against his shoulder, the way you do with a baby, and circled, stomped, swung. Gradually Will's eyes drooped and he dozed off.

'Whacko,' said Jeff, 'here's a new way to tire him out and get him to sleep.' He danced out to the kitchen and bedded Will among cushions inside a cardboard box. Then we all slipped away to bed.

By midnight, William was awake and ready for action. He meeped outside our bedroom door for a while. We lay doggo inside. William began to systematically overturn the chairs. Bang, crash, crack. Then he started pushing them along the lino. Bump, thump, slither. Wearily I got up and went out to see if he wanted food.

His bowl and water dish were full. We had begun to supplement his canine kibble with carrot, apple, oats and lettuce. They did not tempt him much. Too weary to worry about it, I got out dog biscuits, one thing we knew he did like, even if we did not think them appropriate food for him. William settled down on his haunches to crunch his way stolidly through the lot.

I sneaked away and climbed back into bed. Later we heard Will bumping and meeping outside our door but he did not persist. Soon a blissful silence reigned, and we assumed he had gone back to sleep.

We were wrong!

When I came out early the next morning, I saw how William had spent the wee small hours. He had been just outside our bedroom door, chewing a hole in the lino a metre square! The floor covering we had chosen for our kitchen was thick, of a Delft blue that matched the antique platter and cheese dish standing on our kitchen dresser, gifts from Jeff's parents. That lino had been expensive but we figured it would last for twenty years. Now, after less than half that time, there was this huge unsightly scar!

'That does it!' Jeff said. And went off to build a wombatarium.

After Goth and Van left for school, I squared up the chewed linoleum and swept away the debris. Then I went to search through the offcuts from the original laying, hoping to find a piece large enough to cover the wound. There was one but it was now darker than the rest, which had faded from light and scrubbings. We were stuck with a dark patch outside our bedroom door, a reminder of William, who taught me that night a lesson about animals and their potential for destruction if ignored. There are very few shortcuts in wild animal care.

I finished my repairs about the same time Jeff completed his wombat holding area. It joined onto the slab wall of the old dairy, facing into our back yard. The ground surface was boulders bedded in earth – the place where docile dairy cows used to emerge after being milked. Around this, Jeff built a stout paling fence.

It didn't look like a yard a wombat could dig out of or chew its way through. Yet it was very pleasant. Clematis covered a trellis overhead. Sweet grasses grew up between the cobbles. Jeff put in a forty-four gallon drum on its side, with one end cut out. He lined this with hessian sacks, old cushions and woollen jumpers. A chaff bag hung over the opening.

When introduced to his artificial burrow, William went inside at once. After rummaging through the contents, he wrapped his legs tightly around a cushion, put his head under a jumper, and with a vast sigh went into a long and contented sleep.

Jeff and I looked at each other with relief. This looked like a solution to the problem at hand, which was to contain William until he grew familiar enough with this new environment to live naturally in it. We had no idea at that stage how long William would want to stay with us. We thought he was about eighteen months old and we reasoned he should be able to cope on his own fairly soon.

As it turned out, he was most reluctant to abandon human company. Perhaps this was because of the affectionate care he had received from his first foster families. It would be almost a year before he wanted to branch out alone into wider territory. But at least, after those initial frantic days, Will settled into a more placid and less destructive routine at Glenrock Farm.

13

Our bountiful years – the sixties

W hen Eric Worrell learned we once again lacked a stud male for our little band of female kangaroos, he thought he could solve a problem for us and himself. Blind Bruce had lived at the Reptile Park since he was a youngster. He lived a sheltered life in company with other rescued kangaroos, but as the number of visitors increased, Bruce was put in an out-of-the-way yard. It wasn't that he could not be trusted with the public but the other way around. So Bruce's life became solitary, lonely and sexually frustrated. Eric arranged to bring Bruce from Gosford to Foxground. This entailed a drive of 160 miles straight through Sydney's busy heart. Bruce was fully mature, standing over six feet tall, so Eric decided to effect the transfer himself. He tranquillised Bruce, then had him lifted into the back of the family station wagon. Robyn, Eric's wife and principal assistant, drove.

The injection should have knocked out a horse but it only immobilised Bruce for half the journey. As Robyn piloted them through peak hour traffic, Eric wrestled with a wakening Bruce behind her. Arms and legs flailed about and it took all Eric's strength to remain lying across the big animal to hold him down.

There had been a kidnapping that week. Newspaper and television reports told how a couple in a station wagon had abducted a child. It was a nasty crime which had everyone on the lookout for the missing boy. Noticing the Worrells' vehicle with a man in the back clearly restraining a body that struggled to be free, motorists began to honk and stare. Soon a police car drew alongside with flashing light, indicating they must pull over to the kerb.

Nothing could have pleased Eric more. He identified himself and gasped, 'Where is the nearest vet?'

With a police escort, they drew up at a nearby surgery and more tranquilliser was administered. Even this barely quietened Bruce until Foxground was reached. Eric and Robyn handed him over with relief.

Once he was back on solid ground, with lush green grass underfoot and the scent of other kangaroos in his nostrils, Bruce began to settle down. Within a day he had found his way around the yard which formerly contained Big Joe. Grazing by brail, he taught himself the tree roots, fence corners and other obstacles so that he could hop around with reasonable sureness. He seemed to have a super-radar which warned him as he approached protrusions. Watching him get about, you would never have picked him as blind until you looked into his face and saw his white-filmed eyes.

The next step was introducing him to the ladies. They entered his yard willingly enough. Bruce himself was approached more cautiously. He met them halfway, fur rippling, nose outstretched. When they were together, he began to cluck and pat at them. Almost at once, he showed signs of sexual arousal. We, the audience, were delighted. Things were not going to be that simple, however.

Without sight, Bruce did not seem able to mate. He was forever approaching the females from the wrong direction. Somehow, everything was back to front. Opal, Mathilda and Sheila were no help at all. They dithered like girls at their first dance, titivated and skittish and quite silly. Blue Belle was a different species and we weren't sure whether Bruce could impregnate her, even if he got the system right. We wondered if the exercise had been a waste of effort.

Well, not entirely. At least Bruce had a spacious green home with plenty of suitable company and no poke-fingered louts to bother him. And our kangaroos had found a leader, if not a father for their joeys. We stopped dwelling on what was happening in Bruce's yard and went back to writing and tending the farm.

As it turned out, without any help or attention from us, the ultimate goal was achieved. All three mature female grey kangaroos became mothers. Either Bruce figured it out or, as the old saying goes, somehow nature found a way. It wasn't the perfect solution but for the present, it would do.

It is not surprising that breeding and babies were on our minds. 'Natural increase', as farmers call it, was the business of Glenrock. Our cattle multiplied according to plan. Although the carrying capacity of our farm was small, my herd records remind me that we reared thirty-five calves over a period of six years. Some of them were sold as yearlings but others stayed to produce second and third generations of offspring.

Dear Freya, for instance, produced four calves and reared a foster one as well. Being of good Friesian stock, she had plenty of milk for two. The trick, we learned, was to save some of her afterbirth and smear it on the back of another day-old calf bought at the sale yard within twenty-four hours of her parturition. Then you yoked her natural calf to the ring-in, using two collars joined by a swivel chain. With any luck, she would permit both to suckle. But she, and others like Helga and Thoragird, always gave preference to their own infants. The orphan had to learn to drink from the rear, poking its nose in between her hind legs. You can recognise a foster calf by its dirty forehead. I learned quite a lot about parenthood, orphans and fostering through observing and recording our cattle. And also the dogs.

Jim and Laika mated and produced puppies annually, most of which were sold as cattle herders. The first litter arrived very early on a summer morning. Ignoring the comfortable basket we had prepared for her, Laika made herself a nest under the raised floor of the feed room adjoining the blacksmith's shed. Her labour started before dawn. Van was dwelling on her and crept out without waking any of us to watch and help if necessary. He came into our bedroom full of good news. The litter was huge, the puppies each had slightly different combinations of their parents' markings, and all were healthy. He was so pleased with himself, we never mentioned that the knees and elbows of his pyjamas were ingrained with dirt from his patient vigil. The stains never quite washed away.

Because we had no trouble finding homes for Jim's pups and

because it seemed such a good learning exercise, we did not want to have Laika spayed. Unlike the cows, we could fuss over her as she swelled in pregnancy. She was a diligent mother and since she was middle-aged when she met Jim, she did not have all that many reproductive years left.

A curious thing occurred when she produced her final litter, however. The babies looked robust enough but even before their eyes were open, we detected something amiss. Laika seemed restless and inclined to leave them unattended, a neglect unheard of with previous litters. We wondered if she was simply feeling too old for the job. Then, one by one the pups began to cry in pain. Van reported seeing Laika biting at the top of their heads, where the skull bones had not yet fused. Was she trying to ease some pressure on their little brains caused by an infection? Or was she trying to kill them?

It was distressing to watch. When their cries became screams, Laika snapped at them and finally, her patience frayed, she barked hysterically. Jim came to peer at his progeny and then slunk away. While we pondered what to do, Van announced that some puppies were convulsing. We didn't know a remedy for that. Next morning, he awakened us with the news that all the pups had died.

We came to expect Van's early morning reports and always took them seriously because he was intuitive, an accurate observer of natural phenomena. Both he and his brother were early wakers. Van's style was to get out and about – so much happens at dawn in the country – while Goth preferred to busy himself at his desk, drawing plans for some contraption he would build in the shed, or else putting together the model airplanes he suspended from his ceiling on pale fishing lines.

Goth suffered with hay fever, and a tendency to 'colds' which sometimes brought on asthma, both family traits. He learned early to pace himself when he wasn't well, sometimes sitting propped up in his bed reading through the dark hours if he got the wheezes. The Biggles books were among his favourites. It was lucky for him, and for us, that he was literate and creative.

Our sons had perfect boyhoods in Foxground. Balanced against what went on at Glenrock was their participation in farming life down the valley. In those days people helped each other with planting and harvests. Willing kids were always pressed into service at such times. As well as being useful, they got to ride on top of the hay, drop the seed potatoes into furrows, climb up into the loft and help stack bales. The farmers took it upon themselves to school the lads in best practices around a farm. As well as the fun and learning of it, their reward was often a good feed of scones with jam and cream, or maybe a hearty roast chicken lunch.

After work came the creek. Oh, those creeks of Foxground, which down in the valley flowed wide and, in some places, deep. The swimming hole behind Conroys' had platypus living next door, as well as a rope for swinging on and a log for crossing over – or pushing each other off. Even today, the men who swam and played there as lads can set themselves laughing as they remember what they got up to.

On Glenrock Farm, those 1960s years were bountiful. Our stomachs were always well filled with fresh healthy food which tasted all the better because we grew it ourselves on our own land. The boys helped, usually willingly, and learned the sweet satisfaction of carrying back to the house crisp snappy beans, green and yellow squashes, cobs and cobs of sweetcorn, rosy tomatoes picked with their own hands, hands dirtied by the good clean earth of Glenrock, shoes ditto. Pumpkins almost covered the roof of our shed, stored high to escape mildew and rats.

It's simple food that tastes the best. Plain boiled potatoes, just an hour out of the ground, running with golden butter, salt and pepper. The platter – that huge old blue and white platter Jeff's parents bought for us at a second-hand shop, ikon of our country kitchen and our Good Life – heaped, *heaped*, with fried rabbit, meat so plentiful (and so virtuous because we fed ourselves while ridding the land of a declared pest species) that you didn't need to clean the bones, you just tossed them into a dish for the dogs to finish. Stewed fruit from our own trees, topped with gobs of thick cream scooped off the milk we bought by the billycan at the Conroys' dairy.

Our back verandah was always lined with buckets of produce waiting to be processed. I bought a second-hand Vacola boiler and mastered the technique of vacuum bottling, then spent every summer and autumn evening preserving food. The shelves of our walk-in pantry soon filled with plenty to carry us through winter – tall bottles of ruby plums and golden peaches, squat ones of big china pears and tomato pulp, plus bottles of corn kernels yellow as sunshine. Some of the fruit and vegetables went into relishes, chutneys and jams, sending rich, sticky fragrances through the house. That full pantry brought more satisfaction than any fat bank balance ever has.

Friends gave us recipes for making dill pickles, using salt and vine leaves, raisins and sliced bread. For weeks we tended cucumbers transforming magically in the brine. Our great pickle experiments worked a treat. We learned how to make ginger beer, too, and quaffed its sweet peppery fizz – so cheap, so thirst-quenching – while the 'plant' doubled and doubled again. For safety, the bottles matured in the garage, corks tied down with rags and string. Occasionally a bottle would explode and once Jeff had to cover an unstable dozen with chaff bags and smash them with a hammer to avoid a holocaust.

The spare cottage brought us added income and also new friends. I painted it inside and out and planted shrubs around to soften its stark exterior. Then I put two small ads in the *Nation Review*: 'PEACE and QUIET, clean air, fresh mountain water, rainforest; beaut for kids'. From then on it was all word of mouth and the tenants we attracted returned again and again. Their holidays on Glenrock gave us an excuse for a Saturday night party. Almost all were family people. I used to send the children out with baskets and scissors to gather foliage and flowers with which they decorated the tables, where bowls and bowls of fresh salads, stewed fruits, mountains of corn on the cob and platters of meat would stand, an invitation to help oneself. We put music on the record player – The Beatles, Dylan, Creedence Clearwater Revival, plus all the old favourites of folk and blues and jazz, and after dinner we danced, the kids too. Together we made bushwalks and gave bird talks. Those cottage tenants plus other friends kept us in touch with the urban world, being mainly from the disciplines of journalism or science or social work, and we kept them in touch with nature, and also with outback Australia, where we regularly travelled in the course of our writing.

Conversation flowed warmly as the youngsters raced round the garden or went to swim or fish or fossick in the creek. The sixties was an era of new ideas. Our visitors helped us hone our philosophy, as did our subscriptions to magazines and the books we mail-ordered through the Mary Martin Bookshop. We debated nuclear disarmament, dispossession of Aborigines, the vietnam war, and took heart from a growing but bitterly resisted liberalism in America.

Jeff's parents, who came to stay at the farm to look after Goth and Van when we went away to gather story material, bought us a television set. We had hoped to preserve the minds of our sons and ourselves from that intrusive and addictive medium, but Jeff's mother thought this a shocking deprivation for her grandchildren and thrust the abomination upon us. Luckily, but also sometimes unluckily, reception in our buried mountain retreat was poor.

Through snow and ripples, we watched *Shintaro* (action vivid enough to inspire mock fights using strange weapons – star knives and staves – combined with the supernatural and a soft physical beauty set to Japanese music), *Dr Who* (marrying science fiction effects with music – the best of British for kids of all ages), and *F-Troop*, with wimpish Captain Parmenter, Corporal Agarn and their squad of wacky, dumb, innocent Americans who made no pretence about evoking anything but belly laughs. After dinner, to balance those, we studied the news and *This Day Tonight*, encouraging Goth and Van to sit with us for a view of world events.

Thus we heard Martin Luther King speak, and saw marches, night sticks, anger, blood and agony. From a terribly funny, poignant routine by stand-up comic Dick Lester, I learned there had been sit-ins in the south to protest racial discrimination. Suddenly I felt shamed to see how some Americans had been putting themselves on the line fighting racial oppression – the bigotry from which I had fled. I felt a defector from my own land but decided I was too rooted, too committed in Australia, to go back and help now. I must put my ideals to work in my adopted country instead.

When Jeff and I travelled to Central Australia for *National Geographic* and later to research a book, we visited many Aboriginal settlements, mainly in those days still run by church missionaries. We kept our eyes and ears open and formed our own conclusions about what was being done 'for the best' for indigenous people. Whenever possible we spoke with Aboriginal people themselves, establishing contacts which we would renew from then onward. We found it hard to publish our experiences because the prevailing attitude was one of patriarchal tolerance, at best, and outright disgust at worst. I realised that, refugee from my own roots though I was, I could still make a difference in my adopted land, using the skills particular to me.

From our jittery television screen came other news that the times were slowly but surely a-changing. We thought the good guys were beginning to win when the 1967 referendum granted Aboriginal people parity with Europeans, including the right to go into the pub after work for a beer. Ha ha ha.

As we watched footage of big American music festivals, it seemed like the iron hand of conservatism was unclenching. I was amazed to see street dancing in the Haight-Ashbury district of my beloved San Francisco. The face-painting, tie-dyed clothes and public pot-smoking had all happened after I left the States. Bare feet, tresses flowing . . . most Australians I met disparaged the notion of Flower Power, but it sounded all right to me.

We went to see the musical *Hair* in Sydney and, euphoric, went back to see it again taking Goth and Van. Long hair and beards, we had always thought, bespoke volumes about 'natural' life. Jeff had not shaved since the day he resigned from permanent employment and turned freelance. That was in our second year together. My own hair grew long and longer, my vanity being that when I was old, I would be able to sit on it and thereby win a tiny place in the memories of my grandchildren.

Jeff and I must have been the result of the same impulses which were thawing attitudes in North America and Britain, yet we felt our philosophy was born in isolation, bolstered by a handful of Australian friends who, like us, did not see ourselves as a 'movement'. We simply considered issues and acted according to our consciences. Thus we travelled to Sydney and demonstrated for nuclear disarmament. CND (Campaign for Nuclear Disarmament) membership was something noble we felt, even though Jeff was no joiner after a brief, disillusioning affair with the Communist Party in his youth and with the trade union movement during his factory-jobs stage. When the anti Vietnam War protests were scheduled we again took ourselves to Sydney and marched to the town hall. One had to stand up and be counted, we believed. Otherwise, the point of living in a democracy was wasted.

When they were only nippers, I took Goth and Vandal with us as a necessary part of their education, clutching Goth with one hand, pushing Van's stroller with the other. I always dressed us neatly. Many young marchers put on hippy warpaint for the day and cavorted with holiday gaiety, but I felt this was self-defeating. By alienating conservative Australians who were the majority, the real message of the demonstrations would be weakened. Sending troops to Vietnam affected all citizens, so I presented myself and my sons as we were – as I believed we were: thoughtful middle-class protesters. Their grandparents were appalled.

Jeff's father avoided contentious subjects by keeping his mouth shut, unlike his outspoken wife. But their politics were upper working-class conservative. Their hero was Prime Minister Menzies. They hated dissent. So Jeff and I mainly kept quiet when they lectured us about nonconformism. In most things they were very good to us, very giving, so for the sake of peace in the family, we kept our more provocative opinions to ourselves.

Close to home, in Berry where Goth and Van attended school, I was also circumspect, fearing that our principles might rebound on the boys. There seemed no dissidence in Berry, where churches and the RSL reigned uncontested. They were uniformly paranoid about racial threats from Asia and any form of debate was branded communist propaganda.

The fact that our main earnings came from writing and photography had already set us apart. Our neighbours could not comprehend journalism – it wasn't really work and it made them uneasy. Whenever we returned after travelling to gather story material, we were greeted with: 'Another holiday? Did you have a good time?' in tones which combined envy with censure. This used to irritate me some, since we moved fast and slept rough; camping out for reasons both financial and practical, we worked as close to outback happenings as we could, swallowing dust and rising at dawn. But I kept my annoyance to myself.

I tried to affect a low profile, which was easier because we lived on a property. My only contact in Berry was through the primary school where, on tuckshop duty, I cut sandwiches and listened. Current affairs were not then a suitable topic for country women's chat, I found. If subjects like conscription or racial vilification did enter the conversation, I let the bigots and the cheerfully ignorant have their say, leaving my own contributions to the end and keeping them brief and cool.

Even so, I knew that Goth and Van were held at arm's length by many families, because of our unusual lifestyle and what they knew of our beliefs through magazine articles. Pacifism, and conservation of waters, forests and wildlife were considered at least eccentric and at worst treasonous, notions which evoked fear and quite strong anger in many people. Jeff's parents included.

When Goth and Van wanted to let their hair grow, we saw no reason to stop them but warned it would set them apart from their peers, at first anyway. So they approached their teenage years with blond curly locks touching their shoulders. Our only stipulation was that they kept their long hair clean and well groomed. It was their own idea to use headbands to keep it in place, inspired by Jimi Hendrix posters, or a ponytail like the surfer boys wore.

Suspicion of long hair on the south coast was very strong at first, but the fashion spread. High schools vacillated between *can*, *can't* and *maybe, if*. It all came to the point of reconciliation when the father of a pupil at a high school in Nowra frogmarched his rebellious son to the barber and demanded he be given a crew-cut. The lad went home and hanged himself in the garage.

When I related the shocking tale to Jeff's father, he amazed me. With a rare show of naked passion, he said: 'I'm with the father. I'd like to get all those kids down and shave their filthy heads clean!' He was so beside himself that we let the subject drop. Only later did I learn that his attitude dated back to World War I, when soldiers in the trenches became infested with lice. From that evolved the standard short-back-and-sides hairstyle. Dadda wore it proudly until his death.

One of my campaigns which Jeff encouraged was the outward expression of affection. The Australian way in those days was very reserved, very British. Jeff and I believed that love and sensuality should be shown openly, manifestations of human nature at its best. So we encouraged our children to develop their tactility and not be ashamed of emotions. Jeff loved to have his feet – and his head – rubbed, and entreated his sons to oblige him whenever we knocked off working. At nights in the lounge, our family looked like a tangle of caterpillars, with a few dogs and a wombat thrown in. Sensual free expression seemed to rub off on most of our visitors. Our love of flowers and candlelight, coupled with good music and uninhibited dancing, plus our robust use of salty language, 'the living language', made our home famous within our own circle for hedonistic revelry.

Another thing which set us apart was Jeff's love affair with Porsche motorcars. When he bought his little blue C Class, the first of seven Porsches he would own in the next two decades, the local petrol stations didn't know what it was. They thought he had some weird sort of Volkswagen. Once they learned the pedigree of the marque, they began to treat him (us) differently than they did when we drove our old workhorse Land Rover or the one-ton ute. They became jocular and just a tad subservient. They stopped offering us bargains or suggesting ways to cut corners, price-wise, and began to charge us top dollar. Which bothered me because the only reason Jeff could afford a luxury speedster was because of our spartan lifestyle. Almost everyone in the district had better furniture and even a newer house than we did, which was fine by me. I loved our lifestyle. So did Jeff, but he aspired to the best in equipment – cameras, hi-fi, Porsche motors. And this generated in our sons some attitudes which I did not like.

It became clear that they had been infected by their father's selective materialism when one of the boys from the Boys' Museum said, 'Mrs Carter, Goth and Van say their father owns the fastest motorcar on the south coast. Would that be true?' The only honest answer was, 'Probably.'

I worried over this, because it so contravened my own philosophy of being liked for what you are, not what you have. However, I reasoned that our sons had every right to take from our teachings and our examples what appealed to them. They learned to admire speed and driving skills, and to disdain conservative drivers and traffic law. Thor bought himself a Ducati motorbike for commuting between Sydney and Foxground, and he bought Van a hot Kawasaki, even before he was old enough to ride it on the public roads. Jeff paid Phil Conroy to bring his tractor and they all constructed a trail-bike track up the back. For a few years, the cattle were disturbed at weekends by the angry buzz and smell of motorbikes tearing down gullies and up over humps. And so was I.

Several things occurred during the late sixties which did very nearly compromise us in our small conservative dairying district. One was our appreciation of the surfing movement which was spreading along the coast. Jeff was putting together a book about board surfers, who were seen as a threat to the belt-and-reel chaps, members of the militaristic surf lifesaving clubs. While most folks mistrusted the anarchic, carefree and sometimes poetic board surfers, we found them refreshing and were happy to have our sons exposed to them.

The same was true when younger friends of ours asked if they could hold their hippy wedding on our property.

The third event was a psychedelic naming celebration for the child of the bridal couple.

All these happenings influenced our philosophical growth and that of our kids, and all but the last were positive influences. It was that third celebration of what many saw as the sixties' indulgences that nearly undid us and put a sobering cap on what had been our glorious, most bountiful years.

In retrospect, I see that our goings-on at Glenrock Farm reflected a social trend. Part of our wide circle of friends were men and women about ten years younger than ourselves. They came to us through photographer Roger Whittaker, having been his mates at university. No drop-outs, they worked as engineers or teachers, but they shared a common goal: avoid becoming wired into The System. No formal engagements and white church weddings for them, no mortgages, no commitment to long-term careers with life on hold until after retirement. They enjoyed life *now*, which may be why they liked us and our place so well. They, too, aspired to a free and natural life and leant toward an Earth Garden lifestyle. Camping out, canoeing and bushwalking were what they enjoyed, and they came for weekends with boots and sleeping bags, happy to help Jeff with farming tasks, hiked, talked, played records on our hi-fi and taught Goth to pick guitar. Summer came and they asked if they could stage a marriage on our property, designing their own ceremony and celebration, ultra simple and naturalistic. It sounded like fun.

We left them to make their own arrangements but offered to fetch tables and chairs up to the meadow they chose for the event. 'No, no, we'll sit on the grass. Well, maybe one table for food would be good. The guests will bring the eats.'

Having my own ideas about Happenings, I quietly baked a big flat chocolate cake with nuts on the top laid out to form the inter-

twined symbols for male and female. It was so different from the
elaborate tiered wedding cakes of the day, which I always
suspected were iced in plaster of Paris, that I figured it would not
give offence. Ceremonial food, I had come to understand, fills
more than the belly. As often happened, my social instinct was apt.

The guests arrived in the late afternoon, parked their cars near
our dairy gate and, after some milling about with picnic baskets
and salad bowls, began to waft up the hill, trailing tie-dyed chiffon
and whiffs of patchouli. I offered the bride our bedroom for
changing into her finery, whatever it might be, while the groom
disappeared with his kitbag into the studio.

About five o'clock, Jeff and I and the boys walked up to the
meadow. There were weekend tenants in the cottage and I invited
them to accompany us with their children. I sensed this would be
interesting to witness and wanted to share it. An evangelist for the
alternative, was I.

Guests had been arriving steadily from Sydney and about forty
were gathered in the grass, looking very pretty against the
backdrop of trees. Everyone had dressed for the occasion. Some
girls wore spectacular see-through crocheted dresses and many
guys had donned embroidered Indian shirts. Only one wore a suit,
which looked like it had come from a jumble sale. On the still, clear
air wafted the sweetish fragrance of marijuana. Several 'groomsmen' clutched tree fern fronds which they had asked permission to
cut. My portable table was laden with bowls and platters. Organisation was minimal but everyone was smiling and relaxed as we
waited and chatted until the sun dipped behind the western hilltop.

A tall man in a long velvet robe with stars on it prowled about
waiting, I assumed, to perform the nuptials. 'No, that's the Wizard
of New South Wales uni,' they told us. 'He's here for the Invoca-
tion!'

We heard a motorbike revving, labouring a bit as it started up
the steep hill.

'They're coming,' someone called. Round the bend rode the
groom and his pillion passenger the bride. He wore a bright red,
blue and gold military jacket, just like the ones on the cover of
Sergeant Pepper's Lonely Hearts Club Band, and he grinned hugely
through his luxuriant whiskers, which were freshly shampooed
and brushed out full. He was the peacock. She was the nymph.

Riding demurely side-saddle behind him, her frock was simple, Boticelli style – white organza with sprigs of cornflowers on it. Her hair fell loosely round her face and down to her shoulders. On her head was a garland of live field flowers.

Both she and her betrothed were barefoot and she wore anklets of smaller daisies. As they parked the bike and dismounted, everyone clapped spontaneously. The fellows raised their fern fronds and made an arch. The bridal pair walked through it to where their friend waited in his rusty secondhand suit. When they were in place, the fern bearers formed up behind them, making a bower. It was the prettiest wedding I had ever seen.

As if to defuse what might have been a solemn ceremony, light-hearted vows were exchanged amid witty interjections from the crowd and jokes from the groom. Then flour was thrown. The 'celebrant' copped the most, whitening his fine wispy hair and his rumpled old clothes.

Larrikin hijinks followed, until the Wizard suddenly clapped his hands. 'Silence,' he commanded. 'Come.'

We all drifted after him to a knoll at the edge of the clearing, facing the east. After a few nervous twitters, we quietened, compelled by his posture which signalled something impending.

He turned to face the view, just as a huge lighted orb began to rise above the tree-tops, so big, so glowingly red, it made us all gasp. It was the moon. It was a full moon and looked big enough to gobble the earth. As it filled the sky behind him, the Wizard raised his arms slowly until he was silhouetted against glowing crimson, an archetypical priestly figure. 'Rise,' he intoned. 'Rise.' For a few moments, we were primitives, tossed back into super-stition and fear. Had something gone wrong? Could that gigantic moon harm us?

Obviously, like a good shaman must, he had done his homework well, then he and the groom had choreographed proceedings to coincide. So in its own fashion, the hippy wedding *was* structured. But it was a jolly good bit of theatre. I felt deeply affected by it as my family and the cottage tenants trailed back down the hill, leaving the wedding guests to whoop and cavort across the grass until it was time to fall into their sleeping bags. Wedding Flat is what we called that meadow from then on, and still today I am moved by the memory of that evening.

So that was the first outdoor wedding held on Glenrock Farm during our time, but it was not the last. Three more occurred within the next few years and each was imbued with a special lasting magic that tinged all who experienced it. Each was an occasion when people's inhibitions were melted by the special aura of the farm and, if I may say so, of the Carters themselves. An innocent hedonism prevailed at party times and many's the person who remembers that with affection.

Other flamboyant get-togethers and events occurred on Glenrock, many of them involving fancy dress and an expansion of personality. One of these was the 21st birthday party of Thor, involving his younger brothers but also his best mates from high school in Sydney, a conventional bunch who ran wild for the weekend.

One of the good things about partying on Glenrock was its remoteness from neighbours. There was no one within view to complain about raucous fun. Another asset was that Jeff's hi-fidelity sound system could be turned up on such occasions without disturbing anyone. Well, no, I take that back. I'm sure the birds and animals wondered what caused the din those few hours. And I did hear rumours of a mysterious rhythmic beat which echoed into the valley and puzzled farmers down there.

The sequel to the hippy wedding was a sobering celebration for Jeff and me. The bride became pregnant and some of her friends asked if they could stage a baby-welcoming ceremony. Face-painting and kite-flying would be featured. It sounded good to Jeff and me, so on the weekend when sporty cars rolled up and boys and girls in rainbow shirts and gauzy dresses began spilling out from the cottage (where many of them were staying) and across into our front cow paddock, we stopped work and went down to watch the fun.

The kites they had brought were extravagantly colourful. Goth and Van gave them a hand to get them up, having themselves had experience in that sport. Face-painting gave everyone a festive appearance, and when they began yipping and rolling over and over down the grassy hillsides, we applauded. We knew how to play. And sometimes with our friends we got tipsy.

We began to realise that this psychedelic romp was fuelled by more than alcohol, however, and we receded back indoors, impatient for their partying to finish. Jeff and I did not need chemicals to love 'Lucy in the Sky with Diamonds' and it sobered us to realise that other people did.

It all got a bit out of control after dark. Our middle-class hippies began loping about, some ran up the waterfall track and we heard their shouts resounding along the creek as they searched for magic mushrooms and discovered colonies of fireflies. I prayed they wouldn't fall and injure themselves on the rocks. Next morning, when we were told that they had used that weekend to experiment with mind-altering substances, we felt they had used us. Had we been consulted, we would not have given permission. Too dangerous and not the good influence for our sons that I had thought the weekend would be.

Jeff and I were always considered young for our age. For young, read free. Free of social inhibitions. Free of conventional ideas. Able to let go and enjoy. We liked being accepted by people years our junior. But that weekend reminded us that we were parents, responsible citizens, members of a community which was far too conservative to tolerate this sort of rave. We informed our guests that the era of Glenrock as a hippy haven had now finished. And in so doing, we stepped forward into middle age. Thus we entered the seventies with our innocence eroding. Maybe everybody did.

14

William and Gidgea

Whatever else was happening in our lives, our involvement with animals went on, all the time. William the wombat had fitted into Glenrock Farm well enough. No, that's wrong. It is fairer to say that the routines of Glenrock were adjusted and expanded to cater for William's requirements and foibles. Wombats, we began to discover, are creatures of simple habits and strong needs. The trick is to learn these and anticipate them.

By nature, wombats are nocturnal, but William's body clock had adjusted partially to human time. Thus he would graze during the day but he wanted someone to stay with him while he ate. As Will munched, I attended the clothesline, read through mail, even sat on a stool with my portable typewriter on my knees. He didn't mind what your hands were doing high above him, so long as your feet kept handy. If something startled him, he dashed between your shoes and hunkered down with a sigh.

In time, we learned to get him eating strongly and then edge away. But it was only a temporary respite. Instinctually he required a companion. Without one, he panicked and ran to the house, meeping and scratching to get in. We tried snibbing the screen doors but William simply walked through the wire. We nailed masonite over the mesh on the bottom half. If you've ever tried to drive a nail into masonite, you'll know how impervious it is, yet

William spent one happy afternoon chewing a hole the size of a grapefruit through it. His front teeth were like chisels. William's hole in the back door served one good purpose – it made a place where Jim and Laika could hook their paws in and open the door. William, of course, did the same and so did all of his successors.

Jim's bed was in the kitchen entryway. Laika's bed was in the garage but sometimes she flung herself down next to Jim on the cool lino. So if William wanted to enter the house, he had to pass them. As soon as William opened the back door, both dogs growled, Jim especially fierce. William would pause, then let the door bang shut again. Silence. A standoff. Then William would pull the door open again. Same response, another bang, until he found the courage to run the gauntlet. Jim would rise up in his basket, lips drawn back over his teeth, snarling like a Baskerville hound until the wombat scrabbled past, his toenails chattering on the slippery surface, a plaintive little squeak escaping from him like gas.

If we were around, we escorted William through the blockade, speaking reassuringly to all present. We knew Jim wouldn't bite William because he was too wise in our ways by now. But he sure looked scary. Once the wombat entered the kitchen, Jim subsided, grumbling.

During the day, Jeff and I spent most of our time in our writing studio. We had established a comfortable office in the old dairy. William liked to lie between our feet under our desks. This allowed us to get some work done. His problem was climbing the steep stone steps leading from the back yard. Like a rock climber, he strained to reach above his head, scrambling for a finger (paw) hold, then hauled his backside up a face as tall as himself, hind feet clawing the old stones. Going down was much quicker. He stood poised on the top step, tentatively feeling with a front paw the precipice before him, casting about for the best route, then committed himself like a parachutist to tumble downward.

Having written several successful books about outback travels and people, notably *Four-Wheel-Drive Swagman*, *People of the Inland*, and *Wild Country*, Jeff was working on a new book about how our property had evolved into a wildlife refuge. Its title was *Wild Animal Farm*. William was already in it, although we were still novices with wombats. Whatever happened with Will was grist for Jeff's mill. And mine.

When we went up to the vegetable garden, we took William with us, hoping he would accustom himself to the wider world of our farm. He dogged our feet up and back. Once between rows of lush veges, the cultivated earth excited him and he would scrape at the soil with his big front paws. These experimental digs were a sign he was heading toward independence, we thought. But so far, whenever he dug under the back gate, flattening himself and squeezing outside, free and unfettered, he panicked and meeped urgently to be let back in.

At least the cows were no worry. The first time they saw him peering at them through the mesh, they approached, blowing and pawing. Oh no, not another episode like the one Thalos had endured. As we dashed forward to scoop William up, he gathered himself and screamed at them. The cows scattered. And gave him a wide berth from then on.

If we went someplace where William couldn't accompany us, we put him in his enclosure adjoining the dairy. He usually did the rounds of his feeding bowls, sharpened his teeth on his log, then stepped primly into his drum and scratched out his bedding. Next he scratched some of it back in again, wrapped his stubby legs around a cushion and rocked himself happily to sleep. He often slept on his back if it was hot, paws flung to the sides, head back. The hair on his underside was sparse and he seemed to welcome fresh air on his skin. Once a visitor, who'd entered the yard seeking Jeff, peered into William's enclosure, saw him stretched out thus and concluded we had a dead wombat on our hands.

We tried not to keep William locked up any more than necessary. Our intention was always to stage the animals in our care to a free-living state. But we were coming to realise that a friendly habitat inside a barrier fence could be safer for hand-reared orphans than just shoving them out the gate and wishing them 'bon voyage'. In William's case, he was not ready to go. He wanted to be with *us*.

So we stuck to what suited him best – morning graze with Mare near the laundry; breakfast, lunch and tea with the family, afternoon romp with Goth or Van. Evenings, whoever was available took him outside to eat grass. This, of course, was his natural feeding time. And he became more settled during the dark hours, more willing to let us sneak away and leave him munching outside the house. We would peep at him regularly and see the moon highlight his silvery-grey silhouette. His coat was lengthening now, and his face maturing. It was the broadening of his nose, his grainy proboscis, that told us he was passing from adolescence to adulthood, that and the blatantly sexual way he embraced his pillows from time to time.

When everyone went to bed, Jeff or I would try to stay awake because William was still grazing strongly in the back yard. Finally we'd give up and go fetch him, swinging his weight up into our arms efficiently and carry him on his back to the wombatarium.

We often woke up in the morning to hear him scratching, scratching at his paling fence. Wombats are good alarm clocks. 'Meep, meep, meep', William would shout from his stockade across the back yard. 'Okay, Will, hang on, we'll be out in a minute,' we'd call and go to put the kettle on. 'MEEP,' he'd holler, 'Now!'

When we went to fetch him, we'd often find he'd clawed out one of Ernie Staples' boulders from the dairy verandah, or gnawed a paling down to a smaller size. But he never got out and we figured it was better he played his obsessive games in his yard than in the house.

After breakfast in the kitchen, all sociable with the family, dogs milling around too, William took himself out and down the path to a tap at the corner of the house where I kept a heavy concrete drinking bowl ever full for animals. Now, wombats are not really built to drink. I speculated that in the wild they must get their moisture off dewy grasses because their nose protrudes, their bottom jaw is short and their fat tongues do not seem designed for lapping. Water taken in at the front leaks out the sides where there are no teeth. But the kibbled dog food Will preferred to eat was dehydrated; it needed to be followed by water. Funnily enough, Jim disdained eating it, unless it was in William's dish. Then he would gobble it up while William looked on, daring the wombat to object.

Watching William drink was both comical and tedious. It took him so long to snap up a small mouthful of water and swallow, then repeat the action, that we grew bored, and he actually fell asleep on occasions, so that his nostrils dropped forward into the water and he awoke blowing bubbles.

Mornings were too busy, however, to stand watching wombats

drink. Goth and Van had to be driven to the bus stop, for a start. My beautiful old red Essex had long since been phased back, not to nature but to Thor's mother's back yard in Sydney, where he was slowly stripping and renewing it. Awaiting my attention were always farm chores, house tidying, then writing and other business, including account keeping. Plus we received another orphan to rear.

We named her Gidgea, after the native bushes we so admired in the inland. She was about nine months old when she arrived, a very nervous little animal cowering in a bag which Van took delivery of at the back gate. My heart went out to Gidgea from the start. Her recent experiences had taken the bloom off her and her eyes were terrified. She had diarrhoea and her fur was all peaks and rat tails.

By this time I had acquired a 'touch' with kangaroos, similar to developing a 'way' with horses or dogs. You study their behaviour, you know where and how they like to be handled and you avoid things you know will upset them. The positiveness of your approach instils confidence in them and if you are sensitive to their needs, you can win them over easily.

I put my hand into her bag and, edging delicately between her skinny front legs, I rubbed my finger gently along the line of her jaw. My hand came to rest cupped behind her head. She tucked her face into my palm and snuggled down. All the while her donor was telling us her story, which was that, like so many of her kind, she had been plucked from the pouch of her dead mother after a kangaroo shoot on a property in western New South Wales. One of the shooters thought he would bring her home to Sydney as a pet for his children. But the kids were noisy and rough and their mother didn't want her soiling the carpet, so she was passed on to us. Good riddance. I kept my hand on her, not oppressively, but reassuringly. Instinct told me the best medicine for this desperate little creature was close affectionate contact.

For the first twenty-four hours we never left her alone. If I was too busy to hold her bag, Jeff or one of the boys did so. We kept a hot-water bottle beside her, consistently warm, and I fed her frequently using the long fountain-pen bladder teat we had adapted for the other joeys. She drank readily. She must have been very hungry. That first day, I did not attempt to take her out of her bag. At night, she slept on our bed with my hand resting on her much of the time. By morning, she was peeking out. 'Chut, chut, chut,' she went, anticipating breakfast.

After the boys went off to school, I prepared some warm water laced with a few drops of disinfectant. Then, lining my lap with an old towel, I removed her gently from the bag and swaddled her in another soft towel. Propping her on the butt of her tail with her back resting against my body, I carefully sponged off her fur which was matted with faeces. At first she struggled, but the sureness of my touch reassured her. She could not get away so she gave in and let me clean her. I knew by now that mother 'roos spend a lot of time grooming their joeys. Adult kangaroos groom each other, too, especially the places they cannot easily reach themselves, like behind the ears.

Jeff came in for morning coffee and I gave him Gidgea to hold while I replenished her hot-water bottle and prepared a clean bag for her. We somersaulted her inside and she snuggled down, content until her next feed.

By evening she was ready to go into the kangararium. I had cleared it out and relined the floor with fresh, well-aged sawdust. (New sawdust can be toxic, as we discovered once when Opal and Mathilda were small.) The heater was glowing red and beneath it were dishes of water, grass and oats with raisins, apple and grated carrot. It looked very cosy. We hung Gidgea's bag on the wall inside the compartment and left her to explore her new home as she wished.

Before bedtime we peeped in and found her still in her bag, cosy in the glow of the heater. We took out her bag and I fed her on my lap with my hand inside the bag, on her body. She licked my hand and seemed perfectly at ease.

By dawn I was anxious to see how she was. I went out to the front verandah and found Vandal already peeping round the curtains of the Kangararium.

'She's up,' he reported softly. 'She's eaten some grass.'

The sound of our voices alarmed her. She stood up, shivering. 'It's all right, Gidge,' I soothed and hurried away to prepare a warm bottle of milk for her and tea for us, while Van prodded her gently to somersault into her sack. A few minutes later, we were all ensconced around Jeff in the bedroom, sipping tea while

Gidgea drank thirstily from within her bag. That was a typical Carter morning: father propped up in bed with his vital first cup while the boys, still in pyjamas, sat round him, waiting to hear the plan for the day. Jim would push his nose under the nearest elbow or knee, doing everything but climb onto the bed, which he wasn't allowed to do. Just outside, framed in the big picture window that looked onto the garden, Laika would sit patiently beside Ernie Staples' bird feeder, smiling and wagging while the bowerbirds whined and squabbled above her.

Gidgea developed the habit of clinging onto your finger as she sucked, her delicate little paw clenched almost like a hand. We gave her plenty of physical contact at feeding times and she thrived. Fresh grass was something she hungered for. She ate it from our fingers, biting off strands with her front teeth and grinding them deliberately between her back molars. If a piece was tough, she tugged it free by rearing back her head. All we had to do was hold tight, so she could get what she craved, in a manner she could understand.

Each evening she was held on someone's lap while we listened to music. Occasionally we watched television instead. William would be with us, dozing between our feet. If he sensed Gidgea's presence, he would rise on his bandy hind legs and sniff jealously at her wrappings. He looked comical, like a furry hippo. If we weren't on guard, he did his standing leap trick, landing on one's lap, all forty pounds of him. There would be squeals and complaints until someone took either the wombat or the kangaroo. Holding them both was impossible.

Apart from a few sort-outs of that kind, both animals progressed steadily. But neither was eager for the independence we imagined they would want. Both were content to keep to our routines and share our hearth and home comforts.

Gidgea adapted easily to grazing our yard. She was very confident for a 'roo. The chooks did not worry her at all. She flailed at them if they came peck-pecking too close when she was grazing. Her eyes would darken and her fur bristled warningly. Fortunately, and oddly really, Jim tolerated Gidgea's presence better than any other kangaroo's. They would lie within sight and smell of each other without nervousness or antagonism. Later, when Jim lost his wife Laika, he actually seemed to seek Gidgea's company.

At William's approach, Gidgea stood upright and clucked. William would come waddling along, his nose two inches above the turf, his mind a blank. Gidgea would chatter at him, holding her ground until the last minute, then leap aside as he trundled past her. Sometimes she tried to drop-kick him. It was water off a duck's back to William, but we fancied his step quickened to a bustle, as if he were thinking: 'Strewth, what was that?'

When William ran, he rocked from back to front. Goth and Van gave him a romp each afternoon. After a day at school and their long bus ride home, they were ready for a hearty snack, then some rough-and-tumble with the wombat. He loved a game of football; he'd pounce on it, bonk it and, when it rolled away from him, dribble it across the grass with his nose to the shouts of the lads, who then kicked it and raced William for it. William liked leather! Chasings was still William's favourite. As he and the lads tore around the yard, the dogs would look on – Jim with excitement, Laika with disgust – while Gidgea hopped away to a neutral corner of the garden until the hullabaloo had finished.

As dusk slipped down over the hills around us, they would all drift indoors and the evening rituals began. I fed William under the kitchen window, Gidgea on the hearth. Replete, they would settle patiently while we ate our dinner, William tucking himself between someone's feet under the table. The dogs, having been fed outdoors, would stretch out on the lino. Getting to the sink was an obstacle course, but it was all cosy and companionable.

Within a month, Gidgea was grazing outside at night, the front verandah door propped open in case she wanted to come in. I tried introducing Gidgea to the other 'roos. Putting the dogs on the chain, I'd open the gate to the kangaroo paddock and call them. Expecting an extra feed of pellets, they came hopping, led by Opal with her delicate little daughter, Potch, followed closely by Mulga Mick. Mathilda with her gammy hip usually let Sheila precede her through the narrow gate. Blue Belle was always last. She had accepted her position as lowest on the totem pole. 'Poor Blue Belle,' we used to say.

Sometimes Gidgea touched noses with the other kangaroos, but often she was standoffish and lay down near Jim while the others circled the garden browsing before they returned to their bigger, greener paddock. It took coaxing and trickery to get

Gidgea in with them, despite the lush grass there. Once I made the mistake of snibbing the gate behind her, thinking she'd settle if left alone. No way. She became agitated, hopping along the fence dividing off the back yard, calling out. Overheated, she licked her forearms and even her ankles to cool herself. In no time they were dark with saliva. When we hurried to let her back through the gate, she glared as if to say: 'Don't do that again!'

We did repeat the experiment, but each time the result was the same.

Then Mulga Mick began to show signs of sexual maturity. He started following Sheila, Mathilda and Opal, even little Potch, patting at their tails and clicking his tongue. Potch wanted nothing to do with him, but the others became coquettish. To our surprise, Gidgea began hopping along the fence-line as if she wanted in to the paddock. We opened the gate and she entered, no trouble.

Hooray! Soon might begin the population explosion we wished for. Once again, however, our aspirations were thwarted by disaster.

One morning just before dawn, we were awakened from deep sleep by dogs barking. This was a danger signal. We had come to fear the visits of farm dogs out for fun and frolic. Kangaroos are such flightly creatures. They show no sense at all in the face of danger.

The clamour was receding down into the valley as I dashed outside. I noticed the gate to the kangaroo paddock standing open! Hurrying forward, I saw the body of Blue Belle lying in the gap. Poor little Belle. She was stone dead.

I raced back inside to rouse Jeff, changed into boots and went outdoors to find the others. Opal and Potch, Mathilda and Sheila were crowded into a corner of our front garden. They were trembling violently and impossible to approach but looked unhurt so I left them to calm down. Missing were Mick and Gidgea. The boys joined us as we paused by the gate to try and guess what had happened. We figured the dogs must have come up from the creek and panicked the 'roos. For once in her life, Belle reached the gate first. Terrified, she must have banged into it, popping it open but breaking her neck. Poor, poor Blue Belle. The others jumped over her seeking safety in our garden. So where were the remaining two?

We began to comb the paddock. Jagged trails through its long grass and dents in the netting fence told the story of the chase. Van called out that he could see Mick up the hill, hopping about distractedly. He must have managed to clear the fence. Still no sign of Gidgea. Please, oh please, I prayed silently. Then I found her.

She was up in a corner of the paddock behind the chooks' pen, standing like Eeyore with her head almost touching the ground. When I approached her cautiously, murmuring soothing words to her, I saw that her cheeks had ballooned like someone with mumps and her neck was swollen to the size of her shoulders. She must have banged full speed into the fence. Her neck might be broken. Her nose and mouth were dripping with saliva, she seemed paralysed and almost unconscious. To touch, she felt burning hot.

I called the others. Gently Jeff and the boys lifted her and carried her into the yard, ever so slowly to avoid jarring her injured spine. I dashed ahead and, on impulse, opened the door of the little feed room next to the Boys' Museum. 'Hold her,' I called, 'just hold her while I prepare a place.'

Working like a whirlwind, I covered the floor with newspapers and straw, then gathered up as many soft blankets as I could lay my hands on. They brought her in and placed her gently on her side. Jeff prepared a sweet drink and we force-fed her, very slowly, inserting an eye-dropper into the side of her mouth where there were no teeth. I sponged her wrists and ankles to cool her fever. When she began to shiver, I covered her with a blanket.

We rang our friendly vet. George Borys came and injected penicillin against pneumonia. Then he shrugged. 'There is really nothing else I can do for her. More than likely, she will die.'

All through that day I tended her, talking softly all the while. Encouraging, loving, coaxing. 'You can't die, Gidgea, you *mustn't* die.' When evening came, she seemed no better and perhaps a little weaker. Dinner was a miserable meal, scratched together and eaten in silence. Afterwards, Jeff put his arm around me and told me that Gidgea probably wouldn't make it through the night. I should prepare myself to lose her. When I went upstairs to kiss the lads goodnight, they told me the same thing. They'd obviously talked among themselves and were worried for me, as well as for the animal.

Somehow I couldn't give her up. I tried to settle in bed beside

Jeff but it was no good. When he dozed off, I got up very quietly and went out to the feed room with a torch. Kneeling beside Gidgea, I laid my head on her gently, and stroked her as I had done when she first came to our place. 'Don't give up, Gidgea,' I pleaded. 'Just relax and time will heal you. Only don't give up.'

I must have dozed off beside her. Jeff came out looking for me hours later and I woke with a start. I was cramped but Gidgea was still alive.

I spent most of that night with her, giving her sweet drinks by torchlight. By morning, she was no worse. And she let me do everything for her. She seemed to realise how much we wanted to save her. When she was still with us by evening, we began to hope she might recover.

It was four days before she could stand. The boys helped to raise her, so she wouldn't strain herself. The swollen tissue round her face and neck took weeks to return to normal. But gradually, gradually she began to pick at food – rolled oats, chopped grass – then she moved stiffly about and at last she hopped out of the feed room and returned to garden life. I swear Jim smiled and wagged his tail.

The aftermath of that night was twofold. For one thing, the menfolk remained on the alert in case the dogs returned. Jeff put out the word round the valley that any dog found chasing on our place could be shot. As keepers of a wildlife refuge, he was empowered to confiscate or destroy canine invaders.

He learned that our night raid was not common but neither was it unheard of. Farmers lost newborn lambs to marauding dogs occasionally. Worse was when pregnant cows were chased and harassed until they miscarried or fell down dead from exhaustion. The culprits were usually two or three farm dogs, normally disciplined workers, who joined together and went for a wild night out. Some farmers thought the full moon or some other natural factor was the catalyst.

The second effect of that horrific accident was the change in Gidgea's behaviour. For the next year or so, there was no shifting her from our house–studio orbit. She stuck to us like glue, the most people oriented of our adult kangaroos. She acted as if she were now a person, or at least a dog.

15

The 1970s – branching out

As we entered the 1970s, things were changing. Foxground was no longer Shangri-la. Indeed, it felt like the hub of the universe. Through our eclectic stream of visitors, our journalistic travels across the continent and back again, plus what we read and heard on radio, we kept in touch with the wider world and, like good concerned citizens, pondered and discussed. The Vietnam War dragged on, black kids ran blockades to attend desegregated schools in America's deep south, JF Kennedy and Martin Luther King came and went and our chosen lifestyle evolved.

Decimal currency arrived and metric measures replaced imperial, but didn't completely stick. The local farmers never really took to hectares. Acres denoted the size of your land then, and largely still do. Kilos and litres would cause years of head-scratching, but within a decade they did supersede hundredweights and tons, quarts and gallons. When pounds, shillings and pence ceased to be legal tender, prompt acceptance was forced upon us, but an interesting example of human nature occurred during the first few weeks following the changeover. As luck would have it, we sent cattle to the saleyard the day after decimal currency was introduced. The new prices *sounded* twice as much as the old, because there were roughly two dollars to one pound. So as each beast went under the hammer, the buyers grumbled: 'There's no

way I'll pay that. No, sir! That's twice what she's worth!' Thus we
had to bring two heifers home until the farmers' thinking caught
up with the arithmetic.

I began to have misgivings about animal husbandry as it was
practised then. First was cattle branding. Jeff went through all the
steps to create and officially register the word FOX above a line
(Fox-over-ground, get it?). It made a handsome iron, quite large,
but we could never bring ourselves to use it. We relied instead on
tail-tag numbers and our own stud book entries. Living where we
did, our beasts neither strayed nor were rustled. Thank goodness.

Dehorning was another practice we adopted at first. Cattle can
injure each other once their horns grow long. They can also get
caught up in fences. So it was correct procedure to yard them and
run them through the crush while a vet snipped off their horns
with a huge set of shears. We stood by to hold their heads and try
to soothe their fear and their pain. Blood flew from the open cuts,
their eyes rolled white and they bellowed, bellowed for quite some
time after. You were meant to put a sticky substance on the stump
to keep it from getting flyblown and I used to watch those big
beasts, known since calf-hood, shaking their heads and moaning,
tongues licking their big granular noses as if to reach and cool the
hurting.

After a few seasons of this, a thought surfaced which I had
been repressing. It was no different to our visiting the dentist and
having him cut off a tooth just above the roots without anaesthetic.
I mentioned this to Jeff and he admitted that he, too, was not
comfortable with the procedure. So we stopped dehorning our
cattle.

Sending cattle away to the saleyards is part and parcel of
farming. Every week the local livestock carrier made his rounds
of the district, picking up everything from unwanted day-old
calves to mature beasts of several hundredweight. Pushing them
up the ramp into the truck took some doing. The animals balked
and called out, the carter swore. He hit them with a stick, twisted
their tails until they squealed and finally put his boot into their
rumps to cram them amongst the other beasts. It was common
practice. It was awful. Unloading at the saleyards and pushing
them through the selling ring was further trauma.

Looking around our district, we saw that farmers with prize

herds had their own transport and treated their animals more carefully, to avoid bruising and distress. Stud sales were conducted on the property, bypassing the saleyard. Perhaps we would have gone this way had we continued with cattle husbandry. As things worked out, we were not sorry to be free of the crueler practices, which were rooted in a belief that humans are superior to other species. Animals were created to serve men's needs. They did not suffer, or if they did, compassion was unfashionable. Without going to extremes, we began to feel all right about rejecting that premise.

Having said that, I never begrudge those years of trying to emulate traditional farmers. The attitudes I learned then stood me in good stead as I progressed into professional wildlife care. A display of strength, sometimes bolstered by anger, will deflate most fractious animals, including wild ones. It is necessary to pump oneself up and refuse to accept rebellion – for the good of the animal as well as oneself.

The only time this understanding failed me was with Smokey, the demon horse. He was a Welsh mountain pony bought for Van by his grandmother from a young suburban guy who could no longer afford to keep it. He led us to believe Smokey was a gelding. But he wasn't. He was a young stallion, already headstrong. This explained why young Van, who was normally very good with animals, could not control him. He could not stay on him. Neither could Jeff, who knew how to ride but had no liking for horses. Goth and I and the dogs gave Smokey a wide berth. He bit and made free with his hooves, and his favourite pastime was backing me up against a barbed wire fence so he could kick me. I was completely bluffed by him. Yet I disliked myself for fearing him. In the end we sold him to a local riding school, which gelded him and put him to ferrying kids on his broad little back. He lived out a long life, doing that.

My love affair with old-fashioned technology also lost some of its bloom, not because it was too hard but because I hadn't the *time* that Grandma had. At first, that might sound silly. Olden-day folks worked from dawn to dusk. Well, so did we. Our problem was taking on too many activities your normal Foxground farmer would never be concerned with. We had our feet in the past but our heads in the present, and that became our trouble.

A simple life takes time. Wood coppers and stoves do excellent jobs. They boil, bake and simmer perfectly, provided the wood is right, the flue is clean and the ashes removed regularly. If not, it is a battle to keep your fires stoked. Some days I ran from one appliance to the other as my blazes spluttered too low to do their jobs. You cannot neglect fires. For a start, you need good tinder. In our family, as in all families throughout time and the world, getting in the 'morning's wood' was the youngsters' task. It was character-building, because without proper fuel there could be no food cooked, no bath water, no cosy warmth in the evenings. Keeping up the kindling is a lesson in self-protection and also service to family.

Goth and Van, and Thor when he was at the farm, were very cooperative about chores, always willing to provide muscle or leg-power when their father or I needed assistance. They would pose for the camera when Jeff wanted human figures in a shot; ferry freshly harvested produce from the garden; climb the ladder to pick the highest pears or peaches; walk up to the back paddock in search of missing cows or to shut a gate. But nothing prompted excuses – sore leg, lots of homework, headache – like being reminded that the kindling box was empty.

I enjoy gathering firewood. It is a grand excuse to nip to the forest edge and focus on small natural dramas beyond our homo-centric household. In outback Australia I acquired a love for hunting up good dry sticks, putting my boot on them and hearing them snap in two, their promise of a substantial campfire; it stayed with me and is in me still. However, it was one more task to add to an already overloaded day.

So we caved in and installed a small hot-water heater in the bathroom where the chip heater used to stand. Called the Zip, it took the chore out of drawing baths. No longer need we hop into the same warm tub, one after the other, because making four separate ones took too long.

When we first moved to Foxground, on the hottest summer days when physical work was out of the question at noon, I used to take soap, shampoo, comb, towel and sometimes a book, and make my way down through what became the kangaroo paddock to the stream. The sudsy part was done on the bank but the creek was for rinsing and steeping. Between a cluster of big rocks I

dammed up a little pool, shallow enough to be warmed by the sun
but deep enough for sitting in. Its bottom was clean sand and
sweet water changed by the minute as fresh flowed through. After
bathing, I sat on a big warm rock and let the sun dry me, watching
my all-over slick shrink to big, then smaller drops of bright clean
glistening water. It was my idyll. Private, shared with no one but
birds, lizards and insects. Never will I, never should I, forget it.
But necessity now kept me at my desk in the cool stone dairy
during the hot midday hours.

In the kitchen, the technological revolution continued. I did
not entirely give up preparing food on the wood stove, particularly
in winter, but I supplemented it, first with a small table-top electric
stove we brought from Grays Point, and later with a basic gas
range. This made cooking quicker and, in summer, cooler.

When my struggles with the smoky copper in the laundry
ended, I was not sorry. We bought a second-hand washing
machine, a round tub on legs with bakelite paddles that slowly
went swish, swish, back and forth, until you turned it off and
ringered the clothes into the laundry trough alongside for hand
rinsing. Water was heated by a portable immersion heater. It did
make washday, which was almost every day, easier. I doubted the
clothes came out as clean as with a properly boiling wood fire, but
that was probably my imagination. Or a niggling feeling of capit-
ulation. What would Grandma think?

Added to my ambivalence about the new arrangements was a
tragedy that occurred one day when I was trying to work in three
places at once and left the new washing machine running, unattended. Swallows nested in the laundry every year; that day a
pair were sitting on eggs up near the roof. While we waited for the
babies to hatch, it was never too much trouble to enter quietly,
keeping small and non-threatening, because it was such a joy to
observe the parents fly in, twittering and scolding, with insects to
feed their yawping brood. It only lasted a few weeks before the
infants clambered onto the edge of their sculptured mud home and
teetered there owlishly, ready for launch. Then the whole family
flew away together. No problem.

However, this day I returned to the laundry to finish off my
washing and vaguely noticed things were too quiet. The soapy
water had bubbled right to the top with prolonged agitation, and

when I drained the washing machine I saw the sad story. Two sodden little bodies lay on the bottom. The parents must have flown in and mistaken the suds for a solid surface. Landing, they were sucked down and drowned. Oh dear. Oh *dear*! From then on, I kept the machine covered during swallow season.

This was easy when, a few years later, I graduated to a twin-tub washer. Out of the question was getting an automatic machine because they required mains pressure water to activate their cycles. Our water supply was fresh, pure, but slow, and getting slower as the original old pipes grew rust inside. Occasionally the flow stopped altogether. This usually followed heavy rain. The inlet pipe entered the creek above the waterfall, weighted by lumps of old iron wired to it, even bolted to the rock in places. When the creek ran a banker after storms, this contrivance washed out. Torrents roared for hours, or even days. We would discover our pipe wrapped around a tree above the flood, the banks and surrounding bush festooned with debris. Usually we had to wait until the creek receded before we could replace the inlet, so we carried containers up to the first creek crossing and dippered them full. For a day or so, we sparingly used water out of buckets and pots covered with clean tea towels. I never minded. Somehow it satisfied my yen for coping with adversity. For getting back to basics, a lesson I was happy for our children to learn, and a reminder for urban visitors how spoiled they were with a piped-in water supply they took for granted.

Jeff was forever tinkering with our primitive water system, which worked on the principle of a simple siphon, placed high. He extended the inlet, dug up pipes to see if they were blocked. We all took turns on the shovel, good virtuous exercise. Among our 'hippy' friends were several young engineers and much time was spent picking their brains for ratios of height of inlet to length of pipe. They instructed us about corrosion and also about air locks. Air locks – the nemesis of plumbing.

Jeff resisted suggestions that we put in big tanks to catch roof run-off. Our creek siphon system was fine; the streams of Foxground would never go dry, the water so fresh, so healthful, so good tasting, so unpolluted, so cheap. We never begrudged time and energy spent on our creek water supply – and still don't.

However, in most other departments we did need to win time,

so gradually we relinquished our (my) ideals and upgraded to modern conveniences. A septic tank and flushing toilet was one innovation I never objected to. I saw it as a trade-off. People who ride in Porsches shouldn't have to bury sanitary cans. Yet I took pride in being able to do that chore. Other women I talked to, the respectable dames of Berry Parents and Citizens and Red Cross Ladies' Auxiliary apparently neither wanted to, nor had to, dig the hole and wrestle with the slopping, stinking receptacle. Even the farmers' wives of Foxground left that to The Men. I learned the tricks of tipping so the contents didn't splash. And felt good when I replaced the container, hosed clean and odourless, back in its freshly swept and sanitised cubicle. Both down at the cottage and up near our back door, I treated the two 'little houses' as carefully as if they were indoors.

The cottage was my province. I tended its garden, cleaned after each lot of tenants, provided comfort and welcome for the next lot – a pot of homemade jam on the table, flowers, a note. Orchestrating their delight was my pleasure. I handled the bookings, collected the rent money. It was one of my contributions to family revenue.

Another was the Jeff Carter bookshop, which began as a quaint little display in the tiny feed room adjoining the Boys' Museum. From there I fulfilled requests from visitors to buy Jeff's books, which now numbered seven. After I became a licensed bookseller, I expanded my range to include other good outback texts. Next I created a book service for school libraries. In those days, Nowra and Berry were considered too far off the beaten track to warrant visits from book salesmen, so once a month I went up to Sydney and spent a frantic day driving from one publisher's warehouse to the next, choosing books for my country clients. It became my escape, a day when I felt completely self-determined. Making the bookshop pay, and keeping the accounts for the family, farm and journalistic business were challenges I welcomed.

I also gave talks at service clubs to promote Jeff's books. They always wanted a guest speaker for Ladies' Day. I put a lot into preparing displays, maps and photographs. Looking back on how I pandered to the prejudices of the era makes me queasy. They saw as eccentric my involvement with wildlife, our journeys across lonely tracks carrying petrol, water and food because there were no safari stops then, no desert roadhouses, just cattle stations and the camps of miners, drovers and water drillers. I presented myself as the obedient servant, the willing 'little woman', trailing along after 'her man'. Well, maybe that's how it was. Yet I felt an equal to Jeff. Although he was the instigator, my contributions added more than just muscle and comfort. Mine was a worldly outlook for those times. And it was an important element in our family equation.

The articles I wrote for magazines were another source of income, but the more extrovert jobs became my first priority. Nature and nurture. Obviously, I lacked a personal career drive strong enough to keep writing as my principle craft. *Life* was my art form in those days, life on Glenrock and travelling through the inland bush. It kept me busy.

Jeff was always busy too. As well as his involvement with the property, he churned out articles, books and photographs, travelled far to get material for them, then carted his product to Sydney for sale. When I did not accompany him, my pride lay in coping with most things in his absence.

There was only one job I couldn't manage: putting down creatures that needed it. I seemed to have a great antipathy to actually killing anything. I gladly cleaned and dressed the poultry, handling all their organs without squeamishness to assess what had made them tick. My studies in zoology made this a skill I could share with my sons and it was fascinating to observe how a particular chook's behaviour could be explained, postmortem, by finding extra large, or small, gonads, an abnormal liver or heart. One of my happiest days was dissecting a worm with Van, pinning it open on a board and teasing out its thread-like nervous and digestive systems as I'd been taught to do at college.

But when I tried to stretch a chook's neck and dislocate it, as Jeff did in preparation for the cooking pot, I bungled the job, every time. Tried hard, talked myself into the deed in logical principle but in practice, after repeatedly stretching the neck without quite the correct twist, I let the bewildered fowl go and cooked an omelette instead.

When Laika and Jim and their daughter Lulu ran riot down the valley, chasing cattle, it was Jeff who went to fetch them home, took them up to the orchard and, without family consultation, shot two of them. Guess which two? I was glad to have Jim still around, but felt it reflected unfairly on the females, who had been my pets. Lulu had been a silly, excitable little mongrel, but Laika was like one of the family. I pondered her fate and privately fretted over it. On the one hand, to be fair, I knew that once dogs get the taste for chasing livestock (or wild creatures), they will do it again, even if intermittently. On the other hand, I believed in my deepest mind – which was beginning to question the chauvinistic attitudes surrounding me – that Jeff shot the two females for reasons of gender prejudice. Nothing fair about that. Unknown to me, Jeff also had misgivings about shooting Laika but he couldn't admit it, not then, because a man had to do what a man had to do. It was a time of rethinking, like I said. Within a year or so, I defied Jeff's ban on keeping more than one dog by acquiring young Gentle Brownie from the Conroy family. In a roundabout way, she was a descendant of Jim and Laika and she was no trouble, except as a symbol of my incipient 'revolution'.

In most things, however, I went along with the desires of my restless husband. And this is how, early in the 1970s, I found myself a film producer and front person for a documentary film series. It was an appropriate step for me, having grown up near Hollywood with an aunt as an actress in silent movies, my mother a bit player, her sister and most of their friends involved in the industry. It provided good experience for our sons and daughter. And it satisfied Jeff's urge for something new and challenging. But it also ultimately affected life on Glenrock, which changed drastically in the following decade.

For years people had been saying that Jeff should buy a movie camera. As a still cameraman, he had a remarkable facility for capturing people in action. Candid photography was the only sort he liked, and he shot sequence after sequence of people at work or play, catching the essence of what was happening as it happened.

The trouble was, it was largely wasted. Magazine and book publishers used single photos and then, reluctantly. Reproducing pictures was expensive in those days. All Jeff's wonderful series – rodeo riders, sheep herders and shearers, abalone divers, charcoal burners, cattle drovers, opal miners and whale hunters – sat in his files, unused. Jeff felt frustrated about their non-use, although for him it was the taking of the pictures that counted.

So when photographer friend Roger Whittaker urged Jeff to take up cinematography as a natural vehicle for his skills, he succumbed. Television was the glamour medium then, predicted to kill off the printed word. Television hungered for material which could be resold round the world. The incoming Whitlam government, eager to encourage artists of many media, backed the new Australian Film Development Corporation (AFDC). It was to lend Australian film producers money and assist with marketing their product.

We decided to borrow from them, using Glenrock as collateral. Jeff, encouraged by Roger, researched the budding documentary field. Then, with his usual flair, bought the best portable 16-millimetre camera on the market, a lightweight French Eclair, and a Nagra tape recorder plus professional microphones.

We were advised to produce six half-hour films similar to the magazine stories we specialised in. Six was the standard pilot package for a television series. Four of the films would be about the outback life we knew so well and the remaining two would be about people working with nature. One of these would show Eric Worrell and his crew catching wild snakes and milking them. The other would be about our own work on Glenrock Wildlife Refuge.

As usual, we plunged in and then learned to swim. The calf shed, our largest barn, was enclosed, carpeted and air-conditioned to make a new office and an editing studio. We moved our desks and filing cabinets from the dairy and sixteen-year-old Goth moved himself into it, his first pad out of, but not away from, home.

For our series, we decided to use the title of one of Jeff's most successful books and also his long-running magazine column, *Wild Country*. I was to be the on-camera narrator. Thor would be our sound recordist. He was twenty-one now and ready for a change from education and working for strangers. Karen was also taking a break from university studies. She was twenty-four and would help with editing, as well as keeping the farm, family and office functioning while we went away filming on location. Jeff and I would be producers, directors and scriptwriters. The one non-family member of Jeff Carter Films Pty Ltd was Roger. He was the only person with experience in cine production.

There was one other important member of our little team, free-lance composer and music producer, Pat Aulton. Luckily he liked where we lived, he liked our style and he contributed his talent to our project at a price we could just afford, tailoring his fee to suit our budget because he was excited by what we wanted to produce. Not for us the stodgy talking-heads, encyclopedic style of documentary. Ours would be fresh, real and personal, filled with action and backed by Australian country rock music.

Pat composed a great theme song for our *Wild Country* series, which he adapted to the mood of each film, plus other music specific to the subject matter. He knew all the best session musicians in town and the happiest day of making each film was the one we spent in a professional recording studio watching and listening as rock and folk musos put down tracks of Pat's arrangements for our movies. Goth, Van and the rest of us, as music consumers, found it tremendously exciting to see how recordings are mixed and made. Pat's *Wild Country* theme had a great beat and I reckoned the lyrics were apt. They went like this:

Show me a long and dusty road,
I'm gonna pack my travelling load
and go . . . out into Wild Country.
      Chorus: Wild Country:
Places where the struggle's just to live.
         Wild Country:
Where gettin' along with your fellow man
is relative, to what you give
to . . . Wild Country.

Producing the six films would take four years and serious investment of time and money. The ABC was our preferred customer but they moved like treacle and paid abysmally. Commercial networks paid more, so we worked out a formula which we hoped would catch their interest. We visited them all and finally won a tenuous agreement with Channel Seven. Our pilot film captured the imagination of lateral thinker, Bruce Gyngell. Signing a letter of interest in our series was the last thing he did before leaving Australia to work in London. As each film was finished, we had to get them to accept it before we could borrow finance for the next one. It was nerve-wracking. The AFDC was our first creditor, so as fast as we delivered a finished print to the Seven Network and received their cheque, we paid our accounts and the rest went back to the Corporation.

It was a dreadful scramble, but we so loved the new medium that we kept going. Whenever we weren't on location in the outback, we shot what was happening at home. The whole family – dogs, wombats, birds, kangaroos, eagles – all were captured by Jeff's lens, including the beautiful waterfalls, the rainforest, the magic moods of Foxground's lush environment. Overnight, we all became actors. Life as we were living it on Glenrock became a movie. Borrowing another of Jeff's book titles, we called this film *Wild Animal Farm*. We considered it to be a minor part of our series – the wildlife rescue work, the unusual creatures who shared our home, were just how we lived. As things turned out, *Wild Animal Farm* became our most popular movie, our signature film. But at the time, we just made it as it happened.

We began with a montage of hectic traffic in Sydney, long before that became a cine cliché: noise, streams of cars, harassed people, synchronised to wild rock music, which ended in a slow zoom onto one of those signs they use on freeway ramps: STOP! YOU ARE GOING THE WRONG WAY. We then cut to Foxground corner and a sweet version of the *Wild Country* theme song as our Land Rover turns off the highway, drives sedately across the valley and arrives at Glenrock to the scene of me and the boys feeding 'roos, languid in a sunny paddock, Jeff at his desk sharing morning tea with Gidgea. This was a ritual she adored, pleasant and convivial; she liked to stretch up on tiptoes and steal a biscuit off his saucer with her velvet lips, nose twitching ecstatically at the fragrance from his coffee cup. Gidgea was good talent.

If that sounds like we tried to humanise the animals, think again. Never would we pander to the 'Skippy' mentality which was rife then. *Skippy* was a television series in which a kangaroo filled the sort of role played by Lassie and Mr Ed. We thought it was dreadful. And dishonest. Our experience had taught us that kangaroos have none of the sort of intelligence dogs and horses are bred for.

No, Gidgea's intrusion into our daily routines (and into our affections) was her own doing and we simply filmed things as they occurred. Quite a lot went on during that period because word had got about that we would care for injured or orphaned animals and then liberate them to live free on our property. Thus our film included another pouch joey, a baby hare, a possum, an orphaned honey-eater and a kookaburra with a broken wing. An amazing fluke presented us with the opportunity to film a quoll roaming our garden in broad daylight. Quolls are predatory carnivores and they are normally nocturnal. This one turned up for one day only and became a film star. Then we were given a tame wedge-tailed eagle and asked to prepare it for release back into the wild; we filmed the process, step by step. It made stunning footage, very inspiring because eagles are beautiful and intelligent creatures.

The script for this film wrote itself. We rarely knew how a sequence would end, until it did. But we were geared to shoot film every day and whatever occurred was captured by Jeff's lens. Naturally, because we were filming, we chose agreeable venues for events and we did contrive three sequences. The first illustrated how joeys become orphaned.

One morning the boys discovered a dead kangaroo up on the hillside next to the road; apparently it had been hit by a car during the night. Before we disposed of the body, I got an idea about how we could turn this tragedy into a windfall. We rang a neighbour who was a sporting hunter and asked him to come up dressed appropriately. Jeff shot close-ups of him aiming his rifle. Cut to a kangaroo, yawning and stretching unawares in the paddock. Sound of gunshot. Cut to a dead kangaroo supine in the grass, its back to the camera. The hunter's boots move into frame, he rests his rifle on the corpse, steps astride it and, reaching down, brings into frame a baby kangaroo which he tucks inside his jacket. Poignant!

In actual fact the dead 'roo was a male. But from the rear, you couldn't see that. The joey was an orphan I was feeding in the house; we took it out of its warm bag just long enough to shoot the scene. It seemed a vivid way to make the point.

The second contrivance was more elaborate. One of the prin-cipal players in *Wild Animal Farm* was Wally the wombat. To show how wombats are hunted and harried until they end up dead or in zoos or with people like ourselves, we filmed a sequence in which we apparently found one caught in a wild dog trap.

We knew the brothers set traps on their grazing acres up the back, hoping to catch dogs (and eagles) eating their sheep. It is picturesque landscape – which we named the High Country – and was riddled with big old wombat burrows. At that time no one lived there. The brothers drove up from the town every week or so to check their livestock or take out timber. So we set up a sequence in which, on a bushwalk, the Carter family finds this wombat (actually it was William) caught by his foot. Aahh! We free him, wrap up his paw with a hankie and Van rides out of frame on his trailbike carrying the 'injured' animal home. Heart-warming.

The next part of the story followed the wombat settling into (disrupting) the household. Earlier we had shot footage of William in the house which could be used for this, but now he was almost fully grown and was regularly going on walkabout. What we really needed was a younger wombat to show the settling in process. Once again we were lucky. A call came from Sydney offering us an adolescent wombat to rear. The people who had him couldn't keep him any longer. He had to go. Thus we acquired Wally, the real Wally who became interchangeable with William in our movie. Wally, we discovered, was a vastly different character from placid William, but this didn't show up in the script and Wally/William became a movie legend for decades after.

The end of our story had to be when the wombat begins to roam from the household and finally returns to the wild. That took our most complex scripting and was shot over several days in various locations. It made a moving climax for our film.

The wombat-goes-wandering scenes were contrived but accurate. We had been experiencing that process with William for months. When he changed from a sooky youngster into a burly young man, he began to go about his own affairs with confidence. He still came indoors for a meal, a scratch and tickle, a sleep on the hearth, but then he took himself outdoors again. He spent more and more time in the Boys' Museum digging himself a burrow underneath the old blacksmith forge. He excavated an amazing lot of dirt, loosening it with his strong front claws, then raking it out behind him with his bandy hind legs. From the rear, he looked like a rotary hoe. Goth and Van wormed themselves into his tunnel to see where it led. They reported it curved around and was heading for the feed room. Next door was our new sound and film studio. We hoped William wouldn't undermine that!

When he wasn't digging, William began to wander further afield. We knew where he got to, because people kept ringing us up and we had to go and fetch him home again. His escapades on those journeys are worth telling, as are those of Wally as he made havoc within our farmhouse. Some of it was filmed, but not all. Most was hilarious but occasionally these two, singly and together, gave us some heart-stopping moments. Torrid, taxing, yet endearing. More of that later.

When Wally grew into *his* walkabout stage, it was time to finish *Wild Animal Farm*. Our biggest scriptwriting and acting challenge. In fact, it was easy. Day One, we carried Wally to the waterfall track and then Jeff filmed him bravely waddling through groves of tree ferns, across the creek, up rocky hillsides. Then he filmed Karen and Goth, me and Van going over the same ground, calling: 'Wa-lly!'

Day Two, we mounted an expedition up to the grazing lands above our farm, me driving the Land Rover, Goth and Karen as passengers and Van riding his trailbike. Jeff filmed us passing. Wally rode with us in the truck but the camera didn't see that. As luck had it, a thick mist was rolling over the escarpment and cascading like whipped cream onto the slopes. There was a moist, magical silence up there and Jeff captured it beautifully, setting the scene for Wally's return to nature.

The script read like this:

MARE: 'When we couldn't find Wally anywhere on our farm, we decided to return to the high country where we first found him.'

WIDE SHOTS OF GOTH, KAREN, MARE SEARCHING ON FOOT, AS VAN ON TRAILBIKE RIDES OVER ROUGH TERRAIN, SEEKING WOMBAT. CLOSE-UPS AS CAST PEERS INTO WOMBAT BURROWS CALLING: 'Wally?'

DISTANT SHOT, GOTH RAISES HIS ARM AND POINTS. MEDIUM SHOT OF VAN LEANING AGAINST HIS PARKED BIKE, WAITING FOR THE OTHERS TO ARRIVE. CAMERA CLOSES ON WALLY NEAR HIS FEET, HAPPILY ABSORBED IN DIGGING OUT ONE OF THE OLD BURROWS. FAMILY MOVES INTO FRAME. SMILING, THEY KNEEL TO WATCH AS

WALLY CONTINUES HIS EXCAVATION.
MARE: 'Wally was so intent on digging, he hardly noticed us going. But we were content to leave him there. He was back on his own ground, in Wild Country.'
CAMERA PULLS BACK AS FAMILY RISES AND LEAVES WAL, STILL HAPPILY AT WORK ON HIS NEW HOME. THEME MUSIC UP AND OVER.

In real life it happened much like that. What happened before Wally returned to life in the wild is a saga in itself, most of which wouldn't fit into our half-hour documentary. The adventures of William and Wally were a feature film in themselves.

When William began to roam, his route always took him northward, in the direction of Jamberoo on the other side of the mountain. Which was odd, since he had come from the south, down near Jervis Bay.

People kept ringing us. ' 'Scuse me, do you own a wombat? Because there's one in our house and somebody said it might be yours.'

It always was. Wombats had become very rare in our district. Farmers had been shooting them for years because they undermine fences, letting in rabbits or wallabies which eat crops. So William caused quite a stir when he ambled up to someone's house and demanded to be let in.

It happened first on a New Year's Eve. Way up on Saddleback, far from Foxground, William crashed a party. Just before midnight, the host heard scratching at the door. Thinking it was a late guest, he opened up and found William standing on the porch. 'Come in,' the man invited and William obliged. He became the life of that party. He gave them a wonderful night and vice versa. Next morning, he was bundled into a sack and returned to us. But first they took his picture for the local newspaper, and from then on people knew where he belonged and rang us to fetch him home.

The next time he scratched at someone's front door, he was not so welcome. The lady had just recarpeted her house. But William was lured into the laundry with a loaf of bread and then we were rung and requested to remove him as soon as possible.

Once a family of animal lovers kept him for several days. Theirs was an old-fashioned farmhouse like ours and the bathroom had been added late. Here Will was induced to set up camp, feted with all sorts of tidbits, treated to endless cuddles by the kids and bedded on chaff bags arranged in the old bathtub, the sort with lion's foot legs and high sides. It was only because they needed to bathe that the family caved in and informed us where our wombat had got to that time.

Not long after, William became trapped in a pit at the Jamberoo milk factory. This was right in the centre of town, a long, long walk from Foxground. Another night he fell asleep on the front doormat of that town's bowling club. Residents were amazed next morning to find this big furry beast snoring on the stoop. Thor drove to Jamberoo at once. As he lifted Will, still sleeping, and began carrying him to the Land Rover, people came from everywhere. They had been too scared to approach him before, but now eager hands stroked William's coarse fur and fingered his strong claws. Thor was buckling at the knees under William's weight, yet patiently stood while they satisfied their curiosity and William dozed through it all. He was used to adulation by now.

Next, Will disgraced us by ripping the screen door off the mail lady's house. Whatever prompted him to do it, we could not guess. He had never been seen there before, yet this night he awakened them by screaming and clawing at their front portal. They tiptoed in their nightwear to watch their flywire door disintegrating. In response to a frantic phone call, we rushed down in our pyjamas and fetched William home. Next day, full of apologies, Jeff replaced the ruined screen with a new one and we prayed, without confidence, that William would not repeat the performance. Luckily, he did not.

Not everyone tolerated Will's antics so well. He came home with a wound on his head that was clearly from a gunshot. The bullet had creased his skull, nearly severing his ear. As William shook his head in pain, maggots flew out. The wound was flyblown. We put a dressing on it and then Jeff lifted big fat William back into his old enclosure outside the dairy. He settled down in his barrel with a contented sigh, happy to be fussed over and handfed while he convalesced, patient and stolid like he'd been in his younger days. That wound left a pale scar on William's head which in years to come made it easy to distinguish him from other wombats at a distance, padding about our place during the dark hours. When he was healed, Jeff and the boys took him down to a burrow he had dug under the huge slab of rock the cottage stood on, and there he settled for a while.

He visited our house off and on for years, always coming in with complete trust as if he had never been away. His story was, in a sense, the end of the tale we tried to spin in *Wild Animal Farm*. The middle parts were played by Wally, who was the second of a dozen or more wombats we reared and released during the 1970s and '80s. Each had its own personality, within a fairly narrow range of wombat behaviours. And Wally, we discovered, was a vastly different character to our dear doddering William.

It seemed like fortune had smiled on us when the call came asking us to take Wally. We badly needed a younger wombat to intercut with the footage of William for the movie. However, we were not so confident when we met Wally.

He was brought to us in a state of agitation. He had been living with a chaotic family of many kids and they claimed they couldn't manage Wally any longer, he was out of control. After meeting them, however, we reckoned it was the other way around. As soon as they entered our house, it became like a cement mixer. The kids put the wombat down and began shrieking and jumping about. Wally responded by chasing them, which made them run even faster, jumping onto coffee tables and the couch. Plates fell off the kitchen dresser, conversation was impossible. We were glad to see them go, minus their poor addled animal.

Wally will settle down, we told ourselves. He will respond to loving kindness and a firm, quiet routine. Our confidence bordered on smugness after our experiences with William. We discovered, however, that there are wombats and wombats. William had been a stolid character compared to peppery Wal, who was friskier, jumpier, nippier, faster and far more wakeful than William. Well, we told ourselves philosophically, wombats must be just like people. Each one a little different. We set ourselves to learn the needs and tempo of this new animal, around which our lives instantly revolved. It was a period fraught with trials and laughter. Wally kept us always on the go.

Like William, Wally loved a late afternoon romp when Goth and Van were in the mood for some rough-and-tumble after a day at school. However, Wally not only jumped higher than William, he bit harder. William used to sort of mouth your ankle if he wanted your attention. Only rarely did he give you a serious nip. Wally was much more positive. He'd snap his teeth closed on exposed flesh and it hurt. The lads took to wearing gumboots when they exercised him but, unless they were on guard, Wal jumped even higher and bit their calves above the rubber. And where William used to stand up and drag down a chair cushion to cuddle, Wally wanted one to chew! Within his first few days at our place, he had demolished several crumb-rubber pillows, scattering bits in all directions before settling down amid the chaos for a nap.

It never occurred to us to give up on Wally, however. Not just because we wanted to film him but because we were full of wonder at these lumpish Australian marsupials and we saw it as a privilege to have another one in our care. Jeff kept his cine camera loaded with film at all times. The portable lights were primed too. And we retained an attitude of readiness to step in front of the camera with Wally, whatever he did next.

Thus when Wally ate the wallpaper in our bedroom, we saw it as a gift and Jeff rushed to set up camera and lights. One minute Wal was nosing quietly around the floor. The next, he discovered a tiny bit of loose wallpaper, took it precisely between his front teeth and jerked backwards. A foot-long strip of 'cinnamon tweed' came away. Wally settled down on his haunches contently to chew it up.

Soon there was a bald patch in our bedroom and Wal was happily surrounded by expensive crumbs. Under normal circumstances, I would have been angry. The bedroom had just been repapered, by me. But my ardour for home improvements was as nothing compared to my enthusiasm for film-making. This made a beaut cine anecdote and I figured I'd cover the scar with a cupboard.

Now, cupboards. Wally was a devil for getting inside them. It was utterly fatal to leave any door ajar. That blunt nose was as deft as a lizard's tongue for getting things open. Then in would go Wal and out would come everything in the cupboard. He was worse than a possum for chucking things out. Couldn't bear having things in his road. They had to go!

After emptying the cupboard, Wally loved to chew up the shelf linings. Getting hold of him to drag him out was difficult. He humped himself into a round ball you couldn't get any purchase on. He was strong too. Thirty pounds of squirming, straining, stubborn wombat is hard to drag from a bottom shelf. You try it sometime.

It was all grist for the movie mill, however. When I did the ironing, Wally 'helped' by tossing the clean clothes out of the basket. Then he raked them into a bundle and, hugging them beatifically to his chest, he fell asleep at my feet.

When I left the door of the central guest bedroom unlatched, Wally nosed it open and went inside. He leapt straight onto the bed, wormed his way down under the clean sheets and put himself to sleep. He looked so cute I let him do it again. And yet again. Then one day we returned to the house to find that Wally had scratched open the ticking. The mattress had exploded into snow-drifts of kapok. From then on, the guestroom door stayed latched.

When I neglected to put away the box of stale bread I bought off the local baker for the kangaroos, Wally found it on the hearth and chewed up loaf after loaf. I brought the vacuum cleaner to remove the mess and Wal offered me his bloated tummy. For fun, I ran the cleaner nozzle over it and he stretched voluptuously. Jeff captured the whole incident on film and, from then on, Wally loved to be vacuum cleaned.

Head-butting was a game Wally enjoyed. Van used to get down on his hands and knees and offer his skull to the wombat. He soon learned, however, that Wally was much better equipped than he, so that game faded away. Football was Wally's favourite. He couldn't resist the leather. The boys would throw the ball and Wally would chase it, jump on it and try to bonk it. As it rolled away beneath him, he leapt after it. This became a hilarious opening for our film.

When Van went off fishing or rabbit hunting, Goth exercised the wombat on his own. He invented a game he called Matador. Waving a red shirt in front of his legs, he tempted Wally to jump at it. This was easy because his first family had taught him all sorts of aggressive habits. Wally loved Goth's game. He charged again and again, so quickly that Goth grew breathless and had to jump onto a garden table for sanctuary. Goth dropped the red shirt onto Wally's back and he stalked off proudly. The winner! In our movie, we backed this with Spanish bullfight music and crowd sound. *'Olé! Olé!'* It always raised a laugh.

Each evening while I prepared dinner, Wally would be in the kitchen under my feet. If I was slow in getting his food, he reached up very precisely and nipped me on the knee. It hurt and never failed to achieve his objective, which was for me to give him some dog biscuits to munch. Yes, his previous carers had given him that snack habit too. It made good television, but I worried about the protein content for a herbivorous animal.

Like William, Wally had no trouble opening the outside doors. Snibbing them did no good. He methodically dismantled the wooden panels of the dear old side screen door, flung apart the boards and clamoured in through the gap. Luckily Jeff was filming the day the door swung open with him hanging onto its bottom frame. Like a tubby little trapeze artist, he swung back and forth in space until we rescued him. Another funny sequence for our movie.

While Wally was enjoying the home comforts at the Carters', William was off on walkabout. We kept our eyes open for his return, following his trail down past the old oak tree to the burrow near the cottage. He always marked his presence with a large fresh dropping displayed on the track or a rock near his cave. Sometimes we caught sight of him on hot days asleep on his front stoop. His great silvery body would be inside his tunnel but his chin rested on his paws at the entrance, where he might catch a cooling breeze.

After months on his own, William began to revisit our yard. He pushed his way under the back fences. Or bashed his way in through gaps which turned into gapes. Just on dusk, we'd hear 'Meep-meep-meep', and dear old William would come lumbering round the corner of our house heading for the back door.

Instant panic. Where was Wally? We sensed we should keep them apart. However, we also knew we couldn't keep William out of the house. So we would whisk Wal up into the living room and close the adjoining door, while admitting William into the kitchen. We made a fuss of him, gave him some brown bread to munch and then he would meander out again and depart.

Whoever had been minding Wally in the lounge would return with him to the kitchen. Did Wally sniff the lino and paw the floor with rage? No. Nor did William appear to find anything amiss when he came to visit the house. It seemed strange. They both liked to rub their bony backsides on the legs of the dining table and chairs. We had read that this stimulated a gland near their ridiculous little tail to secrete a scent marking their territory. But in practice, within our house at least, neither William nor Wally seemed to smell anything alien. So maybe they just rubbed their backs because they were itchy.

It was when William decided to reoccupy his diggings beneath the Boys' Museum that we had a problem. Wally had been prowling around under there, having a little dig now and again. If William should encounter Wally down his hole, there might be a fight. Jeff decided to construct a barrier of corrugated iron and heavy implements across the entrance to the museum to prevent either wombat from entering. But it didn't stop William. In one night he managed to dig his way under the barricade, making a shocking mess. We weren't sure if he had gone down his hole or where he was, so we decided we'd better put Wally under constant surveillance in case he and William encountered one another.

The next few days, in fact the ensuing weeks, became a nightmare of keeping the wombats separate. William had become aware of Wally's presence now and he prowled the garden, squealing as if in challenge. Wally was stirred up too. Although he was only two-thirds the size of William, he was such a fast and aggressive little character that we weren't sure who might win, should a fight occur.

There were some very close calls. On several occasions we would hear William making his plodding way round the house, meeping and occasionally screaming, causing Wally to stop grazing and gear himself into bristling alertness until someone snatched him up and dashed with him into the house while someone else went for bread to distract William. We were forever dropping one wombat or the other into the Wombatarium, which was strong enough to contain either of them. The one inside would be screaming with rage or frustration (or fear?) while the one outside paced and garumped and pawed the ground. It was nerve-wracking.

It was also time-consuming. The hours between four and seven in the evening became 'wombats time', during which all of us were pressed into service protecting our two friends from each other. We had several near misses. Once I found myself inside the

museum trying to grab Wally by his back legs while William
hurled himself furiously at the corrugated iron barricade held in
place, barely, by both Goth and Van. It took all their strength to
resist his charges until Jeff arrived, swung him up into his arms
– a risky feat since William was gnashing and frothing – and
carried him to the enclosure.

One time Jim got in the road and was tossed halfway across
the yard by William. He yelped and slunk off. We had seen Jim
kicked by cows yet go back again to nip their heels and move
them in the direction he wanted. But he lost his nerve with the
furious wombat. William in a rage could bluff our brave Jim, no
worries.

Finally, a near disaster brought things to a head. It scared us all.
Somehow William and Wally managed to get down the burrow
beneath the shed at the same time. They must have fought underground and their ruckus caused a cave-in. It had been raining for
days before and water must have seeped down under the buildings, perhaps contributing to the collapse of the tunnel. It was
action stations for all hands. Every shovel was put to use, Jeff and
the boys dug furiously to open the shaft and I helped remove the
buckets and buckets of sticky wet earth.

At last, out crawled William. He was coated in red mud and so
exhausted he could hardly flick an ear or lift a paw. I wrapped him
in a big towel and then in a blanket, swept by a wave of affection
for this great simpleton, this trusting booby. Surely we couldn't
lose him, in such a manner, so close to home

The big question was, could Wally still be alive somewhere
down the hole? Van, holding a torch, wormed his way into the
excavation, regardless of the mud. Goth held his legs. When Van
was hauled out again, he said he could hear a faint digging coming
from underground.

It was like a mine disaster. The fellows worked furiously,
shifting dirt. Jeff rigged up his film lights to give them as much
illumination as possible. No thought of filming. This was a life and
death rescue. It seemed that boulders had fallen into the shaft and
Wal was trying to dig under them. When as much earth as could
be reached had been removed, there was nothing more to do but
wait and hope Wally had the stamina to get himself free. Jeff
went down on his belly and stuck his head into the shaft, to 'talk'

Wally out. Coaxing, encouraging, repeating his name over and over, Jeff urged the little fellow on.

At last he wriggled under the final rock. 'He's coming,' Jeff said.

We could all hear the pitiful, anxious meeping of a little wombat, homing in on his loved ones calling to him. The sound was faint and hollow but it was coming closer. At last Wally appeared around a bend and flopped down in the hole, utterly worn out. Someone crawled in and dragged him the rest of the way. His back was red-raw under the caking of mud where he had squeezed past rocks. He, too, was quickly swaddled in a towel and warm wrappings. We had been very lucky to save both animals.

The shock wore off us in about twenty-four hours. It took a lot longer for the wombats to recover, and both had to literally grow new hide where their skin had been rubbed off during their frantic escape digs. Their front claws were broken and they were very subdued, content to be nursed and nurtured.

Jeff blocked up that tunnel inside the museum shed, using big boulders and cement. Then, when William had recovered from his accident, we took him down the track to his burrow under the cottage rock. He seemed glad to be back and trundled down his hole without saying goodbye. We didn't see him again for quite some time.

Meanwhile, Wally began to show interest in going walkabout. He started digging his way out under the gate. At first he stayed away for only a few hours. Then we'd hear him outside the gate, meeping to be let in. He could get himself out but not back, it seemed.

Then one day, he left, and did not return. We went searching for him but found nothing. William also had disappeared from his burrow region. We had no idea whether they might be together, or what. Hours were spent searching and calling Wally's name. Being younger and inexperienced in the wider world, he was the one we were more concerned about. We found neither animal but Vandal refused to give up. He went out with Jim for one more look and heard something down a gully. Jim barked and pointed down a steep bush-clad incline.

'Wally?' Van called.

A desperate meeping came distantly.

Van peered through dense foliage and saw at the bottom of a

steep ravine a furry little football, plastered in mud, screaming with fear, right at the end of its tether. He climbed down and gathered Wal in his arms. The slippery bank was all scratched where again and again Wally had tried to climb up. He had been trapped between the deeply running creek and an almost sheer, muddy cliff. Had Van not found him, he might have perished there. When he and we recovered from *that* shock, we decided we had better stage Wally's return to the wild for the movie camera. He might not be with us for much longer.

So after Jeff had shot all the footage he needed for that final, poignant scene, we let Wally find his way out into the wider world. He began to go bush more and more frequently, staying away longer each time. When he returned, he looked bigger and stronger, as if the experience of being out on his own agreed with him.

Of course we worried in case he struck trouble again. But somehow we all sensed he was able to cope now. And we felt content to see him go. His going was the purpose of the whole exercise, after all.

16

Horace, a truly lovely eagle

The other star of *Wild Animal Farm*, the movie, was Horace, a wedge-tailed eagle. He had been rescued out west while still a fledgling and reared in Sydney. His benefactor was a young man of kindly disposition who did everything he could for Horace. The only problem was his limited resources. He lived in a flat, worked at a factory. Each day he took Horace to work and tethered him in the factory's courtyard. Of an evening, he exercised Horace in the park. Naturally, he could not let the bird off its leash for fear of traffic and the reaction of passers-by. Most people are frightened by the sight of a fully grown eagle. He realised that, for the good of the bird, he would have to seek a more suitable habitat. He contacted the Parks and Wildlife Service and they rang us. Our brief would be to gradually release Horace back into the wild. It was a project which interested us strongly, not only because we saw potential for filming, but also because for years Jeff had championed eagles in his magazine stories and his books.

The cause was not a popular one. Most outback graziers consider eagles an enemy. They claim that eagles kill lambs and calves and maim fully grown beasts if they are weak or sick. The counter-claims state that eagles dine mainly on small animals which would (and sometimes do) reach pest proportions. When eagles are observed eating a larger domestic animal, they are often feeding on carrion. The actual kill has been caused by dingoes, disease or collisions with vehicles or fences. Scientists looked through food residues in eagles' nests and droppings, and found they ate mainly rabbits, small macropods, snakes and lizards, even smaller birds. Jeff publicised their findings. He also condemned the practice, common in rural Australia, of stringing eagles along a fence, dead from gunshots or poison, sometimes six or eight corpses in a row. Was it to warn other eagles away? Or was it a boast, a sort of seven-at-one-blow swagger? Either way, it was barbaric.

So both Jeff and I were eager to observe an eagle at close range, and to try and reintroduce it into our Foxground highlands. Farmers in our district had culled so many eagles that they had become scarce. Gladly we made a 300 kilometre round trip to collect Horace. The rangers put him into a chaff bag with only his head sticking out, and he made the trip to Foxground standing on the rear seat taking in the scenery. Riding in cars was nothing new for Horace.

First we put him in an aviary, left over from the days when Ernie Staples lived on Glenrock. His hobby had been keeping birds, ours was releasing them. But first we wanted Horace to become accustomed to our farm, where he was in no danger of being shot by farmers or so-called sporting shooters.

Next, we conditioned him to associate the sound of a whistle with feeding time. It was a fox whistle, a flat round instrument with a high shrill sound like the squeal of a rabbit in trouble. We blew it each time we approached with Horace's dinner. He replied with a pure, sweet, down-sliding note, repeated two or three times. It was easy to copy and we communicated with him in that fashion.

Each evening, Jeff and Van went hunting for rabbits, which we offered to Horace still warm, whole and uncleaned. We wanted to awaken his appetite for bush meat. When the rabbit was laid across his perch, Horace would hop onto it hard, enclosing its body with his strong talons before eating it. This seemed an instinctive piece of behaviour and we felt encouraged, eager for the time when Horace could be released and given more room to chase and pounce.

While he was enclosed, however, I used to visit him often, fascinated by a close-up view of a bird which had inspired

mythologists and artists for centuries. His profile was magnificent, the prototype of aquiline beauty. What surprised me was his
eyes. They were so large and so knowing. He regarded everything
happening about him with alert intelligence. Because he was used
to humans and to captivity, his manner was one of imperial calm.
He turned his head sideways, then upside down, the better to
examine me standing only inches away but separated from him
by chicken wire. This way of looking was distinctive. It prompted
me to do the same, bending my face toward my shoulder and
looking up at him. It did not improve my eyesight but seemed
normal for him.

Another surprise was the beauty of his plumage. It was reddish
brown, with a shawl of finer, lighter feathers on his head and neck
fanning over his shoulders. His wings looked immensely strong
when he unfolded them to stretch. On hot days, he loved to be
hosed and would spread his wings wide, exposing soft fawn
feathers on his underside. When he finished his shower, he gave
a huge shake, which efficiently flicked the water away. The only
thing which upset his serenity was when birds flew overhead,
calling out in alarm at the presence of the eagle in our yard. This
agitated Horace. He opened his beak and held his tongue erect in
his mouth as he twisted his head to view what was above.

Horace was a thoroughly nice individual to have around. We
were all fascinated by him and Jeff captured his moods regularly
on film. When the day came to liberate Horace from the aviary,
we all stood by. Jeff had his cine camera, I had a still camera. Goth
stepped forward and cut open the wire front wall, rolling it aside
so no barrier existed between Horace and freedom. Then Van
blew the fox whistle and tossed a rabbit on the ground. There was
a string tied round its body and Van twitched it to excite Horace's
interest. The huge bird stared, girded himself, then jumped down
onto the rabbit, talons open. As he landed, Van began to draw the
rabbit slowly outward into the yard away from the aviary. Horace
followed, pouncing and grasping. Then Van swung the bunny up
onto a strong perch we had constructed out in the open. Horace
hopped up on the perch and grasped the dangling rabbit. So far
so good.

He picked at the meat for a while, glancing at us watching him.
Then the notion that he was free began to grow. He swivelled his

head round, stretched his wings experimentally. At length, he hopped onto the roof of the aviary. Step two.

We all felt a thrill to see him standing up high, unfettered at last. The mountains rose behind him. They would be his ultimate destination, if our plans went right. We had no idea what Horace would do next, but in fact he did nothing. He simply stayed on the roof, tramping heavily up and down, his claws creating a racket on the iron. Then he hopped back onto the new perch and began to eat his dinner.

For the next few days, Horace showed no inclination to fly at all. We weren't even sure he could fly. He had never been free in his adult life. So we watched him carefully as he walked around the back yard, terrorising the chickens with his presence. That is, he did not menace them, but they recognised him as their enemy and gave him a wide berth.

Jim was also very leery of Horace. And Gidgea ruffled her fur at him in alarm. But he just stumped about on the ground, allowing us to give him drinks of water out of a deep kitchen mixing bowl. Every few hours when it was hot, someone hosed him down. It was Van's plan to stimulate Horace's hunting instincts by dragging a dead rabbit along the grass on a string, but bunnies had suddenly become scarce. He tramped the hills each evening and returned empty-handed. So he improvised a simulated rabbit and waggled it in front of Horace while blowing the whistle, the way you tease a kitten with a ball of wool. Horace pounced. Van pulled and Horace hung on. Here was progress. They played the game daily from then on, and we fed Horace on beef shanks until rabbits could be found again.

Jeff had constructed a big net, like a butterfly catcher, so that Horace could be recaptured if need be. One morning he netted Horace and carried him down into our front paddock on his arm, as falconers do. Jeff wore heavy gauntlets and a canvas coat and he said that, although Horace made no attempt to hurt him, the padding was welcome when the eagle clenched his talons to preserve his balance. Jeff set Horace on another strong perch he and Van had constructed down there. Then Van blew the whistle from some distance away and jerked his simulated prey. Horace looked, cocked his head and listened intently, looked again, then spread his wings and glided low to where Van stood.

This new game became popular. Van put on the canvas coat and taught Horace to sit on his shoulder while riding down to the new perch in the front paddock. From it, he practised short flights, circling the ground and alighting back on the perch or onto the grass near Van. Jeff filmed the entire process.

One day we heard an eerie call coming from a great distance. It sounded familiar. Then, closer at hand, we heard Horace reply. Rushing outdoors, we watched three wild eagles circling above. They were singing out to Horace, who sat atop the shed, watching them with great excitement. We had no idea what would happen. We prayed the wild ones would not come down and attack our friend. They did not, but they stayed overhead for nearly an hour, soaring in lazy circles while angry currawongs dive-bombed them. At last they rose on an updraft and disappeared over the edge of the escarpment. Horace lowered his attention to us as if returning from a dream.

From then on, the wild eagles visited frequently. One day when only Jeff and I were at home, busily working in our studio, and the farm seemed especially deserted, they landed in trees on the opposite side of the creek. Horace was agitated but he did not attempt to fly across and join them. He was excited, we were aflame! We peeped out the window, consumed by indecision. We didn't want to frighten the eagles away – three might mean that one of them needed a mate and with luck this could spell a happy future for Horace. On the other hand, we weren't sure that the visitors had not arrived to try and kill our wonderful bird. At last we could stand it no longer. We went out and made a commotion. The eagles rose and flew away.

We decided it was time to accelerate Horace's education. He needed to become much more self-sufficient if he were to survive in the wild. Van played a big part in finally staging Horace out into the world. He devoted every afternoon after school and all his weekends to coaxing Horace further afield. He would run through the paddocks of the adjoining farm, which was untenanted, blowing the whistle. And Horace would follow him, on the wing. It got so that Horace took himself for a little fly when he awakened each morning.

One day soon after, he flew away down the valley and we lost sight of him. We had spread the news of what we were attempting up in our hill sanctuary, so before long we received a telephone call from a worried farmer's wife in lower Foxground. 'There's an eagle perched on the tractor,' she said. 'I think it must be yours. The kittens are all hiding under the dairy. The chooks won't come out of their run. And I'm scared to let the kiddies out of the house. Could you come and fetch it, please?'

Jeff donned his protective clothing, grabbed his net and hopped into the Land Rover. He had no trouble whistling up Horace and really felt his heavy gear was unnecessary. Horace sat docilely beside him on the front seat. At the post office corner, a farmer flagged Jeff down for a chat and got a shock to see his feathered passenger.

We sensed the last phase of Horace's liberation was at hand. Jeff had completed his filming for *Wild Animal Farm*. The last shot in the sequence would show Horace circling free in the sky above our farm with the *Wild Country* theme music playing sweet and joyous on the soundtrack. We took some still photos of Jeff holding Horace and gave them to the local newspapers with a little story. We wanted as many people as possible to know that a tame eagle was trying to return to the wild so that if he landed on a property outside Foxground, he might be given a chance.

Several times more Jeff was rung and requested to come and fetch the big bird. Horace had no fear of farmhouses and landed trustingly, once actually walking up to a kitchen door and peering in through the screen.

While Horace was back at our place, the wild eagles appeared again overhead, calling. Horace took off and flew down to our front paddock, away from the house. The eagles circled and called, then they landed further down the hill. Horace flew to meet them. We sensed he was in no danger in their company.

Not long after that, we saw the last of Horace. Nor did we sight the wild eagles again that season. But the following year, we noticed magnificent lazy shapes soaring above the escarpment, kings of the air. The distance was too great to recognise Horace among them, even with binoculars, but there were four eagles in the group and I felt this was a good sign.

With *Wild Animal Farm* shot, edited and accepted by the Seven Network, we needed two more films to complete the standard pilot series of six. To our amazement, the movie we made about

Coober Pedy opal miners, *Jackpot Town*, won the Golden Reel and other awards in 1972. Roger had entered it in the annual Australian Film Institute competition because he had put such a lot into editing its remarkable footage. We should have entered our other films too, because our style was ahead of the trend, but Jeff wanted nothing to do with competitions. He said they were a waste of energy and time.

The truth was, he was feeling the strain of borrowing so much money to make films which, until we could secure an overseas sale, kept us in debt. Although our small team was all family, apart from Roger and Pat, our modest budgets had to include a salary for everyone except Jeff and myself. To maintain a monthly cash flow, Jeff was bound to freelance journalism. We tried to attract a sponsor related to travel and motoring but felt no affinity in city skyscrapers with executives wearing designer suits and board-room manners. The corporate milieu repelled us, as did the Film Development Corporation, whose brief was to make a quick profit. Within a few years, a more realistic approach to film finance came into play, but by that time we had bailed out.

Our fifth movie was to be shot in Central Australia. Before we went on location, the burden of what was still ahead brought Jeff low. 'Right,' I said. 'Okay. We take a few days off and think this through.'

Away we went to the city. 'What we need is to relax, do what normal people do on holidays,' I suggested. No opposition to that idea either. So I looked over the recreation section of the newspaper. Sydney's principal attractions were the zoo, Manly Aquarium, Waratah Park ('Home of Skippy') and Koala Park. 'Seems to be an interest in animals,' I said. 'Maybe we should go and take a look.' Again, no argument. So we drove out of town through tree-filled suburbs on Sydney's north shore. What did we find?

Coaches. Tourists. People with money and cameras in their hands, eager for contact with kangaroos and koalas. We also found the saddest bunch of animals we had ever seen, crowded into grazed-out enclosures, dispirited from too many eager hands patting and prodding them. Also the dirtiest toilets, the poorest picnic facilities, the worst array of bad-taste souvenirs. And at 'Skippy park', we sat on broken old seats to watch reject prints of those weak television 'dramas' we disliked so much.

'We can do better than this!' we told each other. '*Wild Animal Farm* makes *Skippy* look like comic cuts for preschoolers.'

That started us thinking. We needed to build on the resources we already had in order to generate income. The money was partly to continue to pay our children who, for some reason, we felt duty-bound to employ. Thor, Goth, Karen and, soon enough, Van were old enough to earn their keep. We wanted to find a way they could do this on the family farm. Our models were the dynasties on isolated properties which we admired in the outback.

So we returned home with plans to establish a nature park on the front corner of our land, at present a cow paddock which included the big creek fed by the waterfall. We would show the films, which owed us money, as part of the attraction. Ditto the kangaroos, wombats, possums, eagles and whatever else happened to be under our care. Not that we would create a zoo. We were against that, on principle. No, we would simply invite people to partake of the wildlife refuge as they found it. We would give them clean toilets and idyllic picnic spots in the bush, plus a rainforest walk along the creek. And no crass souvenirs, no souvenirs at all apart from a lovely little green brochure with a map of the nature trails and a list of the films which would play, one after the other, all during the day.

It is a measure of Jeff's creativity that he went away exhausted and returned full of energy and enthusiasm for this new project. Within a week he, Goth, Van and Thor were building a long, low theatre-museum, using the hand-hewn slabs from the sheds in our backyard, which included the blacksmith's and the Boys' Museum. Dick Conroy and his son Phil came up to help, making old-style wooden doors, a wooden verandah along the front where visitors could look out over the park, and a counter of waxed brush box planks for the small kiosk we included in the plan – all the timber was second hand and well weathered. They covered the iron roof with tea-tree brush, hidden within which was an irrigation hose. Water trickling over the roof would cool the cinema inside. The lads brushed kerosene and sump oil over the timber so that it looked like it had stood there for generations.

Inside the theatre, I put up panels of still photos showing the six films we would be screening. Over the concrete floor, Jeff spread sawdust from the local sawmill. This gave a lovely resiny fragrance to the cosy interior. We were able to buy some obsolete wooden

theatre seats, old but comfortable, and I brought down the artefacts from our Relics of Olden Days exhibits to complete the
atmosphere and spirit of the place, which we called Wild Country
Park after the name of our film series and also Jeff's book and
magazine column. Reusing the same name in order to fuel demand
for our 'products' was the advice of Keith Finlay, editor of *People*
magazine and one of our best friends.

Of course, we had to spend some money to create this new
enterprise so we asked the bank for a small business overdraft and
they complied. We bought an urn for tea and coffee, a second-
hand drinks fridge, a small freezer for ice creams. By keeping
everything simple and rustic, we created something really characterful, which worked.

The lads and Jeff improved the animal pads along the creek
bank to make a nature trail, and I had discreet signs painted in
brown or green to explain the place. Since we were against clut-
tering the landscape with signage, we kept ours small and few.
Just two enclosures were erected. One was in front of the theatre-
museum, dubbed the Nursery Yard for orphans or injured
animals. The other was halfway down the grassy hill, enclosing a
small dam. This would be the Staging Yard for animals being
prepared for release into free living. Both these enclosures would
be helpful in our work on the refuge, so they were actually necessary extensions of our program of care. We erected a perimeter
fence along the roadside, mainly to keep out dogs, screen the
kangaroos from traffic and funnel the public in through our
modest little front entrance. We wanted to welcome guests personally, partly so they would know what we had to offer them, but
also to let them know that any animals encountered must not be
chased or teased.

Our philosophy was summed up in the little green brochure
which we gave each entrant, along with free bags of animal food:
WHAT IS A WILDLIFE REFUGE?
*On a Wildlife Refuge, everything is protected. This includes the trees,
ferns and plants which give animals food and shelter. The idea is to
preserve the wild habitat which is the natural home of birds, reptiles,
insects and furred creatures.*
*To make friends with animals, walk softly and slowly. NEVER RUN.
Hold out your hand, PALM UP (to show you won't hit). Talk quietly. Do*

*not corner animals against fences, bushes, buildings. Don't surround them.
If they want to move away from you, please let them go.
Animals like natural food and shelter . . . and a quiet place. WILD
COUNTRY PARK provides these things – which we believe people need
also. Henry David Thoreau called it: 'The Tonic of Wildness'.
Please help us preserve WILD COUNTRY PARK as a peaceful and
quiet place . . . for people as well as animals. Thank you.*

Jeff and I hand-signed that statement, which explained that the
park was only 6 hectares out of 43 (15 acres out of 105), the rest
of which were private. The brochure introduced our children and
a little of our history, then included a nature guide to plants and
animals – those easy to find and those in residence but hard to see.
Our aim was to slow people down and encourage them to seek out
the wonders of a natural setting. After our sojourn at Minnamurra
Falls, minding the reserve while Howard and Ivy Judd went
away, we knew well how soothing rainforest can be.

We opened quietly after placing a few modest advertisements in
the local press. As soon as the family were proficient in running the
park, Jeff and I and Thor set out for Central Australia. We needed
to finish our series, so we could try to sell it overseas and recoup
some of our outlays. I talked hard and convinced Jeff we should
make both episodes five and six about the Centre. The network
seemed to bracket two half-hour films together anyway, filling a
one-hour time slot. If we could get away with only one trip out on
location, it would save time and money. Thus our final two films
were '*Two Faces of Central Australia – One: The Locals. Two: The Tourists*'.

Everything went smoothly. We returned to find the trickle of
visitors to Wild Country Park was growing some. People liked
what they found, although most expected a zoo with animals
secure in cages. It would take a lot of talking, plus screenings of
Wild Animal Farm, to get across our message, which was: it can be
more rewarding to see wildlife in its natural state than always
enclosed in wire.

As usual, we were ahead of public perceptions by about twenty
years. The eco-parks we dreamed about even then would not
come into being until people sickened of commercialisation, the
manicured landscape, and longed to experience wildness. We like
to think Wild Country Park played a role in creating that demand.

17

Wild Country Park

The second eagle we cared for came as we hurried to complete the two 'Centralian' documentaries. In Sydney we had met a young Canadian film editor, Steve Weslak, who was glad to edit our movies at Glenrock. Steve, a bushwalker and outdoor enthusiast, was keen to experience Australian life outside the city. The first day he drove down to Foxground established a pattern for his adventures within our refuge.

The Parks and Wildlife Service had rung to say another wedge-tail needed rehabilitation. We asked Steve if he would mind calling by their office in Sydney to pick up something to transport to us. 'Sure,' he drawled.

'It's an animal,' we said.

'That'd be neat.'

Dear Steve. He was a gem of a bloke. All the way down the coast he kept glancing in his rear-vision mirror, meeting the questioning gaze of the eagle perched on his back seat. Although she was securely bagged with just her head sticking out, he handed her over to us with relief, then stood by watching as we settled her into the aviary, the same routine as with Horace. After lunch and an introduction to some of the house animals, we took Steve on a tour of the property, starting and also ending at the editing room in the barn which adjoined our office. He took in our basic little Pole editing machine, our winding arms, film hangers and trim-bins, handmade, inexpensive but perfectly efficient. 'Pretty neat,' Steve said, sitting down at his workbench. 'Mind if I get used to your editor?'

We left him at the Pole and retired to our desks. After about half an hour, he stuck his broad grin round the door. 'Uh, say – is that snake gonna be on the window ledge every day?'

We jumped up to look. There on the sill not two feet from where he'd been sitting, a big fat python was coiled, taking its ease. Shocked, we assured him we had never seen it there before. 'Oh, I don't mind. I jest sort of wanted to know. Ya know?'

What Steve didn't know about Australian wildife was plenty. But he was intensely interested and also unfazed by most things, thanks to his lifelong hobby of camping and canoeing in Canada. During his stays he gladly nursed possums, fed wallabies, stood with the current wombat, while she grazed. At weekends he returned to his wife, Brooke, who had a job in Sydney. As soon as she was free, he asked to bring her down for *her* indoctrination into Aussie wildlife. She was as funny and good-natured as Steve and they became our lifelong friends, Foxground their little taste of rural Aussie bush.

The eagle Steve delivered we named Monica. Her preparation for liberation went much the same as Horace's. She, too, had been raised in captivity and so was in no hurry to leave our care. Vandal hunted rabbits for her and trained her to respond to the whistle so he could fly her and call her back until she was ready to live free. She bonded to him especially and let him stroke her, gently pushing his fingers up underneath her feathers. He was growing a moustache and a little goatee, following the example of his bearded dad and brothers. Van's was very fine, still pale blond. Monica used to run her beak through it, as if to clean him for mites. When he stood quietly beside her perch in the back yard, she would examine him all over, turning her head upside down in the manner of Horace, cooing, teasing out his long tresses with her beak, then she would spread her wings above his head like a protective mother. It was the most beautiful performance, so beautiful that Jeff could not resist filming it, even though *Wild Animal Farm* was complete and screening on television and in our theatre. Later, the Monica footage would find its place in a movie called *Nature Boy* which I put together for school children coming to Wild Country Park.

On Glenrock Farm, the times truly were a-changing. We sold the last of our cattle to finance *Two Faces of Central Australia*, intending to buy some more later. With both films done, our pilot series of six was ready for market. If we could sell it overseas, we would press ahead and make another seven documentaries to complete a full series of thirteen episodes.

During 1973 and early 1974, while we were completing the last two films of our pilot television series, from all directions came a growing inflow of wildlife in need of care. There were three more wombats, two kookaburras, four possums, three wallabies, another eagle, seven emus, a characterful cockatoo plus other parrots. I know this because I kept an animal register with notes about the donors, the animals themselves and what happened to them after they came to the park. Keeping a register was a recommendation made by Eric Worrell and his crew at the Australian Reptile Park. They were required to complete all sorts of paperwork because of their official status. Ours was not so formal. We were not a zoo, we never took flora or fauna from the wild, nor did we aspire to traffic in it. So my little register was simply our protection to ensure that all we did was above board; it was also a valuable reminder of people and creatures and their own special stories.

Of the three wombats we handled during that period, only one stayed with us for any length of time. The first was a traffic casualty found beside the road up on the tablelands. Despite veterinary treatment by Georgie Borys and loving care from the Carters, that animal died.

The second wombat was Gnasher, from Worrell's reptile park, a fully grown male who had turned cranky. Eric asked us to take him and give him his freedom at Foxground. We drove him up to the High Country and let him go near the old wombat diggings where we had filmed Wally. Those burrows still seemed to be deserted and we felt Gnasher had scope for a new life on the hundreds of untenanted acres between us and Jamberoo.

The third wombat was Bippy. She had arrived as a result of my article for *The Women's Weekly* about William, in which I said we thought he needed a wife. By the time Bippy's donor rang us, both William and Wally were away on walkabout, which made it easier to settle her in before they returned. I have to say she was a far gentler animal than either of them had been. We guessed it was because of her gender but it would be a few more years, and many more wombats of both sexes, before we would be sure of that. As it was, Bippy brought us fresh wombat joy but caused us no trouble, which was as well because we were very busy. Along with our writing and film work, and caring for the growing influx of animals, there began a stream of telephone enquiries from people seeking advice about wildlife. We tried not to rush these because we believed ours was a duty to share what we were learning through experience.

Although our park was open only on Saturdays, Sundays and during school holidays, the grounds had to be maintained and the kiosk stocked during the week. On the job, we learned about retail trading, a new experience for us. Our only previous brush with a cash business had been while minding Minnamurra Falls Reserve for Howard and Ivy Judd. It felt quite refreshing to have immediate income, even though it went out as fast as it came in, much of it on feeds, medicines and equipment for the animals.

We had to enclose an area for seven young emus which were surplus at Eric's nature park. He was literally innundated with homeless animals then, and there were very few places where they could go once the zoos were full. We reorganised the kangaroo paddock, which had become redundant for Opal, Mathilda and company after they had resettled into Wild Country Park. The emus had about an acre to live in, with shelter and plenty of water and fresh grass. The fence was waist-high, tall enough to discourage the public from climbing over, emus ditto, yet not so high that the big birds could not escape if they so wished. This was a criterion of the Parks and Wildlife Department, which was in accord with our own philosophy of enclosing but not incarcerating any fit native animal.

As we had hoped and Eric Worrell had assured us, the emus were content in their big area and did not jump the fence. To guard them from temptation, we always made sure visitors had a bag of pellets to offer as they passed them along the nature walk. Emus are curious – they will take glasses from a pocket, pluck an earring from an ear – and can be quite intimidating when they thrust their long necks over the fence, eyes staring hungrily, big beaks eager to peck. This does not hurt, because their beaks are not sharp, but it looks like it might. They are also greedy. If given a chance, they will grab the entire bag and at the end of each public day we had to lean in and pick up crumpled, trampled pellet sacks.

We found this new (to us) species of Australiana fascinating and studied them closely as we daily gave them feed and fresh water. Emus' necks and heads are scantily feathered. You can see their skin underneath. It flushes blue around the head and behind the big ear-holes at the active times in their breeding cycle. The rest of their feathers are dense and long, and rustle drily as they stalk about. Hidden within are tiny buds of useless wings. They are, of course, flightless birds. Walking and running is how they get about. Their feet have three strong, black-nailed toes pointing frontwards. When they fight, they jump up and lash at each other with those toes. They can dodge and weave in mid-air and look quite balletic when they joust or play.

Apart from their physical appearance, the most distinctive thing about emus is their booming call. It reverberates all over the property, like an African drum. When a journalist came to write an article about us and all our wildlife on the refuge, it was the emus she liked best. She couldn't resist reaching over the fence to fondle them and stare into their huge dark eyes. Her story headline was: 'You Haven't Lived Until You've Cuddled An Emu'.

In 1974, at Roger's prompting, Jeff decided we would take *Wild Country* to Cannes. Each year documentaries are shown and marketed at the equivalent of the more famous feature film festival which precedes it. We decided to see for ourselves what was selling on the international television market rather than pay an agent to offer our films to overseas networks, teaching us nothing.

An elaborate roster was concocted to man the fort during our absence; it involved Steve and Brooke, another friend Judy, Karen and Thor. Vandal was still attending high school but Goth had bailed out. At eighteen he underwent a crisis similar to the one experienced by his father at a similar age. Jeff counselled Goth to do what he had done, find work on a coastal fishing trawler, try out his wings, learn to stand alone. After working for a few months on an abalone boat near Eden, Goth hitchhiked to Central Australia to meet up with us while we were filming. He was an instant success in Alice, finding a job within days and performing for the first time in public at the folk club there, a venue popular with young backpacking musicians from round the world. We felt he had found a good niche and left him there with the hope that he had found a new career in one of our favourite parts of Australia.

Actually, I felt quite uneasy about going to Europe, leaving Glenrock with the park barely established, a menagerie of animals, the family growing into young adults and branching out as individuals. However, Jeff was keen to go. For years he had made everyone laugh by standing on Seven Mile Beach and pointing at the wide ocean: 'Don't tell me there's anything out there!' was his standard quip. Now his chauvinism was to be tested.

At MIP, *Wild Country* screened every day in the Palais on a monitor fronting the Australian stand; being fast-cut and full of action – galloping camels, jousting kangaroos and leaping wombats – it attracted attention and we received invitations from eight countries to bring audition prints. In a hired campervan, we visited television stations in Britain, Scandinavia, Germany, Belgium, France and Italy, a three-month round of travel which resulted in agreements to buy some or all of our series.

We returned home modestly proud of ourselves. Both Jeff and I had hated the high-pressured huckstering at MIP. Glamorous Cannes was far from our style and trying to do business in several European languages taxed us. Ditto learning to get around huge old cities, mastering foreign road signs and driving on the right-hand side. But we proved we were on track with our movies. Although payment for documentaries was minimal and would be slow, terribly slow, to arrive, we had secured sales. So while our investment in film-making would be 'in the red' for some time yet, our cultural profit had been huge. Never again would Jeff sling off about going overseas. He was smitten by art, culture, architecture and cuisine.

I saw Foxground with new eyes on our return. Driving down from Sydney airport, the skies seemed so wide and clear, the green paddocks rolled like visual poetry over hills gentle beneath the escarpment. Suddenly we were on that last magic mile of gravel road, slowing to cross the little creeks, passing through the tunnel of rainforest trees leading up to Wild Country Park. My heart swelled as I thought how blessed we were to own such beautiful, uncrowded seclusion. After Europe, the slab hut museum-theatre looked quaint and appropriate to its purpose, the farmhouse small and rustic, especially now that the boys had grown so tall. It was good to be home.

During our absence Thor and Van had acquired another wombat, with initiative which tickled me. A lady up on the table-lands near Moss Vale had rung to see whether she might give us a baby wombat to rear. She sounded very particular about how it should be treated, and nonplussed to be dealing with young men instead of Jeff or myself. Thor proposed they should drive up to visit her, taking Bippy as an example of the good care provided at our wildlife refuge. Stopping in Kangaroo Valley for petrol and a cool drink, they left Bippy on the front seat. When they returned, the Land Rover was surrounded by people eager to see and touch her. Bippy charmed the woman in Moss Vale, too, and they returned with a new little wombat, no bigger than a grapefruit. They named it Winkie because it blinked a lot.

So what with possums in the wardrobes, a new wallaby on the front verandah and two young wombats racing round the house mixing it with Jim and Brownie, it was a lively homecoming. I was content that during our absence the fort had been well and truly held by family and friends. The best news was that Goth was back, tall and suntanned. He had met a girl in Alice Springs – an American lass – who wanted to see Sydney, so they hitchhiked to Foxground. She didn't stay long but he did, for the time being anyway.

Monica the eagle was still around. On days when the park was open to the public, Thor or Van would bring her down to be seen. During these excursions she wore soft leather jesses on her legs so that she could be grasped in a gloved hand to steady her. Some-times they kept her perched on their arm while people looked at her, but often they placed her on a low branch of the big old English oak which had been planted in Mrs Henry's time, halfway down to the creek. This made a shady spot where people could stand and watch the eagle majestically watching them. Monica would walk up and down the branch, shake out her wings, coo a little, and when Van or Thor whistled her, she would fly down onto their arm and be returned to our back yard.

Jeff decided to feed her in the oak tree, so on days when the park was open, he would take a rabbit and drape it over the big limb for Monica to pick at while people stood quietly below, watching in fascination. Thus far she showed no inclination to fly away.

In the Nursery Yard were two new wallabies, growing toward release. On weekends Bippy would be brought down to waddle round inside the theatre. We rang an old cowbell on the front verandah every forty minutes to signal that a movie was due to commence. Most visitors answered the summons and thus worked their way through several, if not all, of our six films. During the show Bippy usually settled down between someone's shoes while they watched the screen, an experience which delighted many but could also startle if she decided to get up in the dark and move through the rows to find a different pair of feet. You had to be sure to warn the cinema audience what to expect.

The icing on the cake arrived when little Winkie was brought down from the house, wrapped in a pretty crocheted shawl, one of several I kept for such showings. I timed this so that she could drink her bottle of milk on the verandah when the audience came out of the theatre.

People really enjoyed the films, but often needed help to comprehend that their hosts were the actual film-makers and also the 'film stars'. Ours was a pretty original commercial enterprise in that respect. However, there was no doubt that everyone expected to see animals when they came to Wild Country Park. They were not quite content with the information that kangaroos lie up during the middle of the day, hidden in shady places of their own choosing. If found, we made it clear the animals were not to be flushed out into the open just for the sake of a photo, or badgered to eat pellets they didn't really want at that hour.

We took seriously our role as teachers of respect and tolerance for wildlife. Apart from screening *Wild Animal Farm* for visitors, the only way to do this was one-on-one conversation. The trick was appealing to an unselfish side of people which prompted them to begin thinking of the animals' good rather than their own. Once they got the hang of what we were offering, most folks returned again and again, bringing neighbours or overseas visitors. They began to come as friends and we liked that. But we still had to field those questions: 'Where are the animals? How many can we see today?'

So we were very pleased with the news that we were to be

given some koalas. Because they sleep peacefully on a tree branch during the day, they would generally be easy to see without any inconvenience to them. More importantly, we could fulfil a life's dream. Ever since we first moved to Foxground and learned that, within living memory, koalas had been common in the valley, we wanted to reintroduce the species, which had apparently been shot out during the Depression of the 1930s, when their skins were in demand and people needed a source of cash income.

We read up on the types of eucalyptus leaves koalas eat and found that of about a dozen species they thrive on, we had at least three within the park, next to the old oak, easily accessible to visitors. Then Jeff constructed circles of tin around the perimeter of each koala tree, which he believed would enable the animals to jump from tree to tree but not run off along the ground. It was important to contain them until they became acclimatised to Foxground.

We purchased two new feed trees and planted them outside the front entrance, a bridge between the park and eucalypts growing along the road, marching up toward the back of the property where the koalas could take themselves when they wished to roam.

On the prescribed day, Jeff and the lads set off for the mid-north coast where an entire koala habitat was to be cleared for a new housing project. While trees were bulldozed down, rangers rushed about, collecting koalas as they dropped and putting them into sacks. It was a privilege to receive one mature male and a young female because koalas were an endangered, diminishing species and people wanted them for zoos but also for private properties.

When they returned to Foxground, Jeff and the fellows climbed ladders and gently released the koalas into the eucalypts within the tin barriers. Fortunately they were content in their new home. When hungry they chomped stolidly on gum leaves, which were plentiful for their needs, and moved quietly from branch to branch, sometimes leaping to a higher perch, agile as acrobats, before settling down to nap. Although we had read they did not need water, we put a drink at the base of each tree just in case. When they did climb down, it was to nibble soil. Jeff nailed a box of earth in each tree for them.

One problem was that the koalas' subtle colour blended so well with the tree trunks that people had trouble finding them. Visitors would trudge back up to the kiosk and swear the koalas must have gone, until we took them down and pointed out the sleepers, usually high in a fork of branches. It amused us to see people grouped round the grove, puzzling and peering and pointing upward. It all seemed to be going well. The only hitch was Monica.

She had grown accustomed to being fed in the oak tree, under the gaze of park visitors at weekends. Now she began to show an interest in her new next door neighbours. One day, to Jeff's consternation, she flew across onto a koala tree and began jumping about on the branch. Ringed by visitors, Jeff had no option but to climb the ladder he kept handy and try to catch Monica. Which he managed to do, just as she grabbed the little female koala. That woke it up! It cried loudly, the visitors gasped, Jeff hung on for dear life, dragging on Monica's ankles and shaking her until she unclenched her grip. Then he quickly climbed down with her and headed for the aviary up near the house. There was a funny side to it, but it also could have been a disaster.

Luckily, that problem was solved for us. Wild eagles dropped in to visit. They landed some distance from Monica's perch and began calling to her. She replied. After almost a day of communicating, she took off and flew down to where they were. We watched and just before sunset saw them fly away together. It was an emotional parting for us. Yet we reminded ourselves, as we continually had to do, that that was the point of the whole exercise.

A good thing about opening Wild Country Park was that more people got to see how orphaned or injured native creatures could be rescued and released back into the wild. Ours was a minority view. In that era, most people wanted to see animals nailed down and fenced in, which soon broke the spirits and often the health of wild creatures. I have faith in the power of personal example; I believed our refuge would do more than lectures or tracts to stimulate a caring attitude to wildlife. As visitors to the Park glimpsed the rehabilitation of little damaged creatures, they would spread the word that Foxground was a place to seek advice or sanctuary.

The final donation that year from Worrell's sanctuary was another grey kangaroo. Strong, healthy, unspoiled, he was a favourite of Eric, who had reared him from orphanhood. We named the young buck after his donor, and introduced him to our female kangaroos.

JEFF CARTER

Mare feeds an orphan
wallaby, using a soft
kitten's bottle with a
specially modified teat.
Such animals were
always swaddled in
woollen knits except
when taken out briefly
for eliminations or a
stretch. As well as
requiring warmth, gentle
cuddling is important
for marsupial babies —
loneliness is anathema
to them.

JEFF CARTER

Mare with William, the first of many orphan wombats reared by the Carters and released onto their wildlife refuge. When on walkabout he crashed parties, ripped off a neighbour's screen door and made himself an uninvited guest at strange homes. Yet his lumbering charm and trusting, thick-headed confidence kept him safe, and the Carters were ever glad to see him home.

Inbuilt in young wombats' brains is the necessity to keep between their mother's feet for safety, and orphans transfer this compulsion to their human foster-parents. We learned to place Jeff's boots on either side of our wombats, thus winning a little time to move freely about our chores.

Once securely bonded with a human foster family, wombats become quite cuddlesome and even coquettish.

Two members of the Foxground Boys' Museum, (L) David Waite
and (R) Robert Binks, sons of local farmers and school mates of
Goth. The lads were justly proud of their busy, authentic exhibits
housed inside our old blacksmith's barn. They showed visitors
around with growing aplomb, learning, and giving, much.

Jeff grooms one of the emus whose feathers had become matted with mud. Emus love a roll on the ground and a swim. We often watched them fling themselves into the dam and paddle smoothly about, nothing showing above the water but their heads.

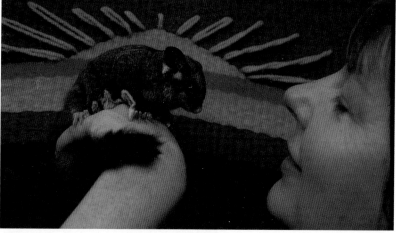

This little possum showed total confidence in our farmhouse until she was old enough to return to her natural treetops habitat. She curls her tail around my hand to steady her balance, hanging on firmly but gently with claws meant for climbing bark trunks. The membrane which enables her to glide from branch to branch rests like a frill along her body.

ATHOL YEOMANS

Jeff thought he could handle Big Joe, a hand-reared orphan buck from a neighbouring property. But when Joe seriously wanted a fight, Jeff had no chance against him.

An animal rescue gone wrong. Jeff suffered severe damage from Big Joe. A lesson well learned: never keep bucks past puberty. Unafraid of humans, they may attack when feeling aggressive.

MARE CARTER

JEFF CARTER

The kindest thing to do with an echidna found near the road, or anywhere, is to let it continue on its way. If it is judged necessary to remove an echidna from a busy highway, put a glove on one hand to steady the spiky end and slip a shovel gently under the feet. Release it in a safe place, as near as possible to its habitat.

JEFF CARTER

Eric the fine grey kangaroo became the patriarch of our Wildlife Refuge. The 'roos were free to come and go as they wished, and, if undisturbed, would lie calmly on the lawns of Wild Country Park. This enabled visitors to watch them close up, feed and even gently pat them.

These days, I have time to sit in the front verandah of Casa Simpatica, birds and the bounty of our fruit trees around me, and, with Annie Rose 'the little peace maker' on my lap, contemplate my wide green world, my private sanctuary, and count my blessings.

Apart from Blind Bruce, who still lived in the pear tree paddock because of his handicap, the girls were again without a husband. Mulga Mick, who we had hoped would fill that role, suddenly turned nasty one day while Vandal was dishing out his feed. He reared up, roared and tried to engage Van in mortal combat. Van was fourteen then, wise in the ways of animals, a big strong lad but never provocative, yet Mick on tiptoe and pugnacious was beyond him. He threw the feed bucket at Mick and ran for the gate leading back into our yard. We heard the racket and went out to find Van just going into shock as Mick bellowed and hopped back and forth on the other side of the fence, frothing, furious, keen to leap the wire and do battle.

Sharp in all our minds was the saga of Big Joe, which is probably why calm, brave Van had been so scared. While I took him indoors, Jeff went for his rifle and shot Mick dead. We all knew it was too dangerous to keep a buck around once he began to challenge humans. So that was the end of our fine male trio. At least we still had Opal, Potch and Mathilda, plus Sheila and Gidgea. Now we had handsome Eric. He took charge of the girls like the leader he was destined to be. Jeff admired him very much.

Of the wallabies we received then, two were quite young. One, so tiny it fitted into the dint of a slouch hat, had been rescued by a woman at Bateman's Bay. She had done a good job of saving its life, feeding it on vegetables and roses and an evaporated milk formula laced with vitamin drops. She bequeathed us her special puppies' feeding bottle with fine black tubing down the teat, and returned to visit us later to see how the little animal had settled in.

The second wallaby was the youngest we had ever raised ourselves, so tender that its pink skin showed clearly through fur that was like tatty velvet. It had been found by a science teacher who'd had the sense to look in the pouch of its mother, lying dead beside the road. She brought it to us the next day. Flash Nick was his name, and he was a good-doer, no trouble to stage toward eventual release, a process taking most of a year.

The third had been well reared by a family near Nowra. It was used to being indoors so at first we let it sleep in the theatre on the sawdust floor until it was ready to progress outdoors into the Nursery Yard. After just a few weeks it only came inside when the weather was cold or wet. When free-living within the park it used to hop out of the bushes to paw at visitors, trying to pick their pockets for something to eat. Finally it migrated across the creek to Wallaby Hill and melded into the bush.

The kookaburras were both traffic victims but each recovered with rest and quiet nurturing. Jeff became skilled at getting them to open their beaks so that he could pop food inside their maws, which would snap shut like traps. They shake their heads vigorously, flicking, cracking the food from side to side, even when it is not alive but only meat from the butcher.

The possums had been orphaned by motorcars. Since they are nocturnal animals, we thought if we built a snug possum house and suspended it at the end of the theatre verandah, during the day visitors could glimpse a furry grey back or bulbous pink nose while the possums slept. The first one, a ringtail, confounded us, however, by breaking into the building and running amok amongst the museum exhibits. Then it settled into a cosy nest of its own making behind one of the film speakers, where warmth was generated while the movies were playing. The noise, apparently, did not deter it.

Lick-Lick was a brushtail with a mind of her own but endearing ways. Unless prevented, she would go along the shelves of the kitchen dresser, the pantry or the mantle and rake and shove everything off onto the floor. Then she would clamber onto your shoulder and burrow into your arms for a cuddle. She loved to lick our skin, perhaps in search of salt. One night when I was home alone she nearly licked me raw. I shut us both in the bedroom after securing everything she might damage, and retreated into bed with my head under the covers. She stomped around, trying to find how to get in with me but finally settled on her own alone in the wardrobe. Next day, Jeff returned home and made her a nestbox filled with straw on the front verandah. We left food for her and water but also propped the screen door open so she could go outdoors if she wished. She began to do this but always returned at dawn. By evening, we would find that she had left her box and wormed her way into the house, curling up to sleep high atop a wardrobe, in a cupboard or behind the hi-fi speakers. She loved the linen closet, when she could find its door open. Fortunately, possums are fairly clean animals and, being largely blossom feeders, their smell is sweet and musky.

Even more adorable was Stripes, a little glider possum. She was a quarter the size of brushtails or ringtails, really petite, with long whiskers and sparkling dark eyes, her ashen forehead marked by a line of dark fur. Her rescuer was Martin, a young timberman working in the forests of Eden, two hundred miles down the coast from Foxground. He had snatched her off a log on the conveyor belt heading into the pulping mill. She must have emerged from her knothole nest just in the nick of time. Martin tucked her inside his jacket and kept her safe within his tent, because the camp was overrun with cats. For five months, he eschewed giving her processed foods and fed her apple, banana, carrots and milk; she thrived. Unable to guarantee her safety further, he made the long drive up to Wild Country Park and entrusted her to us.

We settled her shoebox of cotton wool and cut-off jumper sleeves into our wardrobe, leaving the door just slightly ajar and she slept there contentedly. When she woke up at evening time, she would run delicately along the picture rails high up the walls until she spotted one of us, and then she would launch herself in our direction, spreading her legs so the membrane attached to her body allowed her to glide to her destination. Landing on a shoulder, she would run down your chest and burrow inside your jacket or shirt, peeping out sweetly to receive the tidbits we never failed to provide.

There was a gap beneath the front wall and the roof of our bedroom and we figured she would squeeze outside when she was ready. Finally she did that but returned by morning through the upstairs window of Van's bedroom. He left it open specially for her, after waking to find her pacing the sill excitedly, her nose prodding the glass. Gradually she stayed away for longer periods until we did not see her indoors at all. Much as we missed her, we were content to think she had established a natural home in the forest.

Months later, an extraordinary thing happened. Our old friend Athol came down from Sydney to visit one winter weekend. He was wearing a big woollen pullover, which he began to peel off as the kitchen wood stove warmed him. Standing with one arm in and the other out of his sleeves, he suddenly jumped and cried out. Something had 'flown' onto his shoulder and was burrowing into his jumper. It was Stripes. She must have returned indoors after that long absence and, seeing him standing with his arms akimbo, like the invitations of the boys of old, she launched herself into his embrace. I have to say, Athol did not finish taking off that sweater for hours but sat entranced, cuddling her against his chest until bedtime. He left her on the kitchen bench, still tucked inside his garment. By morning she had gone again.

The most personable creature we received during that period was Herbert, a six-year-old white cockatoo. He had come to live with a Lancashire couple named Kelly when he was just a few months old. They gave him a big cage but let him roam about the house and out into the garden. When called, he would come indoors again.

Herbert could talk. 'Hello Herbert?' he used to say. 'What's that? Eh?' 'What're you doing?' He spoke with the broad regional inflections of the Kellys, high when imitating her, lower for him.

Herbert slept in their laundry until he learned to turn the hot-water tap on. From then on, he was put back in his cage while they slept. Because he could undo any catch and even unscrew bolts, they had to padlock his door when they went out. Why? Because Herbert had learned to unravel electrical cords. He liked picking at the furniture. Mrs Kelly used to flick him with a tea towel and say: 'Tsk, tsk. Naughty Herbert.' This prompted Herbert to dash to a corner where he could hide his tail. Then he would say: 'Tsk, tsk, naughty Herbert!'

He played with an ice-cream container of water in which they floated little toys and boats. He drank from a cup. As well as mixed parrot seeds, Herbert liked chopped fruit, nuts and oats; also corn on the cob, raw pumpkin seeds and freshly mown grass cuttings. The Kellys fed him a bird tonic from time to time. They put a pinch of salt in his food. He liked, they said, to dance to guitar music and could whistle 'Sing a Song of Sixpence'.

At our place he settled in well and grew bolder and bolder about going outdoors, which suited us fine. We had no time for dealing with 'naughty Herbert' tricks. One day he joined a flock of wild cockatoos and flew away. Later, a visitor spoke of being on a Foxground property not far from ours when a mob of cockies flew overhead. One peeled off and flew down, landing on the man's head. It startled him but he was tolerant, guessing it had been someone's pet. We like to believe that was Herbert.

When Wild Country Park was open, some of these animals could be shown to the visitors. Formerly, although Jeff and I wrote about our work at the wildlife refuge, much of it, including what we were learning about native species, was hidden. *Wild Animal Farm*, the movie, told only a fraction of the ongoing story. So we contrived to show visitors our latest rescues, providing they were up to it. The well-being of the animal always came first. Sick or nervous animals remained up at the house. A few of the young and dependent were brought down briefly, always swaddled or enclosed in a comfortable carrier, to be peeped at before being returned to quiet and privacy. I learned that marsupials, even grown-up ones, felt secure when wrapped because they had been accustomed to being in a pouch. Quite the opposite to placentals.

We did a lot of talking beforehand, to calm people in preparation for what they were going to experience. We wanted to make sure they would not crowd too close, would view quietly, with respect for shyness, wildness, the trauma of orphanhood. Our message was that we were not trying to tame the animal, merely to prepare it for a free and naturally unconstrained life on the property and beyond.

Into the Nursery Yard adjoining the theatre-museum verandah went only those able to experience humans passing by without distress. Most visitors wanted to touch but we allowed this only under supervision, if at all; delicately, literally with one finger, they could test the softness of fur, trace the shape of a skull or torso. If the animal was a marsupial, we might arrange a glimpse of the pouch but we never let it be touched. Rarely, after assessing the character and temperament of a person, we entrusted an animal to be cuddled within its bunny rug, maybe even bottle-fed. Oftentimes it was a quiet child with sensitive parents who won this privilege.

There was a lesson in all we did. Our softly-softly approach created a compassionate mood. People left feeling gifted. We knew they would tell others, which we hoped would spread a long-lasting message. It also brought us more and more animals.

18

A voice for the rainforest

Extending the scope of Wild Country Park preoccupied me. The conservation movement was a tender plant in the 1960s and '70s, but it was growing. When people bopped to Joni Mitchell's 'Big Yellow Taxi', I suspect many liked the beat and the lilt as much as her message about clearing Paradise to put up parking lots. So many seemed high on development. Things old were devalued. The new – 'the latest' – was where It was at, and to champion the bush over buildings was cranky if not downright unpatriotic. Nonetheless, the World Wildlife Fund and local groups like the Kangaroo Protection Society, the Gould League for Birds and the Wildlife Preservation Society were spreading a different message.

We felt Wild Country Park could contribute. Heritage was what our place was about, both environmental and human. Four of our films celebrated the ethos of the outback, the other two dramatised nature conservation. Our theatre built of slabs of local timber a century old was itself a museum, which reinforced one of the messages of the films. Souvenirs of our desert travels sat comfortably near natural history exhibits and artefacts of yester-year Foxground. The trick was to make the riches outdoors as easily accessible to the public.

Jeff had laid out our nature trail (which we named the Jungle Walk) cleverly, making use of animal pads plus the remains of the old road which had provided access to the farm in the days of five creek crossings and seven gates. The first part of the walk led people down the open hillside, over soft green grass, past the Staging Yard and its dam. That dam was a miracle in itself; inside a year it had evolved from a totally new pond created by bulldozer into a whole system of rushes and frogs, water beetles and tiny fish, an inviting place for herons and other migrating water birds. We hoped visitors would stop to look for whatever might be in residence there, then descend to a grove of wattles where kangaroos often laid up during the hot hours of the day. It was a natural rest spot for people also, to pause, observe and ponder before proceeding down to the creek to follow the trail along its shore back through the rainforest.

That was the plan and to a degree it worked well enough. We gave visitors their little green map and bags of pellets, our gift so that they would not approach animals empty-handed, otherwise the wallabies and kangas would learn strangers were not worth meeting. The challenge was getting people to go slowly and quietly. After our little welcoming spiel at the front gate, most adults accepted our suggestions and you could see them begin to relax as they set off, uplifted by the view, refreshed by pure air and open space all around them. It was children we had to put brakes on. Show most red-blooded kids a hillside and they will want to race down it, especially if they spy kangaroos at the bottom. Trouble was, the first lot who charge down like wild Indians spooked the 'roos for the rest of the day. Since they weren't locked in, they could easily hop off and hide themselves.

My strategy was two-pronged. First, convince the parents; if that didn't take, then I explained it to the kids in their own language. Never one to ignore children, during my years with the Boys' Museum I had discovered a special wavelength which worked with other young visitors to the property. To use it involves bending or squatting to their eye level, speaking in a sympathetic tone and listening, trying to see things from their perspective – not unlike the technique that works with animals. It was a special skill I used for everyone's benefit. Especially my own.

My aim was to inspire visitors to take time along the Jungle Walk. Human nature urged them to simply cover the distance, getting from beginning to end without interruption rather than pausing to inspect what was in between. And there was plenty to see, even for the uninitiated. A rainforest is a magic place. A creek is a magic place. Two together makes double magic, and how to help people experience it became my task.

From the start my vision was to duplicate something I had enjoyed years before in a totally different sort of park. This was at Wyperfeld, Victoria, adjoining the Little Desert. Wyperfeld had once been a grazing property but the arid climate blighted the hopes of its settlers, who left behind only graves and remnants of pioneer buildings and fences. The Victorian Field Naturalists' Society discovered the area early and by the turn of the century its interesting flora and fauna were being documented, in the then popular spirit of amateur science. Wyperfeld encompassed three environments, where desert melded with mallee grasslands and riverine. In a very modest but comprehensive way, those field naturalists laid out two tracks – one for walkers, another longer one for vehicles – along which were discreet markers pointing out what characterised these systems, as well as relics of human activity. One of the happiest days I ever spent while on photo location with Jeff was at Wyperfeld. The memory of it and their simple, roneoed trail guide remain with me forever. Now I wanted to do the same for visitors to Wild Country Park. But first I had to learn more about our subtropical ecology myself. That term meant little to me as I began my project. Within a decade, it would become the catchcry of my life.

First I consulted dear Howard at Minnamurra Falls. He recited his litany – the basic requirements for rainforest and how our little strip, no more than 70 kilometres long and about 10 kilometres wide, came to nestle between the escarpment and the sea, much further south than was 'normal'. It was knowlege he was happy to share. Doing so was his life's mission.

Sheltering cliffs, high rainfall, volcanic soil, warm climate – these were the elements which blessed us with rainforest. The canopy of tree-tops and vines acted as a giant umbrella, preserving beneath it a humid atmosphere in which thrived layers of vegetation – tall trees, small trees, shrubs, ferns and fungi. Underfoot, nourishing this busy plant colony, was humus composed of leaf matter falling from above, the detritus of rapid life-cycles made possible by moisture and mild temperatures. The bacterial and faunal life sustained within rainforest is so rich. What were its components, its ecosystem (which I learned came from the Greek word *oikos*, meaning house – the home environment of living things where all are interrelated and interdependent)?

At the beginning, my knowlege of what I hoped to share with our visitors was patchy. We had studied the birds fairly keenly from the beginning, but there was always more to learn. The animal and reptile communities, ditto. Insects . . . I knew some but not enough. As for the forest, it was mainly just colour, texture and fragrance to me. Strictly an impressionist basking in pale green shade, I was like a Stan Freburg joke: 'You seen one tree, you seen 'em all.'

During the next few months, I spent every spare hour gathering information. Books were bought or borrowed from the library. Avidly I filled notebooks. I paced out the nature trail, identifying features that would be easy for people to observe. Beside each I would put a small numbered peg. The key to the numbers would be in the nature trail guide I was writing. Included in its ten pages would be not just natural but also human relics and the sites/scars of our attempts to 'stage animals back to nature'. I designated thirty-eight stops along the walk, which would bring visitors full circle back to where they had begun, at the theatre-museum.

The side track to the bottom of the waterfall was not included, being narrow, steep in places and slippery after rain. It was one of my favourite places on earth, the waterfall walk but, concerned lest visitors hurt themselves, we placed small warning signs where it began, and during wet times we closed it off altogether. This super-cautious regard for safety paid dividends. Our accident record was blank.

Meanwhile, it was business as usual and spare hours weren't many. Family involvement, following up overseas film sales, tending the park and caring for dependent and free-living animals kept me fully occupied. And very, very happy.

Goth moved to Sydney for a while. He found employment at the film production studio where we'd first met Steve Weslak. After gaining experience there, Goth applied for a job at the Australian Broadcasting Commission, in the sound department, and got it. It seemed fitting for him to commence his Sydney career thus, serving our dear old ABC, which had blurrily kept us informed and amused for so many years.

Karen was at university in Sydney. Thor was also studying for a degree in science. He worked nights at Sydney's primary cine-film processing house. At weekends he yo-yoed between Sydney and Foxground on his motorbike, helping out with the farm and refuge. A self-taught welder, he built what we needed, repaired what we had. Very strong, was our Thor. Strong, silent, stubborn. And a bit of a daredevil. He and his mates from Sydney used to stage hill-climbs up the winding track, from front to back, driving in reverse! Once when Jeff and I were away for a few days, Thor rolled the Land Rover while racing Van on his motorbike through our front gate. Upside down, battery acid leaked onto Thor's shin. To souse the burning, he jumped into the creek, injuring his leg. They had a student visitor with them, billeted at our place overnight. That city lad went home believing that country life held unlimited chances for adventure. And of course, they didn't tell The Old Man what had really happened to Thor's leg or the Land Rover, not for a long time after. It was innocent fun, after all.

Sometimes Thor took out his big bow and arrows, which still lived in our closet, and went hunting rabbits. As Van stalked bunnies with his rifle at one end of the property, his big brother took the opposite direction, both wary and silent, in tune with the bush, like Indians. Often they returned with meat. Always they brought back news of our back boundaries and the wildlife living there.

About that time, Vandal, without fuss but very firm in his resolve, left high school early, earlier than Goth had and much earlier than I or his teachers thought appropriate to his abilities. Jeff did not oppose his decision. He had done much the same thing in his teens and found no reason to believe an aborted formal education was a deterrent to living a rich and productive life. Van moved into the dairy room and as soon as he could get a licence to ride his motorbike on the public road, he found a job at a small factory in Gerringong.

About once a month or so, Jeff's parents came down to visit and help us out. Always very industrious, they cut back the old garden without being asked, cleaned the house, Dadda invented aids for Jeff's darkroom or sharpened the tools, Nana took over the kitchen. When they went home again, they left us feeling we weren't quite measuring up to the tasks we had set ourselves, but that they, once again, had put us back on the right track.

They approved of Wild Country Park, as well as they understood what it was about, but their bewilderment with our
menagerie of native animals sometimes turned to anger. To us,
teethmarks, scratches, holes dug in the garden beds, pillows torn
or bonked to death – all represented stages in the return to free life
of wild creatures deprived of their natural homes. Where we saw
triumphs of a sort, as well as the basis for many amusing anec-
dotes, Doris and Percy saw wanton destruction. They judged our
careful regimes as wasted time, money and effort. Why not just
lock the varmints up and be done with it? Well, they came from a
different era. Most of our neighbours shared their views.

We did, in fact, need more temporary holding quarters. With
the volume of wildlife arriving, secure quarters for the short term
were essential, to protect animals until they acclimatised and could
be let out. With this in mind, the barn that had housed the Boys'
Museum was rebuilt, one of Thor's projects, assisted by Van. He
laid a concrete floor, erected corner posts from trees felled on the
property and put corrugated iron partway up the walls – a good
strong useful shed like those he had seen in the outback. One day
a gale sprang up before he had secured his new roof strongly to
the walls. As the big sheets of tin rippled like waves, he clambered
onto them to receive the boulders and bits of heavy iron the rest
of us passed up to him to weight it down.

Inside the shed, Thor built a new wombatarium. It had brick
walls about waist high, a metal door and a lift-up lid. It may have
looked like a penitentiary, but it worked well. Inside it was cosy,
with sawdust on the floor, straw to burrow under, a fat hollow log
to sleep in and chew on, a wooden box of dirt for eliminations in
one far corner. When the lid was down, it was dark and safe and
snug, just like a real burrow. The wombats all liked it.

They came thick and fast, after one brought by Bill Graham, a
member of the local conservation society. Her name was Wompy.
She had slept with her head beneath his pillow every night since
she'd been orphaned. He brought the pillow with him and then
asked if he could sleep the first night on our couch, with her. Such
devotion to her resettlement impressed us. Next day, after
patiently escorting her all around the house and yard, he departed,
leaving her the pillow. But he kept in touch.

Bippy was moving about freely by this time. Jeff went out with his shovel and began digging her a 'practice burrow' on a slope below the house. Once she got the hang of excavating dirt herself, he left her to it. Within a week or so, she had tunnelled into the hillside three times her own length, but seemed disinclined to stay within. Next he took her down to Wild Country Park and repeated the exercise in a clay bank beneath the oak trees. She seemed to like this spot better and we encouraged her to make it a proper burrow, which she did. However, at night we called her out and took her up to the new wombatarium. We weren't sure what would happen when she encountered William or Wally, or even Gnasher, but we suspected they would fight for her favour. Later, we learned that females are also combative when roused.

Winkie was growing into a tubby little animal, about the size of a honeydew melon, but she slept in the old wombatarium outside the dairy room. Van had to put up with her snuffling and meeping on the other side of his bedroom wall. Luckily, he was a sound sleeper.

That left us with little Wompy, whom Bill Graham had encouraged to be very placid and people oriented. Jeff and I were too busy to spend much time with her at night – and actually we were quite tired – so we simply popped her inside the bed when we retired. She made her way like a mole under the covers, curling up with a huge sigh at the bottom. On cold nights, she was a little round furry toaster to warm our feet on. The only snag was that toward morning, she would work her way up our legs until she came to the back of our knees, where she fastened her lips onto skin and sucked. It felt creepy, and never failed to rouse one of us; weary and sometimes testy, we took turns to get up and prepare her a bottle of milk formula. I remember sitting up in bed, holding her and dozing while she drank, after which she would settle again and let us sleep out the night in peace.

Through Bill Graham, we received other animals and we met Pat Olbrich, who dedicated her life to native animal care. Pat was just past middle age, stocky and strong, very outspoken, full of humour but also anger. A failed marriage had left her with one treasured daughter and the opinion that animals made better friends than humans. Pat lived on an acre at Mount Kembla, a position similar to Foxground but smaller and steeper. On her little patch of bushland she kept countless rescued native animals. She was the Doctor Dolittle of the south coast, well known to vets and the Kangaroo Protection Society, which handed over to her victims of the road and of bush clearing. She saw Wild Country Park as a good place to pass on her charges.

The orphans from Pat always arrived in good health, with a well-documented and often quite hilarious history. If any hiccups occurred while settling them into Glenrock refuge, we had only to telephone Pat and she would advise us or even drive down to assist. She brought us our first wallaroo, a female. Her name was Lovely, and she was. Her pale soft coat was long and fluffy, like mohair. Of a more stocky build than the grey kangaroos, her wrists and ankles were thicker, her tail was stumpier and furrier and she carried herself more upright than they did. With big black 'liquid' eyes, she was just so pretty.

We also received a euro, which is another *Macropus robustus*, like the wallaroo. He had been living in a suburb of Wollongong, eating chicken meat, cherries, orange fizzy drinks, tea and bird-seed. Once he grew accustomed to nothing more artificial than pellets and was satisfying his hunger mainly with grass, we let him out of the Staging Yard to join the grey kangaroos, but being a slightly different species, they did not welcome him. He preferred to knock around with Lovely, who was more genetically similar.

Not all our projects went well. If you only like stories where everything in the garden is rosy, you had better skip this next bit. But if you can accept the fact that life in the animal world is no more permanent than in the human one, read on.

First there was Lucky, a disabled eagle who had been found shot beside the road out west. Half of one wing was missing so he couldn't fly. He was brought to us with a leather collar round his leg, attached to a light chain. During the week, Lucky stayed in the back yard and slept at night in the aviary, but at weekends we tethered him on a big rock in the park where he could regally watch over visitors without being pestered. We told everyone his story, and several times a day Jeff let him off his chain to move about where he wished. He used to trudge up the hill to the theatre, then spread his wings and spring down again, half gliding, half running. Several times a week we fed him either a rabbit or a shin of beef.

We thought we were giving him a pretty good life, considering his handicap, but then we heard that a local teacher, who had been one of our fans, was turned off the Carters and their park by 'the eagle chained to the rock'. Put like that, we realised Lucky mightn't look so fortunate to outsiders. He was sending out a negative message. So, with misgivings, we removed his tether and left him to make his own way about the park. He liked to potter around the creek, bathing himself in running water. As we feared, when we weren't free to chaperone him he was exposed to undue attention from visitors. A few kids wanted to toss stones at him, or shout at him to make him move. Overseas visitors, especially Japanese, were frightened of him.

In retrospect, we should have given him to a zoo or housed him in a big aviary, but both were contrary to our philosophy. So we persevered with the Free Lucky campaign but finally, as we'd feared, it ended badly. Some predator must have taken him in the night. He had been 'phased back to nature' in the most basic way, as would have happened had he not been rescued in the first place from the roadside.

Another failure occurred when a relative of some Foxground neighbours asked us to accept her young female grey kangaroo, very fondly loved. We put her in the Nursery Yard while she adjusted to Glenrock. Very docile, she still drank milk but also ate pellets and peanuts, sausage rolls (her donor said she would even eat stew!). She seemed to have settled in so we left the gate ajar when the Park was not open to the public, hoping she would venture out and join the other 'roos. They seemed to tolerate the newcomer, but a few days later, one Saturday morning, I discovered she was listless, with mild diarrhoea.

Thinking we might have been pushing her along too quickly, I carried her up to the house and put her in the bedroom with plenty of newspaper on the floor and a heater, too busy with the park to give her much attention until evening. By then she was scouring watery diarrhoea. I crushed a tablet of Sulphadimidine and gave her that in some milk. By morning, she was no better. The Conroys had told me they fed burnt flour to animals as a remedy for 'the runs' so I tried that. On Sunday, another busy day in the park was followed by a worrying night nursing the kangaroo. She had begun to look emaciated, and by Monday morning she was passing black and odiferous liquid. This was a worse affliction than we were used to. I rang Worrell's Reptile Park and described the symptoms; they suggested it might be coccidiosis, a disease they said was always a danger with animals in captivity. The dark colour indicated the presence of blood in the faeces. They recommended Sulphamethazine by injection, so I rang George Borys and he obliged, also prescribing a scours remedy for sheep and cattle.

Most of the next few days were spent tending the 'roo, who continued to be very sick. She was as light as a wraith when I carried her outside. She hopped a bit, I induced her to eat a little grass, forced a bit of earth into her mouth as well, in case 'nature's remedy' would work. Hour by hour I monitored her, sometimes hopeful (a tiny curd formed in her eliminations for a while), at other times dreading what was to come. Her spirit was strong, but physically she just wasted away. Despite force-feeding her fluids with added vitamins and keeping her good and warm, on Thursday night she died.

When I gave the donor the sad news, she told me she was disappointed but not totally surprised. The kangaroo had scoured before. A vet had told her it had lungworm. He gave her a pink medicine which seemed to 'fix it up'. That was a salutory experience, not only because of the time I had spent tending an unsound 'roo but also because we learned that coccidiosis is highly contagious and could contaminate an area where other animals grazed. Not to mention lungworm! We decided to rest the Nursery Yard for a few weeks, just in case.

Another such encounter happened to us before that year was out. A woman asked us to please accept her dear pet kangaroo which lived in her back yard. The day after it came to our place, we saw it had coccidiosis. This time we did not waste any time but had it destroyed. The donor wrote to say she knew it was sick but could not bear to have it die at her place. Her husband had passed away the previous year.

So. There was more to tending a wildlife park than we had bargained for. From then on, we always asked first if animals offered into our care were well and if they had had any history of illness – in fairness to the other animals on our place, as well as to ourselves.

19

Linda's list

Attendances at Wild Country Park started with trickles which swelled like freshets after rain. The turn-off to Foxground had always intrigued motorists along the Princes Highway. Some simply loved the name and remembered it; others turned in and followed the narrow road across the valley floor. Most turned back where the bitumen ended, but after our modest Wild Country Park signs appeared on the roadside, more people followed their curiosity and ventured further.

Each telecast of our *Wild Country* documentaries by Channel Seven in their *The World Around Us* program brought more visitors to Foxground. The local councils put the wildlife refuge into their brochures and recommended it at their tourist offices. On Sundays, farmers were amazed to see a growing stream of cars and the odd bus passing their front gates.

Many drivers arrived at our doorstep shaky and worried until we assured them that, yes, they would be able to get out again. The unsealed road from Mailbox Corner was pretty narrow and the rough creek crossings we so loved put city drivers off. Fewer and fewer felt comfortable without bitumen under their tyres. Jeff growled at their timidity and said the experience of getting to Wild Country Park would do them good. The road was a message in itself. However, the council was keen to attract tourists to the district, so they began to keep the road graded and eventually diverted the creeks through huge drainpipes beneath the gravel. It saved us work at flood times, but we mourned losing contact with those little streams.

Additional 'progress' occurred when more coaches began to venture in and the drivers complained about branches scratching the roofs of their vehicles. The council came to prune back the leafy tunnel along that last stretch of road leading to the park. As soon as we heard the chainsaws, we rushed down and begged the council workers to go easy; take no more foliage than necessary and spare the trunks. Red cedars, coachwoods and other precious rainforest species grew there but it was not the practice then to consider such things. Any tree near the roadside was expendable.

More visitors meant more animals were brought to us. Some were backyard 'pets' whose keepers sought a wider habitat for them. Introducing them to a free life in gradual stages was time-consuming but rewarding. We worked at it with a will, accepting each challenge as it came. Some had fixed habits after having lived in captivity for a long time. Our task was to introduce these animals to native foods they could survive on once released. Others were fresh from the bush, like little Rhubarb Walker, a wallaby who had been kidnapped by a pet Labrador and presented like a gift to its owners. They brought Rhubarb to us straightaway. The little fellow was traumatised and wouldn't graze outdoors unless held by one of us. We secured him in a playpen on our front verandah for weeks until he'd calmed down and could eventually progress to the Nursery Yard.

Three wild ducklings were passed to us after their mother had been shot on Lake Illawarra, a local waterway encircled by houses. We kept them in the playpen too, with lots of newspaper and a dishpan of water, feeding them a 'slurpable' mixture of cooked oatmeal and bran, lettuce and cabbage and later, poultry pellets. They thrived and grew until big enough to live on our dam. To protect them from foxes and other night predators, we built them an island using an inflated inner tube from a tractor tyre, covered with chicken wire and turf.

Percy Noir was a crow blown into a Wollongong family's garden during a storm. His wings were clipped and he had twine wrapped around one leg, indicating he was an escaped pet. With no means of finding the owner, and no desire to keep him captive in their back yard, his rescuers brought him to us. Percy was very quiet around people, accepting meat or a piece of banana from the hand. We conditioned him to expect food from us by repeating the same cry: 'Percy No-waahr', which sounds something like a crow's caw if pronouced right. He perched in the lemon tree outside the back door during the day while his wing feathers grew, but we brought him indoors at night until we were sure he could fly well. Even after his release he returned occasionally for hand-outs of meat, hopping to us confidently when we called: 'No-waahr, Percy No-waahr.'

Two men turned up late one night with an injured magpie they had picked up off the road near Moruya. We put him on the front verandah and kept him warm, wrapped in sweaters on a hot-water bottle. Next morning he was hopping about. We gave him a wide vessel for drinking and bathing – in this case an old saucepan – and for food, to encourage him from the start to get his own, we put down newspaper under a pile of fresh earth containing worms and also small morsels of meat, insurance against the inevitable times when worms could not be found.

On the afternoon of the second day, Maggie began to eat. He picked out the worms excitedly, learned that the dirt-covered tidbits of meat were edible too, and from then on we had only to set before him a heap of soil and he began probing with his beak. We took care not to touch him, approached him seldom and always whistled when we brought his food. Nobody told us to do this, we just figured it out, based on the principles of conditioning and our experience with the eagles. It worked for the magpie and other dependent birds subsequently. Once its injured wing healed, we let it outdoors, providing food signalled by the whistle until it was no longer needed.

Just before Christmas 1975, we received Sonny, a red kangaroo orphan from out Wilcannia way. *Megaleia rufa*. His donor lived in a suburb of Wollongong and, although the 'roo was thriving on a diet of soybean milk plus orange skin, spinach and rolled oats, she did not want him to home in on her back yard.

I haven't interrupted the story thus far with scientific data, but as we were learning then, so you may also feel ready to know a little more about macropods (kangaroos and wallabies). Most of our original 'roos were eastern greys, *Macropus giganteus*. Led by

Eric, they formed into a little band of individuals who took comfort and safety in keeping together. Opal, Mathilda and Sheila all had joeys at foot, as did Potch, and Eric saw to it that their pouches were drooping with new babies. It was interesting to see the 'family resemblance' between offspring and their mothers. Opal's children were like her, fine-featured and rather delicately built, quite different to Sheila's or Gidgea's. Mathilda's had her long face and sleek, fawnish pelt. She may have been a western grey. The western grey, *M. fulignosis*, is built to blend in with a more arid landscape. Crossbreeding happens between western and eastern greys, but not so easily or not at all between wallabies. The walla-roos were a borderline case and I watched carefully to see if Eric could make Lovely pregnant.

Less than a month after Sonny joined us, we received a second red orphan, this time from Western Australia, who'd been plucked from the roadside by a young couple on a marathon drive across to New South Wales. They had a newborn infant and after six weeks of travel felt they couldn't manage him in the car any further – in fairness to him as well as their child. They had kept him alive thus far on a formula of half evaporated milk and half water.

Not long afterwards, a second young wallaroo was given to us. This little fellow ate well on apples, brown bread and grapes, plus three full bottles of fresh cow's milk daily. So all of a sudden, our Nursery Yard was populated by three young chaps with different diets, all far from home but, for the moment, safe and cared for. Rather than upset their digestion, I continued to feed each the milk they were used to, while I pondered their future in our high-rainfall district. The trio made a good talking point with visitors about the consequences of removing orphans from their natural locale and, indeed, the practice of making them orphans in the first place.

The lesson came home to roost on us very smartly. A traveller called in with a fur hat in his hands, the sort of toque Ukrainians wear. He was a tree-feller by trade and he had found a young greater glider possum on the forest floor a day or so earlier. He'd kept it warm in the marvellous hat, turned fur-side in, but had been unsuccessful in getting it to eat anything. Its face and ears ruffled with long soft fur, it was by far the most beautiful animal we had ever seen, and bigger than other possums we had reared. We rang Eric Worrell's place at once and received disquietening advice. The food for greater gliders is very specific: in order of preference, they eat grey gum, scribbly gum and peppermint gum in the wild, and in captivity may come at watermelon, apple or carrot. However, in most cases these animals do not survive when removed from their tree-top habitat.

We scurried round getting as many foods on the list as possible but despite our best efforts, the choicest tidbits, the little chap just sniffed them dully, then tucked his head back into the hat. The fluffiness of his fur disguised the fact that he was fading to skin and bone, but we could feel his lightness and also sensed that, somehow, we were not presenting the food in a way that he recognised. We puzzled and pondered, and rang all the experts we could think of, but could not save that special little animal's life.

Oftentimes, it's the one failure you remember more distinctly than dozens of successes, but we learned from each encounter with native animals. And one thing the greater glider taught us was the fragility of species dependent on a narrow sort of habitat or food source. Such species slide into extinction very easily.

I loved looking after the animals, caring and learning, but in 1976 Jeff was ready to go overseas again. He concocted a scheme which would take us to live in Spain, a country we had come to appreciate especially during our earlier trips to Europe. We would be away for at least eighteen months. Jeff's plan involved selling the cottage. With the proceeds, he would buy a new Porsche from the factory at Stuttgart. He had already ordered it. In fact, I found out the details – his version of them – from an article he wrote for *Wheels* magazine. For *Wheels* articles he often used a special brand of humour which earned him many loyal readers.

He described how he had told 'the cook' (his chauvinistic nickname for me which went over big with readers of a certain age group – his – but which secretly I felt demeaned me) that he thought I needed a change and therefore he had planned this jolly European holiday for us. In fact, it was a means of avoiding import duty on the Porsche, when we returned to Australia bringing it back with us. Nudge nudge, wink wink. But I felt misgivings about being away for so long. Although Van had left school by his own decision, he was still young enough to need support, I believed. But Jeff, having himself left home early, was comfortable with the arrangement.

We had thought that Thor would be living in the cottage with Jennifer, the girl of his dreams. Cousin of a best mate, she came from Tasmania, growing up on a rural property near Hobart. She rode horses and worked as an entomologist. At first Thor began fixing up the cottage for them, but it became clear that she had too much career potential to bury herself at Foxground. They both applied for jobs with the Forestry Commission in Sydney, and were hired, Thor as a photographer. Just before we were ready to go overseas, we all flew down to Tasmania for their wedding, the first in our family. Goth and Van were groomsmen.

So, for the first time, neither Thor nor Karen would be available to run the family business and mind the family home, Karen having moved to Melbourne to follow her boyfriend into academic studies at Monash University. Steve and Brooke had returned home to Canada. Roger was busy making his own films. Luckily, Goth was now eager to move back to Foxground with a new girlfriend, Linda. Van continued living at home, in the dairy. Goth and Linda would move into our places in the farmhouse

Linda was a Sydney girl but she took to the country life enthusiastically. She and Goth expected to enjoy an idyll, free from parental supervision, earning a modest living from Wild Country Park, dining cheaply on the eggs, chicken meat, vegetables and fruit growing on the farm, plus fresh country bread and milk still warm from the cow, bought daily down the road at the Conroys'. If you put the can into the fridge overnight, by morning you could scoop a jug of thick cream off the top.

Fun-loving and spirited, with a bush of wild curly hair, Linda was artistic. I asked her to draw a cover for my nature trail guide, which I sat up late completing the night before we flew to Europe. Her drawing showed a young family of three, little child hand-in-hand on a leafy path with Mum and Dad, whose trousers were the then-fashionable flares. Goth was entrusted with the task of installing the numbered pegs along the walk. Together they launched the new Jungle Walk after we departed.

We told them not to bother accepting any more orphans during our absence if they didn't want to. But they did. Linda fancied being a carer. If they did happen to take in any little foundlings, I asked Linda to enter details in my animal register.

When we returned two years later, she showed me her list. It was full of graphic explanations about donors and animals, a wonderful document which I keep to this day. Under Linda and Goth's management, the residents at Glenrock wildlife refuge quadrupled during our absence.

March 1976 – Crow named Inky, from Martin at Warilla. Kept in a cage for one week, ate eggs, mince, bread, grapes, almost anything. Martin returned to free it the following Saturday, have not seen it since. Maybe it's still flying around. Martin phones about Inky constantly.

April 1976 – Ambrose, our new male wombat from Pat Olbrich. Took over burrow in the park. Had a fight with Wompy about June . . . his back is badly hurt. September, now he's just about better. I think he mated with Wompy in February, '77.

June 1976 – two red-necked wallabies, brought by Bill Graham, and one fully grown eastern grey female.

September 1976 – Wallaby from Bodalla region. Its mother was shot dead. Geoff in Warilla reared it with his dog. Name is Eugene. He eats dog food. He thinks he is a dog. We put him in the Staging Yard. Later: – Eugene seems to be settling in nicely. Doesn't act like a dog anymore. Later still: Found Eugene outside yard, all cut up. Was attacked by something. Brought in house for a few days, now is in Nursery Yard, quite well again. One of his ears droops, but.

October 1976 – given seven little emus from out west, exactly two months old. Raised from eggs by Warilla girl, Debbie. Mother abandoned the nest after a fright by shooters. Debbie is extremely fond of her emus and visits them here frequently. They will have to be moved soon from Nursery Yard. They're growing rapidly and making such a mess. They love apples, pellets and plenty of water. Had no trouble adapting to this environment. November: let them out one night and one strayed away. Unfortunate. Now we have six. They walk around the park during the day and we lock them into Nursery Yard at night until they grow a little bigger. December – a fox came and killed three emus in one night. Now we have only three left.

November 1976 – Pretty-faced wallaby, found near Grafton, mother run over; looks about five months old. We feed it Pro-sobee but we're having trouble stopping it from sucking itself. We gave it a dummy and put bandaids everyplace it sucks. Poor little darling.

More emus given to us. Four stripey babies. Put them in Nursery Yard. They look so cute, people love watching them.

November 1976 – Galah, Nip, female. Came from some snobs at Hunter's Hill. Very smart bird. Was found run-over about three years ago. Her wing was all banged up. She loves cups of tea, wine, is a real character. Loves sitting on Goth's shoulder. She has to sleep in the same room as us, as well. She likes Goth better than anyone else.

And so it went on, pages and pages which told a rich story of how Linda and Goth and Van kept busy during our absence.

1977, January – Twiggy, female grey kangaroo, 12 months old. Eats everything, prefers humans to animals, is far too pampered – very spoilt.

Another grey female, Mathilda. Really nice, very sensible, going well.

May 1977 – three white cockatoos, one has old wing injury, named Ralph. All three sit in big lemon tree and are very good friends.

July – Twiggy died of pneumonia during cold spell. Very sad. Mustn't tell the lady who brought her, she has cancer. Poor lady. Poor Twiggy.

December 1977 – Josephine, wallaby, found at Cape York, mother run-over. Mated with Eugene. Baby in pouch.

A tally of Linda's List told me they had cared for three wombats, seven wallabies, five kangaroos, three possums, twelve emus plus a crow, a hawk, a galah, two seagulls and five cockatoos. Not all their charges survived, but most of them were still in residence when we returned, including Nip, dear little Nip the galah, who liked to sing out from a bush near the side gate to anyone returning from the park. 'Chirrup?' she would say, cocking her head. 'Chirrup?' We would ask her: 'Do you want a taxi, Nip?' If she did, when you held out your hand she'd step delicately but precisely onto it, gently using a beakful of skin to steady herself, then she'd ride confidently with you round to another favourite perch near the kitchen door. She often hitched a ride, otherwise she had to walk and climb using her beak and claws, a slow process.

Goth and Linda had some marvellous times during our two years away. With Van and Glenn and other local friends, they hosted hilarious parties at which everyone dressed up in improvised costumes and danced the Limbo. The old house rocked to the songs of The Eagles and The Stones. One Saturday night a terrific storm began to rage after their guests had gathered and the hijinks were in full swing. Above the music and laughter and roar of the wind, they heard a pounding at the door. On the porch a drenched visitor stood, asking for help with his car which was trapped by a fallen tree back down the road.

In true country style, Van and his huge mate Phil threw on raincoats and boots and went to the rescue. Wind lashed branches, the road was awash, occasional lightning zig-zagged overhead. Out of the blackness they strode, like two Paul Bunyans, tall, bearded, with long blond hair streaming. Clasping the tree trunk in their mighty arms, they heaved it to one side. Through the windscreen of the car they saw horrified faces staring at them and remembered they were wearing make-up and frilly nylon under-garments, their party clobber revealed as the wind blew aside their coats. The car started with a roar, made a precarious U-turn and sped away.

Van and Phil laughed all the way back to the farmhouse; they guessed the strangers would be wondering about their saviours who had appeared out of the storm and darkness to rescue them on that wild mountain road: 'Who *were* those big girls?' They laugh about it to this day and so do I, even though I wasn't even there and only heard the story second hand.

There were some taxing experiences also. Goth records how a white cockatoo flew down to the creek after it was let out of its cage but couldn't fly back, or anywhere else. They had to go down, calling and climbing to catch it. Several times they rescued it from premature attempts at freedom, until finally its wings strength-ened, along with its natural instincts.

There were two great emu disasters. First, someone sneaked into the park at night and stole all four of the new chicks. Linda and Goth had noticed a couple of 'suspicious characters' eyeing them while the park was open and believed the villains returned after dark. There was money to be made, trafficking in wildlife.

Fully alerted now and into protective mode, they discovered one of the older emus dead in the paddock below the house. Something had been chasing it, and this time they guessed the culprit was a fox or rampant dog. Van and Goth took turns sitting up at night with the shotgun. After nights of fruitless vigil, they began to creep away to bed as daylight approached. Another emu bit the dust. Back on full alert, the patrols began again in earnest.

As it happened, Goth was on duty the night a big fox was finally sighted, galloping confidently across the paddock, bounding over the long grass like a porpoise surfing waves and lunging at the emus. Although not an experienced hunter like his brother, Goth did his best. Blam went the gun, knocking Goth over backwards. 'Van-dal!' yelled Goth. He had missed the fox but the ensuing commotion as Linda and Van beat the bushes convinced the predator to stay away in future. In retrospect it struck them as hilarious how Goth went 'arse over turkey' and they laughed about that for years.

They had other bad luck. While we were in Europe, it rained every weekend for a year, which meant the park attracted fewer visitors. Goth and Linda's income was much lower than they (and we) had expected. They were just able to meet expenses. Then a careless driver forced them off the road, causing their car to roll into a paddock. They had to buy another one. Although only second hand, it was an outlay they had not budgeted for.

The responsibility of it all weighed upon Goth, who was only twenty-three. His proclivity to allergy resulted in chronic eczema, prompted by three common triggers for such conditions – stress, eating too many eggs and dairy foods which were cheaply available, plus a great many animals living in the house. By the time we returned, he was a physical and nervous wreck.

Not long after that, he and Linda split up. Goth moved back to Sydney, a bachelor again, determined to make his fortune as a photographer and entertainer. Linda, although very disappointed by the failure of their partnership, did not quit the district. She rented a little cottage near Gerringong beach and lived there courageously with her pup Granite, named because of his markings, a rascal son of Jim and Brownie. Also from Foxground she took unique experience in wildlife husbandry and an ecstatic job reference from me, which she parleyed into a job at Wollongong University's department of zoology and eventually a science degree there. Her bonds with Glenrock and the Carter family remain strong.

In 1978 I felt ready to settle down. After our European sojourn, the promise and the challenge of Wild Country Park excited me. I felt plump and rosy from imbibing art and architecture and antiquities for two years, and on top of all that, four animal parks we'd visited had set me thinking. They were Monkey Mountain in Alsace, Adler Castle at nearby Kinzheim, the new state-of-the-art zoo in Brussels and a reserve for ancient highland animals in Scotland.

At the first, capuchin monkeys lived in a huge community on a wooded mountainside, all ages and stages conducting their affairs while the public walked amongst them. Why were they there? Because their native home in South America had been taken for human purposes. Relocation in Europe gave them a chance to survive as a species. At the Adler park, hand-reared eagles were flown and fed in the air for audiences numbering thousands, entranced at such close views of these magnificent birds in action. When not performing for their supper, the eagles were tethered on grassy lawn. Brussels zoo also gave close access to exotic animals and birds. Solid barriers had been replaced by moats and low electric fences. Vegetation appropriate to the former habitat of the creatures had been planted and they were grouped according to their native continents and climate systems. In Scotland, the small shaggy forebears of modern cattle were in their correct locale, along with lynx and antelope, but they had been reimported, brought back from extinction.

Brussels zoo and Adler park were, in principle, the sort of keeping places for animals which did not interest me, although both those places were immaculate examples of the genre. No, what impressed me so much was the exhilaration of visitors to these popular tourist attractions. They yearned to get close to native species. Because there was apparent concern for the well-being of the animals, an air of righteousness prevailed. The fact that a huge income was being earned by these parks was not what inspired me. I saw a different message for Australians. In Europe, and increasingly in Africa and South America, natural habitat has been corrupted or lost altogether. The relicts we saw in Europe were secondary examples of once wild life and in no way lived free. On our continent, still unspoiled but rapidly trying to emulate more 'developed' countries, primary ecosystems and species are still in place. They are savable, if people have the will to preserve them. I vowed to increase our efforts to promote an appreciation of natural habitat.

First, I commissioned a mural from local wildlife artist Trudi Last, which showed our rainforest in spring, summer, autumn and winter. The modest bird list compiled during our first year on

Glenrock had swelled threefold and we had learned to recognise animal and plant activities which heralded the change of seasons. This information I put onto a page for visitors, to indicate what they might espy in spring, summer, etc. I compiled a plant profile, beginning on the forest floor with ferns and fungi and working up through bushes to understorey trees like the native bleeding heart and plum pine to the red cedars, sassafras and coachwoods of the canopy. 'How Many Can You Find?' I invited, giving clues to identification – height, leaf size, type of bark and so on. To help with this, I dried leaf samples, encased them in perspex and hung them near the mural. Finally, I drew a geomorphic profile of Foxground valley and surrounds, from mountain to seashore.

My inspiration in preparing these nice, simple sheets of artwork and quizzes was Leon Fuller, a south coast man who had spent every weekend for years walking the ridges and valleys of the Illawarra, listing the trees. He didn't wait for a commission or a grant, he just went ahead and did it, a monumental study undertaken on his own initiative, later recognised for the valuable work it was. Like Howard Judd, he was a self-taught botanist. It was his book which finally enabled a tree illiterate like myself to recognise different species. He had just the right touch for words and diagrams. I wanted to emulate him to make people think ecologically. If they could do so at Glenrock, they could do it at home or anywhere.

Thus I became able to invite spring visitors to scan the mountainsides for the reds of coachwoods and Illawarra flame trees in bloom, the pink of new red cedar leaves appearing. Lewin honeyeaters, swallows and green catbirds were nesting, the forest bronze-wing pigeons flapped about the tree-tops while wongas strutted below, foraging the leaf litter. With any luck, an echidna or two might come waddling down the forest trails.

By summer, bowerbirds and parrots would be feeding on the fruits of brush cherry trees, paper wasps would be nesting, cicadas were hatching, fungi were popping up on wet logs and mossy tree trunks, and red-browed finches were tucked in their cunning little nests. It is the time for termites to hatch and fly, provoking amazing feats of upward hunting by grey thrushes, exactly like the take-off of a Harrier jet plane. My all-time favourites, the eastern spinebills, would be sipping summer blossoms and, down at the creek, yellow-throated scrub wrens would build their homes, suspended above the water – they look like flood debris and are called by the locals 'hanging dickies' nests'.

In autumn, when the clematis vines sent down showers of winged seeds like platoons of fluffy paratroopers – Santa Clauses, as the kids liked to call them – the sandpaper fig would fruit, along with the pittosporum, native raspberry, and the naturalised black-berries and lantana, all good tucker for myriad birds. Then could be seen another of my special favourites crashing about under the bushes, the rich brown ground thrush with the so-pretty name, *Oreocincla lunulata* – 'songbird with half-moons on its breast'. And so the lists ran on . . . and on.

Jeff and I were troubled that fewer and fewer visitors knew how to approach a day outdoors. They couldn't light a barbecue campfire, and they didn't wear sensible shoes. They arrived dressed for the beach or esplanade. In just a few generations, it seemed to me the affinity with the bush that most Australians took for granted was being lost. Families no longer had relatives on a property to visit. Kids from urban backgrounds did not recog-nise creeks as places to wade and trees as cubbies and climbing frames. About the only natural feature that intrigued them were the huge boulders looming up from the earth – the rocks in our glens. They wanted to climb them all right.

So I invented The Bush Detective game. Goth had canvassed schools during our absence, convincing some to bring pupils to Wild Country Park. A gifted communicator, Goth sent children and teachers away happy. We wanted to build on this. I longed to show kids how to read something of the landscape, a glimpse of what Aborigines do, and thus discover the wonders of nature.

My first challenge was to divide the Jungle Walk into four 'leaf trails'. That way, a class could be split into four smaller groups, each entering the forest at four different points, as big groups are hopeless for teaching. Each trail was marked by small coloured symbols – the Red Leaf walk showed a native bleeding heart, the Blue Leaf was a sassafras, the Yellow was the Illawarra flame tree, and so on. Each contained all the elements of rainforest and the refuge, but differed in where and how they could be found.

There were colour-coded buckets of pellets and birdseed for each group to take with them, plus a quiz sheet of the appropriate colour for each Leaf Trail. Written into each script were two wombat burrows (and asked them questions to ponder – 'Can you tell if a wombat is at home down there today? How?'), the koala trees, eagle rock, the cedar tree beside the pioneer stone wall, sandpaper figs which Aborigines used to smooth their spear handles ('Just feel how rough the leaves are but don't pick them, please'). 'How many bird's nests can you find? Just look. Share your discovery with your group'. At some stage I invited them to kneel and contemplate humus – smell its richness, observe the life cycling within. I bought magnifiers, which I dubbed 'nature glasses', and lent them to the kids to wear on a thong round their necks. 'Take a good look at lichen,' I urged. 'Peer into moss. See the tiny things living there, courting, mating, giving birth and dying, all within that mini-ecosystem.'

That line was inspired by a favourite book, *The Horse's Mouth* by Joyce Cary. Remember the ant who thought he was the whole universe until along came an elephant 'pissing rainstorms and shitting continents'? From Bernard O'Reilly's *Green Mountains* I borrowed another example: 'If you were in a plane that crashed into bush far from shops and telephones, would you be the one who sat down bewildered to die, or would you know how to look for water, make shelter, find some food?'

I loved those sessions with the kids. If there were not enough leaders (teachers and accompanying parents), I used to guide one group myself, weaving into my narrative things they could relate to: Van and Goth swimming in the big pool; throwing rocks for Jim the cattle dog to dive for; getting lost following the animal tunnels up Wallaby Hill – I knew they would be seeing those scenes later in our movie. It loosened the school children up to realise kids like themselves had grown up here, had played and had adventures. The questions they asked me, I answered honestly and personally; they replied by sharing their own stories. It was beautiful. Like our whole concept, it put them on a personal footing with the park, which I believe helped make our message acceptable.

Providing the weather was favourable, my routine never varied, though I don't believe any of the children realised that. It all worked so well. We had a talk together before they came inside the park, inspiring them to stop, listen, sniff the air, look up into the sky and the tree-tops as well as under their shoes. From those first moments, they became observers, right where they stood. By slowing them down as they poured off the bus, I put them into a mood for discovery rather than rampage. Rampaging can be fun, but our day together was too precious to waste time on it.

Then the Jungle Walk. With any luck, the teachers were by now on side. Not all . . . some thought a day in a nature park was their excuse to sit on a bench and gossip while the kids ran wild. But most, having been primed by mail beforehand, responded from the start, grateful that things were organised for them. They divided their pupils into groups and proceeded to their bench with its coloured buckets and the printed game they would take back to school to fill in the next day. As they set off in their small bands, eager to *find things*, I never failed to thrill, knowing they would return with so much new knowlege and confidence about being in the bush.

Each group returned from the trails really hungry for their morning snack. Then I rang the old cowbell and they trooped into the theatre. I screened for them either *Wild Animal Farm* or *Nature Boy*. The former was a sure crowd-pleaser, being a commercial film, but I felt that the modest, quieter *Nature Boy* had more to teach. It was Vandal's own story and included footage of koalas and the lovely sequence of Monica the eagle mothering him, which the earlier film lacked. Both were feel-good movies, and each was only twenty-six minutes long, so they weren't boring. 'Wal-ly!' they always sang out when the wombat went missing. 'Wah-lly!'

Lunch followed the movie and after that it was up to the teachers and the time remaining as to what they might do. For some this was free time and many chose to return to the creek. We stipulated that the Waterfall Track was not to be attempted without a teacher and warned it was unsuitable for very young classes, so it was an optional extra. One thing was for certain. Those pupils filled every minute and most left reluctantly, thanking us personally for letting them come. Many returned later with their parents.

Jeff and I are still meeting those children, now grown up and wanting to bring their own kids to the park. They thank us for inspiring them and giving them one of their best-ever school experiences.

20

Casa Simpatica

Our stay in Europe planted different seeds in Jeff than the ones which sprouted in me. He wanted to build a new house. The creative idea had probably been brewing for some time, but the initiative was triggered by my mother's announcement that she would live out the rest of her days with us, at Foxground. She was seventy-eight years old and seriously crippled by arthritis, almost at the end of her ability to live in her self-care apartment in California. After some soul searching between Jeff, me and my conscience – my better self – it was agreed she should come. But he would not fix the old farmhouse to make it accessible to an elderly and partially incapacitated person – especially one who, twenty years before, had flounced back to the US after a short, unhappy visit to us at Grays Point, where our lifestyle, delightful to me, was far too primitive for her. Jeff announced his intention to build anew on the back part of our property. The house would blend with the environment, be open on all sides to the bush, and would use natural materials for easy maintenance. It would be, in fact, the 'hose-out' house of his dreams.

His design grew out of our travels. The house would have verandahs front and back with rough logs for posts, like the homesteads we had seen in the Kimberley and along Coopers Creek, but also resembling the farmhouses of Spain. It was a long low building shaped like a U, hugging the contours of what used to be

our back cow paddock. The front of the house faced out over
Foxground valley and the view rolled on to the sea and spread
south over Shoalhaven to Jervis Bay. The back of the house,
which was the inside of the U, cloister style, faced rainforest. In
the centre of a sheltered lawn, Jeff would site a fountain to feed
a moat running round the edges of the courtyard, a sort of mini-
Alhambra. His vision was to borrow the water, which flows
continously from our creeks, piping it in through the fountain,
then out through drains at the corners to let the waters return to
the creek. No pumps, no technology – typical Carter.

From the start, the project was very much Jeff's. I couldn't
understand why, since we had shared so much, but this time he
made it clear he wanted no opinions and no interference. The
rough plan he drew up was his and his alone. Julian Voorwinden,
an old friend and neighbour who specialised in stone and natural
materials, would supervise the construction. I had no say in it at
all, until the end stages. The roof was laid on huge beams cut on
our property and left exposed above slate floors. Tiles from Italy,
Spain and France decorated bathrooms, kitchen, laundry and the
floor of the courtyard verandah. I was offered a say in choosing
the tiles. All else was plain and earth-hued. Inner doors were
arches hung with rough leather curtains. The one big family room
– a combined living room dining room and kitchen – was centred
on a big walk-in fireplace of sandstone quarried on Glenrock, the
mantelpiece a giant slab of Foxground rosewood.

From the start, the new house had an inspiring ambience. We
decided to name it 'Casa Simpatica', which in Spanish translates
as house of warmth, friendliness, relaxed conviviality. A month
before it was finished, I went to California to pack up my mother's
belongings, dispose of all but the family heirlooms and fetch her
back to Foxground. During my absence Jim, our best dog,
suffered a severe and rapid decline in health. He was old by then
and must have contracted cancer. Nearly blind, infirm and in pain,
his suffering impacted sharply on Jeff. The day before I was due
home with Adeline, Jeff carried Jim up to the tea-tree grove
which looked over the house, where he had dug a grave; there he
shot him. It cost him very dear to do that, I learned later. As ever,
he had done what a man was supposed to do, but he had become
sickened by that type of bravado. As a headstone, Jeff placed a

fine sandstone block, left over from the fireplace, an appropriate burial site for a loyal worker and family member.

My mother was impressed with the new dwelling and settled immediately into her bedroom, with *en suite* bathroom, on one side of the U-dwelling facing into the courtyard. Jeff had designed this as granny quarters, for my mother and later his own parents, as well as guest room when not otherwise needed. I, on the other hand, felt some trepidation at moving, twenty years after coming to Glenrock, from the dear old farmhouse up to the rear of the property. However, such was the appropriateness of Jeff's design that the transition was seamless. Within days of relocating, I felt my spirit meld with the new house. The materials were mainly from our beloved farm. We had both shared the travels which inspired Jeff's plan. Our old house, saturated with not only our joys and triumphs but those of its former owners, the Henrys and the Staples, was in place just down the hill. We visited it every day, and were still using the animal barn, the film studio, the dairy room. The house itself would be lived in by family or tenants.

One satisfaction I enjoyed just before we moved out was surprising a wonga pigeon waddling confidently along the back path toward the kitchen door, in exactly the same spot where that Easter hunter, so many years earlier, had triggered in us the desire to create the wildlife refuge in the first place. Wongas and other rare birds had bred up within the protected environment, along with other rare species. To sight a lyrebird was no longer news.

Up at the new house, Jeff decreed there would be no more animals, apart from those free-living ones who chose to visit us. Indoors would smell of nothing but good cooking and incense. Critters were strictly taboo. Ha ha ha.

The first social event in our new home was an engagement party for Van and Kerry. She had been his girlfriend in third class at Berry Primary. I remember her well, fine blonde hair, face open and smiling like a daisy; at school sports, she knew how to win but she also knew how to grin after losing. Following high school they had each tried living in Sydney, in pursuit of work and wider scope, but, independently, each decided they preferred the friendly and familiar back home in the country. Their reunion in Berry was sweet and filled with promise. Kerry was good material for a daughter-in-law.

Their wedding was scheduled for late in November, 1980. A fortnight before it was to take place, Mother passed away. Revealed among her papers was the true story of her marriage break-up with my father, which might have explained her attitude to me, but somehow we had never got around to discussing it. The grief I felt at her death was ambivalent and had to be put on hold until after the wedding . . . and long after that.

Kerry and Van were married at Wild Country Park just before Christmas, in a wedding which everyone remembers as the loveliest ever. The ceremony was performed under a red cedar tree beside the creek. While Goth played his guitar softly, guests gathered in the little pioneer meadow near the stone wall, facing Van and his best men, Glenn and big Phil. The wedding was dress-up time again for those party-loving lads, and they were tickled with themselves in maroon and white, until Kerry began to ascend the steep jungle path on the arm of her father. Like an angel in a long white wedding dress, her face was composed with that inward sanctity special to brides. Suddenly the afternoon became tinged with magic. At the last moment, with great dignity, she kicked her thongs into a bush and slipped on white satin pumps. Everyone clapped. So beautiful she was that even Jeff, hyped in his candid photography mode, was moved.

After vows had been exchanged, the guests drifted back up the hill to drink champagne among the kangaroos gathered on the lawns. Everyone seemed to be smiling. The sun's last rays slanted benignly through the smoke and fragrance of lamb roasting on a spit; the chef was Kerry's dad, who had quickly changed from his father-of-the-bride finery into overalls, brand new for the occasion. I catered the rest of the meal, serving a menu chosen by Kerry – it strained the limited resources of the kiosk, but we managed. Dinner was served in the theatre, using the movie seats and the museum tables, transformed into elegance by white napery, flowers and candles.

Old family friend Athol conducted the formal part of the speechifying. With his usual aplomb, he included in his remarks Jeff's parents, Doris and Percy, whose wedding anniversary coincided with Van and Kerry's marriage. Then Goth delivered a long, clever, funny ode to Van and his bride, composed with his usual lavish use of puns and waggery. I can't tell you what a good feeling prevailed inside those rough slab walls that night. From the rafters, a python looked down bemused.

When the furniture was moved aside and dancing began, energetic among the dancers were Jeff and myself. I needed to release a lot of tension, accumulated after my mother's death and the responsibility of the wedding, which launched my beloved Nature Boy, my last born son, into his own family life.

The nuptials of Van and Kerry inspired two more weddings at Wild Country Park, between friends of ours, both strictly private affairs. Although the ambience of the property lent itself to celebrations, we did not pursue marriage receptions as a commercial venture – despite urgings from our more commercially astute friends and family.

The park did provide a setting for hundreds of parties, however. These occurred spontaneously among our patrons who returned again and again, as friends. By inclination, Jeff and I hosted the park as we had always done the house and cottage before the park opened. We made it especially cordial to 'ethnics'. Our entrance announced not only *Welcome* but *Wilkommen*, *Bien Venue*, *Bien Venido* and so on. Jeff and I greeted overseas visitors with the best we could muster of Spanish or French or German. We saw ourselves as ambassadors for Australia and answered questions about native wildlife as well as outback living and travel, advising guests on how to visit the places we celebrated in our films.

As usual, we were ahead of the times in this, but having learned to make our way around many European countries, grappling with languages not our own, we knew the worth of friendly helpfulness. There were other reasons too. One was the exuberant exchanges Jeff could have with Europeans, especially Mediterranean peoples, which was quite the opposite of his normal, taciturn Aussie manner. With Spanish or Italians he became as ebullient as Georgie Borys, excited and voluble. This released him from the inhibitions which had troubled him since boyhood.

Another reason was my desire to instruct the non-English reading public about nature conservation, recalling still those migrant shooters from Port Kembla who, in all innocence, killed native birds for their table. I paid to have our park brochure translated into several languages. Having been overseas myself, I now understood the problems of trying to comprehend wildlife protection laws and other protocols in a foreign tongue.

The ultimate reason for Wild Country Park's success as a sociable weekend destination was that Jeff and I enjoyed conviviality. We liked sharing ethnic foods and drinks, which are traditionally partaken of outdoors in big groups of extended families on Sundays. The Spanish from Warilla brought the makings for huge paellas, which they cooked on the barbecue. The Italians from Warrawong brought frittata. Wine flowed. Jeff filled his wineskin, purchased in Spain, and offered it around, a guaranteed crowd-pleaser as men, and women, vied to squirt the vino from afar into their mouths. In our role as hosts, we drew Australians in when we could, explaining a food or method of preparation to locals too shy to ask. In this way we evangelised multicultural tolerance before it became the vogue.

The family who bought the cottage as a weekend retreat became part of those congenial gatherings. They were very good company, sympathetic to the aims of the park, and they became friends as well as our only near neighbours. The father, Ian Heads, was a sports writer. He and his wife Joy played ball with their two children almost every day they were in residence. It pleased me to look across and watch the tradition of good clean family fun carry on at the cottage.

The animal population in the park was expanding along with visitor numbers. King Eric now had numerous wives and several young lieutenants to help him keep them in order. With great interest we watched the younger males challenge him for supreme leadership, and fail. The only changes in the hierarchy were hard won amongst the underlings. It was mainly to do with mating, of course. We watched the females closely, too, and I noted how they behaved as oestrus built, peaked and then fell away.

I watched with concern how some were willing to copulate while others were reluctant. Mothers took their young daughters away to protect them from the bucks, but the poor orphan females had no one to stand up for them and they became victims of what can only be called rape. It was pitiful to see a maiden pursued by Eric and his boys, barking and dribbling. Young females cried in terror and fled from one end of the park to the other, then tried to hide in sheds or in the toilet block, all to no avail as the males pounded close behind. While oestrus lasted the bucks never let up, testosterone driven and careless of all but their biological imperative.

I had seen the same relentless drive in dogs and with poultry. The poor silly hens always elicited my sympathy as they stood up after the rooster had finished with them, shook the dust from their feathers, waggled their stinging tails and staggered off to recover. The female kangaroos also suffered pain after being grabbed in turn by five or six bucks and vigorously penetrated. Some were left with blood and even torn tissue leaking from them. Yet, I have to say, those females did not die of peritonitis, which on the day I thought looked a possibility. And not all females were unwillling. Many became coquettish as Eric and his band followed them, sniffing their tails as if testing fine wine to see whether it was ready for bottling. Those males displayed themselves as they waited, and it was impressive to watch. They stood up tall on their hind toes, leaning back against their tails, erections rampant, scratching at their chests and roaring their masculinity.

Fortunately for the sensibilities and even the prudery of our patrons, the more violent mating pursuits usually occurred when the park was closed. In order to continue our writing careers, we still opened only on weekends and during school holidays. The one exception was my school tours, which were pre-booked and finished by two o'clock. While people were around, the kangaroos might court in public but they took themselves outside the park for the nitty-gritty. Mothers and daughters kept together, as cattle do; young males stayed with their mothers and sisters only until adolescence, at which time they joined the male mafia to learn jousting and serve their apprenticeship at the low end of the mating hierarchy.

We recognised successive generations of youngsters by their physical resemblance to their parents. Kangaroos were becoming so numerous that they were hiving off into smaller bands, seeking fresh grass up the back of the property and returning to the park only every few days for the hand-outs of pellets we dispensed morning and afternoon.

Parallel with the 'roos was a band of wallaroos led by Jo-Jo, a fine strong male who had come to us from Pat Olbrich. Shorter and stockier than the 'roos, and also fluffier and quite pretty, the wallaroos had been donated by different people in much the same circumstances as the other animals. They kept themselves separate from the kangaroos, but I noticed Jo-Jo's interest when the female 'roos went on heat. Of course, he didn't line up with the buck kangaroos but when they had done their best and gone, I thought I understood Jo-Jo's intentions from his body language. Eventually I was rewarded by seeing at least one crossbred joey. It looked like a kangaroo and hung around with its mother, but it had the unmistakable shorter arms and thicker wrists and ankles of its father, Jo-Jo.

I was an avid watcher and documentor of animals, believing there was much for humans to learn from their more simple, straightforward behaviours about pairing, about sibling rivalries, about social dominance and recessiveness, about attitudes of mothers and fathers to their offspring. I wrote an article for *The Women's Weekly* called: '*Teaching Children the Facts of Life*', putting forward the proposition that farm kids hardly needed sex education because it was a normal part of rural life. I further suggested that if urban parents were prepared to put in a little extra work, they could assist their youngsters to understand much about the human condition by keeping guinea pigs or a pair of cats or dogs. Most readers received it well but one wrote the following: 'I have just read Mare Carter's disgusting article and thrown it in the bin. I have been a subscriber to this magazine for years but will never buy another copy!' Well, evangelists can't hope to please everyone.

By mid-1981, Jeff had us in Europe again for three months. We took his mother, to distract her from the sudden death of Percy, her husband for fifty-five years. Dadda died of heart attack, which was a fierce blow to everyone. This time we left the park in the care of a canny young Irish woman from Berry seeking agistment for her horse. She brought the horse with her and was pretty good with native animals too, but when we returned we found the farmhouse full of hippies who were reluctant to pay rent, and a baby wombat with a plaster cast on its front leg, broken when someone had carelessly dropped it on the concrete path. Seeing that poor little animal stumping about, meeping after sandals and weedy cheesecloth skirts, wrenched me.

By the time Irish and her mob moved out (leaving the horse behind, but that's another story), the wombat's cast had been removed, the leg was healed but it was an unlucky little fellow. It had been experimenting with the practice burrow in the back yard of the farmhouse, which successive wombats had deepened considerably since Jeff first started it. One afternoon the youngster disappeared down the tunnel and was soon out of sight. Call as I did, I could not coax it out. I never saw it again, but fretted daily about its safety. I felt we had become careless of our obligations.

While I was cleaning up the vacant farmhouse, preparing it for rental again, a tragedy happened. Gidgea was hit by one of the cars which used the road past our place. The timber-getter brothers had subdivided their lands up the back and a handful of weekenders plus three permanent residents were now in place. We thought most of the new chums drove too fast for that unsealed switchback, and I ordered signs painted showing a wombat and 'roo in silhouette, with the words: Please Drive Slowly.

Despite these, one day Gidgea hopped out from the bushes beside the road and was hit by a motorist who did not even bother to stop to see it she was all right. In fairness, he probably thought she was because she glanced off the side of his car and bounded over the picket fence into the farmhouse yard. I found her there, trembling, with her hind feet all raw and bleeding. The vehicle had passed over her long toes. Gidgea was too big by now to take to the vet's, so we called him to visit. Our good friend Georgie Borys had died suddenly but his replacement came and dressed the feet, telling us to change the bandages daily.

Gidgea was now strong and not as docile as she'd been before she became self-determined and roamed the property with the other kangaroos. The worst part was, she had a tiny joey in her pouch. I asked Van if he could come up on his way home from work to hold her down while we treated her wounds. He and Kerry now lived at Gerroa, watching the whales frolic off Seven Mile Beach while they awaited the birth of their first child. Van knew plenty about dressings and medication, having studied nursing the previous year. Despite his best efforts and mine, though, Gidgea's wounds would not heal, and in fact they became gangrenous beneath their bandages. In the finish we lost her, and I thought long and hard about the value of having put her (and Van, Jeff and me) through that daily trauma, for no gain.

The one thing I could do, I did. I painted the following sign and stuck it up beside the track near our house. 'To the driver who hit our beloved 'roo, Gidgea, on [date]: Gidgea died today, after ten days of most awful suffering. The baby in her pouch had to be destroyed. I hope you will think about this, and drive more carefully in future.'

The following year, Jo-Jo also was hit by a car. We didn't witness the accident but noticed him missing from his little band of wallaroos. Jeff went out searching and calling him. On the property next door, he heard Jo-Jo reply. Full of dread, he followed the sound and found our proud buck lying head-down on a hillside above the creek, with a compound fracture of his front leg; he was almost dead. He had been trying to reach the water but pain had beaten him. Jeff scooped him up some water to drink, then went home for his rifle and put him out of his misery.

Although we appreciated that kangaroos are notoriously foolish about traffic, I took this second death of a special animal very hard. It was a wildlife refuge, after all. The people who had bought properties up the back knew what they were in for. They should have been driving really slowly because animals were often on the road, especially at night. I took to springing out whenever I heard someone scream down the hill, planting myself in the middle of the road so they had to stop. Then with dignity (I thought) and suppressing the worst of the anger I felt, I explained the situation to them reasonably and requested that they slow down. I tried to show them what a lot of time and money and care had gone into making Glenrock the delightful wildlife refuge it had become.

In 1982, the year the Green movement began fighting to save the Franklin River in Tasmania, Van and Kerry's daughter Lauren was born; a day of joy in a year of hope. Three months later, they lost their apartment at Gerroa. The farmhouse was again vacant so, to my delight, they asked if they could move in. It was beautiful for me, having them close by. I was able to share so much of Lauren's first year, both the joys and the panics, like the day she plucked an interesting looking plant from the garden which turned out to be a baby stinging tree, one of rainforest's few villains which had seeded there. She howled in pain. Now, the antidote for stinging nettles is to rub crushed dockweed on the affected area, and since 'nature' often grows dock near nettles, getting stung is not much of a problem. A stinging tree affliction is more serious, the acidic poison in the hollow spines more virulent. We soothed

Lauren's pain that day with an alkaline bath, but the experience taught her that Grandma's enthusiasm for examining nature needed to be taken with a pinch of salt – or baking soda.

Lauren celebrated her first birthday on Glenrock. The party was staged under the lemon tree in the back yard, where the Boys' Museum committee used to meet and where so many rescued animals and birds had resided on their way back to a free and natural life. Seeing the balloons and little people round a low table took me back to Goth's cubby at Grays Point. The circle remained unbroken. I felt immensely buoyed by this.

Meanwhile, back up the hill, Jeff's policy of Casa Simpatica remaining an animal-free zone continued, with a few concessions for special cases. There was the matter of the Fox Brothers, two foxes reared in captivity with whom Jeff spent a lot of hours – incurring, in the process, permanent scarring on his hands where they gnawed him – before concluding they were better suited to free life in the wild.

We were asked to release two more eagles. After a couple of worrying incidents we'd had in the park, we thought it prudent to conduct the proceedings up near Casa Simpatica.

Dinah, an amiable young dingo, also came to live with us. She had been confiscated by the RSPCA in a state of neglect from the man who had taken her out of the wild as a pup. We had been a one-dog family since Jim's death. Gentle Brownie, fat and elderly, lived a sedentary life following the sun around the inner verandah, but Jeff felt little affinity with her. He had always been intrigued by the so-called wild dogs of Australia, just as he had been inter- ested to try and tame the Fox Brothers, so when the RSPCA man rang, singing the praises of the young dingo who was 'just too nice to put down', Jeff accepted her willingly.

There are certain characteristics which distinguish dingoes from other domestic dogs. Four white feet, white tail tip, broader skull and the ability to howl but not bark are some of them. In one breath experts will tell you there are no pure-breds left. In the next, they will question whether dingoes and feral dogs do inter- breed in the wild. Certainly microscope tests have established that dingoes' blood is different from other canines'.

What endeared Dinah to us was her alert stance, her crisp yellow coat, ever-pricked ears, intelligent warm eyes always following our movements, live brushy tail. She was smart, loving, funny. Yes, I said that. If canines can laugh, Dinah did. What distinguished her from other breeds was the way she whelped. Ah, yes, she did have puppies later, several litters, and I'll skip ahead a year or two to mention how she looked after them. She always dug a burrow. Then she lined it with leaves or with cloth from her bed, meticulously chewed into small, leaf-sized pieces. After the pups were born she was fierce in keeping us away from her dug-out until their eyes were open and they were tumbling about. As her lip curled away from her big sharp teeth in the most menacing snarl, her eyes watched us with soft apology. She knew she was a changed character in maternal mode, and she seemed to want us to understand and forgive.

When the pups were ready for solid food, Dinah exhibited another trait. She went off, compulsively raided a garbage can or some other unusual food source and gulped down what she could find to eat. Then she returned to her lair and vomited in front of her puppies a soft warm edible mush. I never knew another type of dog to habitually feed puppies that way. Even more remarkable, I thought, was how her son, Lyall, did the same thing. He was part of her first litter and Van took him for his own. Lyall's father was a town dog. Van and Kerry were living in Berry then and we left Dinah with them while we went away. She came into season and although they locked her inside their garage while they went to work, they could not frustrate her biological drive. She worked all day to chew and rake at the wooden garage door with her strong claws, literally shredding it, until she could squeeze out and find fathers for her pups. Lyall's dad had a very long nose and so did Lyall. His patrimony was obvious.

Anyway, the second year when Dinah whelped, she was again in Van's care, this time at Foxground, and they watched her go off to find food for her babies. The puppies were out on the lawn, clearly left in the care of Lyall. He fussed over them, shepherded them round as the sun moved behind the trees and the pups began to whimper with cold but also hunger. Lyall became agitated. At last, he disappeared. In a few moments he was back, and in front of his young brothers and sisters he vomited up something for them to eat. Since he was only about one-quarter dingo, I thought that was pretty good evidence of inherited behaviour.

Dinah came to us accustomed to being on a chain and Jeff wanted to keep her used to being restrained at times, until we had assessed her response to the wildlife around our property. Without too much effort, he trained her not to chase, which meant she could be free most of the time. Dinah was no trouble, except during electrical storms. Lightning made her crazy. Once when we were away for a few hours, a violent thunderstorm occurred. When we returned from shopping, we found Dinah had splintered our laundry door – the only door that wasn't glass – in a frenzy to get herself indoors.

However, during the eighteen months Van and Kerry lived at Glenrock, Dinah and Lyall became a lethal combination. One minute they would be smiling and wagging in the back yard, the next minute they had vanished, silent as shadows. They would run swiftly together up the back, casting around in the forest until they found a wallaby. Then we would hear their voices as they bayed and chased. No matter that Jeff and Van went out, whistling and bellowing at them. They chased for days. At least once, when they finally returned home bedraggled and tired, Lyall vomited up the remains of a wallaby on Van's back doorstep.

It was embarrassing, because we had been forced to adopt a very stern attitude to dogs after a number of disastrous invasions. The worst had happened a few years earlier, when Eric was chased and literally torn to bits by dogs from down the valley, out on the rantan. Jeff cried when he found Eric, who had managed to get his flock of females and young males away to safety by decoying the hounds with himself. They finally trapped him against the bottom chicken wire fence and he had no chance of survival. From then on Jeff was ruthless with marauding dogs. He shot them on sight and soon the message passed round the valley: keep your dogs at home if you don't want them shot at the wildlife refuge.

So with that policy, we could not allow our own dogs to harass the free-living wildlife up the back. Van had to keep Lyall tied up at the farmhouse until they moved back to Berry, and we put Dinah on the chain up at our new house. Several years later, when we imagined Dinah and Lyall would have forgotten their earlier bad habits, we allowed them to accompany Linda on a bushwalk with her dog, Granite. Suddenly she looked for Lyall and Dinah and found they had melted away. Minutes later, we heard them

baying up the back, which meant they had found a wallaby. They
were a fatal hunting pair when together, wild and unmanageable.
On her own, however, Dinah did not harass the birds and animals
around our garden, and in fact she herself was bossed around by
a little animal half her size and a quarter her weight. That was
Tootsie, beautiful Tootsie, the delicate red-neck who became the
house wallaby of Casa Simpatica.

By and large, Casa Simpatica did remain animal-free indoors,
and fairly well organised outside. Seven goldfish bought at the pet
shop multiplied – by a factor of twenty or thirty – in the pure
creek water piped through our courtyard moat and fountain, but
they were under our control, as were the two dogs, Gentle
Brownie and Dinah-the-Dingo. Well, more or less.

Many of the kangaroos and wallabies followed us when we
moved up the hill, hoping for an extra hand-out of pellets but
also, I like to think, because of our sympathetic manners. Special
friends shifted territory altogether to be near us, like Opal the
matriarch grey, and dear little Tootsie. She had been given to us
as an orphan after we had moved up to Casa Simpatica from the
old farmhouse, so she stuck close to us and rarely ventured beyond
the acre that is our 'yard'. Several times a day she fronted up to
the verandah window-doors, peering inside so closely that her
nose left smears on the glass.

She was such a pretty animal. She had the long narrow face
typical of her species, accentuated by black nose hair separating
big almond eyes with reddish eyebrows, eyes that watched you
and locked onto your gaze. Her slim, short-haired tail was long,
longer than her delicate torso, which was beautifully furred in a
rich grey that contrasted with the russet on her shoulders and
flanks. Unable to resist spoiling her, we fed her whenever she
asked for it, including the odd piece of bread which she held delicately but firmly in her fine front paws as she nibbled away.

Not that Tootsie was especially amenable in temperament – she
was her own little person, quite bossy when given a chance. She
was dominated by the kangaroos every morning and evening,
when they fronted up for a feed. Apparently she recognised them
not as oversized cousins but only as competitors for pellets. In a
daily struggle which she always lost, she would growl and bristle
from bowl to bowl, standing back with grouchy impatience until

the bigger hipper-hoppers had eaten and moved aside to ruminate on the lawn. We kept an eye on this process and often went out to top up a dish for her once the rush was over, something she expected and accepted as her due.

Funnily enough, the battles she did win were with the dogs. Old Brownie was easy to bluff but I expected Dinah to hold her ground when Tootsie growled at her. Not so. She often growled at us too, when love prompted us to try and pat her. 'Don't *touch* me,' she clearly said, aversion rippling through her fur. It was only in her later years, after her heyday and her great tragedy, that she relented and allowed us to groom her while she ate, our fingers scrabbling through her fur to rout out the strange fat flies which prey upon marsupials' bodies. Catching them was very hard – they are fast and elusive – but it became a challenge; even when you had one trapped in your fist, it was tricky getting it between your fingernails to squish it to death. The kangaroos groomed each other but Tootsie was on her own, one of a kind, and so she had no one to look after her except us. That was what led to our noble experiment.

As an official wildlife refuge, we received newsletters from Sydney's Taronga Park Zoo listing their surplus animals, and I noticed that an occasional red-necked wallaby appeared on this list. The idea was born to import a male for Tootsie and for Mindi, the one other red-neck still living within the refuge. Mindi was almost as beautiful as Tootsie, though older, slimmer, facially darker and very, very self-contained. Another orphan released to follow her instincts within the safety of our property, she lived all her life in sight or sound of our farmhouse but always kept a wary distance from people. There was never any question of patting Mindi. We took her a bowl of pellets whenever she was sighted, which was usually not long after the lids of the grain bins rattled during our twice daily feeding rounds. She must have been dwelling on us more than appeared, but she never let us approach her closely, daintily eating only after we had withdrawn. She became more and more finicky and self-centred, in manner very like the proverbial Old Maid, which was what she was, there being no male of her species to take as husband. The males we had accepted had all taken off, heading instinctively, perhaps, toward the drier country down south in the Shoalhaven, where red-necks thrive. Up in Foxground, the resident species were swamp walla-bies, heavier and dark-furred. Red-necks do not interbreed with them.

One of our great pleasures in tending the wildlife refuge had been observing diverse native animals in our charge settle and produce young. So many of them had survived trauma. To make babies indicated an adjustment, an acceptance of our habitat. Some of the animals we received remained one of a kind. I was beginning to wonder about the validity of accepting such exotics to our district. We took them in because there was no place else they could go, but times were changing and so were my ideas.

Having said that, I had also observed how species change habitat without human intervention. On Lake Illawarra, a commu-nity of pelicans from the inland lakes now live, driven to the coast by drought. On the opposite side of the coin are the seagulls one finds on outback dams. Blown by the wind? They seemed to have relocated successfully to fresh as well as salt water. Where species could survive within a protected, appropriate environment, could live free without being stuck into zoos, I had no quarrel with the practice. So it niggled when creatures could not pair, either because they were still disturbed, or on-the-outer as new chums, or worse, when there were no members of their species of the opposite sex, as was the case with Tootsie and Mindi. Thus we sought a service offered by the zoo.

There was quite a lot of paperwork to be filled in and a hefty fee. We had to be checked out to make sure we were sound. It all took a few months, but at last we were notified that a young red-necked male would be available to us on such and such a day at Taronga Park. Hurriedly we bought six-foot chicken wire and steelposts, erected a run near the house in Tootsie's favourite area, secured a strong box lined with warm rugs and placed food and water bowls in the enclosure. Then we drove up to Sydney to pick up Tootsie's fiancé.

I was nervous about bringing the little chap 120 kilometres from Sydney to our place, but in fact the transfer was very profes-sional. The zoo had been extra careful, placing the young wallaby in quarantine to make sure he was disease-free. Then he was lightly tranquillised and packaged securely so that his journey would be as stress-free as possible. When we released him into his enclosure, he went straight into the box house to hide for a while. We left him to settle, but watched through the kitchen window. We decided to call him Wasley.

All went smoothly. By the next day he was grazing the fresh green grass in his enclosure and nibbling pellets. We approached him seldom, and always gently and quietly, until his confidence grew. Tootsie kept right away at first, but within a few days she showed herself and he watched her with some interest. Gradually she drifted closer and closer to his run. We watched them avidly and were rewarded by seeing them tentatively sniff noses through the wire.

After a week or so, Wasley had eaten down the grass within his enclosure and we reckoned he was acclimatised enough to be offered an open gate. We withdrew into the house to observe discreetly behind windows, and it was suspenseful. Would he bolt as soon as he found himself free? Fortunately he did not. In fact, he stuck very close to his little yard and his sleeping box and put himself back inside several times. Thus it was another week or more before we removed the enclosure altogether. By that time he had taken to trailing around behind Tootsie and lying down near her in the garden.

He was young, probably not yet sexually mature. And an aura of docility hung about him which we imagined was due to his having been born in captivity and kept closely confined. This probably worked in his favour, at first anyway, since Tootsie made the running with him. She led him, bossed him, growled at him if he got too close to her or dared to put his nose in the feed bowl beside her, and we relaxed a bit, pleased to see two little red-necks out among the kangaros who numbered, on any given day, between two and twelve.

To cut a long story short, eventually he did mature and mate with her. I don't think we actually witnessed much courtship between them, not the first time anyway, but in due course, many months after his arrival, we noticed a little bulge in her pouch. How we dwelled on that! It grew and grew. There was no mistake. Tootsie had a joey in her pocket.

Even better, Wasley had been venturing further and further from the house for some time, hopping down the hill toward the park where Mindi hung out. One day we saw her hopping up the hill, which we had never noticed before. Whether she found him or he found her we never knew, but in due course we noticed that Mindi also had a sagging pouch.

The thrill of sighting first one little head and later the other poking out of the two females' pouches cannot be duplicated. Young red-necks have long faces with noses tender and pink from being clamped round a teat at the bottom of the humid pouch for several months. Their little eyes sparkle with shy curiosity as they confront the world after so long in the dark. Baby wallabies' skulls look so petite compared with the larger, broader heads of baby kangaroos we had grown used to – like porcelain is to pottery.

As the infants leaned further and further out to sniff and then snatch at mouthfuls of grass while their mothers grazed, we looked forward to our first sight of either Tootsie's Wootzie or Mindi's Bindi actually standing free upon the earth. The pouches stretched, the mothers spent more and more time cleaning out their pockets, pulling the rubbery rims wide with their paws and nosing deep inside, diligently licking up urine and faeces.

After another month, our dreams were realised. First Tootsie and then Mindi were sighted with their toddlers standing shakily beside them. Wasley seemed quite amazed by their appearance, bemused even, and kept trying to sniff them before being warned off crossly by the mothers, his two wives. For a season, we were treated to glimpses of our now five red-necked wallabies lying about in the grass. They kept apart from other animals and did not visit the feed dishes without tucking their kids back into the pouch. What joy. A project working so well!

Even more bliss: Mindi's and Tootsie's pouches began to bulge again. Soon our herd would total seven! We knew the first two born were daughters but reasoned that at least one of the second lot should be a male. We visualised a fine multiplication of red-necks, as the wallaroos had also bred up smoothly once their gene pool reached a workable size. But the best laid plans oft go awry. When the second batch of infants were big enough to view the world from their mothers' pockets, riding strong and curious like kids in rumble seats, and their older sisters were tall enough to be mistaken at a distance for their slender little mums, disaster struck. Something began to pick them off. The two maidens at foot were the first to disappear, then Wasley himself (although a male, he was never as bold or alert as an animal born in the wild), then Mindi's baby and Mindi herself – oh, what a wrench to my heart to imagine her demise, after so valiantly fending for herself for such long years.

What was the killer? We never knew but guessed it was either a fox or a native tiger cat, or perhaps a family of big feral cats – maybe even dogs running wild at night. Tootsie hung closer to the house again and seemed very nervous. One morning I saw her baby was half hanging out of her pouch, like a cartoon damsel in distress swooning out a window. I itched to tuck it back in but knew Tootsie was capable of doing that if she wanted to and I didn't want to spook her away. By next morning, her pouch was empty.

After that, the carnage stopped. We were reduced to one single red-necked wallaby. We felt beaten and left things like that. Thus Tootsie became the house wallaby, or rather, the verandah wallaby. She followed the sun round the house, stretching herself out in warm places on the tiles, watching us when we emerged. We spoiled her, of course, talking a lot to her and handfeeding her tidbits of bread. In time she let us gently scratch her in those certain places — between her ears, along her jawbone, in between her shoulder blades — hard for her to reach on her own, the parts of her pelt which friends and family of her own species would have groomed for her. She only tolerated our ministrations briefly, then she would growl and ripple her fur, even try to bite us with her blunt little front teeth if we did not desist quickly enough. She drew blood on the backs of my hands several times, looking darkly into my eyes as she bit, as if to say: 'I *told* you, cut it out!'

In winter she hung about the glass doors of the house, peering in, plainly asking to enter. Several times we weakened and let her in for a few minutes. She roamed around, sniffing everything. Once or twice she made straight for the soft Greek shag rugs and laid herself down with a sigh. When we came over to admonish her audacity, she did not spring up but lay watching us calmly, as if to say: 'See? This is what I am made for. Why can't I live indoors and enjoy the fire, like the dogs do?' Yes, the master had weakened and on the most wintry evenings, he did allow Dinah and Brownie inside. Briefly.

But rules are rules. When we moved to Casa Simpatica Jeff had said: 'No more wild animals in the house.' And truthfully, marsupials do let go their droppings and their urine when and wherever they feel like it, just like cows and horses. So even nice, sleek, clean, adorable Tootsie had to spend most of her time outside.

She took to bluffing Dinah or Brownie out of their baskets on the inner courtyard verandah. Brownie, elderly and weary as she was, used to give up easily with a sigh. But Dinah-the-Dingo, I thought, would have been a harder one to bluff. Tootsie managed it. Daily Tootsie confronted her, snarling until she bullied Dinah out of her basket, then she would hop in herself. She looked comical yet serenely at home, sitting on her spine with her tail stretched out between her long hind legs. In cold weather she would grasp her tail with her front paws; I reckoned this was to warm them.

For several years she was the closest thing to a pet marsupial I ever knew, even though I still maintain what I said at the beginning: wild animals cannot be pets in the easy way that domesticated species can. With Tootsie being on her own – small, neat and, toward the end, dependent – we were able to learn her ways and she ours enough that we fitted into each other's lives tolerantly and with great affection.

21

Changes in the Garden of Eden

The work of Wild Country Park settled into a routine, one with which I, at least, felt very comfortable. During the week, playing the Bush Detective game with school excursion groups, I realised my dream of awakening children to the wonders of the rainforest. They learned some survival skills and gained a little of the confidence and ease in the natural world which earlier generations of Australians took for granted. Teaching them kept me attuned to nature also.

What I taught the kids was matched by what they taught me. We used to pad along the Jungle Walk, silent as primitive hunters, senses totally alert. It was marvellous the things they discovered, with their excellent eyesight and their innocent, unfettered curiosity. A python coiled around a branch. Strange galls, insects, droppings, footprints. Something bizarre caught in a spider's web. I praised them highly for their discoveries and often told them quite truthfully that they had spied out things I had not seen before. Like the time they found a stocky bird, about as big as a thrush, with a bright yellow beak. The poor thing had its mouth open; the vivid colour was inside, too, probably meant to scare off predators. It seemed exhausted and did not attempt to fly away as we stood watching it. Later we looked it up in the bird book and learned it was a dollar bird, a migrant which annually flies thousands of miles between Asia and Australia.

How I loved those school excursions. Never was I too busy to answer the plea: 'Mrs Carter, come and see what we found!' I still had faith in the power of naivety. I believed it encouraged lateral thinking. Society had become too sophisticated for its own good, I thought. People were too calculating, too inhibited, scared of revealing weakness by being fresh, spontaneous, by playing. When I galloped after the kids to see what they'd discovered, as if I were twenty-three instead of fifty-three, I imagined I was setting a good example somehow. But I was ever given to such vanities and foolish notions. I would soon learn a hard lesson.

Meanwhile, the park took in Benson and Bats, a pair of wombats who had been reared together. I suggested we cut a trapdoor in the floor of the theatre verandah. Wombats always went under there from the Nursery Yard and had excavated a little burrow. While allowing them to follow their normal inclination to sleep underground by day, we could give the public brief glimpses of them by raising the trap, without really disturbing them. The system worked a treat.

They were as amiable as brothers, Benson and Bats, although they were not related. They cuddled together when at rest, ate together without jealousy, romped and bonked each other in play for months as they grew toward maturity, my ideal for 'keeping' animals without suppressing their potential for a free and natural life. Eventually, however, Benson, the older one, tired of his friend. For a day or two, he chased Bats around the Nursery Yard, snarling, snapping and squealing until poor Bats went and hid his head in the farthest corner, presenting his bony backside to the world (the wombat method of defence). Then Benson dug his way out of the Nursery Yard and made off. Bats had the burrow under the floor all to himself. Next, Benson dug his way back in. More commotion. This time Bats went walkabout and Benson stayed home, taking himself out under the fence at night but returning by morning to sleep under the floor.

Strangely enough, after six weeks or so Bats returned and the two wombats settled down again, together. Eventually they both went out under the fence simultaneously. Whenever we catch sight of two wombats waddling about at night in tandem, we imagine – we hope – they are Benson and Bats.

Our experience of wombats on Glenrock has been that in our

area, humid and wet, they usually live alone, establishing themselves in a burrow and following a grazing round marked by a
succession of spoor, left prominent atop a rock or in the centre of
a track, as foxes do. After a time they move on to another locale,
then another, working their way around to the first territory again
in about a year. My theory is that they seek fresh grazing land, but
also need to rest each burrow for a while, to cleanse it of the para-
sitic mites which can cause the mange wombats are prone to in
other areas. Fortunately, we only saw one example of that scourge
at Foxground.

Further investigation showed us that once a burrow has been
vacant for two or three months, a different wombat takes it up for
a while. Thus new trail markings appear, sometimes an adult
dropping with a tiny infant one alongside. It thrills me, when I find
that. I know that the baby will stay close to its mother until it is
old enough to wander away and fend for itself. Most nights, on
different parts of the property, you can see a wombat trundling
about its business, and we have to warn visitors to drive extra carefully until they gain the main road.

Mornings, we were often faced with big piles of fresh soil where
a wombat had dug its way in or out of the park or farmhouse yards
during the night. These had to be plugged with big stones, gravel
and earth. Sometimes, by the next morning the plug would have
been scratched out again and repairs needing redoing, stronger
this time. The refuge was fenced only on the road side – the public
or car-park side. At the jungle end and up the back past the farmhouse, we organised things so the public were kept out but animals
could come and go as they wished.

We resisted breaching our big roadside fence at first because we
feared marauding dogs might get in or kangaroos might pop out,
putting them in danger from traffic, but after years of filling in
tunnels in inconvenient places, we constructed swinging gates in
that strategic fence, with little confidence the wombats would use
them. Wombats rarely go around barriers. They batter their way
through or dig under, which is why farmers hate them. We chose
good spots, however, and the wombats used the gates, no worries,
probably following a trail of scent. The kangaroos did use the
gates also, but squashing down and squeezing through slowed
them enough that motorists could see them emerge and stop.

We were little troubled by visiting dogs by then, but when we weren't looking our own dogs used the wombat gates to seek food. However, since the kangaroos always cleaned up most of the pellets and since we religiously emptied the rubbish bins at the end of each trading day, there was little to tempt them inside the park. If caught, they got into bad trouble.

Our policy of daily picking up litter never slackened. We found that because the park was always clean, people were more careful about dropping rubbish than in other places, even in those days before litter awareness. With an eye to public safety, the tracks we kept well maintained. That super-careful policy of ours worked well. We never had a visitor injured. We never had an accident claim, nor did anyone fall. The worst thing that happened was when a teenage boy was bitten by a snake.

Now, snakes were one subject I steered wide of, with the exception of pythons, which are harmless and deserve a more than even break. I wrote into my nature list both black and brown snakes, just to remind people that ours was a natural environment, not a sanitised one, but I didn't believe in fuelling the general fear of reptiles. I did sometimes see venomous snakes crossing the park during quiet times, and it scared me. Kids walk so softly and love getting about in bare feet. For this reason, we kept the grass trimmed short around the barbecue sites and underneath the benches. But one busy Good Friday morning, while passing the emus' yard, this lad stepped off the path into long grass where a snake was hiding. He was wearing thongs and suffered a bite on the instep. When his little cousin came running up to the kiosk to tell us, Jeff refused to believe it. That was the worst part for me. His scepticism at times could be exasperating. And inappropriate, to my way of thinking.

I didn't waste time but hurried round and found the little group in tears, the boy included. He had unmistakable puncture marks and he said he had been bitten before so he knew what had happened to him. While appearing calm, I did all the wrong things. We tried to carry the boy but he was too heavy. I knew it would be hard to rouse Jeff to help, so I suggested we support him while he hopped back to the kiosk. Even faced with the wound, Jeff was still unconvinced that it had been a dangerous snake. But I felt certain. Jeff tried to ring Nowra, then, for an ambulance. The trouble was that the highway was choked with Easter traffic pouring south down the coast. I said I would drive to meet the ambulance and the family should follow in their car as best they could.

Before we left, I begged Jeff quietly to go round and beat the grass for the snake in case it was still beside the trail. The park was already very busy. Reluctantly, he got his shovel and then the nicest thing happened. A patron jumped the counter and said quietly, 'You go on, Jeff. I'll mind the kiosk while you're away.'

So I laid the boy onto the back seat of my station wagon and headed off, against cars streaming up our narrow road to Glenrock. As I drove, I tried to reassure him and he responded well. When we reached the highway, it was clogged as I had feared. Cars inched along, bumper to bumper. There seemed nothing to do but drive on the wrong side of the road whenever possible. Luckily most people were motoring southward, toward the beach holiday sites, the same way we wanted to go. I honked my horn continuously, so that the other drivers would know something was wrong and let me in when a northbound car approached.

I realised this must be alarming my patient when he should have been kept calm. Within a few kilometres, he told me his vision was blurring and he felt nauseous. I had put a bucket in with him and told him to be sick into that if he needed to. I began feeling desperate. Then an ambulance passed, siren blaring, going the opposite way to us, heading in the direction of Foxground. Was it our ambulance? It had passed before I thought to flash my lights. Oh, what a mistake. As I berated myself, I heard the siren coming back. Someone in the stream of traffic must have indicated for the ambulance to turn around. I pulled off onto the verge with relief and medics were soon lifting the boy onto a stretcher. As the traffic snailed past us, I saw faces at every window, people comprehending then why I had been driving so rashly.

Knowing the lad's family would meet him at the Nowra hospital, I judged it best to turn out of that slow-moving chain of vehicles and return to the Park. Jeff had not found the snake so we were confident it had crawled away. When I rang the hospital I was told antivenin had been administered and the boy was comfortable. After the park closed, I wanted to drive down to the hospital with comics and encouragement but Jeff was adamant. He ordered me to keep right out of it, in case my attendance implied admitting liability; that would nullify our public risk policy. I couldn't see how this would be but, scared to oppose his theory, I complied. Inwardly I felt troubled by this difference of approach to the crisis – I felt rebellious, even, a portent, had I realised, of what was to come. At least Jeff took the mower and cut a wider path along the emus' fence. We agreed the snake must have been there for a drink of water, or perhaps to hunt the little mice which scooted through the grass, picking up spilled pellets. We never saw a snake there again and never had anyone else bitten.

Once while we were away and Goth was minding the park, he had a scary experience when a brown snake slid in under the gap in the kiosk door. A film was screening and, because it was hot weather, Goth had left the door into the theatre open to catch the breeze. To his horror, the reptile slipped into the cinema. What should he do? Clearly it was too dangerous to do nothing, so he turned up the lights in the theatre, turned down the movie sound and quietly spoke to the patrons, telling them to please vacate their seats. He opened both doors and shepherded them outside before telling them what was wrong. I wonder how many were game to return to see the end of the movie, after he cleared out the reptile.

I nearly had a repeat of that experience on another hot summer's day a few years later. People were inside watching the show, and outside it was very quiet. I heard the umistakable continuous slither of a sizeable snake moving toward the kiosk through the leaves beneath bushes screening the fence. I dashed out and verified that it was, in fact, a big tiger snake. What it thought it was doing there, I'd no idea, but clearly it wanted to come inside.

With my ear on the soundtrack of the film, knowing it would finish in about six minutes, I began to stamp on the ground. This usually works with snakes and it deterred this one to the extent that it reversed out through the fence, but it was still questing for another opening. A teenage boy came up toward the kiosk, probably wanting to buy an ice cream. He asked me what I was doing. I sized him up as being sensible and also, like most lads of his age, in the mood for adventure, so I told him quietly and asked if he would help me. Stamping heavily from two directions, we were able to shepherd the reptile back across the road. It was reluctant, we were careful but implacable, and just as the film ran out, it entered the undergrowth which led to the creek on the opposite side of the road. Dashing back to my duties, I loaded that young man with free ice creams and lollies for his trouble, suspecting that the experience itself was worth far more to him than treats.

Considering the number of snakes there must be in our ecosystem, with its many birds and small animals, it is fortunate people did not encounter more snakes at the park. One they did see was a python which took a fancy to the rafters in the theatre. No doubt there was good hunting in there when the visitors had gone because they dropped chips and 'roo pellets into the sawdust, which attracted mice. But also it seemed to appreciate the warmth from a floodlight attached to the beam. That python remained in place, week upon week, every winter for several years. I was delighted to see it there because I knew it could not harm anyone and it was another typical species of wildlife, free-living, which visitors could observe. I used to wait until a film had finished before telling the audience to look up and see something interesting. If I'd told them before the movie had started, many of them would have refused to sit down. But as it was, not too many declined to return once they'd viewed the snake from all angles and observed how sedentary it was on its high perch. Years later, people were still fronting up asking: 'Is the python hibernating in the roof today?'

A close encounter of a different, potentially dangerous kind happened with another eagle we were given to prepare for release. She was nearly ready to go and made her way freely around home and park, perching on the roof of the theatre to the delight of visitors. Jeff was very reassuring to those who had been taught to fear eagles. Always sceptical about other people's danger stories, he completely rejected the odd claim we heard of eagles stealing babies.

Goth himself had a friend who grew up believing a story of his mother's near abduction. She was lifted from her pram by an eagle, in the back yard of her parents' country home. Her mother beat it with a broom until it dropped the infant. It sounded convincing to me but not to Jeff. A few other such tales were told to us but Jeff rejected them all. Until the day he saw the light and narrowly avoided a tragedy.

The eagle then resident in the Park was full of confidence around people. Prompted by Jeff's reassurances, visitors would stop and look up at her on the roof, talking to her and taking photos. If she flew down onto the ground, they learned to step around her, encouraged by their host. He, however, began to notice that the eagle was developing rather too strong an interest in toddlers. Little persons waddling and flopping about obviously excited the big bird. Disquietened, Jeff kept her in view at all times and contrived to shoo her away from the kiosk area where parents intent on buying ice creams tended to relax their vigilance.

One busy Sunday afternoon when folks were starting to straggle back to their cars, slack and happy after a day of eating and drinking and walking in the fresh air, Jeff saw the eagle dwelling on the departees. He saw her fly across to the exit gate and perch on its crossbar. Poised, she stared down at people passing beneath her, people made confident by Jeff's earlier assurances. Now he was not so sure. In fact, he was certain the eagle was going to pounce. A big extended family approached, distracted by the task of rounding up their kids and picnic baggage. They had a tiny child with them, barely able to toddle. Jeff saw the eagle fix her sharp dark eyes on it.

Harumph! Jeff leapt the kiosk counter and hurried to stand between the baby and the bird. Making a barrier of his body, he dodged and weaved until the family passed outside, quite oblivious to what he was up to. Then he whistled the eagle onto his arm and, grasping her firmly by the ankles, carried her up to the aviary behind the farmhouse. When the park closed, he put her in the Land Rover and drove her up to Casa Simpatica, where she was tethered until we could figure out what to do with her.

Compulsive communicator though I was, I kept quiet about those few near-misses. Also about the lyrebird's nest I discovered down in the creek above the swimming hole. Finding it, quietly observing and photographing the chick inside, was one of the high spots of my life in the rainforest. Because the nest was down low and vulnerable, I did not tell the public about its location. But I did inform them that near there, a lyrebird could sometimes be seen and often heard running through its repertoire of bird imitations.

One day a succession of visitors proudly reported seeing an

orange wombat on the trail near the koala trees. Usually sceptical, Jeff became intrigued at so many reports of an unlikely
sighting. He went down to see for himself. When he returned, he
was laughing. They *had* seen an orange wombat. It was Wompy.
She'd always liked that burrow under the oak and returned to it
from time to time. It had been raining, however, and the clay had
turned to mud. Red mud, the colour of ferric metal. She was plastered with it but having been hand-reared, she was happy to pose
for photographs and accept hand-outs of pellets from visitors.

Telling stories was part of our business, a teaching tool. For all
the tales we related across the waxed wood counter of our kiosk,
we received back gold as visitors shared their own recollections.
Two of my all-time favourites involve bowerbirds and a dog who
got caught by a wombat.

The first was the experience of a man who had grown up in the
Illawarra before moving interstate and marrying there. Returning
home to visit his parents with his own kids, he led them up into
the bush behind the house where, in his boyhood, there used to be
a bowerbirds' bower. The site was still being used, after almost
twenty years. There among the objects arranged by the birds for
courtship was a little blue truck he had lost as a boy. The birds had
been recycling it, year after year, until the present.

The second story came from a cheerful family group whose
grandparents lived on a farm. We were talking about wombats and
how they defend themselves against attack by foxes or other
enemies trying to follow them down the burrow. When pursued,
wombats will raise their bony back plate – like solid hip bones –
up against the roof of their burrow, effectively crushing the
intruder. I was telling these folks how I'd tried to hook out a
young wombat we called Billy Hughes ('the little digger') before
he disappeared down a tunnel, to fetch him into the house for his
own protection. Forgetting to be careful, I grabbed at his back legs
and he 'hoiked' his bottom up against the roof of the burrow, just
missing my hand. He would have broken it, had he connected,
even though he was fond of me and didn't really mind coming
indoors. It was just an instinctive action.

'Yes, yes, that's what happened to Grandpa's dog,' said one of
our visitors excitedly. 'Remember old Toppy? He had that crooked
face? Pop said he followed a wombat into its burrow once and got

squashed for his trouble. His skull was lopsided for the rest of his life.'

It was Billy Hughes who solved the mystery of poor little Ben, the unlucky wombat cared for by Irish. One day he decided to dig out the practice burrow in the back yard of the farmhouse. It had fallen in and become waterlogged after prolonged rain. He dug, and dug. All day he happily tossed out earth, his back feet churning like rotary hoe blades. Out flew a small brown skull, about the size of my hand. Unmistakably it was the missing infant, who must have been caught down the burrow, probably by Ambrose or maybe Wally. Poor little devil.

I kept that skull and used it in my nature talks. It gave me a queasy feeling each time I handled it, but it was a useful addition to my collection. Asking what, who, where and why were all objects of the Bush Detective game. By getting kids to regard the teeth of various animals, it was easy to assess if they were herbivores, like kangaroos, wombats, cows and horses, or omnivores, like possums (and humans), or carnivores. I had been lucky enough to pick up the skull of a feral cat once, and its sharp canines and molars were plainly a contrast with the grinders and nippers of grass-eaters.

Feral cats were a big problem for us. People liked to dump their unwanted pussies on quiet country roads like Foxground's. The trouble was, those abandoned felines met up with others, mated and, before you knew it, you had a pack of hunters on your property. I actually met a woman in the park who told me, in all innocence, how her daughter had brought her cat and let it go just outside the park. According to her daughter, 'Those Carters are so nice to animals, I knew it would be a good home for Tiddles.' Even as she was telling me this, the woman's face began to fall. She realised what she had said, and how potentially harmful her daugher's action was.

The easiest prey for domestic cats gone wild were the birds, which were unused to predators other than foxes, snakes or tiger cats. A feral domestic cat was far more lethal than any of them. And after a generation or two of eating only live meat in the wild, feral cats grow grossly muscular. Linda was able to lend us a cat trap used by Wollongong University, until I could obtain one of our own. Ironically, there was all sorts of red tape you had to cut through before you could be issued a permit to buy a cat trap. We caught quite a few. Some were freshly dumped and we took these down to the Berry Rural Co-op, where Van now worked. He released them in the grain shed to catch mice . . . a pretty good end for an unwanted suburban pussy. The completely wild cats had no future, however, and Jeff shot them.

Any feral cats that escaped our diligence probably helped clean up the remains of the rabbits. The release of a particularly effective strain of myxomatosis killed off most of them but the odd few usually survive and become immune to the virus. After a few years, rabbits could be seen once again in ones and twos along the road or up the back in the high country, but Glenrock remained free of them. We thought it might be because we had long stopped shooting foxes or tiger cats, coming to espouse a policy of letting nature balance the books (feral cats excluded, of course).

Striking the ecological balance, allowing ourselves to find an appropriate place in it rather than trying to dominate and orchestrate the landscape and its inhabitants, became our mission. We stopped using fertilisers, weedicides and pesticides for the first time in almost twenty years. We also let the bush regrow.

This policy was aided by Jeff's passion for going overseas, which took him out of farming mode for many years. In 1983 we went to Europe again for four months. That was the last time I accompanied him, although he made five more trips there in the next decade or so. Distracted as we became by this and that, and often absent, we let the bush grow back on the paddocks and hillsides Ernie Staples had worked so hard to clear. Sometimes this was by design, as in the case of Wallaby Hill, which we judged too unstable to remain cleared. At other times the tea-trees and wattles encroached stealthily but relentlessly, a natural process of regeneration. Thus we lost sight of the fine stone wall on our southern boundary and also the plough share in the rock which had anchored Ernie's famous flying fox. We even lost our view from Casa Simpatica out across the Shoalhaven.

When we wanted to restore that by removing some regrown acacias and eucalypts, we found there were tree preservation orders in place preventing it. That was how times had changed by the 1990s. Ironically, we found ourselves hoist with our own petard.

22

One last wombat

Down at Wild Country Park and on the rest of Glenrock's protective acreage, the grey kangaroos had bred so well that there were always between ten and thirty fronting up for pellets each morning and evening. After eating they usually lay around for a while. It was so lovely that visitors could see those marsupials reclining confidently on the lawns. Some of my most satisfying times came in the late afternoon when visitors, relaxed after films, picnic and bushwalk, sat peacefully among resting 'roos. They had grown accustomed to people but not to loud noises. A backfiring vehicle or the sound of a tractor grinding up the road could send them flying in panic for shelter along the creek or up the back, which was exasperating if we were expecting a coachload of tourists or school children. However, we persevered, confident now that the refugees would settle into whatever routine was the most natural to them.

After the death of Jo-Jo, the wallaroos migrated gradually up to the high country, following their natural inclination toward steep, stony places, but occasionally a young orphan was given to us to care for and, believing it would have its own kind to join up with later, we accepted it. One of these was Wallaroo Rocky who, for want of her own kind, gradually emigrated up the hill to Casa Simpatica. She was pretty but aloof, and this fitted in with our new policy of minimum, rather than effusively maximum, care. We fed her twice daily and that was all, after which she lay about on the lawns, or hopped deftly atop one of our huge boulders beside the house, decorative but not exactly a friend.

Poc Roig, the gentle little red kangaroo who grew to manhood under our care and had a brief flirtation with Blind Bruce, was also pretty much on his own. Note the Catalan name, which means Little Red. (Sorry, Banjo, we lapsed, influenced by our nostalgia for north-eastern Spain, where we had lived a full village life for two years.) Poc Roig gravitated toward the western, drier side of Foxground, as the other reds had done. I often used to see him when I drove home through the valley, catching the last rays of sun on a hilltop. He looked so beautiful, lit like a bronze god, a joy for all to see there. One afternoon, a local farmer shot him. Popped him off where he stood. Just because he was accessible. Shot him as vermin. Good riddance. We had a policy that we would stand firm about protecting animals within our wildlife refuge but that when they strayed onto other people's properties, they had to take their chances. So we let it go – but I hold it against that man to this day.

The antipathy down in the valley and surrounding districts to what we were trying to do did not properly come home to me until the mid-eighties. I rang a new property owner about a matter and when I identified myself, he said: 'Oh, I know who you are. You're those people who're flooding the place with pests.' He hung up in my ear. Thus I learned that even as urban public opinion swung toward the protection of wildlife, preservation of habitat, concern about acid rain and holes in the ozone layer, country people were bitterly opposed to 'Greenies'. Bitterly. It was a schism which seemed unbridgeable.

Even among local friends, I discovered that little sympathy existed for what we had done. My good old neighbour Mrs Conroy often fretted about seeing kangaroos in their paddocks. So did another former neighbour, now living on the Gerringong side of Saddleback Mountain. The old notion of native wildlife robbing sheep and cattle of grass was still strong. Kangaroos from the Carters' had spread like a plague. It was a scandal.

Interestingly enough, with all the kangaroos and other herbivores on our property, we never ran out of grass. Ten, twenty, fifty, a hundred 'roos ate their fill for years and Jeff still needed to

mow. We bought two steers as grass-cutters. They grazed unconcerned next to kangaroos and wombats, but still we had to get the
paddocks slashed at least once a year.

By 1985 Wild Country Park was generating a momentum of its
own. All sorts of visitors made it part of their regular itinerary,
including vulcanologists seeking the cores of old volcanoes –
Saddleback was thought to be one of them – and air-crash collectors who solemnly trekked up to the site of the bomber wreck or
another, later, plane disaster, found nothing, and trekked back down
again, content to cross those off their list. There was also a sixth form
from a prominent Sydney boys' school which annually had a
bushwalk and camp-out in the high country, and annually got lost.

The park ran like a well-tuned engine. I shopped for the stock
foods and kiosk supplies while Jeff kept the paths and picnic
areas mowed and the nature trails in good repair. We both tidied
the outdoors as if it were indoors, skipping down through the
open grounds and back along shady tracks before the arrival of
each day's visitors. We used to pick up everything, including ciga-
rette butts and the tiniest scrap of lolly wrapper, united in the belief
that if our place looked as if it were pristine – even though it
clearly wasn't – people would love and respect it. On Saturday
and Sunday mornings, Jeff would prepare the park for opening
while I tidied up the house, often in anticipation of guests that
evening. He put out birdseed and pellets, hosed out the toilet
block, then opened the kiosk and theatre. Jeff had a system of
raking over the sawdust in the theatre – sprinkling it lightly with
water if it were a dry, dusty time of year – then rubbing eucalyptus oil over the log uprights and the edges of the museum tables.
This created a fragrance and ambience of woodsy antiquity which
was very comforting.

Most afternoons, feeding the animals was my job and that task,
too, had been honed to a routine which suited everyone, particularly the animals. Our jobs were interchangeable, but that was the
most common division of labour. The strong shed Thor had built
for us in the back yard, replacing the blacksmith's and Boys
Museum shed, was fitted out with an electric jug for heating the
orphans' milk formulas, and an old fridge which kept meat and
fruit fresh. There were cupboards, a small sink and rat-proof bins
for pellets, birdseed and stale bread.

A typical feeding round went like this. First I would pop the current young wombat into the wombatarium where it settled happily, munching pellets behind its impregnable door, a dark secure environment which caused it no distress and kept it out from under my feet as I did my rounds. Then I would fill two buckets with grain and on top of these would go dishes of chopped meat or fruit, or both, plus a loaf or two of stale bread. Bottles of milk for the orphans were nestled among the pellets to keep them warm. The menu was the same depending on what animals were based in the park at any particular time.

Supplies in tow, I would then visit the big paddock which once once housed the kangaroos but now was home to the emus. 'E-mu, e-mu, ee-moo,' I called loudly, sprinkling wheat and pellets liberally along the feeding trough inside the fence. Then I stood back. Seven small wispy heads would appear over the distant rise. 'E-moo, ee-moo,' I'd warble. The seven heads, on very long necks, would come bobbing and stretching up the hill, feathers waggling on fat oval bodies, strong long legs galloping like those of a racehorse. It was hard not to flinch before such a ground-shaking charge. Little useless wings akimbo, beaks ajar, big eyes staring greedily, they would arrive and fling themselves down on their haunches round the trough. Their agile necks darted in and out as their beaks snapped up gobs of feed. I did not wait for them to finish – that might have tempted them to try jumping the fence – but gathered my buckets and let myself through another gate into the park.

Here I would usually find Opal, Potch, Mathilda and their children grazing near the big round dishes made from plough-shares, where the droppings of bowerbirds showed me that any crumbs left over from the morning's feed had not been wasted. Further down the hill would be other 'roos quietly grazing. 'Roo-ee!' I would call loudly and begin filling the bowls with wheat and pellets, topped up with some chunks of bread. The trick was to use the same words, same tone of voice, and never vary the routine. Easy.

Leaving the kangaroos gathered round the bowls, crunching stolidly, I would attend to whatever animals were in the Nursery Yard before proceeding down the hill. Sometimes there would be one or two, or more, wallabies in care, and if each needed to be bottle-fed, this might take some juggling. I'd leave pieces of meat for an injured hawk or magpie, some fruit for the possums, and a heavy bowl of pellets for the wombats when they woke up later.

On the dam within the Staging Yard there lived for some years three wild ducks and Henry, a bossy mallard who'd come with them. Normally we did not accept domestic animals but Henry was part of a package we could not refuse. Our hope was that the wild ducks would attract others to nest on our pond. Feeding the three native ducks was easy, but Henry was a handful. 'Quack, quack, quack,' he used to shout garrulously, attacking your ankles in a very annoying manner until you could fill his dish with grain.

With the Staging Yard dependents fed, I could make my way slowly back up the grassy slope towards the theatre and, beyond that, the farmhouse. I can still conjure the sweet feeling of contentment as blue shadows slipped down over the sheltering hills and I turned my thoughts to serving dinner to loved ones. Or one. That was, I realised later, the pinnacle of my life. Or one of them, anyway.

Those years until the mid-eighties, tending Wild Country Park filled me with a variety of satisfactions I had never foreseen, had never imagined possible when I arrived in Australia thirty-five years earlier, nor even, indeed, during the early 1970s when we made our films. It was interesting to watch people relate to our documentary series. Even when we, the 'stars', had aged, when clothes, vehicles and to some degree the format were passé, people still laughed at the funny bits, gasped at the dangerous bits, and emerged from their seats stimulated. Some actually applauded as our end credits rolled – Jeff and Mare smiling into the lens, then fade on a windmill. We watched to see whether people would talk among themselves during the movies, indicating boredom, or even walk out. This would have been reasonable, we thought, and if it had become the rule, we probably would not have continued to show the films as frequently as we did. But it simply didn't work out that way. People saw our pictures through. Those on return visits made a point of viewing their favourites and, if they had brought friends to see a particular film – especially *Wild Animal Farm*, *Tiger Man* or *Jackpot Town* – they set their watches for when those would be playing, to make sure they returned in time from the Jungle Walk. And we continued to ring the old cowbell, signalling a screening, at least once an hour.

It was a rare opportunity for us as film-makers to test the validity of our product. Most movies go out into the world and screen or die, unseen by their makers. Showing them ourselves was a very reinforcing experience; we constantly replayed our past life. On the other hand, we had to suffer the errors of judgement we had made in scripting or editing. They weren't many, but they glared at us.

Had we continued making documentaries, our approach would have evolved into a style different to the one we chose for our six pilot films. At least we were able, after a decade, to recoup the money we had invested in making the series, but that involved actually projecting the films, rewinding them, splicing them when they broke, plus all the other business of Wild Country Park, which came into being because of the films. Most movie-makers would not dream of doing what they consider the donkey work of film distribution, as we did.

It was also interesting – and natural – that we created the park to build a continuing business for our offspring, but in time they headed off in their own directions, leaving Mum and Dad to man the fort. They were always able and willing to step in and help when they came home, but gradually their paths led them away – sometimes far, far away – from Glenrock, a good base to return to, bringing their own children to imbibe wildlife and waterfall, the creek and the dear old farmhouse, small, handmade and scarred with memories. So as Jeff and I carried on at Wild Country Park, I began to see it would be a pleasant retirement business for us, keeping us active and sociable. Unfortunately, Jeff did not share my vision. Or my satisfaction.

He began rushing into a series of innovations which he thought would keep old age at bay, including bigger and better hi-fidelity sound systems. He filled one end of our living room with state-of-the-art amplifiers and music players, and studio monitors placed on huge tree-stumps for stability. To soften the acoustics of the room, he covered our window-walls with drapes and bought fokati rugs for the slate floor – all the extras he had disparaged for so long. Casa Simpatica stopped being a hose-out house and became a sound lounge.

Club sports-car racing was another enthusiasm which overshadowed life on Glenrock. Jeff bought a special racing Porsche, space-age helmet, fireproof suit. On our mantelpiece, beside the Condamine Bells, emu eggs and lyrebirds feathers, a small rash of car-club trophies began to grow.

Wild Country Park did not finance Jeff's glamorous new hobbies. It never did more than roll smoothly along, a self-funding parade. No, Jeff's toys for old boys were paid for by the teaching he was now doing, by royalties from his books, which now totalled almost twenty, and the sale of his various Porsches, on which he usually managed to make a profit. He began to hive off his income and activities. Work and social life which for thirty years had been 'ours' now became 'his'. I could sympathise with his desire to fly high while there was still time, and to establish a persona which was not tied in to the past. Happily engaged as I was with Wild Country Park and the grandchildren, I hardly noticed him slipping away.

While I had fun with the school excursions, Jeff filled his midweek days with a new career. He was asked to teach photography at a branch of the National Art School which had opened in Wollongong. It turned out to be a disaster for J Carter – and for me. The wrong place for a man who had unfinished business carried over from his aborted teenage years. Jeff fell in love with one of his students, a girl in need of a father figure, and that was the beginning of the end for Jeff and me, for the family as we had all enjoyed it, and for Wild Country Park. He was fifty-seven. I was fifty-five.

Caught in the oldest trap on earth for ageing men, Jeff gave himself to his new love, thirty-eight years his junior. What happened to him in 1985 and the following few years broke our marriage and resulted in Wild Country Park being sold two years later. It wasn't that having an affair was the worst sin in the book (certainly not the newest) even though it broke Jeff's own implacable taboo about fidelity. What undid me was that in order to justify what he was drawn to do, he demolished my strengths and talents, what I had thought were my achievements, and this plunged me into a crisis which was as unplanned for as the successes had been. Suddenly I had to rethink. To regroup. To survive in a whole new ball game.

The cataclysm coincided with our acceptance of another wombat. She arrived in a supermarket box stamped with the 'no-name' brand and was left like a foundling on the doorstep of the park. We decided to call her Little No-name, Noni for short, and make her the co-star of a modest film with two-year-old Lauren, Van's daughter. Jeff had begun a second flirtation with cine photography, which really was his forte, only this time he bought a new super-8 format camera which was lighter and cheaper to use. Roger Whittaker assured him the quality of this latest technology would be almost equal to what he had achieved earlier in 16 millimetre.

Transformed into a typical macho man of the eighties Jeff, in tight jeans, black leather jacket and expensive joggers, rejected grandparenthood; what I embraced as a bonus of family life, he saw as only for old guys. He insisted his seven grandchildren call him 'Abuelo', which was Spanish for what he was but untranslatable by most people. However, he could see the potential of cute little Lauren and Noni, growing up side by side through his lens. So filming began.

The project stalled when Van and his family moved from the old farmhouse to Berry, just before Lauren's brother Hayden was born, and foundered altogether as Jeff hurtled along his new road. However, we were stuck with Noni, so we reared her as best we could. Her growing up was totally different to that of any of the other orphan wombats we had known.

I have always believed in a synchronicity. Serendipity, ditto. Both seem to be a sort of grace, which I have been blessed with most of my life. Thus it was that when Jeff headed off in his new directions, an old friend presented me with an unexpected gift. It was a bedsitter in The Rocks, cradle of early Sydney. In a nice old crumbling terrace down under the Harbour Bridge, I found sanctuary from my domestic disasters, which compounded around me for the next decade.

Jeff and I agreed to take turns caring for Wild Country Park, leaving him free for his new life on alternate weekends. Thus I had someplace to flee to on my weekends 'off'. The Rocks room satisfied an unfulfilled dream of a bohemian pad – the direct antithesis of my spacious green home at Foxground – and it brought me new friends. I drove up there fortnightly and Noni travelled with me. Our luggage was a series of baskets, one lined with sheepskin for her bed; another, smaller, holding her feeding bottles and formula; spare bunny rugs, plus lots of newspaper rode in a third; and of course I took the dear old battered playpen, which folded neatly into the back of my station wagon. I soon had the routine down pat, as one does when travelling with a baby.

So long as she was kept warm and in touch with a loving foster mum, Noni didn't mind the new lifestyle one bit. It was made easier by my discovery of Wombaroo, a new product then on the market. Developed by an Australian scientist, it was a series of infant milks biochemically suited to orphans of different species. Designed originally for zoo animals – exotics like lions and tigers – the range was expanded to include Australian natives, and there were products aimed at the newly born, older infants and so on. It was a brilliant concept and made the task of rearing orphans so much easier. Never again did I experience the worry of scours.

City people made me and my baby wombat very welcome. They found Little No-name delightful. The problem began when she grew some and needed a ramble before settling back into her playpen and basket. Because she did not urinate or defecate indoors, she was allowed to roam people's lounge rooms. The worry was when she wanted to sharpen her teeth – a typical wombat habit. Chair rungs were just allowable (depending on the quality of the chair), but it was her fondness for chewing electrical extension cords that kept us on our toes. I worried lest she crunch through the insulation and change in one flash to a blackened effigy, but we always caught her and deterred her in time.

Exercising Noni in urban parks was easier and gave pleasure to passers-by, especially local kids who otherwise had no chance of playing with a native animal. Noni always drew a crowd and I found myself answering questions much as I did at Wild Country Park. I didn't mind because it seemed another chance to plead the case of dislocated wildlife.

The two biggest 'shows' Noni and I ever put on were both near Circular Quay. Once, when I was exercising her on Observatory Hill overlooking the Harbour Bridge and my Rocks room, a big party of school pupils spotted her and came rushing over. Her outing became a spontaneous ecology lesson for theirs.

Another day I set her down on the grass at the Domain, where a constant stream of tourists comes to photograph the Opera House. Within cooee of the Woolloomooloo docks where I had landed in 1950 and had my first glimpse of Sydney, my adopted home, Noni frisked and scampered on the same green lawn which had so captivated my eyes after six weeks at sea. It was one of those sparkling, sunny Sydney Harbour days, and lunchtime strollers stopped to smile at the antics of the little wombat, oblivious to the attention she was attracting. Then a huge tourist coach rolled up. The driver spotted Noni and asked if his passengers could take pictures of her. I scooped her up and held her, lest she be frightened as sixty Japanese visitors snapped us in unison. The sound of their shutters was quite loud and it tickled me to think of us forever smiling out of albums in Osaka, Tokyo and wherever else.

City people generally were hungry to see at close range an Australian native. Especially the Japanese and Germans, who poured from tourist coaches around the Rocks and Circular Quay, snapping frantically in their few moments of freedom. The Opera House, The Bridge, Sydney Harbour, and a wombat on a blue bunny rug. Had I put out a hat like buskers do, we could have earned heaps. Little No-name found her way into hundreds of photographs until she grew too big, too strong, too restless for the travelling life.

Driving regularly between the city and Foxground, I watched with regret the lovely soft foothills of the Illawarra change from dairy paddocks to clusters of houses. Subdivisions spread like eczema across the landscape. Incomplete poems of protest sprouted in my mind as I drove the familiar miles. Henry Lawson, Banjo, where are you now? And what would you make of this? Playing in my head, as well as on the car radio, was that haunting song from the Vietnam War; *What have they done to my song, Ma*.

I cried many tears as Noni and I beat our path back and forth between the Big Smoke and the Rainforest Retreat. Change is painful.

In 1987, I had to let Wild Country Park go. It was the nature of the business that made it impossible for me to continue. The prospect of daily, weekly seeing our formerly idyllic life projected onto the big screen was too painful to bear. Fielding questions, ditto. The business was bought by a family from Sydney, with their own dream of tending a wildlife park. They moved into the old farmhouse and became custodians of the waterfall, which were part of the fifty acres we had to sell.

Freed of the responsibilities of Wild Country, taking turns with Jeff to mind Noni and the other animals around Casa Simpatica, I threw myself into a period of intense activity, travelling the outback routes I had first covered with Jeff, sometimes with a friend, often alone, making my own pace, finding my own stories, taking photos, recording notes. I wrote two books about Central Australia and numerous magazine stories about the lives being lived beyond gates and grids. The New South Wales Riverina, the central deserts, the Top End, and western Queensland became again familiar, beloved territory. Those trips brought me a kind of ecstasy. I proved to myself and the world that I could do It on my own.

Not that the world cared. It was preoccupied with the bicentenial celebrations – which I watched from my Rocks balcony, a sanctuary in a flood, a deluge, of excited people – and other navel-gazing which I thought was appropriate and healthy for our adolescent nation. My adopted country, my chosen homeland, which had at times discouraged me in its rush to embrace the worst of the American commerical culture I fled from as a young woman, now seemed to be shaping up in a good way. Aboriginal people were gaining title to their land – a process necessary but foreign to their beliefs. They know where they belong without pieces of paper to tell them. Immigration had made Australia a multi-cultured bazaar. Shops and restaurants displayed the best of the Old World, presented in a New World way. One didn't need to travel overseas to sample what the earth had to offer. I pondered a great deal, that decade after Jeff wrote me out of his script, growing my own new persona.

As luck would have it, I received a helping hand through re-entering the workforce, after thirty-six years of being self-employed at home. I was sixty-one when I realised I needed a Day Job to augment my spasmodic earnings from travel journalism – my hobby, my vanity. No point in demanding work as a veterinarian, or even a business manager, which I had been. You win no degrees or certificates for a life like mine. I took the easy path and applied for three part-time domestic jobs, one after the other. I got them all, which lifted my life onto a solid footing once more. The first was washing dishes in a local French restaurant. As a passionate foodie, it thrilled me to be so close to the aromatic sizzle and chop-chop, professional knives and wonderful copper pans, and to watch the classic dishes in preparation.

My second job was tea-lady in a private Sydney hospital. I had always said: 'Never be too high and mighty for lowly work.' If it is honourable, it is never demeaning. Thus I sailed through the wards with my trolley, bringing far more than drinks and plates of food. I was a cheerful visitor, arranger of pillows, bearer of messages, picker-up of dropped and mislaid personal possessions, receiver of confidences and anxieties, all of which are important parts of therapy. Suddenly I felt better. The patients loved me and I loved them. I earned a regular wage (undreamed-of in the hand-to-mouth world of the Arts). Back in my normal mode as care-taker, doing what I do best, my confidence began to return. And I made some wonderful new women friends among the nursing staff.

My third part-time job put the icing on the cake. I was asked to look after a small girl in Berry while her mother, a schoolteacher, was at work. I had known her mother years before when she went to school with Van and Kerry. Her little girl, Harriet, looked just as her mother had done when she was young. I became surrogate grandmother, she my almost granddaughter. We kept each other going, growing, cheerful, learning heaps, for four excellent years, until she started regular school. I was happy to see her do that, even though I would miss her sweet company. As with the native animals, my determination was to see her move on appropriately. My own philosophy translates to nothing less.

As a parent, my impetus had been similar. Blessed to have encountered the writings of Khalil Gibran even before I became a mother, I saw my children as my flowers, never my chattels or creations. The opposite of my mother, I encouraged them to develop and trust their own judgement and when this conflicted with mine as they grew older, I schooled myself to accept it grace-fully, to let them go, to rejoice that they were developing their own personalities.

The one time I forgot this wisdom was with my husband who, when we first got together, was shy, socially inept, stubbornly iconoclastic, sometimes to his own detriment. I saw my role as smoothing his (our) path, cushioning him from what might deter him from his (our) unorthodox journey to the top of his trade.

Women did that sort of emotional work in my time, and in the isolated Carter household, there was more of it to do than in some others. So I grew him up. He was my creature (and I was his), two very interdependent persons. In middle age, he found himself ready to fly alone. He had learned the skills with me but wanted to practise them without me. Fair enough. My trouble was that I had for so long considered what was best for his development, I forgot to build my own. Umbilical twins no longer, our free and natural lives became quite separate and different. I had realised for some time that I was building my castle on sand, not a wise thing to do but, once started, I felt the best course was to keep going, for the good of all concerned, and it became quite an elaborate edifice. However, inevitably, when the king tide finally rolled it, everything I had worked for began to crumble. And I could think of no one to blame but myself.

I won't go into the rights and wrongs of the split between Jeff and me. It always takes two to make and to break a partnership. Blameless, I wasn't. Perfectly adjusted, ditto. I had a lot of growing to do and it didn't become necessary until the last third of my life. Fancy that! But, like Pollyanna, I have to say that in the end, it was a good job done. My biggest regret was the damage it did to our family structure. It was very hard for our adult children to remain loyal to both Mum and Dad and to adjust to us being separate entities. But like the solid, warm characters they had grown into, they managed to give us equal support and to get on with their own lives and families. Glenrock became a less attractive place for them to visit for a while, that was the worst of it. And almost all our old friends felt the same.

Down the hill from Casa Simpatica, Wild Country Park and the old farmhouse slid into a state of neglect and ruin. Sadly, I had to watch this progressive deterioration as I drove past each day. Eventually the house was abandoned.

During the week I sometimes roamed the back yard of my old home. Jeff was away a great deal of that time, travelling both overseas and across Australia with his new young love and – after his idyll with her collapsed, as such idylls do – with other young women who fooled no one but J Carter into believing that he was anything but who he was, an ageing man afeared of death. Memories crowded my troubled mind. Prowling the wrecked garden, I conjured Tuppy, son of Tippy, peering down excitedly from the kitchen roof now buckling and rusty. Ghosts of Ralph and Claude, two mistreated cockatoos who became pals, perched in the old lemon tree, itself now gone. Cranky Beryl, a spinster 'roo who took over the farmhouse garden after Gidgea died, haunted the ruined lawns. She had been rescued by a milkman from a back yard near Wollongong. Kept for years in a concrete chicken yard, she was up to her ankles in her own droppings, foot pads distorted like old boots. Her personality was set by the time she came to Glenrock. Irritable and fussy, she never mated, never let other 'roos near her and tolerated us churlishly. Yet we grew fond of her and successive residents of the farmhouse pandered to her needs.

I had to smile, recalling all our innocent good times. Once we were invaded by a motorbike club – which didn't seem so funny at the time. It was an Easter weekend when dozens of bikers took over upper Foxground invited – unwisely we thought – to camp on the brothers' land. A rival club camped down on Seven Mile Beach. The mob from up the back shanghaied Van into driving them to Berry for more grog. He had just gotten his licence. Jeff, Thor and Pat Aulton (who had come for the holiday weekend) followed them in another vehicle to back Van up if he had any trouble, then remembered they had left all us women, including Pat's two young daughters, home alone. They rang, told us to go inside, lock the doors and get out the rifle. We were not molested, but two girls from Berry were raped at the beach and two of the bikers camping up behind our place were bashed and burned. One of them died.

Other memories greeted me as I entered the deserted and neglected park. Those were melancholy days as I poked about the remnants of my life's work, a sort of self-punishment for letting go too easily. What was the line from that good old song? 'You never know what you got till it's gone.' How true.

Returning up the hill was my salvation, to the peace and green surrounding the restful verandahs, where often I sat and pondered where I had gone wrong. At my feet would be Dinah-the-Dingo, and dear little Tootsie, and reclining among the birdlife was Rocky, the so beautiful but so unrewarding wallaroo. And what about Little No-name? She was bedded in straw on the inner verandah, enclosed by the warm brick walls of Casa Simpatica and a strong fence, a Taj Mahal of a wombatarium. She thrived but now, having rather saturated Glenrock with wombats, we had to keep orphans secure for longer than formerly, until they grew big enough to fight for some territory. Eventually she made her way out confidently into the free world, as her predecessors had done. I hope she is among the mature wombats who front up nightly for bowls of pellets I leave on the front verandah. And of course, Noni wasn't really my last wombat. There was Duchess Ruby – poor, addled, mistreated little beggar – but that's another story.

In a sense, Tootsie the red-neck wallaby was my last beloved foster-cared native animal. She was my final tie to the property. While she lived, I did not feel free to move away or stay away too long. But sad to say, she turned up one day injured, probably from banging into a fence or even the side of a car. I did everything I could to heal her but she just faded away. Another beloved friend buried in the tea-tree grove.

The good news is, lyrebirds have become pests in the garden, leaving large white sploshy droppings on the Spanish tiles, their courting songs so loud that visitors complain – until told what they are hearing. Rosellas and king parrots jostle scores of finches at the fountain, bowerbirds squabble round the pellet dishes vying for spilled crumbs, wongas waddle the verandahs where grey thrushes and martins nest above their heads. They make a bit of mess and their chatter is so loud you can hardly hear yourself think sometimes, but it's a small price to pay for living in the midst of abundance.

You won't be able to see all this, unfortunately. If you turn onto the Foxground Road these days, you will find a different picture from the one I have painted. There are no more working dairy farms in the valley. Most of the old families have moved away. New houses spring up like mushrooms. Riding horses idle where cows used to graze. The final dramatic mile to Wild Country Park is now bitumen, which no longer ends at the old farmhouse but snakes on up the hill to where more new houses are being built.

You won't find Wild Country Park at all. It has closed. The family who bought it from us sold it again after a few years. The new owners of Glenrock did not want to continue with what was left of the business. They tidied up the rubbish, mowed the grass, but left the old farmhouse a sad relict of its once proud state.

Fearing its fate would be a bulldozer, I prepared myself for the worst and tried to let go.

However, take my word for it. The story I have told here is true, and hanging about in the quiet air are the sighs of thousands who have visited and gone away refreshed, leaving the ghosts of the Carter family, the Staples and Henrys, along with the descendants of Opal and Mathilda, Big Joe, Gidgea, William and Wally and Wompy, and all the rest of the cast, most of whom have spread out to live the free and natural life.

Epilogue

Hang on, that's not the end of the story. Two excellent things happened in 1999 which were totally surprising. The first concerned our decrepit old farmhouse. Mrs Henry's garden had been razed, Ernie's picket fence and stone wall were also gone; standing naked on bare ground, the old homestead was unprotected from rambunctious children, animals and weather. Torn flyscreen flapped in the wind. Broken wall panels and rusty roofing let in rain, which created decay indoors. No wonder the second owner after ourselves made no repairs. He clearly thought the old place – the *dear* old place – wasn't worth salvaging.

Fortunately a family in Foxground thought differently. Friends of Van and Kerry, the Godfreys, fell in love with the farm and approached the owner, pleading to buy. He accepted their offer and they set about selling their own property down in the valley as quickly as possible. Thus, having schooled myself to expect the worst, I was suddenly gifted with the best, a scenario I had ceased daring to hope for. Now as we drove past, we watched a miraculous reincarnation take place. Not only did they repair the old dwelling, they reclad it in cedar slabs, opened up the verandahs, returned it to authenticity and its initial unpretentious glory. They took it back a century, and so there it stands, a quaint and cosy reminder of three families who lived in it and loved it for one hundred and thirty years. And a source of joy to its new owners, who have made it into livable art.

Phil Godfrey is a musician. Di Godfrey is a craftswoman of national repute. Before the sale was finalised, she used to come and sit in the deserted kitchen, listening to the farmhouse 'talking to her'. Now the slab theatre–museum has been transformed into Di's workshop and teaching studio. A whole new circle of life has begun for Glenrock Farm.

The second resurrection was triggered by Van's suggestion that I get another dog. After Dinah-the-Dingo died of old age and was buried in the grove, I resisted seeking a replacement for quite a while but as time passed, the idea took hold of me. The little girl I was caring for, Harriet, and I, during our last year together, spent many happy hours studying dogs-of-the-world books, looking at pictures, reading about breeds and their requirements in the way of care. We settled on a small Australian terrier, or something similar – shaggy, quiet in temperament, amenable to training, easy to travel with.We even named her in advance, assuming she would be a shaggy russet with grey streaks (or vice versa): Ragged Rosey. So what did I choose, when I finally went nervously to the dog pound? A tiny, springy, smooth-haired cross-bred with huge alert ears and bright eyes, a long slim tail and smiling mouth. She was yellow, and I guess she reminded me of a miniature dingo. She threw up in the car all the way home to Foxground.

We arrived just on dark. As I led her along the verandah on her leash, wagging and leaping, Jeff came out of his study and said: 'What the bloody hell is *that*?'

'This is Annie Rose, my new dog,' I said with dignity, naming her on the spur of the moment and hoping he wouldn't make a fuss. We had come way past the era of asking each other's permission to innovate, but kept to our own space at opposite ends of the house and cooperated in matters of maintaining our property, distant, reserved, careful not to fall to arguing. Annie Rose changed all that.

From the start, the only one of my criteria for the ideal dog she met was her size. She was petite, but that was because she was so young. The pound lady told me she was fully grown, about eighteen months old. Ha ha ha. She lied. I don't blame her, she saw a chance to unite a nice lady offering a good home with a sweet puppy.

Annie Rose was three months old, and had no adult teeth at all yet. In fact, she trebled in size during her first year, which still makes her a small dog but not the toy I had planned on. Along the way, she went through all the phases of puppyhood. Jeff became her trainer. I had forgotten how good he is with animals, maybe because he is pragmatic, he keeps commands simple, and combines uncompromising rules of behaviour with kindness which is palpable. He fell in love with that little dancing doggie and she with him. It totally changed the ambience within Casa Simpatica. We took from mothballs the sweet and sassy talk which used to prevail in our household, before we learned to communicate in a way which stuck to business, gave no offence, nor personal details of plans or feelings. Out came physical caresses which once had been standard but had been carefully locked away, lest either of us got 'the wrong idea' about the other's intentions. Annie Rose received hourly pats and hugs, and cuddles were the order of every day, especially each evening as we settled down to a taciturn dinner while watching television after our day's work in our separate offices.

Annie Rose jumped from one lap to the other. She laughed and tried to lick. Excitable sometimes, ever ready for a game of tug-of-war, she could change in an instant to a tired young person needing a snuggle and a snooze.

'Go and see your mother, she might give you a bone,' Jeff began to say. 'Ask Dad to take you with him down the paddock,' I might rejoin. He had only to ask, 'Up the bush?' and she would prance on her hind legs in anticipation of an expedition. I fed her, kept her bed in my room, but Jeff taught her to ride in his Land Rover obediently, to wait until he told her to move, to follow him when he called. Given our past history, it is not surprising that a lovable little animal broke the drought that had fallen on us. We began to consult freely about her growing up and this led to other pleasant discourse. It seemed like we had come full circle, at long last.

It was a relief to me because I felt the example we set during our time of estrangement was bad for our children and grandchildren, because it was out of synch with the principles on which they had been reared. All four reflect these values but each has made an individual life of their own choosing. After some years working in Sydney, Thor and his Jenny returned to her home state of Tasmania. Thor is a photographer and research officer at the Hobart CSIRO Division of Fisheries. Very caringly they parent three bright daughters, whom we see seldom now because of distance. We keep in touch by phone, by photo and by mail.

Karen married a man who mistrusted families. He carted her and their two children – our first-born grandchildren – all round Australia and overseas, before settling them finally in Tasmania. Which kept them geographically out of reach, and without support, most of their formative years.

Goth did not marry until he was in his forties, but he had several rich, long-standing relationships with smart and stylish women, each of a different ethnic background, who were, for a time, my daughters-*ex*-law. He never had any children and his marriage broke up. Photography, music and comedy are his fortes, along with romancing women. He is good at all of these. When he decided to take up an offer of dual US/Australian citizenship in 1993 and moved to San Francisco – once my beloved stamping ground – I applauded his courage, but miss his good, quirky company. Now he lives in Japan.

Van is the only one of our children living within reach of Glenrock. He and his wife Kerry are settled in Berry where they went to school. Their two children, Lauren and Hayden, were both captains of the local school – as their dad had been in his time – and they are smart, warm, funny, artistic, sportive youngsters, like their parents. Nature Boy and Nature Girl, Mark II, but they have many other talents as well. Van, a musician, played in a country rock band for years. He is also the store manager at Berry Rural Co-op – with a million dollars a year turnover and a chance to monitor the pulse of the district through his customers. His extraordinary gift with animals remains strong and he is part-owner of a racehorse, which he helps to train. It is my joy to watch him and Kerry live out rich, satisfied lives, handy to Foxground.

What about the rest of the family, friends and mentors? Percy, Jeff's dad, died suddenly in 1981. He'd not been feeling well for a year or more and spent his visits to Casa Simpatica pottering at the jobs Jeff did not enjoy. He set up a workbench in a shed and he laid a set of stone steps up through the steep back garden. 'My memorials,' he called them once, which signalled to me he felt sicker than he was letting on. Jeff said Dadda didn't mention death often but told him he didn't want any fancy burial ceremony. 'Just hang me up in a tree somewhere,' he said. So Jeff scattered his ashes along his stairway and across to the grove. He hooked the plastic box the remains had come in on a tea-tree bough, which looks a bit off but means a lot to us.

When Doris died, a good fifteen years later, Jeff did the same for her. She never lived in the 'granny quarters' first occupied by my mother, but continued in her own self-care unit in our district until ill-health overtook her. She mellowed after Dadda died and I like to think I was able to give her the support she needed at the end of her life. Once she stopped disapproving and admitted how proud she had become of her son, Jeff was able to treat her with more tenderness than earlier in their uncomfortable relationship.

Howard and Ivy Judd soldiered on, struggling to cope as Minnamurra Falls grew to be a favourite of locals and a must for tourists. The reserve became an annual destination for primary and secondary school excursions, sometimes six or more every day. Howard stretched himself to lead each group personally, putting his message into the ears of the young. As visitor numbers increased to a flood, Howard literally worked himself to death. The happy part is that before his health failed altogether, he was able to visit the Amazonian rainforests and broaden his knowlege of a subject he came to by chance and made his own through inspiration and old-fashioned dedication. The National Parks and Wildlife Service took over Minnamurra Falls from the local council, guaranteeing its preservation as a state treasure. Ivy lives with her daughter Bev in a quiet green backwater of Sydney Harbour, at rest after a life of service to nature conservation and kindness to the general public.

Eric Worrell's story is similar. He did not live to see old age, his health undermined by the after-effects of several deadly snake bites. He did have the satisfaction of seeing Australian wildlife gain the respect he had lobbied for all his years, especially the unpopular species, his own chosen focus. The Australian Reptile Park persists as a popular destination for locals and tourists, a source of education as well as recreation.

Roger Whittaker and Steve and Brooke Weslak achieved international success in film-making. Pat Aulton's career as a music arranger flourished.

What of Georgie Borys, the Ukrainian vet who did much to thaw local prejudice against foreigners? George died young but not of overwork. He died of cancer. With great dignity, he wound up his affairs quickly, efficiently, even planned his own funeral. The speaker was a long-standing friend and client of the veterinary practice, a distinquished breeder and judge of cattle. His eulogy summed up the respect and affection felt in the district for Georgie and his Czech wife, Mila. Their warmth, exuberance, passion, European love of music and good eating helped mellow the sobriety, piety and stern, stubborn conservatism of Shoalhaven society. An annual George Borys memorial trophy for excellence has been endowed for Berry Agricultural Show.

Ernie Staples, the blacksmith, lived out a long life, his enthusiasm undimmed. His fine old bellows, forge and anvil had pride of place on the verandah of Wild Country Park, memorials to his years at Foxground, until they were taken away by the people who first bought Glenrock from us. I felt intense disappointment to see them go. We had not 'sold' them, had merely passed them on as artefacts of the rich pioneering lives lived on the property. It never occurred to me that they would not remain in place forever. Another example of my naive belief that everyone values heritage as I do. Ernie's daughter Valda and her now adult children – all of them brave, outdoor adventurers – keep in touch with Glenrock, their roots.

In Foxground valley, many changes reflect those in other agricultural districts. Waites, Cullens and Conroys all were forced by circumstances to leave their properties. The Conroys' farm, which they worked but did not own, was bought by a man who did not permit trespass, not even for nostalgic visits to the swimming hole by boys grown into men. I hope the platypus still survive there. Dick Conroy died from illness exacerbated by overwork and a lack of purpose once dairying ceased, leaving his son Philip in Foxground on a small holding, a fount of knowlege about bush skills and animal husbandry which, sad to say, is drying up in our part of Australia.

His mother, Eva – Dick's widow – lives with Phil and his wife Jessie and their expanding family, daily tending their garden and one remaining cow, a stubborn Friesian named Maisie. In 1995 I recorded Eva's story, and her recollections about her life in this district now reside in the National Library Archives in Canberra. Eva's experience began in an era when travel along the Princes Highway was by horse and sulky, when her mother went shopping only once a year for cloth and threads to sew them clothes, when soap and butter was made at home, food was hand-grown and eaten fresh or preserved simply, and when 'doctoring' was done by Mum using wild plants and poultices. Eva and I both have time now to be friends in a fashion unimaginable before we both retired. We link each other to happier, richer times.

Other farm families moved away, land has been sold and divided up into smaller parcels, houses grow where cows once grazed, paddocks have become front yards and flower gardens. The evolution of mechanised 'scientific' agriculture, which was beginning as we moved to Foxground, caused the demise of family subsistence properties, a bad direction as things have turned out. When work dries up in cities, people yearn for small supportive communities, soil to plant their roots and a few veges in, chooks and maybe a house cow. At least you rarely starve to death when you have some ground around you.

Having said that, I have to concede that not many youngsters today want to spend a lifetime up to their ankles in mud and manure, foreheads pressed to the flanks of steamy-breathed beasts. In 1997 the last working dairy in Foxground closed down – one of a diminishing number in the Illawarra-Shoalhaven district. It is far more lucrative to turn acres into dollars than labour every day of every year milking cows.

Our part in the changes to Foxground were wrought by making the place known to thousands of people, through our writings, our films and Wild Country Park. A curse or a blessing? Some of the visitors fell for the place and came to live here. Most of the newcomers are more sympathetic to wildlife and the rainforest than the farmers, who saw it first as a source of usable, marketable timber, and thence relentlessly encroaching bush, a challenge to be met and beaten without shirking.

For a few years there was no place to meet and foment friendships, after the tiny crossroads post office closed; mail is now delivered into roadside boxes. Carters and Conroys are among the few 'old residents'. The new ones do not know us, and we do not know them. However, a bushfire brigade has come into existence in recent times and in the simple fire station, residents can get together for socialising and for local business. The sense of community which marked Foxground when we first came is beginning to bloom anew.

At the annual Christmas party in the fire shed, we sometimes hear reports of wildlife we once cared for on our property. Most of them just blended into the bush. You catch sight of kangaroos in twos, threes or twenties in distant paddocks. At night, wombats amble about. When marsupials are ready to die, they seem to take themselves away somewhere. Unlike the secret ivory-rich grounds of dead elephants we used to read about, rarely did we find corpses, or even skeletons, so their natural habit must be to secrete themselves deep in bush at the end.

However, those special cases I have written about were different, more people oriented and so we often knew what happened to them. Opal and Mathilda – after producing many generations of offspring, most recognisable by facial likeness and by their coats – both lived long lives on Glenrock. As they aged, their faces became jowled and they developed double chins. Mathilda disappeared first, and we feared she might have become caught up in a fence, as she used to do. She was always handicapped by the bullet wound she'd received in her thigh as a youngster. We searched but did not find her. Opal lasted to be a very old lady. Very old. She became thin, grey, infirm. Finally she brought herself to stay close to us at the new house. We spoiled her with tidbits of wholegrain bread but we could see she had not long left on this earth. When she finally lay down to die, it was out in the open, within sight of the house and the mountains, an atypically public end which lasted all day, attended by her family, the Carters. Opal is buried in the grove.

The koalas? The mature male was the first to ramble off. When we saw how easily he jumped from a branch of his gum tree to the ground, we realised our circles of tin had been less of a protection than we imagined. Apparently, the koalas stayed put the first year simply because they had enough to eat and were comfortable. After quite a few months alone, the young female forsook the park also. For weeks she hung about in the two feed trees we had planted outside the entrance. We used to rush out and waylay anyone who drove up in their car – whether they intended to stay or not – just to see her. She ate those young trees nearly bare. Then she followed the old fellow up the hill. We encountered them sometimes in eucalypts beside the road leading to the high country, placidly eating or dozing. Then we lost sight of them. I like to think that one day we will hear from one of the new residents in upper Foxground that there is a colony of koalas up there. A thriving colony of koalas. Why not?

If it sounds like some of our efforts were a waste of time, think again. Remember the hundreds of kangaroos which survived, descendants of Gidgea and Opal and Mathilda and the rest, progeny of proud Eric and his lieutenants, spread out over Foxground and Jamberoo and environs. Count the pigeons, lyrebirds and others once seriously endangered, now re-established here. Remember the little glider possum Stripes, the tiger cats which were dragged back from extinction here by our moratorium on shooting them.

And never forget the wombats, formerly characterised on our part of the coastal range by old empty burrows. Four healthy adults now come to feed most nights on the verandah of Casa Simpatica where I leave out dishes of pellets. One is a huge old fellow, bigger even than William. Two of the animals come together and will eat side by side, after a certain amount of cautionary huffing and squealing. Benson and Bats? If the feed runs out, a wombat will root beneath or stand up to claw at the metal garbage bins in which I store the grain. On occasion, they succeed in overturning them. More usually, I hear the ruckus and jump up from sound sleep to go out and refill their bowls.

I am building barricades of fire-logs round the bins to insulate them from assault, but I suspect it is all in vain. I will have to relocate the pellet bins indoors, unsightly though they appear. Another example of how we let animals run our lives. I don't begrudge the trouble. When I look down the paddock and see a red fox unconcernedly crossing the grass near a wallaby cleaning her pouch, when I watch eagles soar in lazy circles overhead, keening as they hunt, when mobs of hipper-hoppers graze on Glenrock and its neighbours, when lyrebirds scratch up my flowers and wonga pigeons bob unafraid along my verandah, when the descendants of William and Wally and Wompy crash and bumble about outside my bedroom at night, when these things happen, and they happen often, I know it was all worth it. The wildlife is here to stay. Vermin are winning!

Having cared for dynasties of marsupials and the whole, still wonderful flora and fauna of our special property, having reared four generations of dogs and now involved with a fifth, Annie Rose, it must tell you something about the age and stage Jeff and I have come to. It took a lot of strain away once we began talking freely between ourselves. Now that Jeff and I can converse less defensively than in the near past, we spend our mealtimes together discussing what we read in the broadsheets, hear and see on the ABC and SBS. There is plenty to talk about. Many things have changed in our world during our lifetime as watchdogs. Sometimes we think the good guys are indeed winning, but we both suspect the bad guys hold the best cards in their foreign boardrooms, anonymous and uncaring about the common people in a little second world country called Australia. We lament that there is not too much we can do any more to change things down here in our yellow submarine, or rather, our personal green refuge high above the highways and urbanisations, the fumes of traffic and the sound of next door's television. We do what we can, harangue our friends, write Letters-to-the-Editor, ring up. And, as we enter another millennium, we ponder and discuss between ourselves, still able to wonder about the directions society is taking. Appetite for life still strong.

A trend we both agree to disagree with is increasing urbanisation. We both favour less rather than more of it, and question the ethos of city existence. Having lived in Europe, we know the small caring village unit works. Self-determining. Self-nurturing. Even the folks who forsake their city homes and move to small communities like Berry – or Kiama, or wherever – often bring in their baggage the careless attitudes of urban anonymity, including arrogance. Self-centred and self-protective, they maintain city ways are best and up-to-date. As my mother used to tell me: 'A hundred thousand people can't be wrong.' Oh no?

What we experienced in Cataluña was three and four generations living intact and close at hand, a source of shared strengths and talents. And mutual respect. Is it ironic – and even hypocritical, my greatest bugbear in my youth – that Jeff and I, with our uneasy childhoods, now espouse the strong family structure? The nimble legs and impish tricks, the endearing innocence of the youngsters at one end, the slow but steady elders at the other, minding the memories, plenty of spare time to help. And in the middle, those still gifted with energy and will and courage, their sense of conquest still intact.

My dream was to found a dynasty rooted on Glenrock Farm, a source of strength and security. My inspiration, the words of a Pitjantjatjara wise man: *We feel sorry for them (white politicians); they have no country. They were born in one place a long way away; they grow up in another place; and when they grow old and sick they just die anywhere.* In an era when many people disparage families, my vision is out-of-step with current thinking, the move-fast and move-on generation. But nature balances. Time will tell whether non-commitment and the philosophy of 'me for myself alone' work in the long term. With more choice than perhaps ever before in history, people's deepest needs will determine, soon enough, the shape of modern society, whether roots still count, and whether rolling stones naked of moss are more than a passing minimalist fashion.

The questions mesh with my profoundest belief that a balanced ecosystem maintains a respectful relationship with a whole environment. Natives – flora, fauna, human – have knowledge about survival and harmony. Wild species contain tremendous secrets and scientists are learning more and more ways to unlock and decode these. Itinerants feel loath to breed. So, for pragmatic reasons alone, it is in everyone's interest to preserve what human and natural heritage is left on this planet. Nothing is expendable. It is *un*developed places which let people experience aloneness, space, fresh pure air, high clear sky, sweet natural water. The tonic of wildness remains a healing draught.

During the past decade, what held me here has been completing this memoir *in situ*. It celebrates the good life we lived here and our earnest endeavours, which I believe contributed to this district and to Australia – our modest but sincerely offered 'personal example'. As physical evidence of this mouldered away down the hill, I was spurred to finish my task. And when Wild Country Park closed altogether, I knew my recording had been justified. The

25 000 people who used to visit us annually may wonder how it could all just vanish.

With the manuscript in the final stages of completion, I began to pack up and readied myself to move. To seek a new start, in a new home. As luck so often has it, a series of bountiful seasons began to embrace Foxground. As all the fruit trees, flowers and vines we had planted bloomed, everything came good and rosy in Casa Simpatica's garden. It had never looked so lovely. The idea grew that I need not give up too soon this lush green spaciousness, this clean air, this privacy, this fresh pure water, these animals who visit me daily or nightly, whose ancestors I knew well. Glenrock Wildlife Refuge is mine. I have paid for it with my labour and my money. It is irreplaceable.

Similar conclusions motivated Jeff to change his lifestyle again. Thanks to a little yellow dancing dog, we found the goodwill to stay and caretake our property, harmoniously. Meanwhile, recognition comes to us slowly. Jeff's years as a chronicler of life in outback Australia are being recognised. His photographs from the past half century now reside in the national and state art galleries and libraries. All those meticulous candid series from the 1950s and 1960s have become national treasures. Good! I feel mollified that the quality work he did by choice and creative drive is being seen for what it is, a valuable archive of life among the battlers, the true backbone of this humble but superbly endowed young country. My stories also find a place in the patchwork of our history and Jeff applauds that. The completion of this memoir brings us both great satisfaction. Begun as a personal record for our grandchildren and their grandchildren, it can now serve in published form as a wider memory for all those who recall Wild Country Park and the 'crusades' of the sixties and seventies, when ideals rated higher than dollars. It may even prompt the so-called sea change generations to create their own model of self-sufficiency. Their own refuge.

As for Jeff and Mare – the Old Boy and the Old Girl as the family likes to call us, affectionately but also diminishing our power to mystify and terrify, a natural evolution of elders – one day the phone will ring and Van will learn that one or both of us have passed away. He will contact Thor and Karen, and Goth up there in Japan, and step forward to do his duty by the farm. The four of them will have to decide whether to sell up or hang onto the legacy which their parents leave them, a sanctuary in times of trouble, a bit of dirt on which to grow your own when times turn bad, when air grows foul and water ditto. My own observation is that money leaks away, while land goes on forever. But that's the romantic peasant speaking.

What do you think?

Acknowledgments

There are many, many people to thank for what is in this story. Some I have known for decades, others for just an hour, but all added richness to the shared experience. Some of those involved are included in the account but by no means all, which does not lessen my gratitude for their gifts and their friendship.

Three people deserve special thanks for helping to bring this onto the printed page. One is Jeff Carter for his vivid photographs and his support and professional advice during the past year. The other two are publisher Alex Mohan and editor Jo Jarrah. Their warmth and encouragement, as well as their professional expertise, are greatly appreciated.